RUSSIAN ASSIGNMENT

RUSSIAN ASSIGNMENT

By

LESLIE C. STEVENS

VICE ADMIRAL, USN (RETIRED)

Naval Attaché at the United States Embassy in Moscow
1947–1949

WITH ILLUSTRATIONS BY VERA DRASHEVSKY

An Atlantic Monthly Press Book
LITTLE, BROWN AND COMPANY · BOSTON

Published October 1953
Reprinted December 1953 (four times)
Reprinted February 1954

ATLANTIC—LITTLE, BROWN BOOKS
ARE PUBLISHED BY
LITTLE, BROWN AND COMPANY
IN ASSOCIATION WITH
THE ATLANTIC MONTHLY PRESS

Published simultaneously
in Canada by McClelland and Stewart Limited

PRINTED IN THE UNITED STATES OF AMERICA

FOREWORD

THE OFFICER WHO PRECEDED ME as naval attaché in Moscow told me that when he returned to America he did not intend ever to write or even talk about Russia. "Why not?" I asked, in some surprise. "Most people are tremendously interested in Russia. It will be difficult to avoid."

"I know," he answered, "but there are greater difficulties in getting people to believe the contradictory facts."

I eventually realized how right he was. Russia is so far removed from our normal experience that life there is like what it must be on an alien planet, continually slipping out of the grasp of one's comprehension even when seeing and experiencing it. The standards by which judgments are validated in Europe and America simply do not obtain in Russia. Moreover, due to the restrictions that are consciously or unconsciously placed on Russians themselves as well as on foreigners, there is no way of viewing Russia by either native-born or foreigners that lies within a framework of experience normal to Westerners. It can only be seen as through a glass, darkly.

The glass in all the Russian windows is so badly distorted that everything that is seen through it becomes warped and twisted. Living in Moscow is like living in a glass house, with the glass all like that of the Russian windows. It is often difficult for the inmates to draw clear conclusions from what they see and experience, but though the glass is dark and twisted, it can still transmit truths.

Sometimes it seemed to me as though we ourselves lived in an aquarium made from that sort of glass. The medium in which we lived was so different from that of Russian life that it added its own measure of distortion. We had the same lack of privacy as fish in an aquarium, and almost the same lack of freedom. Although we could be watched and studied in detail, we wondered at what went on outside our range of imperfect vision. The barrier that kept us from Russia sometimes seemed as real as that of the glass walls, and it seemed probable that even if we could get out we would be like fish out of water.

Nevertheless, one can come to know a great deal about Russia and the Russians. Although it can be highly consistent and authentic, much of this knowledge is indirect and inferred. When one points this out, as one must, it is disturbing and baffling to be regarded with polite disbelief by those who know things that either are not so, or are true only in a very limited way.

The disbelief is not always polite, as on the occasion when Smitty, the red-haired, intense young assistant military attaché, addressed a group of reserve officers soon after his return from Russia. He showed some photographs of Siberian towns and villages which he had taken, and was finally interrupted by an obviously sincere gentleman in his audience, who said: "I think that this speaker is an impostor. Although I have never been there, I know enough about Siberia to know that it is not at all as he says it is."

Many of life's incidents and impressions, and particularly the atmosphere and feel of their settings and surroundings, fade so rapidly that they are beyond conscious recall, like dreams that must be trapped at the moment of waking if they are to be remembered. Almost all of this book was written solely so that the vividness and color of Russia would not fade for me personally. It was written at the time the daily incidents it describes were taking place, and is now made into a book and published because it seems to contain much of the indirect lighting by which my own ideas of Russia have become clear. Perhaps it may serve as a partial substitute for those who cannot see and experience Russia. In it are no revelations, no sensational discoveries, no stirring events, but rather bits and pieces of my own daily experiences from whose fragments and flavor others may take some pleasure in assembling their own mental mosaic of Russia.

The Russian sphinx first fascinated me at the time of the October Revolution when I was a midshipman at Annapolis. Its barbarity, its color, and the subtleties of its contradictory mind were always to me more intriguing than its social meaning, and possibly this in itself kept me from one common sort of emotional bias. From the time in 1922 when I first picked up a Russian grammar in London, the intricacies of the language were a continual source of entertainment, something after the fashion of jigsaws or crossword puzzles. When the United States and Soviet Russia first established diplomatic relations, it was decided to send me there as an assistant naval attaché. Plans were changed, and I ended up in England instead, with a feeling of disappointment that, although England was an extraordinarily pleasant place in which to live, it did not exert the peculiar fascination of Russia, nor would there be even the mastery of a foreign language to show for the tour of duty.

From that time on, the possibility of being sent to Russia was always just around the corner, and both my wife and I read continually about the country. The sincerity of much that I heard and read was apparent, but it seemed that there was always something elusive, even missing, that the whole pattern of the fabric had not been made clear. The mystery of the country was compelling, together with its seemingly unpredictable nature, which arises from what are regarded as contradictions and inconsistencies. Yet I was impressed with the assurance with which Nell, who had gone to Russia on an Intourist trip in 1936 while I was occupied elsewhere, contradicted nearly all the experts when the Germans first invaded Russia in 1941. "Just wait," she said. "The Germans will never conquer Russia. It is not like France. The Russians will fight for what they have been told is their very own — the fields, the factories, the very cobblestones in the streets, which they think are theirs. They will never be defeated." My wife had no Communist sympathies, and Marxism was only a dreary morass to her. The next year I heard a newly returned military attaché who could speak Russian and who had spent many years there say with equal conviction that Russia was completely finished in the war.

In short, my desire to go to Russia grew largely from the fact that I did not know what to expect there and had no points to prove. In the spring of 1947 the Navy wanted to send to Moscow a flag officer who knew the language and who had had some experience in intelligence. It was decided that I met those qualifications.

Everyone who tells of his experiences in Russia must make certain decisions which are rather different from those which all writers who deal with foreign lands must probably make. Russian law deals with the citizen from a viewpoint that is at variance with that to which we are accustomed, for it is not intended to protect the individual from the state, but rather to protect the state from the individual. Those laws are purposely very broad, and their application is a matter for administrative interpretation. There is ample evidence that the law which forbids a Russian to give any information of significance to a foreigner can and will be interpreted by the Soviet state in such fashion as to punish severely the Russian whose remarks are eventually published in any way that conflicts with the interests of the state, including its propaganda. In common decency, it is therefore necessary to protect the Russians with whom one has talked, for the arm of their police is long. Even in cases where those Russians were completely innocent of any disaffection, names and circumstances have been altered in such a way that, while accuracy in other aspects is still retained, those who were involved in anything which might conceivably be held against them cannot be identified.

It is possible that, even with these precautions, the more Russians are quoted for publication, the more they will tend to be silent in the presence of foreigners in the future. The Russian people, however, have a great sense of what is right and wrong, and it seems to me that they are more appreciative of justice, understanding, and sympathy than they are fearful of personal danger.

Another decision which must be made also has a bearing on the opportunities of others in the future. One obviously should not write things which will disclose to the Soviet government repairable holes in the iron curtain which they have drawn between their people and foreigners. There are few ways in which that government stands in need of instruction in this respect. It has known for a long time that any unsupervised conversation with any of its subjects carries with it the strong probability that the foreigner will learn things which are at variance with what the regime would like him to believe. The only remedy is to isolate the foreigner completely from all contacts, or to see that he is always adequately accompanied. The restrictions of recent years have come close to just that. Yet the one thing which the regime dislikes more than the small gaps which still remain in the curtain is the ultimate necessity of baldly admitting the uncivilized isolation which it must practice. Its propaganda position is too intimately involved.

Only the other day all missions were notified that foreigners could visit only cities which were provided with Intourist facilities. Although this negatived the opening up to travel of huge areas which had been made accessible in 1948, it can be explained propaganda-wise on the grounds of solicitude for the welfare and comfort of foreigners. The regime seems to hold all the cards, but its task is not easy, and it is highly probable that it will continue to walk the tightrope between security and propaganda advantage. Certainly it will learn from these pages nothing that it does not already know about how to handle foreigners within its borders.

So, in the words of Pushkin's Onegin,

I have looked all these pages over carefully. In them are many contradictions, but I do not wish to correct them. . . . Go forth, my newborn creation, and earn for me the reward of public attention — wry remarks, noise and abuse.

L. C. S.

CONTENTS

VII THE BORDERS OF ASIA

VIII "FAREWELL, UNWASHED RUSSIA"

PART I. ACROSS FROM THE KREMLIN

1. THE BERLIN-MOSCOW EXPRESS

A LOUD-SPEAKER BEGAN TO BLARE lively music, much too loud for comfort. It hung in the passageway that ran alongside the individual compartments of the international wagon of the Berlin-Moscow express.

"Yes, you will like Russia," said the woman with the tired brown face and the bright brown eyes who had given Nell and me space in her compartment for some of our luggage which seemed to have spawned en route. "It is a golden land, and it must be held firmly in the hands of the people." She cupped her thin hands as she spoke. "Yes, in the golden hands of the people."

"Please say it again, but more slowly," I said. "My ears are not accustomed to Russian sounds. I can read almost anything, without a dictionary, but when it comes to speaking and understanding, I can only try."

Her face lighted up with a smile that washed all the tiredness away. She spoke more deliberately, lingering over the stressed syllables as though she loved the sound of them. "One day your tongue will become untied, but understanding comes from the heart as well as from the ears. Do you know what it means when I say that the people of Russia have golden hands?"

Fortunately I did. Golden hands are as effective in all the manual tasks of life as a green thumb is for a gardener. She was a doctor, going back home to Russia for a much-needed vacation and rest. Before we had pulled out of the Silesia Station in Berlin, the soft voice of this stranger had taken charge of the complexities of stowing all the boxes and bags, each wrapped in canvas, wired and sealed — to prevent pilfering, on the advice of American headquarters in Berlin. The compartments of the international sleeping wagon were roomy, but in addition to the clothing and belongings that Nell and I would need for the unknown period until our freight shipment might show up in Moscow, we had food for five days and a huge ten-gallon tank of fresh water. Nobody knew, nor could find out, when we were due in Moscow. The best guess was five days.

We watched the wreckage of the outskirts of Berlin slide past. Suddenly came flat pine woods, looking much like northern Florida, only, instead of palmetto on the ground, there were, in similar profusion, old shell holes and bomb craters. For the next three days, almost to the outskirts of Moscow, one could never look from the windows more than a few moments without seeing somewhere such marks, or old trenches, foxholes — or crosses.

Two or three of the passengers examined the loud-speaker, trying to find some way of diminishing its volume. "There's no use trying," said the woman porter calmly. "It's either on or off. Now it must be on." It was with us all the way to Moscow, except for a few blessed hours in the deep of the nights. Somewhere on the train must have been the Russian version of a disc jockey who fed it records, for it put forth no news or discussion, only popular entertainment, whether the passengers wanted it or not.

Sometime during that first night some one rapped at our door. The train was stopped. "What is it?" I asked sleepily.

"Your documents, please."

I swung out of the upper berth, fished around for passports, and handed them through the door. Someone took them and went away in the darkness. Soon there was another knock. Another swing out of the berth to unlock the door.

"Where is your Polish visa?" came the question.

"No one said anything about a Polish visa being necessary. We are going to Russia, not Poland."

"But you must have a Polish visa to cross Poland."

"Then why did Intourist sell us tickets for this train? They had to have our passports before they would give us tickets, and they must have checked to see if they were in order."

There was a whispered conference outside the door, and then footsteps died away in the passage.

"Suppose they put us off the train?" asked Nell in a small voice.

I do not know how long the Berlin-Moscow express lingered on the Polish border, for the next knock woke me again from sleep. Our passports were handed in without a word. In the morning, examination showed that they had been newly stamped with Polish visas, but by whom, was not clear.

All the way across Poland were endless grainfields being harvested, with women and children tending the cattle and goats. Whenever the train stopped, ragged boys, girls and women ran alongside or jumped on board to sell bacon, lengths of sausage, salt pork, eggs, tomatoes, cucumbers and small apples. Headquarters had been right, for the train carried neither restaurant car nor water for drinking or washing, and we had no local money with which to buy the food at the villages. At every stop, the woman porter and her dark-eyed young girl assistant washed down the floors, for it was very hot. They did their best, but with no running water in the washrooms there were unpleasant limits to what they could do.

Warsaw was as badly wrecked as Berlin, with great vacant spaces in the center of the city. The train seemed to pause there aimlessly, for the station was completely gone.

The Russian passengers were well-mannered and amiable with us. A colonel of artillery with a crooked nose and big brown eyes asked me for something in English to read. When he was offered a current magazine, he said that that would do, although he would much prefer the *Naval Institute* or the *National Geographic*. He was too self-conscious of his English to try it on me, but volunteered the information that he, coming from Gorky, spoke Russian with different vowel sounds than one meets around Moscow. Two or three officers gathered round to teach me the distinctions in those sounds.

Once a portly general addressed me in English. He spoke slowly and stiffly, but correctly. He said that he had learned his English from listening to the Voice of America and the British broadcasts, and advised me to listen to the Moscow radio continually. The loud-speaker on the train was no help, for it seemed only an incoherent jumble of unrecognizable sounds. It was possible to pick out a few words of one oft-repeated song which they said was an Air Force song. It dealt with the wide blue yonder and girls, in Air Force fashion the world over.

Although the long train was crowded with sweating, swarming humanity, nearly all the passengers in the international wagon were Red Army senior officers and their families. One burly, sullen-browed man in civilian clothes seemed to avoid me, although he talked from time to time with most of the others. Once as I went along the passage he was standing at the end with his back to me, engaged in an earnest conversation with the artillery colonel who had a preference for serious literature. He was saying, emphatically and authoritatively, " — but you must not talk with him about any-thing political!" As I passed, he stopped abruptly and turned to the window. From the look on both of their faces there was no doubt that I was the subject of their conversation, and a bit of a shadow went over the bright July day.

Late in the long summer afternoon we came to the Bug River and the Russian border. The train jerked slowly to a stop on the Russian side of the river. I was about to go out on the sandy road-bed to stretch my legs on Russian soil when a soldier locked the door of the wagon in my face and took his post in front of it. The bayonet on his gun was very long, and needle-sharp. Katya, the porter, closed and locked all the windows, and we sweltered there for the better part of two hours. Not one passenger left the train, for there were soldiers at each end of every locked wagon. The frontier guards began their inspection, swarming above and be-neath every car. An uneasy silence fell over all the passengers.

Through the windows could be seen a wrecked bridge spanning the river, with a rusty locomotive nose-down in the water in a gap between the spans. On both sides of the railroad overlooking the river were green, grass-covered hills which were not really hills, but fortifications, for everywhere could be seen parts of under-ground forts and concrete pillboxes, with the black protruding muzzles of guns. Here and there soldiers with rifles lay on their bellies in the grass watching the river banks through binoculars. There were searchlights for illuminating the river at night.

At the border were only those bristling hills with blue and white flowers in the grass. Instead of a town there was a camp of frontier guards. Its entrance showed the first characteristic sign of the Soviet Union — a sort of bower, hung with green, painted red and blue and white, with big slogans saying "Glory to great Stalin!" and other signs urging vigilance. Within the camp, soldiers lay on the ground, studying or reading, or were gathered in little groups for instruction. There seemed to be something makeshift and poor about the scene, yet it was subtly disturbing and menacing.

Armed guards patrolled alongside the train, and also alongside were hundreds of German war prisoners working on the railroad, bare to the waist, wearing their German forage caps. A supervisor gave signals — one — two — and at a rolling "*rrrrr*" a gang would heave a rail to right or left. The men were dusty, sunburned and gaunt, and the ribs and bones of their bodies stuck out in a way that was beyond mere thinness. A bemedaled officer on the train unlocked a window, lowered it, and shouted something at the captives, who gave him black looks. Katya came running up and again locked the window.

It was evening when we at last pulled into Brest-Litovsk, a short distance further on. A slight, smooth-looking man, accompanied by a squad of porters, came immediately into our compartment and addressed us in English. Katya and her girl helper politely refused the cigarettes that we offered them, saying they did not smoke and did not know anyone who did. The porters gathered up all our gear with amazing rapidity, and we were hurried out and along the long platform of the station. As we went, I saw that not one other person had yet been permitted to leave the train. We were taken upstairs in the station to a dark but comfortable waiting room, furnished with deep leather-covered couches and chairs and a table covered with Soviet magazines and newspapers. The Intourist porters gravely refused cigarettes, and we were left alone in the waiting room. Hoping that someone would let us know when the Russian train was ready, we went down into the station. It was packed and crowded with people. The wooden benches were overflowing, and women and babies and soldiers sat and lay on the floor among heaps of bundles and luggage. Everywhere was a restless movement of people, drifting aimlessly back and forth.

We went outside the station and strolled around in the last of the daylight, past plasterlike statues which gave the same hopeful but amateurish effect as the little entrance bower at the frontier. Against a strip of light sky in the distance rose some dark onion-shaped domes. Everywhere were heaps of luggage, heaps of humanity, mostly soldiers, resting or sleeping. My dress khaki uniform, which was worn for the occasion of crossing the border, attracted much attention — too much. Some groups of soldiers would jump to attention and salute smartly, others would hesitate, not quite knowing what to do, still others would just stare, but all were curious. Whenever we stopped, we would soon become the center of a small crowd. We doubtless were eying them just as curiously, but they had all the advantage of numbers, so we went back up to the Intourist lounge. On the way we passed a special waiting room for generals and other Soviet VIP's but it was a cut below ours in its appointments.

It was a long time before the Moscow train was ready, but at last a different squad of porters appeared, one of them with a fan of bristly red mustache like Old Bill in Bairnsfather's cartoons of the First World War, and we followed them into the broad-gauge train. We went to sleep in as comfortable a sleeping car as there is anywhere — made in Germany. Russia may be able to make them, and perhaps she does, but this one had German markings on all its specially designed plumbing, and undoubtedly came out of Germany and not out of the communist economy. But there was a Russian-made blanket, long-haired and luxurious, which I was glad to pull over me before morning.

Nell woke me quietly. "Look out of the window," she said. The train was stopped in some small town of western White Russia. Wisps of fog made the eerie half-light of early dawn still more mysterious. A bare dirt area, surrounded by a high picket fence with wire along its top and bottom, was opposite, serving as a waiting room, and huddled and grouped throughout this area were human figures, motionless and massed as though in the composition of some despairing painting. They must have been asleep, for their heads were all bent low. The women had drab gray shawls, coarse as if made from coffee sacking, pulled over their bowed heads and bent shoulders. It was evidently chilly outside, for most of the men were wrapped in ragged overcoats. One figure, quiet as death, wore a soldier's overcoat and wrapped leggings, but its feet were bare. Many had legs and feet wrapped in coarse sacking. There were two or three gypsies in bright shawls. Scattered around were huge dark bundles, which must have been their belongings, but I have never seen such evidences of utter poverty as in that clothing. I was suddenly conscious of the pinched, haggard face of a small boy uplifted under the window and heard his thin voice, ghostly thin through the glass — *"Daitye khleba! Dyadya — daitye khleba!"*

A shiver ran down my back, for from his appearance he was not just a beggar, and those were the famine words — "Give bread, uncle! Give bread!" — which are familiar to everyone who has read of the great famines which Russia has periodically suffered. It was surprising to hear that in this land, two years and more after the end of the war. Also it was the first time I had been called "uncle." While we were rummaging around for food to give, it grew lighter without, and the huddled figures began to stir. A gypsy woman balanced a heavy bucket on her head and walked along the tracks. People began to drift towards a thing that looked like a pump but which was not a pump, and which gave forth hot water. By the time we had found our food there were a dozen little children outside the windows, wailing the same cry. And there was no doubt about the need, for their eyes were unbelievably hollow and their ribs stuck out through their rags in a way that made the German prisoners seem well-conditioned.

All that morning, wherever the train stopped in the countryside, it was immediately surrounded by swarms of such hungry children and old women asking for bread. It was a broad, open countryside, more unkempt than Poland but with miles and miles of grain that was not yet ready for harvest, great fields of potatoes blossoming blue and pink, and heavy crude windmills on the horizons. There were many thatched roofs and the doorways and window frames began to be carved. Birdhouses were perched on tall sticks outside the peasant houses, and on one new house was a fir tree like a Christmas tree. There was no farm machinery in evidence, and I have never seen such worn, thin, wicked-looking blades as those on the many, many scythes.

One village offered an unexplained contradiction. A sign there said: "WALKING ALONG THE RAILROAD AND TRADING IN PRODUCE IS STRICTLY FORBIDDEN. PUNISHMENT — 50 TO 100 RUBLES FINE." And, although there were the same swarms of obviously half-starved women and old-faced children, baskets of berries, milk in a big tin can, and even a roast chicken were offered for sale to the passengers.

The Russian train was vastly better than the one across Poland. There was water, and even a restaurant wagon. There were white embroidered headrests on the seats, and at every station there was hot water from the things that looked like pumps. The porters brought us tea whenever we asked for it, in cut-glass glasses mounted in silver holders, like old-fashioned glasses for ice cream sodas.

Minsk and Smolensk looked more like struggling frontier settlements than cities, because of the great areas that had been burned and destroyed, with the rubble now hidden by long grass. At Smolensk the artillery colonel brought us from somewhere two ice cream cones, which he gave us with a deep bow. Nell gave a small boy at the station her last orange. He smiled, smelled it, bit off a tiny bit of peel and then stuffed it inside his shirt. After he had passed a guard, we saw him take it out, eye it proudly, and sell it to a soldier on the train for a handful of paper money.

It was very hot. A colonel from an elite regiment, perspiring freely and smelling strongly of vodka, came into our compartment, sat down, and began talking volubly, asking us about America and telling us about his family. When he went out, several of the passengers expostulated with him. Soon he came back in again, but two of the passengers came in and led him out.

"Why don't they let him talk with me?" I asked the woman doctor. "He is doing no harm. I won't talk politics with him."

"Oh, it's not that," she said. "It's just not fitting that he should talk to distinguished foreigners while he is in his shirt sleeves and a little drunk."

It was a little difficult altogether to believe her, for nearly everyone on the train, including myself, were in their shirt sleeves, and, although there seemed to be a general desire to create a good impression, he did not seem sufficiently drunk to create a bad one.

Some time during the evening we passed a prisoner train on a siding. It was filled with Russians, not Germans, and boxcar after boxcar was packed with people, the men stripped to the waist and the women barefoot. Gaunt faces peered out between the barred slits. On the outside of each car were guards with guns, and also, strangely enough, flowers and bunches of green leaves.

The next day there were no signs of hunger and not even a beggar to be seen at any stop. The country was increasingly unkempt and wild, with long stretches of forest of birch or pine. The villages, both large and small, were made up of log cabins like those of Abe Lincoln, and almost always there were the onion domes of a church to be seen somewhere against the sky. Everyone was excited at the proximity of Moscow, and as busy packing up their things as if they had been on a transatlantic journey. Suddenly, with no more warning than if we were coming into another big village or town, we were in the Moscow station.

2. THE KREMLIN

We had not seen Johnny Maples, who was being relieved by me, and Marge, his wife, for many years. Although Moscow seemed to have agreed with them, they made no bones about how pleased they were to see us because it would permit them to be on their way to the outside world within less than forty-eight hours. After well over two years in Russia they certainly had no reluctance in departing.

We left others from the Navy office to take care of all the uproar and confusion over our luggage and drove to the Embassy. The streets were crowded, but less with automobiles than with swarms of people on foot. They overflowed from the sidewalks and thought nothing of walking in the middle of the road, so that the air was full of a continual din of horns. Moscow seems to have been completely untouched by war damage, and I was thinking that its substantial buildings looked like those of many another city when, in the midst of all the façade of modernity, the Kremlin came into view.

It is fantastic and mysterious, vast, strong and beautiful, a walled town within a city. At the angles and corners of the mighty walls are medieval towers, no two alike, tiled and decorated and exotic as might have been the towers of Karakoram. The soft rosy brown of the old brick walls ties those towers together, giving a sufficient unity both by its color and by its long lines of deep, regular crenelations. Each tooth is notched at the top and slit for archers. The pattern is Asiatic, not European, and, though medieval, it gives no museumlike impression but rather one of living vitality.

Rising above the walls are masses of creamy-yellow palaces, with Renaissance columning and windowing as though they had been brought from Venice or Siena. In a way, they have been, for they were built under the supervision of Italians. Low, flat domes surmount some of these buildings, but soaring above them is a multitude of the lily-bulb domes that are so peculiarly Russian, varying in shape and size as do living bulbs, but all of them shining golden in the sunlight, and over all, the tall, onion-topped tower of Ivan the Great.

The fairy-tale effect which the domes and towers give to the Asiatic medievalism of the fortress is changed into something still more Russian — yet surely not Soviet — by the forest of crosses with which the domes are surmounted. Each dome is crowned with a big golden cross, sometimes bigger than the dome itself — not the plain Roman cross, but that of the Greeks, with a lower crossbar set askew as a reminder of the broken bones of Christ. Each cross is stayed with chains, which sag ornamentally if not effectively. In spite of their size, the crosses give an effect of soaring lightness, for they are filigreed and complex. Sometimes there are crescents worked into their designs, giving them a very Oriental appearance.

The bizarre, glorious picture is completed by a great blood-red banner which floats from the top of the biggest and flattest secular dome and by huge red stars at the very pinnacles of the fantastic towers. Those great ruby stars are said to be mounted in real rubies for bearings, on which they turn in the wind like weathercocks.

Across a broad plaza and facing the Kremlin is Mokhavaya House, the American Embassy.* At one end of the plaza is a long low yellow building, girdled with a frieze of medallions in bas-relief which look remarkably like West Point crests, which was once a training hall for the Tsar's horses and from which the plaza gets its name of Manezhny Place. The old hall is now the Kremlin garage. The other end of the plaza runs into the entrance to Red Square, and Red Square lies along another side of the Kremlin.

Mokhavaya House was built for an art school, and, being at the very heart of old Moscow, its foundations are believably thick with old bones. In it are the offices of the Embassy and apartments for most of the Embassy personnel. It is seven stories high, but of a puzzling layout, for many of the rooms of the apartments were intended for studios and are twice the height of normal rooms. Like

---

* Mokhavaya is no longer occupied by the American Embassy. Towards the end of 1952 representations were made by the Soviet government that it was badly needed for the expansion of Moscow University, and the Americans moved away from the Kremlin area to new premises which were offered on one of the ring boulevards.

many modern Moscow buildings, it has little depth, and the northern studio walls are great expanses of coarsely mullioned windows which look out over a paved court that is used for the Embassy's automobiles. The Mapleses' apartment, which we hope to inherit after it is redecorated, runs unpredictably on both sides of the building on the two top floors. It consists of two of those studio rooms with their mighty windows overlooking the court, a kitchen and a low room with a narrow stone balcony on the Kremlin side, and a bedroom on the next level above. Meanwhile we are quartered temporarily in a similar but smaller apartment.

Ambassador Bedell Smith, to whom I presented my credentials, has his residence at Spasso House in the Arbat section, some ten or fifteen minutes away. Senior diplomatic personnel, most of the girls who do office work, and the naval, army and air attachés live at Mokhavaya. The assistant naval attachés have a house of their own in the general direction of Spasso which they call Spirodonovka House, and the comparable army and air force officers run their own establishment known as Khlebny. Enlisted men from all three services and male clerical personnel live in American House, which is a rather barrackslike building not far away on the Moskva River, which flows past the Kremlin and through the center of Moscow.

Since the Soviet government owns and controls everything, one cannot just go out and make a deal for a place to live. As a result, living quarters are extremely difficult to get, for they are assigned by the government, and the Embassy is always in difficulties trying to house its personnel. There are two or three other small places and an occasional hotel room which are held on very uncertain tenure. Even Mokhavaya and Spasso are leased on an annual basis, and the renewal of leases is always a time of troubles.

All of the Americans have been most cordial, hospitable and friendly. It was very late when we looked out on the Kremlin before turning in. Dance music was still coming from the tall Moscow Hotel across Gorky Street at the end of Manezhny Place — Danube waltzes, and "Alexander's Ragtime Band." The moonlight was so bright that the domes of the churches and cathedrals within the Kremlin still showed golden. The red stars on the pinnacles had swung around in the wind and glowed eerily in the moonlight.

Dominating everything was the great crimson flag, picked out by a steady shaft of light from somewhere within the mysterious reaches of the Kremlin.

Twice during the night the rattle of machine-gun fire wakened me. Each time I went to the window, but there was nothing to be seen except empty streets, dreaming peacefully beneath a low moon.

In the morning, looking out across the courtyard, I got a shock. It is bad enough to see a horse staring at you from a window of the topmost floor of the building opposite, but this horse — with no pun intended — was a genuine nightmare. It had been flayed, and all its muscles were abominably evident. I did not fully recover until someone told me that it was occupying the premises of the Medical College of Moscow University, which adjoins the Embassy.

The difficulties of understanding spoken Russian disturb me. Every Russian talks much too fast, spouting it out like a machine gun, so that it is seldom possible to catch more than an occasional word. The radio is nothing but a confusing babble of incoherent noise. There is little difficulty in saying anything I want, although it is frequently necessary to hunt around for words — "to go through my pockets," as Nina, my new language teacher, says.

The first day in Moscow, Nick de Tolly, the big, handsome, dark-faced acting air attaché, had a large official luncheon at one of the hotels for all the foreign air attachés. At the same time Alice, his lovely wife — she should be lovely, for she is the daughter of Alice Joyce and Tom Moore of the wonderful days of the old silent movies — had a luncheon to which Nell went. Nick's luncheon, which I attended by virtue of my wings, was impressive. There were two or three high-ranking Russian officers there, in addition to General Serayev, who heads OVS, the office of military liaison with foreigners, and some officers from OVS whose duty it probably was to go.

The luncheon lasted until half past five, and there was much vodka and many speeches. Few of the foreigners speak good Russian, so Nick acted as interpreter. He came by his Russian honestly, for he is a direct descendant of the Barclay de Tolly who was one of Kutuzov's generals in the Napoleonic War. Sometime during the speeches Nick introduced me as a new arrival. Probably a bit unsteady on account of my bad knee, a burning desire suddenly seized me to make a speech myself, so I got up, told Nick that no interpreter was necessary, and did it in Russian. A hard-faced Russian general showed his appreciation by banging on the table and shouting *"Molodyets!"* which is a high expression of admiration and encouragement. But I had no sooner sat down than I was conscious of more than one grammatical mistake.

There is only one thing sure, which is that I shall get nowhere until this damnable language can be really mastered. It seems to me that a Russian who goes to the United States without the ability to understand English could not help but get a distorted idea of America, and to be in a similar position here is not attractive. So that same evening at a party at American House which combined a farewell to the Mapleses with a welcome for us, and where there were several striking Russian girls who said they were language teachers, I promptly and enthusiastically hired Nina, the prettiest of them, for a daily lesson. Although here there is no other way of learning the spoken language than by getting a personal teacher, this precipitation seems somehow to be regarded rather coolly by Nell.

There were low clouds and rain at the Vnukovo Airport when we saw the Mapleses off for the outside world. Several of the foreign attachés were there, still impressed with my speech of the day before. So was I, but not altogether favorably.

Sergei, my driver, is a sleek, broad-faced Russian with very blue eyes and long fair hair which gives him an air of unusual smoothness. He is unique in being able to speak a fair amount of English. He obviously wants to practice his English on me, while I want to practice my Russian on him, so some difficulties can be foreseen.

Later in the day we drove out to Khimki, a few kilometers to the north of Moscow, which is the closest point to Moscow that was reached by the German tide during the war. Khimki is on the Moscow-Volga Canal, and it has a pretentious station for the river traffic of which the Russians are very proud. The waiting room of the station had a huge map of the canal, and there was a row of medallions of Russian industrial activities which was very colorful against the granite walls.

There, on an open terrace overlooking the canal, we had our first Russian beer. I decided to be democratic in this land of a classless society and asked Sergei to join us. He was quite at ease. The beer was without sparkle and rather sweet, but cold and strong enough.

We came back through Sokolniki Park, which was rather unkempt and bedraggled. There the oppressing classes once practiced falconry, according to Sergei. We passed a great building of the familiar creamy yellowish-brown stucco, which was a hospital built by Catherine the Great. Sergei shrugged his shoulders at my remark that she was one of the oppressing classes.

"There they have the finest doctors in the world," he said. "One of them is an American."

On the way home we passed two women walking in the street, and under the arm of one of them was a small coffin.

When I later asked Vaughn and others in the Embassy if they knew of the American doctor in Catherine's old hospital, no one had ever heard of him.

3. SERVANTS OF TWO MASTERS

I WENT OUT INTO THE CROWDS, around the corner, and up Gorky Street. There is a street for you! It was broadened by the Soviets from the old Tverskaya, and the process must have destroyed many an old historic landmark. Canal Street in New Orleans, which has always seemed to me to be an extraordinarily wide street, could be laid in it twice over.

Everywhere were women, with kerchiefs and shawls on their heads which gave color to otherwise drab and even poor clothing. They seemed greatly to outnumber the men, who could claim no comparable touch of brightness to their shabby clothes. Certainly the women do all the work. Big, strapping, rosy-cheeked young women and little frail old ones swept the streets with brooms. They were besoms rather than brooms, for they consisted of bundles of twigs on the end of a handle, just like those the witches ride. One group of women was working on the streetcar tracks, and I was fascinated by the expertness with which one of them operated an acetylene cutting torch. They never wear overalls or slacks, but always short, grimy skirts. The faces of men and women alike were hard and shrewd. One never sees a fat and soft-looking individual.

The windows of the food shops are filled with the most implausible and unappetizing dummy hams and sausages I have ever seen. The famous Russian talent for illusion must lie in other fields. Attracted by another kind of window display, I stopped in at a second-hand bookshop, but found it disappointing. Apart from a counter which was crowded with Russians, all the books were stacked on shelves behind the trade counters, just far enough away so that it was impossible to make out their titles. One cannot browse through the shelves, but must know what one wants and then ask for it. Being run by the government, as is every shop and enterprise, it had a "complaint book" at the cashier's desk for criticisms.

On the open counter I finally found a book on Russian engraving, illustrating, and black-and-white drawing, rich with beautiful reproductions of Russian work in these techniques. It was expensive, but it was apparent that used books were generally valued higher than their original prices. It was necessary to stand in line to pay the cashier, who deftly did her sums on a primitive abacus, and then again to stand in line to present my receipt and get my purchase. That abacus was so intriguing that I bought one on the way home, only to find that it was not as tractable in my hands as under the stubby fingers of that Russian cashier.

Although the book appeared never to have had a previous owner, the pages being still clean and unmarked, one picture had been partially removed, not by cutting it from the page, but by carefully scraping or slicing it away from the surface of the paper. It was in a chapter on the portrait silhouettes by Kruglikova, who was a professor in the Leningrad Academy when the book was written. There were several other silhouettes of people such as Pasternak, Blok, Kropotkin and Lunacharsky, but the head and even the name had been removed from this particular one. I looked at the date of publication. It was 1928. It could only be concluded that my missing portrait was one of Trotsky, Zinoviev, Bukharin, or someone else who had been caught in the Great Purge and whose very name and face had been expunged from all record. It was too neatly and expertly done to have been malicious. Just impersonal thoroughness.

In addition to Sergei, who is supposed to have one meal a day in our house and usually manages three or four, the household which we inherited from the Mapleses consists of a cook and two maids, all of whom sleep at their own homes. Natasha, the cook, is little and gnarled and wizened and old, but she is very shrewd and they say she makes lovely bread when flour is to be had.

Zoya is young, with a husband who works in a factory. She is not particularly pretty, but her trim little figure looks very well in her maid's uniform, and better still when she is all smartly dressed to go home, for she manages to look much better than most Soviet girls. She always has a bright smile, and is remarkable in the way she can understand what Nell tries to tell her.

Valya, the other maid, is just a dark, heavy ox, almost surly in comparison with the other two.

In addition, there is an adolescent long-haired gray-and-white cat with huge eyes, which seems to have lost its mind, if it ever had one. It is an extraordinarily playful cat, whether or not it has anyone with whom to play. When it is not elaborately stalking some unseen object, or, with twitching tail, watching the sparrows through the big windows, it is making mad leaps about the apartment, startling everyone out of his wits. Nevertheless, it is a lovely little beast.

"What is its name?" I asked Natasha.

"It has no name. Just call it Koshka."

No foreigners can just go out and get themselves a servant. All Soviet employees of any sort must be satisfactory to the Soviet government and registered with Burobin, the office which is responsible for all dealings with foreigners that come under the general head of housekeeping as distinct from diplomatic or military affairs. They tell me that every Russian employee, including servants and teachers, is required to report back to his government on everything he can regarding foreigners — their interests, their characters and abilities, and what they are up to. Too many employees have either thoughtlessly or deliberately told of this for there to be any question about it.

Although no reference is ever made to this circumstance, the servants know that we know this. They have no choice in the matter, and are very apt to be reported on themselves, so no one has any particular feelings about it. Sometimes it is a good thing to give them something to report. Nevertheless, it is a strange relationship, by our standards, and one to which it is difficult to accustom oneself.

Also, there have been too many established cases of wiring for sound for one to feel comfortable even when there are no Russians about. One feels safe in talking only in the presence of noise, or when one is outdoors. It would be naïve and foolish for a foreigner to fail to observe these precautions, whether or not he believes in their absolute necessity under all circumstances. Perhaps the reporting system will reflect a clear conscience, and so establish a reasonable amount of confidence in one's intentions.

OVS, the Soviet military liaison office, is located three or four blocks away, over in the direction of the great Lenin Library. I made my formal call on General Serayev, and was taken through corridors that were strangely empty and silent for an office establishment to a dark, bare room with only a long table about which were a few chairs.

I remembered Serayev well from his previous tour of duty as military attaché to the Soviet Embassy in Washington. He is a chunky, mild-mannered man, snub-nosed and blue-eyed. Although he speaks good English, we talked in Russian. He was neither formally stiff nor affable, but soft-spoken in a noncommittal sort of way.

They say that no Russian can have a foreigner in his home, nor are they permitted to accept informal social invitations. Although I had known Serayev well enough to make such exchanges natural, there was no indication that they would be forthcoming. Perhaps it was because his wife was out of town.

I told Serayev that I regarded myself and my naval personnel as guests in Russia, and that we would conduct ourselves as such. As soon as the spoken language could be brought under control, I hoped to be able to visit some of the famous and interesting places in Russia, particularly Samarkand and the Asiatic Republics. He said to put in a request whenever I was ready, and they would tell me whether or not it would be permitted.

I also told Serayev that I would like to pay my respects to any of their senior officers in all cases which he considered appropriate, and would await word from him. This is another thing which they say is not permitted in Russia. All the time we were talking, a silent Russian took stenographic notes of the conversation.

Near Sverdlovsk Square, two or three blocks from the Embassy on the other side of Gorky Street, is a theater which shows nothing but three-dimensional movies. Nell and I walked over there, through the swarming crowds of bright-eyed kerchiefed women and strong-faced men. I have never before seen such interesting faces in such quantity. One feels that almost every Russian is a real personality. Many of the men have their heads completely shaved, which gives them a peculiarly brutal and savage appearance. Their stainless steel teeth do nothing to soften this effect.

The theater, belying its big sign, was small, and the seats, made of cheap thin veneer, were hard and uncomfortable. The customers were first given group instruction in how to watch the movie without eyestrain, consisting of a brief lecture based on a printed handbill which was given to each guest. I read the handbill while waiting for the lecturer to begin, and then was much encouraged to find that nearly all he had to say was easily understandable. Perhaps the Russians who tell me that it will be possible for me to handle this language soon are not merely being polite!

No visual aids were used to get the three-dimensional effect, which seemed to be mainly a property of the screen, in somewhat the same manner as occasional window displays one sees in America. One should sit relaxed and shift one's head and body slightly from side to side until the effect appeared, shifting again if it was lost.

We filed into the projection room with curiosity fully aroused. The picture was *Robinson Crusoe*, and almost immediately it came to life. It was easy to lose the effect, but with a little experience it could be held almost continuously. We were gliding in a boat under trees canopied with Spanish moss. It was not clear what Spanish moss had to do with Robinson Crusoe, but, rather than appearing on a screen, it seemed to hang from the roof of the theater all about and even behind us. Birds would fly from the screen out over our heads, circle, and return. Then would come long sequences where the three-dimensional effect seemed to be very weak. It became apparent that its drama lay only in motion that was approaching or receding, like an onrushing train. But occasionally the effect was terrific, as when a panther crawled out onto a limb over our heads and sprang into the back of the theater, making the audience duck and squeal delightedly.

When it was over, we had the feeling that although it was interesting it was not fully developed, and that it would be very difficult to devise action to take much advantage of its possibilities. There was a curious feeling that even if there was good and sufficient reason why similar entertainment was not available in the Western world, we had seen something in Russia that we could not have seen elsewhere.

On the way home I bought a couple of lovely little bars of ice cream. They should have been good, for they cost something over

a dollar in our money. The Russians love ice cream, but it is difficult to see how they manage to eat much of it at such prices.
Mikoyan introduced from America the modern processes of making
in. He was probably responsible also for the automat which I saw
near Sverdlovsk Square, and which I shall have to visit some time.

Captain Vaughn, the bluff, precise, rather scholarly-seeming
naval doctor who takes care of all Americans and most of the other
foreign embassy personnel in Moscow, kindly offered to lend us a
case of whiskey to last us until my shipments arrive, as there is
nothing but vodka to be bought here, and the price of even that is
astronomical. There is a shop not far away which deals in Georgian
wines. They are about as good as the carafe wine one gets in France,
which is very good indeed, particularly when compared with the
harsh wines of Armenia and Azerbaijan. With a little experimenting with the different sorts of these Georgian wines we should make
out quite well, although some of those which are said to be the
best are in short supply.

Sergei is a red-hot football fan. As a result of his artful suggestions, we took him with us to see the Red Army play Dinamo, the
team of the MVD, the famous police of Russia who are the direct
descendants of the Cheka, the OGPU and the NKVD. When the
NKVD was changed recently from a people's commissariat to a
ministry, the initials merely reflected the change. Several more or
less ominous buildings in the neighborhood of the Embassy have
not got around to making the change, and carry both sets of initials.

Soccer is played by the Russians, and their big-league teams
create as much enthusiasm and have as big a following as the corresponding soccer teams of England. The crowd in the Dinamo
Stadium must have included at least eighty thousand people, with
no empty seats. The red flags and bunting with which the stadium
was decorated and the roar of music from all the loud-speakers
added to the excitement.

The seats which Sergei had gotten for us were about halfway up
the stands, and it was convenient that he was along when we
pushed and scrambled through the crowd only to find that someone
else was occupying them. However, the usurpers moved readily and
obligingly enough. All around us it was evident that people were

having the same difficulty claiming their seats. There was many a voluble argument, but in no case did it lead to bad temper. People just moved over, until soon even all the access ways were filled.

When the teams came out on the field, admirers from the stands — mostly girls — jumped over the parapets and ran out to meet them, holding out large and small bouquets of flowers for their favorite heroes. The big, tough-looking players accepted them, grinned, and held them until a group of small boys took them and piled them in a colorful mound behind each goal net.

Soccer is a nice game to watch, with its head punts and its fast action. The crowd thoroughly enjoyed it, roaring at every play, shouting *"Molodyets,* Nicolai! *Molodyets,* Sasha!"* They acted much like a crowd of Americans at a big baseball game, but always there were those shrewd, interesting faces. Not even a brief downpour of rain dampened their enthusiasm. Although everyone who did not have a coat was wet to the skin, no one made a move to leave. The Red Army team was clearly the favorite, but that does not seem to me necessarily to argue dislike for the police. When I suggested that possibility to Sergei he professed not to understand my Russian, and I did not labor the point.

When the game was over, there was no crowding or disorder trying to get out. There was a good reason for this, for the crowd was channeled into the Metro subway through long lines of MVD horsemen, spaced so closely that no one could slip between their ranks. What it might have been was evident in the struggle that went on around the booths that sold ice cream and postcards of the football heroes.

4. "HE WHO DOES NOT WORK SHALL NOT EAT"

THE FAMOUS GORKY PARK OF CULTURE AND REST was a bit of a disappointment. It lies along the river a mile or so from the Embassy, and was neither as elaborate nor as large as I had expected. The amusements were on about the scale of those of a traveling carnival at home. Such thrills as the catapult gun that shot people into a net, which Nell remembered from her previous visit to Moscow, were gone. The Russians love such things, but there was not even a roller coaster — only a Ferris wheel and a whirligig of twisting gondolas, with which they were having much fun. There was a merry-go-round whose animals were those from all the Soviet Republics — camels, polar bears, reindeer and such.

Much more space was devoted to culture than to relaxation. There were two or three lectures going on in crude theaterlike enclosures, and several exhibits of elementary science, including one which showed in rather grisly fashion how babies come into the world. There were few people in the reading rooms, but a chess pavilion was filled. A large exhibit of captured enemy aircraft occupied several acres. Except for two or three Japanese ones, they were all German aircraft, some of them quite interesting, each carrying its own placard which gave its characteristics and sometimes its history.

There were some untidy little lakes in the hot, dusty wooded part of the park, where some desultory boating went on. Most of the people seemed content to stroll around through the paths of dirt and gravel. One very handsome woman sat on a bench, looking at the water. A Red Army officer, apparently her companion who had been on some sort of errand, stole up behind her and seized her by the arm. "*Vashi dokumenty!*" he said (Let me see your papers!). Her hand flew to her breast and she went white. When she turned and saw who it was, her relief was only too apparent. They laughed and walked off arm in arm.

I shall be glad when the theatrical season opens, for the theater

should be of help with the language, and theater tickets are cheap
enough — about two dollars and a half — to be one of the things
we can afford. There seem to be only a few shows on in the summertime, and they are mostly musical. We went to one of them the
other night in a summer theater in the Hermitage Park. The way to
get good seats is to write a very polite letter to the theater, asking
if they would be kind enough to let the bearer have seats for the
use of the signer, and then to add not only all the titles one can
claim, but the seal of the Embassy. The request will not be honored without the seal, and one's seats depend on one's importance.
This system works, for although the theater was completely filled
we got seats in the fourth row on only one day's notice.

We went last night to an exhibition of folk dancing put on by a
troupe from the Tatar Republic. I expected to see something rather
barbaric, but the dances were as formal and stylized as those one
sees in Spain. The costumes were sometimes peasant ones and sometimes their Sunday best with long silk dresses. They were elaborately
embroidered, with headbands of golden lace, and each dress was a
different color. They were more Russian than Asiatic in pattern, but
the colors were often those peculiar off-color shades of cerise and
pink which both Russians and Asiatics seem to like.

Many of the dances had a motif of restrained, highly proper
coquetry between men and women, with much use of embroidered
shawls to maintain a barrier between pursuer and pursued. The best
dance was one in which one of the girls carried a yoke with a
bucket on each end. Her boy friend picks up the yoke when she
isn't looking, and eventually uses it to capture her around the
waist. One or two of the girls were very lovely, but for the most
part they seemed to have been sent to Moscow for their ability to
dance rather than their faces. One of the songs had an endless refrain of something that sounded like "titty-daddy, titty-daddy, titty-
daddy" which has been going through my head ever since.

One thing that Nina, my Russian teacher, makes me do is particularly valuable. Starting at the very beginning of *Eugene Onegin,*
every day she makes me memorize an additional stanza of fourteen
lines. I have long known the usefulness of memorizing Russian
poetry. It adds permanently and almost painlessly to one's vocabu-

lary, automatically provides proper stressing, and gives one endless ready examples of good grammar. Nina says in her birdlike voice that *Eugene Onegin* is a part of every Russian's education and that it has scores of phrases which are continually used by Russians to make a point, just as we use expressions from Shakespeare and the Bible. Onegin is not only typically Russian, he inspires many a youngster to try to be like him, weaknesses and all. It is probable that he may even have something to do with such things as the Russian love for the ballet.

It is not difficult to memorize each day's stanza, but the days pass swiftly and I have visions of an early breakdown in trying to keep the rapid accumulation intact. *Onegin,* though of full book length, is cheerful and full of lighthearted moods and words. Nina never fails to throw back her mane of thick russet hair and laugh heartily at such indelicacies in the lines as *"Chort vozmi!"* (Devil take you!).

Nell has undertaken the project of trying to make Spirodonovka more attractive, and the young naval officers who live there seem most appreciative. "Spiro" is a two-story stucco house directly on the sidewalk, furnished by Burobin and by whatever has accumulated through the years. In addition to our own apartment being well equipped, we have some duplicate things in our forthcoming shipments, so she has sent them china, silver and odds and ends, and is now making them some curtains. Which is a labor of love, for she hates to sew.

My office is very shorthanded at the moment, there being only two or three assistant naval attachés. Before coming here, I made it clear that no assistants were acceptable who could not handle the language. One of them, Frank Levy, is of Russian parentage, so he fills the bill nicely, and is quiet and reliable besides. Lieutenant Colonel McMillan, a good-looking Marine with a fine reputation, is on his way, and we have been promised a graduate of the current course at the Navy language school. There is also a lieutenant named Dreher in charge of a branch office in Odessa, which takes care of American shipping, but now that the relief shipments of UNRRA are ending, the Russians have served notice that we must soon close that office. It would be nice to get to Odessa before then, but it seems to me that such a trip would not be very profitable until I am more at home in speaking and understanding.

All of the officers living at both Spiro and Khlebny are followed wherever they go by the secret police in plain clothes, to see if they are engaged in espionage. There is no doubt in my mind that I myself am not followed, probably because the Russians think that the younger officers would be more apt to try to get away with something, although my call on Serayev may have had something to do with it. There is also no doubt in my mind that Levy thinks that I'm just not bright enough to know whether I'm being followed or not. Every time he sees me he tells me how he has been trailed, and how to catch them at it, for they never follow openly. One of the principal amusements seems to be to try to evade the *slezhka.* I have told my officers that the best thing to do is to ignore it completely and act normally, for as long as they try to shake off their *slezhka* they give grounds for suspicion that they are up to something. Perhaps such evidence of a clear conscience is why I have been let alone.

The Embassy has a *dacha,* or summer place, near Tarasovka, a village near the northern edge of Moscow. *Dachas* are very popular in Russia, and, although only the mighty can have their own personal ones, a great many groups and organizations have them all around Moscow. The Embassy *dacha* is set in a grove of pine trees with a little stream that flows past below a steep, wooded hill. It is used principally for picnics, and for gardening by those of the Embassy personnel who want to raise their own fresh vegetables rather than pay a dollar and a quarter for a pound of tomatoes. There are tennis and badminton courts, horseshoe pits and tables for bridge.

Sunday the whole Embassy had a picnic at the *dacha.* Even within the city limits, every foot of space along the road is taken up with little plots of vegetables, mostly cabbage, and everywhere people were cultivating these little gardens. Before entering into the picnic, Nell and I went for a long drive in the countryside beyond the *dacha.* The summer comes to an end early here, and already the trees are yellowing in the dust. None of the roads are paved except the main highways that run radially from Moscow to other big cities, and even the Leningrad road is potholed and often atrociously cobbled, far inferior to the average third-class state highway at home. The dusty country roads twist through the fields, beginning nowhere and ending nowhere. They must be impassable in wet weather, for Sergei, who is an excellent and careful driver, often had difficulty in getting around some of the enormous chuck-holes and wallows.

Pajamas seem more for summer sports wear here than for sleeping; more than once we passed dignified Russians strolling by a stream or pond decked out gaily in such attire. The countryside was bleak and colorless, with little charm. We came to the edge of one of the big reservoirs that supplies Moscow with water, and it was unwooded and stark.

I saw a small factory in a fold of the long hills, and asked Sergei what they might be making in such a place. He shrugged and looked unhappy at the suggestion that we might ask someone. Once I stopped and talked with a fisherman, who showed me in friendly enough fashion what he was using for bait, yet the feeling is growing that as far as the Russians are concerned, foreigners must make their own lives.

So we returned to the picnic, with its barrel of beer and its baseball game. From a neighboring *dacha* came the sounds of a loud-speaker playing Russian popular music. The high point of the day was when, towards evening, Walter Cronkhite, the smooth and able United Press correspondent, led us all in a typical Russian parade with much throwing out of chests and chanting of *"Slava! Slava!"* (Glory! Glory!).

I find that I am ex officio a member of such Embassy committees as those which run American House and the commissary. Durbrow, the Minister-Counselor, is next senior to Ambassador Smith, and he does much of the internal managing of the Embassy. He is short and plump, and, since this is his third tour of duty in Moscow, he is a mine of sensible and sensitive information.

The commissary is not supported by the government, but is a co-operative effort of Embassy personnel to provide American food and supplies, for no one can regularly afford the Russian prices. Food has become a genuine problem here, for the Russians are refusing to release our commissary shipments from customs. Each

Embassy was given an annual allowance of 900,000 rubles equivalent in duty to cover everything to be imported. No one can find out what the customs rates are, but the first shipment to be released was one of office supplies. Since we have a large Embassy — some hundred and forty people in all — it was a large shipment, and it ate up 840,000 rubles of our year's allowance. Although newcomers have been told in the past that they should not bring food, it was decided that from now on every new diplomatic arrival should bring with him a year's supply of food. The initial household shipments of those few of us with diplomatic passports are admitted with no reference to our customs allowance, so in this manner we may be able to feed the great majority of Americans who are not in a diplomatic status.

This in itself is sufficient reason for having to depend on Russian servants rather than bringing in American ones. We simply could not feed American servants. As it is, the commissary supplies are strictly rationed and insufficient for ourselves, so that we must depend partly on the Russian market and must feed our servants entirely on Russian food.

With a ration of only two pounds of American sugar a month and with Russian eggs at fifty cents an egg, Nell has found it necessary to put a stout padlock on the supply cupboard and makes Natasha come to her every time she needs anything. One can almost as easily afford to feed them caviar at seventeen dollars a pound.

It seems to me that the many foreigners who consider Russian servants dishonest because they make away with food are doing them a bit of an injustice. A northerner who goes to live in the South may regard Negro servants who take food home as dishonest, but southerners know that the Negro is much more apt to regard a little toting as a perquisite of the job, and so think nothing of it. In spite of the widespread problem of food, Russians are traditionally generous, even prodigal, and so are apt to consider our necessary prudence as a sign of meanness.

Primitive peoples often show qualities which have something in common with what can sometimes be seen in children, a *khitrost* or cunning which they are apt to consider admirable, a flattering of those in power, and a certain amoral orientation which is nevertheless strongly tinged with spirituality.

At any rate, Natasha always looks grim when she comes around for supplies and when she produces scraps of paper filled with highly illegible Russian writing to show what she bought in the markets. In spite of the fact that there is nothing on which you can put your finger and that they are respectful and know that the *khozyain*, the owner or boss, can do as he pleases, there is a feeling that we are not fully accepted by any of the servants, but are regarded with a sort of suspended distrust. Alone among the three military services, the Navy's allowances have been set up by Congress so that all servants — and their food — must be paid from one's own personal funds, if any. Valya has been told that she must go, but neither of us like her very well anyhow.

There are some things about the Soviet system whose implications are difficult to grasp. All wages are paid by the state, so they can be doubled overnight or cut in half, merely by decree. Similarly, the price of food can be doubled overnight or bread can be given away free. In the long run, though, the regime must be up against the same problems that exist in other economies. If people get more money than there are things to buy, the prices cannot be held in line, and black markets spring up. The Soviet government apparently tries to keep such a balance between wages and prices that every citizen must use all his energies to make both ends meet. The principle that "he who does not work shall not eat" is backed up by controls which make it necessary that every individual of a family work in order to keep that family in food.

It is strange to be in a place where bread is so important. Bread in Russia is not an optional and complementary item, it is food itself, heavy-textured and satisfying.

The weeks go by, but the redecoration of our new apartment makes little progress. Nell has herself been doing a bit of supervising on that job. One of the painters told her that the reason they were so slow was because they were weak from lack of food, saying that one of the men had fallen from a ladder from sheer weakness. There is a divergence of opinion on the question of feeding such workmen, for some say that if they are fed they will never finish. Nevertheless, they are all now getting soup and bread from Nell's jealously guarded stores, though even Natasha is not sure it is the quickest way for us eventually to get settled.

5. DISTURBING PATTERNS

IMAGINE A CITY BIGGER THAN Chicago or Philadelphia, with all its office buildings, factories, warehouses, shops and stores. If you then imagine what it would be like if every one of all those buildings was a government office, you would have some idea of Moscow. Not far from the Embassy, for example, is a big building which covers about a city block — the Bureau for the Repair of Sewing Machines. The scope of universal state planning is difficult to grasp. Someone has to worry about the stocking and distributing of spare parts for sewing machines and keeping them in order, but it is not done on a self-regulating system of supply and demand, but by a conscious bureaucratic planning process. Since it must all be based on data of some sort, everywhere special voluminous records are kept of everything as a basis for that planning. The overhead involved must be tremendous. The Soviet papers are full of exhortations about trying to keep down the continually mounting overhead.

I have been walking around the city, stopping in at bookstores and doing shopping errands. The biggest and best department store in Moscow — there are not many of them — is comparable in size to those at home, but it is a rare exception to see any article in any of the stores that is excellent, and most of them would not be salable in the cheapest American market. They are either of sleazy or inferior material, faulty design, badly made, clumsy and awkward in whole or in part, poorly proportioned, poorly styled, badly finished, or just plain unattractive. The Russian people, who crowd eagerly into the stores, and who are as excited as children with buying new things, deserve better than they get.

Yet the other day I hunted up a shop which dealt in uniform equipment, to buy for an officer back home some ribbon of a Russian decoration which had been awarded him during the war, and there everything for the military — ribbons, gold lace, rating badges and fabrics — was well made and of excellent quality. The answer seems to be that the Russians can make anything, but they can't make very much of very many things. The Russians like their decorations. They wear their full medals, rather than merely the ribbons, on all sorts of uniforms, and even on civilian clothes.

Most of the civil servants with whom the stores and shops are staffed are obliging and polite, particularly when they realize that they are dealing with a foreigner. They seem to have a natural desire to be helpful. Yet there was a much higher proportion than anywhere in the West of those who were indifferent and uninformed. It was noticeable that this was not because I was a foreigner, for those same people were the same way with the Russian customers.

There is a stamp collector's shop in Kuznetski Most, and it seems to be the only one in Moscow. I had a long list of Soviet stamps that people back home wanted, and the attendant was endlessly patient, finally taking my order for a complete set including one of every stamp he had in stock for what seemed a very reasonable price, although stamps are not my hobby. While I was talking with him, someone took me by the arm. I turned in surprise, for although I am always a center of curiosity no one had yet been that familiar.

It was the crooked-nosed artillery colonel of the Berlin train. He was friendly as could be, telling me how his family was getting along, asking about Nell, and saying that my Russian had already improved greatly. This seemed an unusual opportunity, so I asked him if he would bring his wife to have dinner with us, but he became ill at ease and full of excuses, and left almost immediately. On thinking it over afterward, it seemed possible that there was nothing sinister about the incident, but that he was not in a position to repay any hospitality, and I have already learned that this is a very important point with a Russian. Also it was just as well that he did not come, for he might have made trouble for himself with his own people.

I have tried everywhere to get a map of Moscow. A series of irregularly girdling boulevards divides the city into rings that center on the Kremlin, and between the rings the streets run confusingly in all directions. Although at first incredulous, I finally had to realize that there are no maps of Moscow to be had. Moreover, there is no telephone directory.* They probably go on the assumption that if you have legitimate business with anyone you will know his telephone number. My first reaction was to put the absence of maps and telephone directory down to the secret and suspicious nature of the Russian government. On the other hand, there is no private initiative to meet any demand, so such items must fit in with the grand plans. Perhaps the planners consider other things more urgent. Since Russia is a complex country, the answer is probably a complex one, and not so simple as being either one thing or the other.

When one gets away from the few straight new streets that have been ruthlessly driven across the city by the Soviets, one senses that Moscow is a very old city. Occasionally there is a glimpse of beauty, as in the fantastic golden domes and chained crosses of the churches, or in some carved and mullioned window looking out on a courtyard, but for the most part one has the feeling that its age is one of decrepitude and decay. Most Moscow houses in the more central portions of the city are covered with stucco, which has often fallen off in great patches showing the wattle beneath. The stucco is sometimes left in its natural gray or yellowish-gray color, sometimes covered with a thin wash of ocher or off-color pastel pinks or blues. Many of the houses are out of plumb, and their edges have lost their sharpness and become blurred. They disintegrate and flow like a ripe old Brie cheese, and often they have the same creamy red-brown color. Everywhere are alleyways and courtyards, unbelievably dirty and untidy, and there is everywhere a feeling of mystery, secrecy and something hidden.

I went into some of those courtyards, and found that they led to other courts beyond. They also had several small, discreet doctors' signs, saying "VENEREAL DISEASES TREATED." The Soviet press says that venereal disease is nonexistent in the Soviet Union.

It is customary among attachés for a newcomer to call first on all the other foreign attachés. I have consequently been gradually

* A telephone directory for Moscow was eventually published in 1951–1952. It is obvious that unlisted numbers, for the convenience of the state alone, are utilized much more intensively than in America.

working through the list. Today I called on Colonel Hjelle, the big-nosed Norwegian who is accredited as army, air and naval attaché. His office is his room in one of the older hotels, and its windows look out on the headquarters of the MVD. "So they can keep an eye on me," he said. MVD headquarters is just like a big office building, and it seemed to me fortunate that there is something like the Kremlin, which is intriguing to the eye as well as to the mind, outside my windows.

The Dutch Ambassador had a big reception at the Grand Hotel, in a room whose ceiling is deeply paneled with Wedgewood-like blue and white scenes of Moscow. One of those scenes is of Mokhavaya House, which was easily recognizable by its lofty columns and the narrow balcony which runs past the French windows of our apartment, although the familiar yellow color was necessarily missing. The reception was lavish with caviar, smoked salmon, *pâtés* and French wines.

At parties I always seek out someone who can talk Russian with me, such as the brown, gentle Mexican Ambassador, who has a natural gift for languages and has been very encouraging. At this party I found a girl who not only could talk with me, but who had big brown eyes, a wealth of brown curly hair, and a waist as slim as Scarlett O'Hara's, set off by a billowing dress. She was Tamara Gilmore, the Russian wife of the Associated Press correspondent. She was very pretty, and her soft Russian speech was just as pretty in its way. Eddy, her husband, is bald as an egg and plump, but always neat and well-dressed. He won the Pulitzer Prize not long ago. Tamara was a ballerina when Eddy married her.

"They tell me that you speak Russian," she said.

"No," I answered, "perhaps some day, but now I only try."

We talked for a while. Then she turned to me, her eyes wide. "You can talk Russian now. Beautifully! And it is so pleasant to find an American who loves the Russian language."

It was obvious that she was flattering me up to my ears, but she is the first Russian who has said "now," and not "by winter," "in a month or two," or "soon." It did wonders for my self-confidence, and ever since I have been much more glib.

Probably nearly everyone likes to read the morning paper leisurely. One of the compensations of duty here is to go to my office
and sit down with a completely clear conscience to an hour or
two of reading the Soviet press. But there is no rose without its
thorns, and after each bout one is well lacerated, because of the
unprincipled and venomous attacks on Americans with which the
papers are filled. When I first began to read the papers it seemed
too bad that the American public could not be given a complete
translation of two or three of them, just as they stand, for a single
week, in order to see the willful falsity of the never-ceasing attacks
on the capitalist system as embodied by America, but I soon came
to believe that, if that were done, the American people would
clamor for war.

Attacks on Wall Street and the lynching of Negroes were to
be expected, but not a long article distorting and twisting the
President into another Hitler, imputing to him worse motives than
those of the Nazis. Zaslavsky and Ehrenburg are two of the most
vicious of the hatchet men. It is not only our system that is
attacked, but Americans as such. *Komsomolskaya Pravda* has
just come out with a couple of articles on the conduct of American
Marines and soldiers in China. One article gave an account of the
delight with which a group of them pushed Chinese into a pond
at bayonet's point and laughed to watch them drown, and the
other told of systematic and deliberate infection of the Chinese
populace with syphilis. A fine thing for teen-agers to read — for
Komsomolskaya Pravda is the paper for Communist Youth. And
yet many Americans still think that the reason why we can't get
along with the Soviet Union is somehow our fault.

To get the full impact of these things, one must realize that it
is not the same as items appearing somewhere in a vast mass
of reading material such as an American Sunday paper. *Pravda,*
the greatest paper in Russia, consists of a single folded sheet, thus
providing only four pages to be read. The first page contains nothing but greetings to Stalin and reports from various cities as to
how the current competition to speed up the Five Year Plan is
getting along, the second page has editorials on the principles of
communism, the third page special articles, largely attacks on
America with occasionally a few letters to the editor on minor

malfunctionings, and the last page more of the same and slanted
Tass dispatches from all over the world that usually quote the
local *Daily Worker* version of foreign news. Nothing else.

Our translators prepare a press digest for those who don't read
Russian, and who consequently receive their propaganda abridged
and in sample lots. Even so, the effect on Americans here of continuous exposure to such groundless abuse is very noticeable. It
gets on everyone's nerves and is depressing.

General and Mrs. Macon had a dinner party for General Guillaume, the French military attaché, who is leaving after several
years in Moscow. He is a fine type of the French professional
soldier, with a total of fifteen years' duty in North Africa. He
speaks Russian with complete ease, having been thrown with
Russians while a prisoner of war. He told me that the one thing
that had really made him at home in the language was the Russian theater, which he had attended regularly. He advised me to
go to the speaking theater at least twice a week, saying that if
I took it seriously as an exercise in the language I could not help
but soon become proficient.

The Swedish naval attaché, Willy Edenberg, and Captain Hill,
the British one, have a *dacha* for the summer twenty-odd kilometers out the Arbat. It is surrounded with cow pastures through
which flows a small stream. Anywhere else it would be a tiny
farm on the edge of a city, but here it is a *dacha*. The Edenbergs
are a dignified and handsome couple, he with his typical oval
Swedish face and thick bushy reddish eyebrows, and she with all
her pleasant calm and her beautifully coiffed silver-blue hair.
Hill is a bluff ruddy Englishman, with a composed and lovely
golden-blonde English wife.

It was a showery day for their party, but between showers we
wandered through the wet pastures and took turns rowing a little
boat. There was just enough water in the little stream to float it
through the watercress and lilies. A troop of German prisoners of
war came through the meadows, scattering on their way a herd of
huge savage-looking red swine. The Chinese Ambassador, a suave
smiling man with a little nervous chuckle at the most surprising

times, went out with his movie camera to take some pictures of
them, but was brusquely repulsed by the young Russian guards.

We had some excellent ice cream that was covered with little
colored flowers of frozen whipped cream, and then, on the way
home, went for a long drive through beautiful rain-swept woods.
Perhaps the rain, which certainly did away with the dust and
turned it to yellow mud, softened the scene in other ways, for
the countryside seemed much less bleak than it was beyond the
Embassy *dacha*.

On the Street of the Twenty-fifth of October is a puppet theater.
There is a larger and more sophisticated puppet theater which has
not yet opened for the season, and this one that I have found is
primarily for children. Nell and I went there to see Hans Christian
Andersen's *Snow Queen,* and again to see the purely Russian
skazka, or fairy tale, *Koshchei the Deathless.*

Ever since I was a small child I have loved the *Snow Queen.*
It has a touch of melancholy and loneliness about it that lifts it
out of the usual run of children's tales. The play was done with
true puppets, manipulated by hands inside them, giving a more
natural effect than is achieved with marionettes.

It began with a stage scene wherein real live actors took part,
as in any play on the stage. A big blond man, with buckled shoes
and a cloak such as might have been worn in Andersen's time,
comes into a cottage and starts to tell the story to a small girl who
drowses in front of the fireplace. Then the lights die down and the
puppets take over. It was a lovely thing, with spirited lifelike
reindeer and an extraordinarily tough and terrifying robber band.
It was all there, the icy splinter from the broken mirror, the talking flowers of the woman who could conjure, the Finland woman
and the fragments of the frozen lake in the Snow Queen's castle.
There were also peculiarly Russian touches, such as the long Mongolian horns that I have seen pictured only in rare old books.
It was all so carefully done that I learned things about the language
that I did not know, just from watching the position of the creatures' mouths that accompanied their pure musical speech.

At the very end, the scene comes back to the real live actors
by the fireside in the cottage. The illusion of reality that had been

given to the puppets had been so vivid that the living figures seemed suddenly abnormal. The cloaked teller of tales seemed a ten-foot giant, and it was some time before he shrank to everyday size.

Koshchei the Deathless was not as faithful to the original *skazki* as the *Snow Queen* was to Andersen's story, but departed from them to give suspense and bizarre entertainment. The winged Koshchei was made just enough of a villainous monster to bring squeals of apprehension from the small fry in the audience, and there were shouts of relief when the egg that held his death was finally broken. The effect was more like that of a comic-strip version of the more malevolent creatures of folklore.

Incidentally, there are no comic strips in Russia, for they are regarded as bourgeois manifestations. Although there was a time soon after the Revolution when fairy tales were also regarded as bourgeois, it is not true that they are now forbidden. Like so many Russian words, *skazka* does not have a completely satisfactory equivalent in English. "Fairy tale" will not do unless it is used in the genuine folklore sense of Grimm's fairy tales, which seldom have anything to do with fairies. The *skazki* are the old stories that have been told over and over again by countless generations of those who are close to the soil, and which are still current and loved in Russia. They are rich and imaginative tales, full of magic and terror, colorful, intricate and gorgeous, and yet often with a somber quality which seems to come from the desolation of the forests and the dark northern nights. They are of importance to anthropologists because of their ancient racial memories, and give many a clue to the understanding of the nature of the Russians themselves and the many and subtle differences which the latter place on such values as cunning, courage, family loyalties and other qualities.

They follow their own pattern, usually beginning with "In the thrice-nine kingdom, in the thrice-ten land, lived an old man and an old woman who had three sons," and ending with a great feast: " — and I was there, and drank beer and honey-wine, but all of it trickled through my beard and not a drop fell into my mouth." Which is proof positive that the whole tale is to be taken with a grain of salt. The language is peasant language, salty, strong, imaginative and often none too squeamish.

The Russians now take their *skazki* seriously and really study them. I have one book which contains a collection of *skazki* that was made in an isolated valley of the Tunguska River in Siberia, and side by side with each story is the stenographic record of the same tale as told by the same narrator ten years later. This is obviously important field work in the study of oral tradition. Sometimes the *skazki* are twisted to serve the ends of the regime, in such ways as to provide a glorification of Stalin or of collective effort, but such perversions lack skill and are easily detectable. There was nothing of that in what we saw at the puppet theater.

Most of the audiences were children, and never have I seen such well-behaved children. There was no scuffling or skylarking, but each child, regardless of age, was as quiet and well-mannered as an adult. Their faces fairly shone with intelligent goodness, and the little girls in particular, with their pigtails neatly curled around their heads, were models of every propriety. During one of the intermissions a mother next to us unwrapped a little package of bread and gave each of her children a slice, which they ate solemnly and quietly. It was just bread, black bread, with no jam and no butter.

Sergei is due for his annual month's leave, which he will spend in the Caucasus. I shall be very happy to try another driver, for several reasons which could not very well be explained to him. For one thing, it will be more comfortable to have a driver who does not understand any English, although I suppose one must still be careful of what one says in the hearing of any of them. Sergei, while an excellent driver, is not much of a mechanic. Yesterday we went out into the country, and the brakes, which he had apparently tightened too much, froze so that we had to sit by the road for half an hour until they cooled off enough so he could loosen them.

Nell and I walked down the road and gave chocolate bars to some children who were playing in the dust. The way the wrinkled old face of their *babushka*, the Russian grandmother who is so useful and who reaps so much affection, lighted up as she thanked us made us wish that we had something special for her. Along the way were fences of light metal that seemed to me to be most unusual until I realized that they were made from the sheets from which knives and forks and spoons and dishes had been stamped, probably by some small factory in the vicinity. We also saw several huge wooden drums on which wire cable had once been wound. They were stenciled with American markings.

On the way back, we drove past the Novodevichi Monastery, whose squat half-ruined towers and Kremlin-like walls brood over a bend in the Moskva River. In some ways Moscow, with all its mixture of old and new, seems very like a big overgrown country town. It is not uncommon to see cows and goats driven through the city streets, and much of the traffic is made up of loads of vegetables and hay. For weeks the city has been getting cleaned up and decorated for a *prazdnik,* or celebration, in honor of its eight-hundredth anniversary.

As we neared home, I realized that I had never seen the prison of which everyone who has ever read of Moscow has heard and which was only too well known in the days of both Tsars and Soviets.

"Sergei," I said, "where is the Lubyanka Prison?"

"Never heard of it!" he said, shrugging his shoulders, his face taking on the blank, baffling look that annoys me more than anything else about him. Maybe it's just bad luck to talk about it.

I have requested a driving permit for myself, but everyone in the Embassy is most discouraging about my ever getting it. Among many other requirements, one has to take elaborate examinations on the theory and practice of internal combustion engines, and they say that foreigners almost invariably fail in them. Perhaps there are peculiarities about Russian engines.

A Russian girl who has been teaching one of our assistant attachés and who has been helped by him with food and such has ended up by getting into trouble with the Soviet authorities, or so it seems. She has been threatened for some time by the authorities, and has now disappeared, sending word through others that she will be sent to Siberia unless he can come to her assistance in some way. When she first began to be threatened, he went to the Ambassador with the story, and the Ambassador showed me his statements.

The amazing thing about the case is the way in which she has implicated a considerable number of Americans in one way or another, including such statements as "please do not have anything to do with so-and-so, for he gives information to the Soviet police," and "do not tell such-and-such a person about this, for he is being used by the police, although he doesn't know that that is the case." I know enough about some of those who were involved to be absolutely certain that what she had to say was false. The whole thing seems to be deliberately intended to sow suspicion among Americans. It is so full of inconsistencies that it is impossible to tell where the truth, if any, begins and ends, to tell how willingly she may have said these things, or even to ascribe motives. It is the sort of thing that would be full of trouble if it were known and discussed through the Embassy.

There are many things that happen that only the Ambassador, Durbrow, and two or three of the most senior people know. They are the only ones who are ultimately responsible, and usually there are Russians involved who are so vulnerable to Soviet power that they must be protected. If all of the others knew of them, it would be impossible to protect them, and the place would blow up. Sometimes it seems to be only a matter of nerves, and other times psychopathic personalities are involved, but there is a curious pattern running through it all that is very disturbing. Much of it can only be explained as due to complex intrigues of the Soviets. In any event, one lives in a strange and unhealthy atmosphere which cannot be handled in the normal open American way, and one soon gets to view everything both good and bad, with suspicion. My respect for the complexity of the problems and my admiration for the way in which the Ambassador and the senior State Department people handle them continue to grow.

Durbrow showed me the file copy of a long dispatch which George Kennan, then acting ambassador, sent more than a year ago in reply to a query from Washington for an appraisal of what to expect from Soviet Russia. It is probably the most profound and brilliant analysis of the Soviet Union that has yet been made, capably and even beautifully phrased, as is all of Kennan's work. It added up to the statement that we can expect nothing but trouble unless and until the regime changes its innermost nature, and it reaches this conclusion without doing violence to any informed viewpoint. It was to me extraordinarily just and satisfying, answering many of the subtle questions with which few seem able to deal. Although its logic is irrefutable, it seems probable that one must live long and thoughtfully in the Soviet Union in order to reach a full appreciation of the excellence of his appraisal.

6. THE EIGHT-HUNDREDTH BIRTHDAY

THERE IS AN AIR OF EXCITEMENT OVER MOSCOW because of the approaching *prazdnik* to celebrate its eight-hundredth anniversary. Moscow is doubtless much older than that, but the first dated record of any mention of the city was just eight hundred years ago. A full-length portrait of Stalin at least thirty feet high has gone up on the front of the Historical Museum at the entrance to Red Square, and the top of the Moscow Hotel has a row of gigantic portraits of the Politburo. The very size of those portraits gives one a peculiar sensation of power behind them, even though one knows that the intent behind it all is to create just that psychological impression. Since there is no speculation or comment in the press regarding possible changes in individual power, everyone, including the Russians, is tremendously interested in seeing whether or not the portraits of any of the Politburo are omitted, and whether or not Molotov and Beria will retain their positions next to Stalin.

All Moscow is hung with flags and bunting like an old-fashioned Fourth of July, but here every flag and decoration is a lurid, exciting crimson. Troops of soldiers sing as they march through the streets, and everywhere there are crowds out to see the decorations and the arrangements. At each end of the plaza outside our windows big platforms have been erected for speeches and entertainment. Up Gorky Street a monument has been erected to Yury Dolgoruky, the Muscovite prince who first used Moscow's name for the benefit of posterity. His name means "long-armed," and the Russians say, off the record, that that is an apt name for any Muscovite in power. Our servants have always been remarkably sober, even abstemious, yet today little old Natasha said that we should all have some vodka with which to drink to the *prazdnik,* so I sent Valodya, the new chauffeur, out to get some.

Nina, who has been obviously ill with a heavy cold for the last few days, was in today to say that the doctors had told her she should have a vacation in the Caucasus. Some of her recent remarks have made me wonder about her motives, and though she is a beauty as well as a good teacher her prospective departure came as somewhat of a relief. I told her that since the language was of such importance to me, another teacher would have to be obtained to replace her. Somewhat to my surprise, she was not at all taken aback, but seemed to expect it. That seems to shoot the theory that she was specially detailed to work on me. Perhaps they had decided that I was not vulnerable, but if that was the case, she had not tried very hard before reaching such a decision. There is still a good chance that she was actually what she represented herself to be, but in any case it is something of a relief that she is gone.

By the eve of the *prazdnik* the crowds had thickened until it was difficult to get through the streets. Bands and music from the loud-speakers gave everything a carnival air. The two platforms in Manezhny Place ran a continuous entertainment, and it was solid entertainment, with no political speeches — wrestling, boxing, choruses, bands, comedians and dancers. Dense crowds gathered around the platforms, and in the more open areas little eddies of people were dancing with each other in the streets.

As it grew dark, the lights came on. Although there had been plenty of workmen in evidence for days, we were not prepared for the effect. The whole vast outline of the Kremlin was picked out with lights which followed faithfully the crenelations of the walls and the outlines of all the fantastic towers. All the bridges across the Moskva River were similarly outlined with strings of lights, and as far as one could see in all directions were similar illuminations. One whole side of the Moscow Hotel consisted of an electric fountain which danced and sprayed in colored waves of light.

Nell and I wedged our way through the crowds into Red Square, which was a blaze of light from fixed projectors as well as from the thousands and thousands of lights on the surrounding buildings and the Kremlin gates and towers. In Red Square is the Head Place where the execution block and gallows stood for centuries, and where, in the Time of Troubles in 1606, the body of the False Dmitry, with a vile mask on his belly, a flute in his mouth and a bagpipe under his arm, was flouted by the mob with the placard, "YOU, SCOUNDREL, HAVE MADE US PIPE OFTEN, NOW YOU PIPE FOR OUR AMUSEMENT." Now the Head Place was a great bouquet of rippling red banners in the glare of the searchlights.

The orderliness of the crowds was very noticeable. There was no rowdyism, no contagious bursts of extrovertism. It is not that the people were apathetic, as some foreigners say, for they were interested and curious about everything. Perhaps the police keep crowds here from becoming bumptious, but whatever the reason, the people were dignified and self-contained as they strolled about with their children of all ages, and at the same time they were full of smiles and good-nature, with eyes that danced at the spectacle. Once two hard-bitten little Cossacks with their wide trousers stuffed into their boots, suddenly, for no reason at all, decided to do a wild Cossack dance. They paid no attention whatever to the crowd around, but had a grand time all to themselves.

Two or three times I tried to talk with some of the people who were drifting around, but soon gave it up. Perhaps those Russians were hesitant to get into a conversation with a foreigner in public, but whatever the reason, they seemed uneasy and turned away.

The day of the *prazdnik* the crowds were enormous, and all day long the continuous entertainment went on on the platforms in the plaza — singers, orchestras, and dancers. There were stamping peasant dances, sailor dances, Cossack dances, Circassian sword dances. Masses of people surged with uplifted hands around big trucks in order to buy ice cream and little pies.

Half-organized little parades went past. One consisted of three or four small trucks hung with scarlet bunting and decorated with evergreens. In the leading truck was a little band playing valiantly against all the noise from the amplifiers and loud-speakers, and each of the little trucks that followed was piled high with potatoes, cabbages and harvest produce. It gave such a childish home-made effect that it was almost touching.

In the afternoon, driving through the crowds only with the greatest difficulty, we went to the Sports Parade at the stadium. The edges of the stadium and all the aisles were outlined by the blue caps of the MVD, seated or standing close together. Whole blocks of people in the audience were vivid with the national costumes of the Republics, blue, cerise, and green, with long, full, heavily embroidered skirts and white puffy peasant blouses. Even the babies had elaborately embroidered headdresses.

The parade itself was tremendous, with endless formations of hundreds of young athletes. I counted sixteen hundred people in a single formation. There were acrobats and tumblers, gymnastic teams, cyclists and motorcyclists, and teams that did acrobatic trick riding on motorcycles, all performed with beautiful precision and timing. The figures that were formed were intricate and shifting, full of color and unexpected developments. Once the Kremlin wall was formed in the middle of the field by human figures. Flower bearers gave bouquets to the winners of cross-country bicycle and motorcycle races which finished in the stadium.

Perhaps what drew as much interest as anything was two horsemen, one a Cossack in long skirted coat with cartridge pockets across his chest, who put their beautifully schooled horses through their paces at opposite ends of the stadium while other acts were going on. Throughout the whole show the crowd roared *"Slava! Slava Stalinu!"* (Glory! Glory to Stalin!) in a tremendous chorus. The football game which ended the show was tame compared with all that had gone before.

When we got home we found that the crowd in the big squares around the Kremlin and in all the streets leading to it had grown until there were no open spaces left, except that held by mounted troops. There were at least one million people to be seen from the balcony. They were packed so tight that they were like a solid pavement. The upturned faces that watched the dancers and jugglers made circles of white around the platforms. In the center of Manezhny Place a sound truck poured out music for street dancing, but the dancers were choked in the throng. New checkered taxis, which have recently appeared in Moscow to the admiration of the people, were unable to penetrate the crowds, and stood like cars bogged down in snow.

As night came on, the lights began to blaze on the outlines of bridges, walls, domes, spires and towers, the colored fountains began to play, and the floodlights made occasional weird silhouettes of dense masses of people. Suddenly there was a simultaneous flash in all directions, and then from all over the city rockets rushed upwards in a complete fiery encirclement and burst into glory against the night sky, followed by a crash of gunfire. After a moment of silence and before one had recovered from the glory, there was another salvo, synchronized in color as well as in time. Once the rockets would be all green everywhere, then all red, then white, and then varied, cascading and hanging in great lurid bursts in every direction as far as one could see, glittering, drifting, shimmering, dying, while the salvo of gunfire echoed through the city. And with them came the searchlight dance, straight bars of white or colored light, upright like a field of trees, and then weaving and swaying together throughout the sky. In occasional intervals of darkness, high up in the dark sky one could see the huge numerals "800," red flags and pictures, doubtless suspended from balloons. Someone, seeing Stalin's portrait in the heavens, murmured, "Oh my! They forgot to put on his wings!"

The regular salvos of rockets and guns lasted for a long time, and then, as if they had suddenly gotten out of control, the synchronization ceased and the rockets went wild, filling the sky everywhere with blazing color for what seemed like an endless time. Even after the main display of fireworks was over, one could see occasional bursts and minor displays against the horizon. I do not know how long it all lasted, for the music was still playing and the crowds were still there when I went to sleep.

Early in the morning, the broad streets and squares were empty, but completely clean and neat. It was hard to believe that all the litter and trash left by well over a million people could have been done away with so rapidly, but someone said that when the crowds finally went home, thousands and thousands of women turned to everywhere with their besoms.

It is difficult to evaluate the effect of such a display. There was general agreement that the only thing which could compare with it was the celebration on V-E day. The great majority of the people obviously enjoyed it hugely — certainly I did, for I had never seen anything like it. I heard an occasional Russian say that it was a pity the government had not put all that expense into making food easier for the people to get, but it seems to me that one might have heard the equivalent of such remarks if comparable lavishness had occurred in any other country.

Valodya, my new driver from the Navy pool, has it all over Sergei in blunt honesty of manner. Although he was born and raised in Moscow and has never been anything but a mechanic or chauffeur, he seems to be much more of a peasant type than the smooth, smiling Sergei. In answer to my question why one sees so few Cossacks, he said that large numbers of them had gotten into trouble with the regime, whereas Sergei would only have shrugged his shoulders. Valodya's shock of brown hair parted on the side, his weather-beaten face, his clear, honest-looking blue eyes, and his smile that shows three or four stainless-steel teeth in front, all give an impression of sturdy openness. At the same time, there is no question but that he is completely loyal to the regime. One never trusts anyone here, but somehow Valodya inspires less distrust than Sergei.

Today was overcast and dreary, with little flurries of cold rain. We went to see the great Tretyakovskaya gallery of paintings, but found that almost all of it was closed for some reason or other. So we drove aimlessly around the city. When Valodya is asked a question, he draws in his breath with a hissing sound and then holds it while he ponders his answer, but when the answer comes it is reasonably straightforward.

We passed some barracks with a parade ground in front. It was apparently a cavalry post, for twenty or thirty troopers on little restless horses were having some saber practice. One by one they would ride at full gallop down an irregular lane of tall wands that had been placed in the muddy earth, slashing with their sabers to right and left to cut down the wands. The shaggy little ponies were excited and nervous, but seemed to thoroughly enjoy the charge, when they twisted and turned like polo ponies.

After every trooper had had his turn at the wands, they took turns at piercing small rings with their sabers while galloping past, and were amazingly skillful in doing so. Two things impressed me about the scene: one, the style and *élan* with which each man put on his act, as though he were on the stage and enjoyed being there, and the other, the fact that not one Russian man, woman, nor even child, stopped to watch, although many were passing by. Athough they are a curious people, the idle crowd that always watches a steam shovel in action in America seems to have no counterpart here.

When one encounters the real greatness of the Russian theater, there is no mistaking it, just as there is no mistaking the greatness of old Egyptian and Assyrian sculpture. We went to see Chekhov's *Cherry Orchard* at MXAT, the Moscow Art Theater, and I have not been so impressed since seeing my very first play when a small child. In fact, there was something in common between that early childhood wonder and the effect created by this Russian production — a deep delight that such a thing was possible. It may have been due in part to the fact that I had just finished reading the play, so that I caught almost every word at the show itself. Never before has the Russian language been so beautiful and understandable to me, so it is quite possible that that had something to do with the sensation of looking into a completely new and different world. There was an unusual clarity in the speech, for MXAT sets the standard for diction in the Russia of today.

But the sweeping away of the language barrier by no means accounts for all of the glamour, for it was a matchless production. Every actor lived his part, completely submerging his personality in it. If it had not been for that tremendous sincerity, one would have said that they overacted, for there was a dramatic sweep and confidence about every gesture that made it almost stylized. It was the sincere acting of great talent within a pattern, just as Shakespeare and Keats and Millay express themselves within the pattern of a sonnet, and it was tremendously moving.

As the program, which one buys for half a ruble, shows, eight of the twelve actors and actresses who had significant parts had received Soviet decorations for their artistry. There is a hierarchy in such decorations, which are awarded either by the separate Republics, such as Kazakhstan or the Ukraine, or by the RSFSR, which is the largest and most important division of the USSR and includes the Great Russian nation. One actor held a decoration for his work in other aspects of the theater than acting, and the other seven had all been decorated by the RSFSR. Three of them had received the Stalin Prize.

All of the Russian theaters play repertoire, and apparently almost any actor can and does take almost any part, no matter how important or how small. They do not operate on the star system, for no part is permitted to overshadow the other roles. It would perhaps be more accurate to say that every actor is a star. I have never before seen such a varied and fascinating portrayal of character in the theater. One minor part in particular, played by a young actor named Byelokurov, that of a lackey who had once been to Paris, was made so boorish in its studied refinement, so utterly revolting, that the audience was laughing all the time he was on the stage. But interwoven with the laughter were tremendous currents of sympathy for the impractical, lovable, but vanishing types which had tragically outlived their time.

And the stage settings and effects were out of this world in their skill, spaciousness, realism, and frequent beauty, from the cherry blossoms outside the windows of the house to the dull sounds of the axes that eventually cut them down. When the furniture of the old house is all dismantled in the last act, there are faded spots on the walls showing the shapes of the pictures that once hung there. The scene of the ball has a tremendous living room in front, with a ballroom on beyond in the background, and the distant strains of the *Sobre las Olas* waltz gives an atmosphere of indescribable nostalgia. I have never dreamed of such enormous stages, in depth as well as in all other dimensions.

In spite of the sympathy with which the disintegrating bourgeois family was portrayed, the social significance was not lost. There is a part which is so minor that it was scarcely noticeable on reading the play, that of a tramp who mildly ruffles a peaceful scene in passing. On the stage, that moment somehow becomes a portent of all the violence of the Revolution that was to come.

The audiences are always interesting, and this one was no exception. Behind us sat two remarkable middle-aged women, with over-marcelled manes of hair, one gold-red and the other dark-red. They had on more make-up than Russian women usually use, and they wore small, smart, open shoes (*toofli* to the Russians) which certainly did not come out of Russia, with clothes of very good materials but strangely provincial and old-fashioned in cut. There was nothing common about them, for they had a great deal of dignity, but absolutely no flair or style. They were too studied, not casual enough, and yet they would have attracted attention anywhere in the world. They were not pretty, but their faces were very Russian. The face of one of them in particular was very white and pale, but strong-boned and not at all delicate, with huge, dark, hollow eyes. We guessed that they were wives of officials or army officers, long stationed in some provincial city.

And next to us sat a couple of nice boys. One of them, about sixteen years old, got something in his eye at the very beginning of the play, and it utterly ruined his evening. Before the intermission, he had rubbed it until he could hardly see at all. I felt so sorry for this lad that I volunteered some advice, and showed him how to use one set of eyelashes as a brush. He had never heard of that before, and was most docile and grateful, asking me to look in his eye and see if I could see anything. I doubt that I at his age would have been so willing to trust a stranger.

Today we went for a long drive in the country. When we were well to the west of the city we left the main *chaussée* and followed some narrow country roads, some of which were, for a change, paved. There seemed to be an unusual number of soldiers standing guard on those roads, and Valodya said that there were *dachas* of Soviet dignitaries in the vicinity. The autumn coloring is not brilliant here, as it is at home and in Canada, for there seem to be only two general kinds of woods, birch and evergreens, but the sun was warm on the golden birch leaves and there was a mellowness in the air that one seldom feels in Russia.

We came through a dark wood of pines that was so closely planted that it looked like the Black Forest. There was deep moss on the ground, and the big roots were so old and gnarled that they looked like an Arthur Rackham illustration. We came at last to the river, which was crossed by a strangely high wooden bridge. Valodya stopped for me to look at the river. I had brought some fishing gear along in case we should find just such a place as this, so we pulled off the road and I rigged a casting rod and went down to the grassy banks below the bridge and began to cast.

From only a little distance, the high wooden bridge looked completely fantastic, for its piers were protected from the spring ice by great plowlike wedges of dressed logs, sheathed with metal, which were so sharp and shaped at such queer angles that they looked like the hulls of warships. Even the arc of the bridge itself against the sky was queer, for it was humped up and curved in such a way that there was a Chinese suggestion to it.

Although I did not really expect to catch any fish — I seldom do — my interest was soon heightened by seeing several nice ones slide past like shadows in the dark, clear water, but no lure in which they showed any interest could be found. Valodya came back from his errand and tried to be of help in changing lures, but succeeded only in getting the line snarled up and his thumb caught on a hook. Suddenly a voice shouted from the very crest of the bridge.

"Are you wanting to catch some fish?"

I looked up. A soldier, with gun slung over his shoulder, was leaning on the parapet. "Yes!" I shouted back.

"I'll help you!" he roared, and unslung his gun.

Then came a few barks from the rifle, each accompanied by a splash where the bullet hit the water. He peered down into the river, took another try, shrugged his shoulders and walked off across the bridge with no further comment. After that there were no more fish to be seen, let alone hooked.

There is a chubby little curly-haired brown-eyed Russian girl, Elyena, who is married to one of the chauffeurs at Spasso House and who is willing to give me lessons. She says that she was trained as a pianist and not as a teacher, and she is not registered as such with the Soviet authorities. In order to be registered as a teacher one must have been through the Foreign Language Institute, where, besides languages, one is taught how to deal with foreigners. She also says that she knows more than most Russians because her father is a purist in Russian usage and because her husband does nothing but read when he is not driving. All that I want is someone who will talk to me and correct my speech, so I am very pleased to try her. She may be able to get by without being registered, because she has entree to the Embassy through her husband.

Also Nila Magidov has promised to come to talk with me every Wednesday afternoon. Nila is the dark, handsome Russian wife of Bob Magidov, the American representative in Moscow of the McGraw-Hill Company. She is very Russian and very proud of her peasant origin. It is pleasant and attractive to find someone who is proud of the fact that she makes her own clothes, which she does beautifully, giving the effect of being one of the best-dressed as well as best-looking women at the big embassy receptions when she appears in a well-fitted evening dress with great billowing skirts.

Today Nila brought a copy of Lermontov, and had me read poetry to her by the hour, checking me every now and then to correct my stress or to call attention to some peculiarity of Russian speech. She loves the language and takes an almost sensual pleasure in its very sounds. Some say that those rustling, murmuring sounds which give it beauty owe their origin to the sound of the wind in the great forests.

7. HORSES AND SWANS

MOKHAVAYA HOUSE GETS ITS HEAT from the same central power plant that supplies the Kremlin, so we should have plenty of heat this winter. However, the regime, like most bureaucracies, is seized with the importance of routine economies, and the heat is not due to be turned on for weeks, although the weather has turned raw and so cold that you can see your breath.

We have been in our apartment for some time, and at last our shipments have arrived. Everything but our liquor has been released from customs, and that is tied up because of the customs wrangle. The apartments are furnished, so the things that came were winter clothes, books, rugs, silver, linens, and personal things. The things that were released were supposed to be under diplomatic immunity and so not subject to inspection. However, Bender, the strong-faced Russian expediter for the Embassy, rather shamefacedly brought in my silk hat in one hand and its box in the other hand.

"You see," he said, "when they took it out of the box in customs to find out if there was anything else in there, they couldn't get it back again."

Last night we went to MXAT to see a modern Soviet play. Several of the main theaters have "filials," which are separate theaters in different parts of town, but whose casts and policies are often completely interchangeable with the parent theater. *The Cherry Orchard* is put on at the MXAT Filial, but last night we were at the original MXAT. Apart from the more elaborate exhibitions of programs, settings and pictures of past productions with which the promenade and the waiting rooms adjoining the theater proper are lined, the two are almost indistinguishable.

The play was Simonov's *Russian Question,* for which he won the Stalin Prize and which develops the theme that there are two Americas which are in conflict with each other, one that of Lincoln and Roosevelt which is sympathetic with the aims and ideals of the Soviet Union, and the other that of Wall Street and the reactionary power of the capitalists. One would think that the regime which is so intrigued with blackguarding America would be confronted with a propaganda difficulty here, because it is rather obvious that there is a real freedom in the United States which makes such conflicts possible, as opposed to the complete suppression of all opposition in Soviet Russia. Perhaps the supposed rightness of their regime is the way by which they avoid this dilemma, but it is highly probable that the Russians are capable of dualities of thought that are beyond Westerners and at the same time have conceptions of liberty that are governed by values that are entirely different from ours. The two or three Russians with whom I have talked about this have nevertheless given me some reason to believe that the dilemma is still there, although not necessarily for everyone.

Although the play was much more restrained in its propaganda than expected, it never came to life. Wonderful actors as they are, they have their limitations, and they were completely out of their depth in trying to portray American types. Perhaps they would have been able to overcome this if the play had had any real greatness or even insight, for it seemed that the actors themselves were aware of its phony qualities. Also there was a feeling that they were playing to us, for we sat in the first row. Although I had not read the play beforehand, about eighty per cent of the lines were completely understandable. Perhaps it was because I missed an occasional line, but whatever the reason, it had none of the magic and aroused none of the sympathy that had been so exciting in the purely Russian *Cherry Orchard*.

Also there were many empty seats, which had not been the case in *The Cherry Orchard*. No one is permitted to enter the theater when the curtain is up, but when the doors were closed just before the play began there was a general rush to take the better unoccupied seats. Apparently the audience knew that all the seats would not be filled, for there had been an unusual amount of confusion beforehand in routing people out of their seats in favor of the rightful owners. Soviet custom permits anyone to take an unoccupied seat in a better location, and some citizens had jumped the gun in the hope that the seats they had taken might turn out to be unclaimed.

Colonel Crockett, the gray-haired long-faced assistant military attaché who has been here for years, had a party which included a box at the horse races. The Russian betting system is complicated. It requires picking two horses, and if either of them fails at least to show, the better loses all his money. Eddy Gilmore had a hot tip on which everyone lost so much that we did our betting thereafter between ourselves. The racing was harness racing, and it was difficult to find out what was going on in all the confusion. My Russian is coming along so well that everyone relied on me as interpreter, and it was usually possible for me to find out at least which horse had won in a close finish.

I went to the betting windows to try to find out more about the system of odds. Although the state takes a tremendous proportion of all bets, there were plenty of customers. Behind the windows was a big open room in which two or three hundred clerks were busy totaling the bets and figuring the actual odds, and they were doing this with — of all things — those ancient Chinese abacuses! It was fascinating to watch the twinkling little counters, and amazing to hear the odds announced within a very few minutes of the end of each race. It had been noticeable that the abacus is generally used in shops and stores, but one would not expect to find it in such a complicated operation as this. Although the Russians say that a skilled operator can get results as rapidly as with an adding machine, to me it indicates something of which I have been increasingly conscious — a general lack of machines of all sorts.

The Russian crowd was endlessly interesting, but most picturesque of all were those who were watching some jumping that was going on in the middle of the arena. The riders of these horses were Cossacks, Uzbeki and Caucasians, and their supporters seemed largely of those nations — if one can call the Cossacks a nation. The Cossacks are a complex group that has developed in the last few hundred years from free adventurers and settlers on the frontiers of Great Russia, and they include a large proportion of Great Russian elements in their mixture of border tribes. The *dzhigiti* of Asia and the Transcaucasus are trick riders par excellence.

One of the riders, an erect, military-appearing elderly man with a close-trimmed gray beard, came away from the jumping with a long bearskin cloak thrown about his shoulders. With him was a fine-looking woman, wrapped to the heels in the same sort of bearskin cloak. One wonders where such individuals fit into the Soviet scheme.

Elyena, my new teacher, wants me to translate some English into Russian. When I expressed my agreement, using the single word *"ladno,"* she told me that such peasant expressions shouldn't be used, as they weren't refined. Since then I have delighted in digging up as many of them as can be found — the *skazki* are a wonderful source — for her especial benefit, and at last she has come to the point where she will tell me which of them are obsolete rather than which are not what corresponds to Park Avenue talk. Many Russians have a tendency to be pretentious, and it is the complete absence of this in Nila that is so attractive.

One of the major difficulties in Russian is the complete lack of adequate dictionaries. Next to English, it is the richest language in the world, with its vocabulary estimated at something over half a million words, yet there is not one dictionary for Russian alone, let alone a bilingual dictionary, which even attempts to be inclusive of all this wealth. Russians themselves are often puzzled by words in their own literature.

Elyena has given me the interesting bit of information that clocks and watches have embodied in them the souls of families. Her mother had a watch which had been in the family for three generations, and, because of this, during the hard times of the war she refused an offer of four thousand rubles for it. Elyena herself had been married to a handsome and romantic young leader of an orchestra. One day her own watch was missing, and the following day her husband died.

The Bolshoy is the most beautiful theater I have ever seen, perhaps the most beautiful in the world. Its great Greek columns stand at the head of Sverdlovsk Square — the Theater Square of the old tsarist days when the Bolshoy was built. Within, it is a solid blaze of gold and crimson, with a big fountain of a crystal chandelier in the ceiling and smaller ones here and there on the sides. There are six horseshoe balconies, one above the other, with no other colors but their massive golden curves and decorations and their scarlet velvet hangings matching the scarlet velvet chairs. The crimson and gold curtain is made up of countless repetitions of the slogans of the proletariat in the revolutions of 1871, 1905 and 1917. The stage seems to me to be the largest I have ever seen anywhere, both in breadth and in depth, and they make full use of its enormous size. It is the theater for ballet, and there we saw Tchaikovsky's *Swan Lake.*

It is the custom in the Western world to give only a single scene from the great ballets, combining scenes from various ballets into an evening's diversified entertainment. The Russians look down mightily on the West for this custom, and rightly so. They would never consider presenting anything but a complete ballet, feeling that the bits and pieces are as meaningless as isolated scenes lifted from a play. Nearly all ballets provide enough variety by including stories within stories or some such thing, and in this one a note that is completely different from the main legendary atmosphere is struck by the scene of the palace ball, where the prince is to choose a bride from the Russian, Spanish, Venetian and Hungarian women who dance in turn for him.

Swan Lake is based on the ancient *skazka* of the transformation of maidens into swans by the spells of an evil sorcerer and the destruction of those charms by the power of love. The Russians are masters of illusion, and the sweet, powerful, mysterious music of Tchaikovsky did its share in building up the atmosphere. The scene where a storm comes and the lake overflows its banks was sheer magic. Unlike so many things in Russia, the costumes were crisp and fresh, immaculate and beautiful. The great wings and feathers of the Black Swan were both imaginative and convincing, and the final struggle between him and the prince was an outburst of elemental savagery. There is no doubt that the ballet as well as the drama of Russia is genuinely great. One advantage enjoyed by state-owned ballet is that they can have casts much larger than a private venture can afford. There were over a hundred dancers on the stage at one time in *Swan Lake.*

When the ballet was over and we left, the old Theater Square was almost as magical as the theater itself, with the glass-domed roof and the colored mosaic walls of the Metropole Hotel and the fantastic rooftops beyond what is left of the old Chinese Wall on the far side of the square.

Sergei has returned from his vacation in the Caucasus, and he has been permanently replaced by Valodya. The arrival of General Carter, the new air attaché, gave me a good opporunity to make it definite. Since Carter knows no Russian, it is almost necessary that he have a driver who knows some English, for one cannot always have an interpreter at one's elbow.

So I told Sergei of the general's need, suggesting that he work for the Air Force instead of the Navy. But it wouldn't do. After some troubled thought, Sergei told me that he would prefer to work in the pool of Navy chauffeurs, so that is where he is. One might infer that Sergei has been assigned to the naval attaché's office by the regime, and so has no option but to stay on even though demoted. One can never tell. I heard Natasha muttering "Poor Sergei!"

"Why do you say that?" I asked.

"It is a disgrace for him," she answered, throwing her head back defiantly.

"But he hasn't done anything wrong. Valodya just suits me better. And Sergei could have driven for the new general instead of me."

"You are the *khozyain,* the boss, and if you want Valodya you should have him. But it is nevertheless a terrible disgrace for Sergei."

They are putting in new, well-grown trees all through the central part of Moscow. Today there was a big gang of women, without one single man except for a planner with a roll of blueprints, hard at work chipping up the pavement on Gorky Street with chisels, sledges, picks and shovels. They were a sturdy, sunburned lot, many with bright dresses, big gold earrings in their pierced ears, and braided pigtails. The Russians always say that the reason one sees so many women at such hard labor is because they lost so many men in the war, but there were several men and not one woman standing around watching them.

A chance Russian on the street told me that all this tree planting was in answer to the criticism of soldiers coming back from central Europe, who were always wondering why Moscow was not as beautiful with trees as the cities they had seen abroad. Most foreigners remark cynically that the trees probably won't live.

Being a naval aviator, I must fly at least every three months or I will not long remain an aviator. There is an airplane assigned to me on the books of the Navy Department, but it is now clearly inconceivable that it could ever be brought here. Somewhere at the heart of the regime is a suspicion of foreigners and an antagonism to them that is so great that it is in effect one of the laws of nature of the Soviets. Even the Ambassador's plane must be kept outside Russia and its infrequent trips are extraordinarily difficult to arrange and are surrounded with many formidable thorns and hooks. So, in the rosy light of sunrise, Nellie went with me to Vnukovo Airport to see me off for Sweden, a free country where my necessary flying could be had.

There is naturally a difference in the sunsets and sunrises in different parts of the world, and this sunrise was an Asiatic one. The flood of rosy light had in it enough of blue to give it the same off-color effect that one sees so often in Asia. In spite of the sun, it was so cold that Nellie wore her fur coat.

Before we left, Natasha had us all sit down for a minute's silence, saying that no journey would prosper without such contemplation, which in the old days ended by everyone making the sign of the cross. There has been an easing in the intangible atmosphere of tension with the servants, and for the first time I felt that we were fully accepted by them.

Vnukovo was crowded with waiting passengers, most of them asleep on heaps of luggage. Dominating the waiting room was a great shining map that showed the way the Soviet airlines served all the Russias. The loud-speakers announced the departure of planes to such improbable places as Baku and Tashkent. Asleep on a bench was a very pretty woman in a big fur coat, and beneath the fur coat she wore graceful silk trousers that might have come from the Arabian Nights. They were patterned with irregular purple spots such as used to be seen on Easter eggs in my childhood.

There was little to see from the air, for the clouds grew thicker as we went north until there were few breaks in the overcast. The city of Leningrad was invisible, shrouded in cloud. Its airport, whose runways were paved with huge hexagonal concrete blocks, was dusty and ruined, with buildings, like those of most European airports when the war had just ended, gaunt and burned out, or pocked and gaping with shellfire and bomb damage.

All there was to be seen of Finland was the Helsinki airport, but the restaurant there was a resplendent sight, so unbelievably clean and neat after the general griminess and stains of Russia. The blue-eyed Finnish waitress seemed infinitely closer to American civilization than any Russian, but perhaps that was just because she spoke good English, whereas English is practically unknown in Russia except for Intourist — at least in any usable form.

Stockholm was a delight from the air, and from the ground too, for that matter, with its red roofs crowning its cream and white houses set thick in the pine woods that cover its many islands, its bridges, the green patina on the metal roofs of some of the big public buildings, and its outlying great houses which have the neat simplicity of pictures in a child's book of fairy tales. We came in to Bromma Airport between the big rocks that separate its sloping runways, and I stepped out of the plane into a world that was as different from Russia as if I had come from another planet.

Although the next few days were pleasantly crowded with friendliness and hospitality from Swedes as well as Americans, I was impatient to get back to Russia and subordinated everything else to my flying. Captain Gallagher, our naval attaché, plump and gray and pleasant, kept me busy with parties and calls, including calls on senior Swedish military personnel whose counterparts in Soviet Russia, to which I am accredited, I have never been permitted to meet. General Nordenskjold, the head of the Swedish Air Force, the great-grandson of that Nordenskjold who discovered the Northeast Passage, is slim and straight and aristocratic, with a long straight nose and smooth black hair, looking ten years younger than his fifty-six. He told me that if I would come back to Sweden next summer he would take me into Lapland north of the Arctic Circle in search of trout. May that come to pass!

Nevertheless, I found myself half resenting all the time spent away from Russia and the break in the continuity of all the things that interest me here, so I caught a plane back as soon as my minimum flying was finished. But the Russian plane which was supposed to connect at Helsinki was canceled — the Finns said that there was some sort of Soviet holiday and that the crew was too drunk to fly, but that cannot be verified — and there followed another period of hospitality and friendliness. And now, back in Moscow, I wonder why I chafed.

PART II. PATTERNS IN THE FROST

1. A LOOSENED TONGUE

It is the custom in Russia to seal up all the windows to keep
out the bitter cold, but when the heat from the Kremlin power
plant was finally turned on it was so plentiful that we soon broke
our seals. Koshka, the cat, when not trying to help me typewrite
or chasing "little hares," as the Russians call the glancing reflections of sun rays, stands on her hind legs in the window watching
the birds fly around the cornices of the roof. Her tail twitches, and
you can almost see her drool over them. Last night there was a
soft, fluffy snowfall, but the windows must have been still open,
and Koshka must have succumbed to temptation, jumped for one
of the birds and slipped in the unaccustomed snow.

However it came about, I was dressing when the uproar began
among the servants. I hurried downstairs and found Valodya with
the poor little beast bloody and battered, but still breathing. She
had fallen seven tall stories into the paved court below, where the
snow was not deep enough to break the fall. Valodya was told to
telephone to see if he could find a veterinarian who would take
care of the kitten. With the help of the central information office,
he soon located one, so I sent him away with Koshka and a hundred
rubles to pay for her care.

In the middle of the morning Valodya came beaming into my
office. "The veterinarian says that there are no bones broken, and

that all Koshka needs is vodka interlaced with milk through an eyedropper, and blue light."

"We can manage the vodka, the milk and the eyedropper," I answered, "but what do you mean by blue light?"

"Oh, that is very good for anyone who is ill. Just blue light. And here is your hundred rubles. We Russians are very kind to animals, and the veterinarian would not think of taking any money for helping one of them!"

When Nellie went to get an eyedropper from Dr. Vaughn, he confirmed the Russian belief in the virtues of blue light and gave her one of several light bulbs which he had painted blue and kept on hand in order to improve their health.

After many difficulties the Odessa office has been finally closed and Lieutenant Dreher has been brought back to Moscow. He is a slender, handsome bachelor with a deep and genuine sympathy for the Russian people. He says that although there was no mention in the papers, there was a real famine in the Ukraine last summer and that on many an occasion he had seen truckloads of people brought to the hospital suffering from it.

He is also in a position to explode the theory that foreigners are followed in order to give them protection. That may be true for ambassadors, but not for anyone else. The authorities in Odessa had given him the protection theory in reply to his questions as to why he was continually trailed. One night he came out on the street to find the tires stripped from his car and the thieves hard at work on the instrument board. Across the street, the Soviet car which always followed him was parked, and its plain-clothes men were sitting in it, idly watching the scene. Needless to say, he got no satisfaction from them or from his complaints at police head-quarters, beyond the doubtful satisfaction of throwing the protection theory back in their teeth.

Elyena was so pleased with what I brought her from Stockholm that she says she would like to give Nell language lessons for free as long as she wants them. Nell is not apt to want them for very long, for she says Russian can be learned by ear, like playing the piano.

Elyena, being a Komsomolka, or member of the Communist Youth League, knows all the answers. When she was telling me how happy the people of Russia were under their form of life, I told her that I myself had seen some who were not happy. Without waiting for me to go further, she flared up and said, "Yes, and not one of them deserves to be called a Russian. They are thoughtless little fools who are discontented just because they can't get nylon stockings, and they will complain about that to everyone who comes along. They are not politically educated, and they are selfish. But you will not find any mature people who think like that." It seems to me that Elyena confuses maturity with being "politically educated," but it is easy to see that the differences in the meaning of words in this country and at home go deeper than anything that can be solved by a dictionary.

We have been reading Fadeyev's *Young Guard*. It is a novel of the young Russians who were caught behind the German advance in the Ukraine and the ways in which they continued to fight the Germans. Fadeyev is now under attack because he does not spell out with sufficient clearness that their tragic fate was an isolated case of abandonment by the regime, and also because he portrays some reasonably human characters in the Red Army instead of making them all stainless heroes. The book will probably have to be rewritten. Elyena says that this should be done to insure the proper education of the young. When I tell her that the young should be brought up to be able to make up their own minds about facts, she replies that that would only end in confusion, for there is only one viewpoint which is right, and therefore only that viewpoint should be permitted to exist.*

Today Nell and I went to Lenin's tomb. There is always a long

* A new edition of Fadeyev's *Young Guard* appeared in 1951. It was extensively rewritten in an even more revealing way than expected, subsituting Bolshevik control for the spontaneous courage of the abandoned youngsters, and changing the scenes of disorder and confusion incident to the Russian retreat to ones of purposeful grimness under Party leadership. There is an analysis of the rewriting with comparative passages in an article by Boris Shub in *Problems of Communism*, No. 2, 1952. Since all secondhand bookshops in Soviet Russia are owned and operated by the state, it is virtually certain that no copies of the earlier version can henceforth be legally obtained there.

queue of people, six or eight abreast, waiting to get in. The line stretches for blocks along the length of Red Square, past the Historical Museum and along the Kremlin walls outside our windows. On Sundays and holidays it is much longer. I told Valodya that I would like to see Lenin lying in state. He said that the Russians, who were always courteous to strangers, would be very glad to let us go in ahead of the line. We parked the car in the square and Nellie and I followed him to the head of the line, rather diffidently, for we were not sure he knew what he was talking about. Sure enough. at a few quick words from Valodya, the officer at the entrance saluted and held back the Russian pilgrims until after we had entered.

We went down a few steps and along a long twisting tunnel of polished black stone. It was diorite from the Urals, and its blackness was lit by flecks of electric blue, like the blue of a butterfly's wing embedded in the stone. Every few feet stood a soldier. The long line moved slowly forward, their voices hushed in the somber half-darkness. Although it could not have been far, it seemed as though we had been there for a long time before we turned another corner and started up some steps.

Then suddenly we were in the tomb itself. We came into a blaze of light that seemed itself to be bloody and crimson, for the walls were now made of red granite in a forceful jagged design and the chamber was draped in red. In the center was a glass case where Lenin lay in scarlet, quiet and peaceful, but so real that one could almost see him breathe. The Tatar cast to the corners of his eyes and his eyebrows was more noticeable than I had expected. The soldiers with fixed bayonets at the corners of the bier seemed like a perpetual watch over the dead leader, like the sons of George V who stood guard over his body in Westminister Abbey. The sudden transition from weird semi-darkness to that ominous but exciting blaze was so dramatic that we still felt its impact when we came out into the weak sunlight.

At last I have had a definite reward for my concentration on the Russian language. Up until now it has seemed that I was always in the hands of other peoples' opinions, and it was easy to see how those opinions might be affected by strong considerations other than the real nature of things. After months of immersing myself in the language, talking it at every opportunity, reading almost nothing but Russian, putting in endless hours at the theaters and listening to the radio, and coming very close to antagonizing Nell as well as many others with what must have seemed to them to be an overemphasized interest, the point has at last been reached where the barrier of language is being washed away and I know what is going on around me beyond that barrier.

There are many reasons why Russian-speaking foreigners do not really mingle with the Russian people. One of them is that they frequent the better places, such as the bars of the big hotels, and there they are always subject to surveillance. It takes a strong stomach and there is even an element of danger in going alone into the swarming second-class or third-class restaurants and bars where one never sees another foreigner, yet in such a place, alone, one is much more approachable and accessible to Russians.

Last night I decided to launch out on my own, so I walked through the cold windy streets until I found a combination restaurant and bar of the sort that might be frequented by taxi drivers or laborers in America. It was early and the place was only about half full, so I sat down alone at a small table in a corner and ordered some cheese and a big heavy mug of the sweetish Russian beer. The restaurant began to fill up, and soon a thin-faced man in his thirties with bright, tormented black eyes sat down at my table. He wore a soft white shirt with no tie and his clothes were shiny and threadbare, but he was no different in appearance from many others around us. He ordered beer and pulled from his pocket a little package of sausage and black bread. We sat in silence for half an hour or more, replenishing our beer from time to time.

At last, when he had finished eating and had carefully restored to his pocket what was left of his sausage and bread, he started to fish around for a match. Without a word, I offered him one, and he lit his cigarette with only a nod of his head in acknowledgment. He sat back in his chair and there was another long silence while we surveyed the people at the other tables.

Then he looked at me and said, "Are you a Lett?"

"No," I answered.

There was another silence, during which he became more interested. "Perhaps a German?" he asked. "Your clothes are better than ours."

"No," I said, "American." I offered him a cigarette.

"Thanks." He looked at me curiously. "What are you doing here? Do you work for the Soviets?"

"No. I work in the American Embassy."

"Might I see your papers?" he asked, eying me suspiciously.

I showed him my Russian identification papers and told him who I was. In return he told me that he was an agricultural expert from a collective farm and showed me his own papers, although he seemed to be thinking about something else. His name was Petrov, and he had come to Moscow to check up on the delivery of some equipment for the farm. He was married, but had no children. His wife worked in the administration of the farm. But all the time he was distracted, twisting nervously in his chair, his eyes darting from table to table. I decided that he was afraid of me because I was an American, and when the conversation died down, fully expected him to leave.

But suddenly he made his decision. He looked swiftly around him, hitched his chair over close to mine, and the floodgates were opened. He spoke quietly but urgently, and so rapidly that several times it was necessary to ask him to go more slowly and to repeat, and all the time he was looking around and glancing over his shoulder to see if anyone was noticing us. It was perhaps the first time in his life that, because of my position, he was absolutely sure that the person with whom he was talking would not betray him to the secret police.

"You cannot possibly realize the unhappiness and discontent that is everywhere in Russia, particularly in the villages and on the farms, nor the dog's life which we lead. I have seen parents, unable to feed their children, deliberately do things that would get them sent to the prison camps, for then the government will give the children food. The whole land is ripe for a new revolution, and we would rise up against our leaders overnight if we could only get our hands on the means with which to do it. But we cannot organize ourselves to do a single thing: we Russians cannot talk about our sorrows with other Russians. There are so many spies and informers that we do not know whom to trust."

His hatred of the regime was so impersonalized that it added greatly to my feeling that his was not a highly individual reaction and that he knew whereof he spoke. He did not so much question the sincerity of the Soviet leaders or damn their motives but railed against their stupidity. Again and again he repeated that they were mixed up and confused. "They are not the caliber of men who should be in charge. They have neither the education nor the intelligence of real leaders, but are themselves nothing more than revolutionary conspirators. The problems of the Russian people are completely beyond their ability to solve, and some day they will be swept away."

He gave me a picture of Soviet life which was full of deprivation, frustration, unfulfilled desires and, above all, violation of all instincts of decency, and through it all was no complaint of his own personal lot. "I myself," he said, "can manage all right. I have a good position and do not live badly, but it makes me boil to see what goes on all around me."

I was worn out with his intensity and with the strain of having to pay close attention to his low, swift words. "There are many things I would like to ask," I said. "Meet me in this same place one month from tonight and I will be better able to put my questions into Russian words." Since he came often to Moscow on business, Petrov said that he could easily do that. We both wrote the date on our documents so that we would not lose it and drank in vodka to our next meeting.

On leaving, we both stopped in the washroom. It was smelly, dirty and disorderly, and had no claim to distinction other than that it was tiled. Petrov looked about with an air of genuine pride. "*Ekh, kulturny!*" he said.

I do not think that I overrate the importance of last night's conversation, and it has had a tremendous impact on me. It seems very significant that my first real opportunity to talk with a chance Russian who had not previously been oriented with reference to foreigners should have brought forth such strong evidence to support one viewpoint on Russia with which everyone is familiar. Out of the millions of Muscovites who might have shared my table, my chances of having encountered an exceptional case seem extremely remote. And what a country this is, where it is so extraordinarily difficult to find out things whose counterparts are common knowledge in any country in the West! That in itself is a damning commentary on Russia.

2. MOLOTOV ENTERTAINS

NEAR PUSHKIN SQUARE IS A SMALL JEWEL of an old church. I do not know its name, but it is done in pale green and rose and cream, and it is a complex little mass of lily domes and arches, weighed down by great crosses and heavy golden chains. I wandered past it this afternoon and stopped for a long time just to look at it. It is such a strange combination of loveliness and bizarre structure that it seemed that with pencil and paper some of its complications might be solved and perhaps enough of its form caught to serve as a basis for a drawing which would help me to remember it.

Across the street was the deep embrasure of a bricked-up doorway. It should be possible to stand there for a few moments and make a quick sketch without attracting the attention of the crowds that were hurrying past in the cold twilight. I gave it a try. I was so much out of sight and the light was so dim that nobody noticed me but one small boy, who, when he saw what I was doing, much preferred to throw stones at the crows. All at once a uniformed militiaman appeared beside me and thrust his long nose close to my rough sketch.

"What are you doing?" he asked.

"Sketching," I replied.

"Why?"

I explained to him that I was trying to get the layout of the domes and cornices so that perhaps a more pleasing drawing could be made when I got home.

"You can't do that," he said.

"Why not?"

"It is forbidden."

"I don't believe it. Why should it be forbidden to make a sketch of a lovely old church like that?"

"It's forbidden." He was in no mood for argument, so I put away my pencil and paper and moved on, consoling myself with the thought that it was getting too dark to see in any case.

Now that I am home, it is hard to understand my resentment of this minor interference. Every precaution had been taken not to draw a crowd, and successfully, for only one small boy had paid attention. After all, it's their country, not mine. Yet the incident seemed symbolic of Russia.

Tolstoy is a common name in Russia, and a great one. As well as novelists, dramatists and poets, there were Tolstoys who were ambassadors, governors, statesmen, physicians, archeologists, generals, sculptors, critics, composers and artists. One of them, who put into practice some ingenious ideas on how to keep education a privilege of the upper classes, was a nineteenth-century predecessor of Beria and Yagoda as Minister of the Interior. It was he who forbade the study of medicine to women, with the result that many women went to study in Switzerland, which soon became the headquarters of the Russian revolutionary activities abroad. A gray woman who is a translator for the Embassy is a Tolstoy. Another Tolstoy, who lived for a time in San Francisco, was a famous gambler and swindler. He was known as "the American," which perhaps had something to do with the complex image of America that shaped itself in Russian minds.

Serayev notified me that in response to my request on arrival an appointment had been made for me to call on Admiral Panteleyev. He is well down in the echelons, being the Director of Training for the Navy, but it was pleasing to be able to meet even one Russian other than those in OVS, so I canceled another engagement and went to make my call.

The gloomy old office building where I found Panteleyev was apparently a major Admiralty establishment in Moscow, for there were sailors on guard at the doors and in the corridors. The passage through which I was taken had case after case of models of old sailing ships. They were remarkable ship models, for their great sails were made of sheets of pure silver.

The admiral seemed to be a scholarly old fellow and the call was pleasant enough, although rather stiff and formal. The only thing that we seemed to have in common was that we were both pipe smokers.

Klin is a small city some sixty or seventy kilometers from Moscow on the road to Leningrad. It was there that Tchaikovsky lived, and it was from there that he went to St. Petersburg to conduct the first performance of his Sixth Symphony and to die of cholera. There is often a touch of the miraculous in Russian life, for they say that although long lines of people looked on his body as it lay in state and kissed his hands and face, not one of them caught that terrible Asiatic scourge.

Elyena had been a pianist for a year or two in Tchaikovsky's home in Klin, providing background and educational music for the school children or grownups who go there in large numbers to see the house and the mementos of the wonderful composer. She went with us when, all bundled up in furs and sweaters, we too went to Klin.

The roads were icy with snow that had melted and frozen again, and there had been a fresh snowfall that would have made the countryside very beautiful if there had been even a touch of sun. But the sky was a steely cold gray and even in the middle of the day it was like a mournful twilight. Russian drivers never use chains until they get in trouble, and there is some justification for this here because the traffic on the roads is so light that a good driver is seldom blocked by others who have gotten stuck. Nevertheless, I insisted on chains, and was glad of it, for there were long stretches of road where the continual wind had swept away the snow and left nothing but bare, slippery ice. The Russians have a special word for that sort of ice. As might be expected, the language is very rich in words for all sorts of ice and snow and frost, as it is for varieties of horses, different aspects of drunkenness, and for the family relationships that we have to express with hyphens in English.

In winter, children and even a few grownups get around Moscow by skating and skiing in the icy streets. It is generally easier to get around the countryside with skis and sleds than it is to slug through the chuckholes and mud of the country roads in summer. All along the way we passed low wagons on runners, filled with people or with brushwood, and drawn by shaggy little horses with big wooden bows over their shoulders. On the horizon were always black dots of people on skis, making their way swiftly across the fields.

Klin had been occupied by the Germans for twenty-seven days, and even now, five or six years afterwards, there were so much rubble and ruin that it looked as though the Germans had just left. Tchaikovsky's house is the Russian version of a comfortable but not luxurious Victorian small-town home, set on the edge of the little city and surrounded with trees. Its windows were steaming when we got out of the car. Elyena's face was all aglow as she affectionately greeted her friends.

Davidov, a nephew of Tchaikovsky's, took care of us while we were there. He was a gray man, with a clipped gray beard like his uncle's and the dignified, precise graciousness that one finds so often in the older generation. There was such a strong family resemblance that one felt as though one were talking with Tchaikovsky himself.

The loving care with which the place is maintained as a sort of national museum was obvious. Much furniture had been taken by the Germans, and part of the paneling had been torn off for firewood, but Tchaikovsky's manuscripts, his piano, desk, bed and cabinets were all as he had used and left them. There was something pathetic about the little trinkets which had pleased him, but which were of no value now except for their associations. He left a tremendous amount of musical manuscript which is still in process of being neatly catalogued and filed. Outside the windows of his study were three birches, graceful and lovely in the dim winter light. The peaceful surroundings were such that it was easy to see how a Russian could put so much of Russia into his work.

Two or three bus loads of school children arrived to be taken through the house, but Davidov continued to talk with us as though they were not there, and as if we were friends who had dropped in for an hour or so. He said that Tchaikovsky corrected Moussorgsky's manuscripts before they were played, and he told of how Tchaikovsky had wanted to do the same for Rimsky-Korsakov. Rimsky-Korsakov was the president of the Petersburg Conservatory, and Tchaikovsky finally told him that his work was so full of flaws that he should study in his own conservatory. This Rimsky-Korsakov did in all humility, and eventually succeeded in overcoming his technical deficiencies.

Then we had tea around a big silver samovar. At Elyena's suggestion, we had brought sandwiches, cakes and candy. Davidov and his household and Elyena said that they were not hungry and only nibbled politely at a cake. But when we were through I happened to glance into the room where the samovar was and saw Elyena and some of the others doing full justice to all the food.

It was dark long before we reached Moscow. The wind moaned and howled around the car, blowing the loose snow into sinuous dances in the headlights. The sense of the vastness and remote loneliness of Russia was heightened by Elyena's account of being lost in a snowstorm. When her first husband died, she was so grief-stricken that she was sent to a sanitarium on the shores of a large lake. She told of the peace that she found in driving a sleigh across the frozen lake — a peace that was intensified rather than disturbed when she had lost all sense of direction and there was nothing to be seen around her but snow.

The preparations for the Revolution Day parade have much in common with those for the eight-hundredth anniversary of Moscow. There are the same huge portraits of Stalin and the Politburo in the same places, and everywhere are the same scarlet flags and decorations. The same two platforms for entertainment are in the square outside our windows, but due to the weather the crowds in the evening are much smaller. For several days the weather has not been too bad, but today, the day of the parade, it turned thoroughly miserable with first heavy fog and then mist, hail and snow.

Our tickets did not arrive the night before, but we were not disturbed, as tickets for such things usually arrive at the last moment. We dressed warmly and sat around until it became clear that for some reason the American military were not to be invited. From some hints that Serayev dropped, this is probably a retaliation for American failure to invite Soviet attachés to some affairs where other foreigners were included.

So we watched the parade from our windows, and were really glad to be warm and dry. The Soviet military have been practicing for the parade for days and weeks, usually at night until two or three o'clock in the morning, so we knew what to expect. Massed bands, infantry, artillery, tanks, more massed bands and more tanks, were impressive. The cavalry made a brave sight, particularly a troop of white horses with red banners. Behind the horses came the women who sweep the streets, plying their brooms.

The civil part of the demonstration had been forming up for hours, and when the military had vanished into Red Square, their lines started pouring in from five or six directions. It was a colorful sight, for there were groups in white sweaters and caps, in red, and in yellow, bands and banners and balloons, portraits and slogans, all slogging through the slush. Long before it was over, groups of foreigners who had been in the diplomatic stands in Red Square began to arrive in the Embassy, half-frozen, and there was hardly an apartment that did not have a party in full swing.

In the evening we went to Molotov's reception at Spirodonovka House — the authentic Spirodonovka House, which is kept by the Soviets for just such occasions. There was a great congestion of cars at the entrance gate, with a veil of snow shining in the headlights between cars. Before we reached the entrance the police opened the doors of our car and verified our identity.

Molotov has a remarkably large square head, a pale color, and a brisk assured air. He and his wife stood under the gleaming bell of a big crystal chandelier to greet the guests, who came pouring in in evening clothes or uniforms dripping with gold lace, with an occasional Russian in drab day clothes. I recognized Rybalko, the great general of tanks during the war. He is an enormous man, with a big, naked, shaven head.

The house had much paneling and carving, and there were good rugs on the floors, including one wonderful Persian hunting rug. Cocktails were passed, and then rows of chairs were placed near a white-and-gold grand piano. Nellie, Duncan Hill and I found ourselves in an adjoining room among the artists who were to entertain. Bassos and tenors paced back and forth, trilling and exercising their voices during the applause, and the great Oistrakh tuned and exercised his fingers on his priceless violin.

After the concert an orchestra played Strauss waltzes for dancing in the ballroom, and the supper rooms were thrown open. There were roasts and game, salads, fish, caviar and wines, and later, ice cream and champagne. Molotov passed from room to room, followed by attendants with trays laden with bottles and delicate glasses. Everywhere he stopped, a group of Russians would gather around him, the attendants would fill the glasses for everyone, and Molotov, all smiles and heartiness, would drink bottoms up with them. The amount of champagne that he consumed thus was impressive. The last group he came to included Voroshilov, still a handsome man, with a diamond star at his collar.

When Molotov left we followed him out and got our own wraps while Madame Molotov wrapped herself in a handsome mink coat and a lace head scarf. Our car was announced, and we left through a cloud of snowflakes.

We drove home through Red Square, which, although the crowds were thin, was a blaze of scarlet banners and electric lights. The Kremlin's walls and towers were outlined again with myriads of electric lights that twinkled through the falling snow. The Alexandrovsky Gardens beneath the Kremlin wall were a remarkable study in black and white, for the bare branches of every tree were loaded with hundreds of huge black crows, thick as leaves against the snow.

"What do they all eat?" Nellie asked.

Sergei, who was relief driver, misunderstood, for he answered, "They aren't very tasty!"

"No. How do the birds get enough to eat?"

"It's very difficult," he said, shrugging his shoulders.

"Like everything else in Russia!"

We laughed and Sergei joined us feebly, doubtless thinking that the light remark was not in the best of taste.

3. TEN RUBLES FOR ONE

TODAY WAS SUPPOSED TO BE NATASHA'S DAY OFF, but she showed up as usual, saying that it was warmer and more peaceful here than in the one room where she lived with her daughter's family.

"Natasha, what happened to your husband?" I asked as she chopped some cabbage with a long sharp knife.

"Dead!" she said, her wrinkled face a bit grimmer than usual.

"Has he been dead long?"

"He died in 1923."

"I should think that a handsome woman like you would have had more than one husband since then."

Her face wrinkled still more into a toothless grin. "I could never find anyone as handsome as he! Oh, but he was a fine specimen of a man!"

"How did he happen to die?" I asked.

"He was a Chechen, a tribesman from the mountains in the Caucasus. He died because he was so handsome." She continued her chopping, knowing that I would urge her on. When I did, she went on. "We were married here in Moscow, and then he took me to Tiflis. You can see the snowy mountains from Tiflis, and we had not been there two days until he said he was lonely for them. I knew that he was lonely, not for the mountains, but for a girl that was among them. But what could I do? He went up in the mountains to his own tribe, to see this girl. And the next time I saw him he was all chopped up in little pieces."

"What do you mean?" I asked, horrified.

"Chopped up in little pieces, just like that!" she said, demonstrating vividly on a piece of cabbage. "They laid the pieces in little packages on my doorstep."

I went today for an aimless ride on the Metro. It is a very good subway, with each underground station done in a different pattern and design with different colors of Ural granite. It is difficult for me to get enthusiastic over utilitarian art, however. A long-haired, bright-eyed lad in a leather jacket sat next to me, and when I asked some questions about the Metro he took great pride in telling me all about it. He was a student at Moscow University, and when we finally got off at Sverdlovsk Square we went into a bar on Gorky Street for a mug of beer.

The conversation inevitably reached the stage of comparisons between America and Soviet Russia. He did not question my remarks until I said that we had freedom of speech in America, whereas the Russians did not.

"What do you mean?" he said. "Someone has been telling you things that are not true. We have freedom of speech here, just as in America."

"But no one has freedom to disagree with the regime," I said.

"But yes! In the University there is one evening every week that is set aside for debate. Anyone can get up and say anything he wants. He can disagree with what the government does, ask questions about anything, and speak his mind freely."

I was frankly surprised, and told him so. But he went on. "Of course our government is very wise and very good. If anyone criticizes it, there are people in the University who are specially trained to answer criticism. They answer all such questions and put him straight."

"But suppose he does not agree with those answers?"

"He must agree with them, because they are right. And before the debate is over, he must admit in public that they are right."

"But what if he still cannot agree?"

"If he does not admit in public that he was wrong, he cannot stay in the University. We cannot have such wrong-thinkers in such a place, when there are thousands who would like to be there for whom we do not have room."

It was no use trying to explain freedom of speech to the young Soviet mind, for the roots of our differences go very deep.

For weeks one of our people has been trying to arrange to bring some Russian friends of his, ballet dancers at the Stanislavsky, to our house for dinner. Two or three times the dinner party was all set, only to be called off at the last minute because they could not come for one reason or another. Today the ballerinas sent him word that not only they could not come at all, but that if he should chance to see them on the street or in the lobby of the theater he was to give no sign of recognition.

I returned to the restaurant for my appointment with Petrov, the agricultural expert, but was not surprised when he did not show up. There are many reasons why none but the most naïve or the most reckless Russian should pursue an acquaintance with an American, and Petrov seemed to me to be neither naïve nor reckless. I sat alone over a mug of beer.

However, the evening was not lost. At the table next to mine sat a grizzled little Georgian. He had a thick roll of ruble notes of good-sized denominations and was apparently out for a good time. With him was an amazon of a woman, gaily dressed in a way one does not see in Moscow. The little man caught my eye, raised his glass to me, and winked. I moved over to their table. He was inclined to be talkative, and when I asked him how life was in the Transcaucasus, he launched into an elaborate statement to the effect that it was pretty tough. The red-faced amazon beside him caught him up short and told him to be quiet. Two or three times he tried to return to the subject, but his companion, eying me suspiciously, would not have it.

Meanwhile a brawl started across the room. I do not know what started it, but I was conscious of a sudden burst of loud words. A big bull-necked fair-haired young soldier was half out of his seat and banging the table with his huge fist, thrusting his face into the face of his companion, who was only a slightly smaller edition of the same type. Suddenly the big lad seized a heavy, half-empty glass mug of beer and threw it, beer and all, at his companion. The mug crashed against the wall, and two or three neighboring Russians ducked under their tables. Shouts went up egging them on, and everyone looked on excitedly. One of the waiters joined the argument, trying to make peace, and apparently was successful, for things soon quieted down. But not for long, for in a few minutes the two soldiers were again shouting and shaking their fists in each other's face.

This time a neatly uniformed militiaman showed up and told the soldiers they would have to get out.* "Where to?" asked the big blond lad belligerently, and a shout went up from the onlookers — "Yes, where to?" The policeman looked a little at a loss for an answer, shrugged his shoulders, and started to talk quietly with them. It was the better part of an hour before I left the place, and even then the two soldiers were still arguing as though the militiaman were not there, their argument occasionally rising to a crescendo of table banging, while the militiaman hovered rather helplessly around.

The last time I saw Elyena I translated for her an article in the New York press which said that an investigation of police brutality was being undertaken there. "Would such an article be published in Russia?" I asked.

"No," she answered promptly, "because there is no police brutality in Russia."

"And no crime, I suppose?"

"No, no crime."

She ended the ensuing argument by telling me that I could not help being completely reactionary because of my capitalist environment, and that when people reached my age it was impossible for them to grow and change. It is becoming increasingly easy to predict her reactions to almost any statement involving the Soviet Union or America.

Her father has been seriously ill, so she has not been here for several days. She says that all sorts of completely new diseases of the heart and of the nervous system have appeared in Russia as a result of the war and that the Soviet doctors have done wonders in identifying and treating them. Remembering the vogue of the blue light, I wonder.

Elyena's father has died. We sent some flowers, and it seemed

* Uniformed members of the MVD perform all the functions of the uniformed police forces of the United States. They have long been called *militsionery* or militiamen. They have no analogy with members of the "militia" in the United States, nor do they have any connection with the armed forces in our sense of that term. On the other hand, the MVD, of which they are a part, not only comprises also the secret police, but is itself an armed force for internal security, having its own artillery, tanks and aircraft.

that it would be a good gesture to go to the funeral. I should have remembered that no Russian likes to have his connection with Americans advertised, for Elyena's husband, who had borrowed his embassy car for the occasion, was so obviously annoyed when we met them on the edge of the cemetery and Elyena herself was so disturbed that I merely spoke to them a moment and went on away.

Perhaps there may also have been an element of embarrassment for other reasons. Coffins, like all consumers' goods here, are in short supply, so that often they are rented for the occasion and used over and over again. Priests, too, are in such short supply that in a city the size of Moscow they have daily mass funerals — with the caskets all open. It is interesting that Soviet law requires an autopsy in every death whose cause is not direct and obvious.

There is another mystery in this city of mysteries. Elyena's father was a gardener, and the place where he worked sent an unusually fine and elaborate wreath of evergreens to the funeral. The family had wired and anchored it over the grave so securely that a major operation with heavy tools would have been required to move it, yet the morning after the funeral it was gone. Two days later it appeared in place again, as well secured as in the beginning!

Comment by a Soviet citizen on the state of the nation:
"We used to have Greek stores that sold sponges and olives, and Italian stores that sold spaghetti. Now the government takes care of the stores, so we don't have such things any more!"

A letter came from the States thanking me for the Russian stamps that I had sent. My letter that had accompanied them had told my friend that all shops were a state monopoly, and that since the only stamp shop in Moscow had been covered, there didn't seem to be much else I could do to fill in the gaps in his collection. His letter shows how difficult it is to grasp conditions in the Soviet Union, for he suggested that I advertise, since in that way it might be possible either to pick up some more stamps directly or find a Russian who was a stamp collector. Now another letter must be written to tell him that, except for an occasional exhortation by the state, there is no advertising here, nor is there any medium for advertising, and that even if there were, any Russian who would seriously consider riding such a hobby with an American should have his head examined. It is easy to see how difficult it is for one who has not been in Russia to visualize conditions here.

The Embassy makes a consistent effort to keep its skirts clean, and there are strict orders against any black-market dealings in rubles or supplies. There are several good reasons for this. One of them is the possibility that the Soviets really believe that we are motivated by money to the extent that they say we are, and another is the propaganda hay they can make whenever anyone gets caught. Also, black markets are a corroding influence, for they set up divisions between those who deal in them and those who either cannot or will not do so. Under wartime conditions such considerations did not apply, but there still may be people around who do not realize that conditions have changed.

Consequently I have been under the unpleasant necessity of serving as a member of a board which the Ambassador has appointed to insure that our skirts are clean and stay clean. The board is interviewing every member of the Embassy, and it is encouraging to know that even under the pressures which undoubtedly exist here there are almost no cases where there is any blame to be attached.

Rumors are thick around Moscow that all of the present Soviet currency is to be called in and replaced with new money at a new and lower value. As a result everyone has been trying to spend their money before they get caught. The stores have been so jammed that the militiamen had to be called to manage the crowds, and now the five largest stores have closed their doors. With characteristic Russian deviousness they are closed "for repairs" or "for inventory," but everyone knows that those are not the reasons. Another rumor is that bread rationing will end. Maybe so, but without a free press all Russia is continually shaken by rumors.

Last night the radio announced that as of that moment the existing money is no good, but it can be exchanged in the morning at the rate of ten old rubles for one new one. There will be no change in prices, and bread rationing is abolished. Already there are queues for blocks outside the bakeries, but most of them are completely sold out. It is easy to see the reason for the currency reform, for it is one way of controlling inflation. It shakes down all the people who have made and kept any money, and probably many of them made it illegitimately. However, it works a tremendous injustice on anyone who has any money that he came by honestly. It is just before Christmas, and countless Russian families are done out of the possibility of buying anything for Christmas. I do not think they will soon forget it.

It also will be a long time before Nell forgives the Soviets for what they have done to her. I put enough faith in the rumors that have been going around to have gotten rid of all my rubles, but Nell had about a hundred and fifty dollars worth that she was saving for Christmas, and they are now worth fifteen dollars. In addition, we were having a dinner party last night, which always means an extra girl to help serve, who gets the equivalent of five dollars in rubles. So that girl's pay for one evening cost Nell fifty bucks.

Up until now we haven't been able to get any new rubles, and since we have used up all the old ones we can't buy any food. We are living on spam and Vienna sausages. There is an additional shadow for this merry Christmas in that the rate of diplomatic exchange has been cut from twelve to eight, which means that everything we buy here will cost us fifty per cent more than it did before.

Such decrees show why Soviet prices in terms of American money are meaningless. There is no free market in rubles anywhere in the world and, without that, there is no standard of comparison. The only way of understanding what prices mean to the Russian is to put them in terms of how many hours or days he must work in order to buy a given article, and on that basis prices are even higher for the Russian than they are for the foreigners who are here. I tried to buy a pair of the soft fur boots one sees occasionally and was told that they were so scarce that there would not only be much difficulty in finding them, but that if a pair could be located they would cost well over a hundred dollars. That is too much for me, and to a Russian it would mean a month's pay.

4. GRANDFATHER FROST

NOWADAYS IN RUSSIA Christmas is a season rather than a day, with four high points in it. Although the modern calendar has been in effect ever since the Revolution, a great many Russians, particularly the older ones, still think in terms of the old calendar, which is thirteen days earlier than the new international one, so they are forever translating dates back and forth. Also the government tries to shift the emphasis from Christmas, with its religious connotations, to New Year, which has always been a holiday occasion. As a result there are two Christmases and two New Year's Days, old style and new.

The Russian Santa Claus is Grandfather Frost, who is so close to the old elemental personifications of the people that he is all mixed up with their folklore. His bearded white figure is to be found on all of the big Christmas trees with which the main squares of Moscow are decorated. Manezhny Place outside our windows now has only one platform for bands and entertainers, but the whole plaza is outlined with fir trees and there is a huge one in the middle, gay with shifting colored lights, dolls, balls and decorations. Beside it is a merry-go-round that spins continuously.

Pushkin Square is the most elaborate of all. There a fair has been built, a village of little booths with peaked roofs, gaily striped and painted, where one can buy cakes and shoestrings, tiny utilitarian buttons bearing Stalin's picture, and the poor trinkets — papers of safety pins, celluloid combs and tiny fabric cats — one sees in the stores. It is a shame that the government cannot or will not give its people more, but any lack of things to buy in Pushkin Square is compensated by the decorations. The stately tree in the center is a living, glowing fountain of colored lights, now red, now blue, now many colors, but always boiling and bubbling with light. There is a gigantic cuckoo clock, and up its side creeps a huge cat, always pouncing on the cuckoo that emerges, and always just missing it. It is done partly with lights and partly with moving mechanisms, and it is so ingenious and intriguing that it would be a wonderful sight even in Times Square. There are polar bears and black bears, rabbits and reindeer, to the delight of grownups as well as children.

All of the foreigners are having parties, big ones and small ones, so that for days one just goes from place to place and eats and drinks. Christmas dinner at Spasso was a real Christmas dinner, for Ambassador Smith has just come back from Germany with a profusion of hams, turkeys and presents for the occasion. There has been a heavy snowfall, and the trees and shrubs at the entrance to such places as Spasso and Khlebny look like a Christmas card with their

sparkling loads and tufts of fresh snow. About the only thing one misses is fireplaces. One would think that there would be plenty of them, since wood is a principal source of heat, but the *pyetch* or built-in stove is almost universal, and an open fireplace is a rarity.

We had a party at Spiro for the children of all the Russians that work for the Navy. Seventeen or eighteen youngsters were gathered there, solemn-eyed and well-behaved. While waiting for things to begin, the children played the universal game of run-sheep-run, but they called it "Goosey, goosey, ga-ga-ga" as they chose up sides to Russian nursery rhymes.

Dreher had been gotten up with pillows, red flannel and a beard as Grandfather Frost, with a big bag of presents on his back. He had slipped out the back door and gone around the block so that he might make a satisfactory entrance through the front. Apparently the Russians do not go in for such personifications, for he said that he excited a great deal of curiosity on the street, two or three youngsters looking at him open-mouthed and then taking to their heels, either in terror or to spread the news of who was abroad. The MVD guards at the door also looked at him with open mouths, uncertain as to whether they should ask Grandfather Frost for his documents. Before they could make up their minds, Dreher had brushed past them and made his entrance.

The Russian children could hardly believe their eyes. Most of them were still at the believing age, and Dreher, who speaks beautiful Russian, acted his part splendidly, saying that he had come from the forests all the way to Moscow just to see them. He swung his pack off his back, and dozens of tennis balls, salvaged from the debris of wartime athletic gear, bounced all over the room, followed by the wide-eyed children in a wild scramble.

After each child had been given his individual present of clothing, toys and candy, we had some movies of Walt Disney animated cartoons and finally ice cream, cake and things to drink appropriate to young and old. Then each Russian child got up and did a little act, reciting a little poem, singing, or some such thing, evidently prepared for it in advance by the parents. Not to be outdone, I also spoke a piece, the prelude to Pushkin's *Ruslan and Ludmilla,* which I had long known by heart because it is such a wonderful epitome of Russian *skazki.*

The windows of Spiro look out directly on the street, and as it grew dark quite a crowd gathered outside to look in through the windows at the lighted tree and the children. Even the MVD guards were among the crowd, and one of them, with a scarred and ugly face, grinned from ear to ear as he pressed his nose flat against the glass.

On the way home Zoya's little niece Irochka was still talking about Grandfather Frost. "He pleased me," she said. "He was so alive!"

The Russians have a well-developed sense of pride and independence, and feel that they must pay their way. (This does not apply to Russian servants who have been spoiled by their American employers.) At this Christmas party the little acts and recitations that the children put on were by way of recompense for the party. One important aspect of this Russian turn of mind is that if a gift is of real value, or seems so to them, they are very apt to become suspicious of the motives of the giver.

Tolstoy's *Cossacks* has an illuminating passage in this connection. Olenin, the traditionally spendthrift and generous serf-owning Petersburg gentleman, is posted to a Caucasus regiment. He admires the dash and skill of one of the young Cossacks in his regiment so much that, when he learns that the young man cannot marry the girl he wants because he does not own a horse of his own, he presents him with a horse. This action, instead of inspiring gratitude, arouses nothing but suspicion. The Cossacks naturally assume that by such an overwhelming gift Olenin is trying to gain power over one of them, for unknown but doubtless sinister purposes. They also assume that an old hunter, who has wheedled the gift of a gun from the careless and generous Olenin, has practically sold himself and the entire neighborhood as the real price of the gun.

The Russian nature, which is itself capable of genuine generosity, is suspicious of it in others when it cannot be repaid in exact measure. It is unfortunate that this trait does not always seem to have been appreciated in some of our dealings with the Russians toward the end of the last war.

Russian help is becoming increasingly difficult to get, and more and more of the Russian employees are leaving the Embassy. There seems to be some sort of unrest, perhaps pressure, among them. Elyena's husband has quit as a Spasso chauffeur, and now Elyena herself has failed to show up as promised.

For Christmas she gave me one of the very few really fine things that come out of Russia today, a Palyekh lacquered box, with a *skazka* scene on it that is so delicately worked into the lacquer that little flecks of gold and blue and scarlet seem to float down in its depths. There are many little lacquered boxes to be had in Russia, but those made by the workmen of Palyekh, who once were famous for their ikons, are head and shoulders above the rest. One is not supposed to open a gift in the presence of the giver.

5. LENIN MUSEUM

MOST OF THE TIME THE BIG THERMOMETER in the archway at
the entrance to the court of the Embassy hovers around zero. Once
or twice it has gone as low as eighteen or twenty below. Even without looking at the thermometer, one can recognize the below-zero
mark. Zero weather is fairly comfortable, but when one steps outside into temperatures below that, one knows it. The air bites and
hurts when you take it deep into your lungs, and you can feel your
nostrils freezing up with each incoming breath and thawing when
you exhale. The snow gets hard and brittle, and of course all the
automobiles are broken down and hours late because of starting
troubles. The people on the streets, wrapped in rags and makeshift
clothes of all sorts, look pinched and blue and miserable. Russians
have no more resistance to the cold than any other people, and
sometimes, on seeing their obvious misery, it seems to me they have
less. Inside the apartment the windows are covered with frost patterns — forests of ferns, and wonderful scenes that I haven't seen
since I was a child.

Occasionally there comes a brief thaw, and then there is sometimes an interesting element of hazard in walking through the narrow streets, for big blocks of ice and snow slide off the steep-pitched
roofs to crash onto the sidewalks below.

Today, after such a thaw, it was twenty above, and the skiing
enthusiasts said that it was just right for skiing. So we drove out
in the country and looked for a likely place where I could try my
hand — or feet — and decide in private as to whether or not I
would ever want to go skiing again. At last, off the Mozhaisk
Chaussée, we found a quiet stretch of forest of breath-taking beauty.
The snow-laden pines were so thick that one wondered how the
snow ever reached the ground below, and the white birches with
which they were interspersed seemed almost dark against the clean
snowy background. Ice on the twigs gleamed like diamonds in the
low, level sunlight. In these high latitudes there are in winter

slanting shadows even at noon, and all day long it seems as though it is very early morning or late afternoon because of the low sun.

With Valodya's help and some more or less useful advice from Nell, I succeeded in getting strapped onto my skis. They were ungainly things, and they seemed to grow longer and longer all the time. Also, when I stood up on them, I seemed to be getting further and further from the snowy ground. The first surprise that I had was that they were as slippery as greased pigs, and were as ready to go sidewise as forwards. Shutting my ears to the stream of questionable advice in both English and Russian, I crept gingerly off at a snail's pace, and soon lost myself in the trees, where there was some real privacy.

At first I didn't like the things, but soon saw that they had possibilities. By the time of my return to the car I was covered with snow, but was slogging along like a veteran — perhaps a veteran of the Crimean War rather than the German one, but nevertheless, getting around.

It was eighteen below when, wrapped in heavy sweaters, a leather coat and fleece-lined boots, I finally got off for Berlin and some flying, after five days of getting up at four o'clock in the morning and waiting at Vnukovo for flights that were never cleared. The Russians have an excellent record of international flights free from crashes, for they just do not fly in questionable weather.

We had a tail wind, and in five and a half hours were away from the snow and the bitter cold and over Berlin, with its peculiar honeycombed effect of vast areas of bombed-out city buildings, its railroad yards crowded with burned-out, rusty coaches, and its rivers spanned with broken-backed bridges drooping into the water. There I luxuriated in the quiet hospitality of Admiral Schuirmann and Jinny, his wife, at their house in Wannsee with its enormous plate-glass power-operated windows that looked out on the placid green river lapping up against the grounds of show houses — some of them badly wrecked and ruined, but still show houses. I slept in the big bedroom in the guesthouse, with its yellow porcelain stove, its balcony overlooking the formal garden, its French windows, blue-green tiled tables, and particularly its fabulous, triple-sized, low French bed and its blue and rose rug crowded with hundreds and hundreds of formalized animals — camels, horses, chickens, dogs, women, and some beasties that were so enigmatic that one could only wonder.

Berlin was very pleasant, and so was London, where my flying took me. I thoroughly enjoyed the unbelievable luxury after Russia and the talking with old friends, and I was most appreciative of the hospitality and help which everyone, regarding me as something of a hardship case, extended. I did not chafe as before, but still wasted no time in getting back to Moscow. In order not to rouse the entire Schuirmann household incident to a before-dawn departure, the last night was spent at Harneck House. There I had bacon and eggs punctually at four in the dark winter morning, served in my room by a slim, black-eyed little German lass in a butter-yellow starched frock, looking like a picture from *Jugend*. And now back in this apartment overlooking the Kremlin, it seems as though I had never been away.

The old red brick Historical Museum stands at the entrance to Red Square that is nearest the Embassy, and at the other end of Red Square is the Cathedral of Saint Basil the Blessed. It is a pity that Saint Basil's is just out of sight of our windows, for it is a wonderful sight. It was built by Ivan the Terrible in the sixteenth century, and its cluster of lily-bulb domes and its commanding position make it seem the most Russian sight in Moscow. Each dome is radically different from all the others, yet they all have that bulbous shape that is so characteristically Russian. One is fluted, another twisted like a chocolate bud, others scaled like fish, and time has given their variegated colors a wonderful softness that keeps them from being garish.

The Cathedral has been closed for repairs for a long time now, but I have been twice to the Historical Museum without seeing more than a small part of all the variety that is in it. Without its tall pinnacles that rise from massed cusps of stone it would seem more German than Russian, but those *skazka* towers make it fit well into its surroundings. The sort of things that make all great museums interesting have here an enigmatic touch that is part Russian and part Asiatic, but whose very unfamiliarity makes them the more interesting — beautiful Scythian carved cups of semiprecious stone, banded and fringed with gold, huge, strange, half-formed idols with a peculiar unhuman savagery to their skewed eyes and teeth, and whole rooms devoted to the mysterious vanished cities of the Khorazm and Central Asia. There are also many rooms filled with more familiar things from the time of Peter the Great and Catherine. One who likes museums can spend days here.

Beyond the Historical Museum is another big red brick building which is the Lenin Museum. It is worth seeing, if for nothing more than the way it illustrates the Russian flair for dramatic effect. Its rooms are numbered serially, and you get the full effect if you go through them in order, as you are supposed to do. The first room deals with Lenin's family and the background into which he was born in Simbirsk, on the Volga. The next room covers his childhood, then his youth, and so on, so that one sees his life develop before one's eyes. One must be intimate with Bolshevik history to get the full impact of seeing the first issue of *Iskra* or Lenin's draft of an historic speech at one of the party congresses, but one needs no particular background to feel the reality that comes from the clothing and personal objects that were there, and which make Lenin seem very human. Clothes that are threadbare or neatly mended make the sort of life he lived vivid and real. It was surprising to find how interesting was the fact that his shoes showed that his feet must have been extraordinarily small and delicate. None but the Russians would have thought of showing the coat with Dora Kaplan's bullet hole still in it, and the sight of it had a curious emotional effect. The manuscripts that were shown were probably selected with the same skill, and they show that Lenin, like most of us, was given to doodling. If it is true that doodles tell much about the subconscious, there is a great field for the doodle analyst there.

As you go through the later rooms, you feel somehow the scope of the power that he wielded, and yet the touch of humanity is always shown. The amount of space given to Stalin in those later rooms is extraordinary in view of his insignificance in Lenin's time, but it is hardly surprising. If it had not been for the final room he would have been well on his way towards crowding Lenin out. But that last room brought everything back into focus again. After the parade of cases of documents, clothing and objects of association, it was as dramatic as Lenin's tomb itself. There, in the same sort of scarlet atmosphere, lying in the same sort of state, was a death mask of the man himself. It bursts on you with all the drama of death.

There are dozens of theaters in Moscow, but with the exception of half a dozen or so they are bare and uncomfortable. The Bolshoy and the Red Army Theater are the only ones that are luxurious. The acting, like so many things in Russia, goes to extremes, for it is either excellent to the point of greatness or it is very amateurish. In addition to the regular theaters, nearly every big factory or organization goes in for its own amateur productions. We saw some competent acting in one of Chekhov's plays at the Railroad Workers' theater, and a distinctly amateurish show at the famous Gypsy Theater. If the degree of state support is reflected in costumes and scenery, the Gypsy Theater is having its troubles.

One thing that the great theaters do is to reproduce in careful detail the types and costumes which are shown in old pictures and illustrations associated with a play. There are some fine old illustrated editions of such things as Gogol's *Dead Souls* or *The Inspector-General,* and it seems as though their pictures were taken directly from MXAT. If they were to put on *Alice in Wonderland,* there is no doubt that the Tenniel illustrations would come to life as never before.

Last night we went to see *The Pickwick Club* at MXAT, and the costumes and faces were like old English Christmas cards. Yet unless the Russians have something fairly authentic to guide them, they often go far astray. Every American Negro in their plays looks and acts like the end man in an old minstrel show, and the Deep South of Lillian Hellman's *The Little Foxes* was given a weird atmosphere by surroundings of giant cactus.

The back lots and open spaces that in America would be parking areas for automobiles are flooded with water in Moscow and turned into ice-skating rinks. I tried one of them today, but with indifferent success. Perhaps it is true that anyone who has once learned to skate will always be able to do so, but the skates of today are different. They have evolved sharp prongs on the ends of the runners. After a few exhilarating moments, when it would seem that things were going all right, one of those prongs would dig into some little irregularity in the ice and stop with amazing suddenness, sending me sliding across the ice on everything but the skates.

There was no lack of help and advice from the Russian skaters of all ages — "Uncle! See how I do it!" — but it did not take me long to decide that Valodya would have to do a major operation on those devilish little prongs before such a public could be faced again.

The Russian help at the Embassy continues to disappear, and there is an intangible tension and unrest among the servants, as though someone was directing them at cross-purposes. Bender, the Spasso expediter, has been jailed for some unknown reason, and the Foreign Office would not even discuss his case with Durbrow. "What do you mean," they said icily, "by taking up your and our time by talking about the petty affairs of a minor Soviet citizen?" It meant nothing to them that Bender had worked for the Americans ever since we have had an embassy in the Soviet Union and that it would have been unnatural for us not to try to help him in any way we legitimately could.

That this ominous atmosphere is not a product of our nerves is shown by the fact that Elyena has sent word that she is all right and not to worry about her. Language teachers are harder than ever to get, for the few that are left are of course fully booked. Nila Magidov, who still comes to talk with me every Wednesday afternoon, is a great help.

Nila's knowledge of English is just about the same as my knowledge of Russian, which means that we can supplement each other's blind spots well. She likes T. S. Eliot's verse, which is difficult enough for an Englishman or an American, so we have translated poem after poem into Russian. She is able to tell me when I have hit on expressions that convey the meaning and the feel to a Russian, and which translations would be only puzzling to him.

I have also been trying my hand at writing Russian poetry. Nila took a couple of sonnets home with her, smooth drafts that I had pecked out on a Russian typewriter. It is difficult to catch the feeling of Russia without ending on a somber note. There was nothing the matter with these sonnets, but somehow they turned themselves into the lament of a loyal Soviet citizen who has been sent to the prison camps and separated from his sweetheart.

"Can't you write on any other subject but that?" asked Nila when she brought them back. "It's dangerous to write things like that."

"I don't see how it can be dangerous. There is nothing wrong with that subject — it happens every day. And there is no complaint or criticism of the Soviets at all."

"Just the same, it's dangerous."

I have been working crossword puzzles from *Ogonyok,* the Soviet poor-relation equivalent of *Life.* Although they are much simpler than American crossword puzzles, even the Russians find them difficult. This may well be due more to the lack of definitive dictionaries than anything else.

Nila told Nell that her mother had once made her some shoes of chair leather, with rope soles. Her mother would only let her have them to wear on Sundays. Nila loved to dance, so she gave her sister her daily piece of bread to "stole" the shoes for her so she could go dancing. One night she came home from a dance to find the door locked. She climbed through a window beneath which her father slept, holding her breath for fear she would wake him. As she stepped softly over him, he reached out and pinched her ankle, but never said a word.

I shall be very sorry to have Nila go, for they are soon to leave Russia. Bob is out in Berlin now making some arrangements for his next job, and Nila is disturbed because she has not heard from her mother for a long time. She also says that she is being followed.

At last, many weeks after Christmas, the Christmas surface mails have arrived. They have been held up by Soviet failure to provide visas for our couriers. When we took advantage of the first opportunity we had to become sticky also over visas for Soviet couriers, the trouble promptly disappeared.

And also the elevator in Mokhavaya House is at last running again. For four months it has been broken down with a burned-out armature, and we have had to climb up six long flights of stairs to get to our apartment. From the continued efforts of the Russian workmen and their distress when the elevator continued to go bad, it is probable that this affair is a chronic and characteristic symptom of Russia and the way it operates, and not a devious attempt to make life uncomfortable for foreigners. There is no stock pile of spare parts for machinery in Russia, so the armature had to be rewound.

There was one period when the workmen proudly had it working, during which I was in it for an hour when it got stuck between floors. It was also during this period that Nell had a long-delayed dinner party, for she did not like to ask high-ranking guests to climb so far for their food. Just before her party, the thing broke down again. Nell apologized for the elevator to an elderly Englishman as he came puffing up the last flight of stairs. "Think nothing of it," he said. "You know, we British are not as lift-conscious as you Americans!"

6. STALIN SPEAKS

WE WENT TO THE TRETYAKOVSKAYA GALLERY, and, although Western critics are inclined to look down their noses at Russian art, it seemed to me to be one of the great galleries of the world. Except for one or two pictures, there was nothing worth seeing among the paintings done in Soviet times. However, there were not very many Soviet pictures, those that there were being mostly scenes with Lenin or Stalin. But the nature and quality of the pictures from tsarist times were "from a different opera," as the Russians say.

There were several Repins, including the famous one which shows Ivan the Terrible holding in his arms his son whom he had just murdered. The picture is bright with Oriental rugs and gore, but never have I seen such stark suffering shown in a painting as that on the Tsar's face. All hopeless unhappiness and all regret are in those wildly staring eyes, and that face has haunted me ever since.

The Tretyakovskaya was crowded with pictures that are familiar to anyone who has read much about Russia: Vereshchagin's epic paintings of the Napoleonic Wars and his colorful and picturesque ones of Samarkand and central Asia, Shishkin's great northern forests — the one with four bears is found in Soviet hotels, restaurants and waiting rooms almost as often as portraits of Stalin — and the peaceful, almost melancholy landscapes of Levitan, which are so characteristic of the land that I was almost sure I had seen the identical places he had painted. One must have lived in Russia for a time in order to be fully sensitive to the social satire of such older artists as Fedotov and Perov, but it is easy to see why they were in trouble with the authorities of their day. Perov's "Village Procession of the Cross on Easter Sunday" is remarkable for the contrast between the faith and fervor of some of the faces and the drunkenness of others, including that of the priest.

The picture of the Princess Tarakanova is there. Tarakanova had appeared from nowhere in western Europe, wealthy, aristocratic

and well-mannered, lacking for nothing, but claiming the right to
the Russian throne. Catherine the Great had Orlov lure her on
board a Russian warship at Leghorn in the Mediterranean. Once she
was on board ship, she was brought straight to St. Petersburg and
thrown into the Fortress of Peter and Paul. There she bore a child,
supposedly Orlov's, and she clung calmly and steadfastly to her
claim until the end. One story says that she was drowned in her
cell in one of the floods which used to plague Petersburg, and the
picture by Flavitsky in the Tretyakovskaya shows her, fine, dainty
and very beautiful, crouched against the wall on her bed of sheepskins and straw while the rats swarm about her, driven by the
ominous water that swirls through the barred window and rises
about her bed.

The Russian people love the gilded domes of their churches and
the white birches of their woods, and the Tretyakovskaya has many
lovely pictures of both of those very Russian subjects. Juan, in particular, catches the play of light on both of them and the touch of
nostalgia that is almost sadness.

But of all the pictures there, those of Vasnetsov pleased me most.
They have little in common with great art, for he painted pictures
from the *skazki,* but they have a great sweep of imaginative realism
coupled with much charm. His mysterious and lurid "Three Queens
of the Underworld" and his picture of Ivan Tsarevich riding with
the Tsar-Maiden on the back of the gray wolf through the dark
forest were made of the same stuff as the *skazki* themselves.

Last night we went to a party at Eddie Stevens's. He lives in his
privately owned house in the south part of Moscow, with a Russian
family occupying half of it. Eddie is tall and boyish and blue-eyed,
and has been in Russia for years. He is the last of the distinguished
line of correspondents for the *Christian Science Monitor.* Most of
the American correspondents, except Eddy Gilmore, whose Tamara
is still a Soviet citizen and so cannot get an exit visa,* are leaving
Moscow, because their papers do not think that enough news gets

* In mid-June, 1953, Tamara Gilmore was granted an exit visa. It seems
probable that the Soviet Union withheld visas for Soviet wives of foreigners
until such time as favorable action would fit in with a general policy of seeming to be co-operative with the West.

by the censors to pay their way, so Eddie Stevens's house is being offered for sale.

It is possible to own a house here, but not the land on which it stands, so the state can and does put a squeeze on people by taking over the land, leaving them the almost impossible task of having to move the house to other land which is also owned by the state. It may be argued that the Western principle of eminent domain is essentially similar, but there is a great difference in the use of power. Moreover, in the West, the power of the state is granted to it by the people, but in Russia it is seized and maintained in the name of the people.

Eddie's house is attractive within, with its paneled walls and ceiling, its grand piano, its Russian pictures and its shelves of Russian books that he has accumulated. His Russian wife has been in Berlin for many months, for, although like Nila Magidov she has American citizenship which has been recognized by the Soviets, there seem to be endless difficulties in getting visas for her to return. Meanwhile Eddie stays on his job here with his little daughter and his mother-in-law. Eddie himself is a very sincere and genuine person, and we are very fond of him. Last night we decided to form the "Stevens Protective Association" for our mutual benefit.

John Steinbeck was at Eddie's, looking very prosperous and assured. He rates high in the Soviet Union because he has so often portrayed the seamy side of American life — the "contradictions in the capitalist system," as the Soviets would put it.

I found a stretch of rolling country south of Moscow that looked as though it might be within my embryo skiing capabilities, so I left Valodya in the car by the side of the road and started off cross-country. While I was still trying to get the hang of the thing, a big, deep-bosomed, rosy-cheeked peasant woman came past. She stopped and watched me for a moment. Then she shouted, "Go more boldly, uncle!" and went on her way laughing.

She must have inspired me to bolder efforts, for soon I was sailing down the little slopes in fine shape. Apart from a brush with a pack of dogs, it was a good day. The dogs came snarling about my heels, and it occurred to me that my skis would be more of an embarrassment than a help if the dogs really meant what they were saying. Some sort of choice had to be made, so I turned on the yapping little beasts and chased them into their village, for they turned tail as soon as they were faced.

Everyone who can really ski goes to Tsaritsino, where, in the grounds of what was once a palace of Catherine the Great, there are some proper slopes. I hope I don't get ambitious and give Tsaritsino a try, for its hills look like mountains to me. It should be enough just to be able to go cross-country on fairly level ground, for I suspect that one has to be born on skis. Right now I am too full of aches and pains to be much interested in anything but bed.

Senta has agreed to make some sort of space for me for regular Russian lessons. She is an Armenian, with thick jet-black bobbed hair and black eyes to match. She is a very intelligent girl, vivacious but businesslike. After talking with me a bit she said that I did not need lessons, but I now know exactly what is necessary, and when that was explained to her she became interested. She has agreed to read aloud to me, to tell me things that are not in the dictionaries about the appropriateness of Russian words and expressions, and to correct my stress and accent. She is thoughtful and sensitive, and I like her very much.

Last night we were invited to the Bolshoy Theater to a special program in honor of the thirtieth anniversary of the Red Army. It was a full-dress occasion. Stalin and all of the Politburo were there, in a box by the stage. Stalin's appearance put to rest the rumors that are always rising up about his bad health. It was a long evening, beginning at six and lasting until nearly midnight, with many speeches and with spectacular dancing and excellent choir music put on by the Red Army. When they began to show a movie that was to trace the thirty years of development of the Red Army, Stalin and the Politburo left their boxes. Most of the foreigners left the theater then, thinking that the evening was practically over. But Stalin had merely shifted to another box at the back of the theater, from which the movie could be seen to better advantage.

At the end of the movie there was another speech, mostly in

praise of Stalin, and when it was over, the audience turned towards Stalin and applauded long and loudly. At last Stalin got up, and made what seemed to be an impromptu speech. His voice was thin and rather high-pitched, giving an effect that was incongruous with his swarthy face and his squat, broad-shouldered figure. He thanked them for their praise, and said that it was not he alone who had won the war — after all, the Red Army had something to do with it! This brought a somewhat surprised but genuine laugh from the house. I must have been almost the only Russian-speaking foreigner who had stayed on long enough to hear Stalin speak, for this morning the press correspondents were swarming to my office to find out what Stalin, who almost never speaks in public, had really said.

Today everyone was startled to see a letter in the Soviet papers signed by Annabelle Bucar, an employee of the American Embassy, which they obligingly published. It said that she wished to give up her American passport in order to find happiness in the Soviet Union, the only country where plain people could find conditions that could give them happiness. She also said that the anti-Soviet feeling in the American Embassy had helped her make up her mind. The letter was couched in such clichés that few of us believe she actually wrote it herself, although she may have signed it willingly enough. A few know that she had recently married a tenor in the Operetta Theater, and those who knew her said that she was seeking her happiness in him rather than in anything else. Of course, the tenor was not mentioned in the letter.

Annabelle Bucar is a Czech by birth and background, but nevertheless she was an American citizen. I have seen her only once, on the occasion of the black market board, and the impression she gave then was one of being a rather earthy person who would be apt to be more interested in men than in their ideology.

It has been a regret to me that I missed seeing *The Stone Flower,* the Soviet movie which was showing in America before I came to Russia, and which received unusually favorable reviews from the American press. It seems to be almost unknown here, for although I have asked several Russians about it few of them have seen or heard of it. There was a notice in the paper saying that it was showing in a small theater in a remote part of town, so Nell and I went out to see it.

We got to the movie theater well before the next showing was to begin, so we went into the waiting room which is usually provided. It was filled with small children who were receiving a lecture on all the benefits that flowed to them from the talented hands of Stalin. At the end, they all sang a many-versed song about the great Stalin. The words of the song were flashed on a screen so they might learn them, and the occasion was of some service in improving my own Russian accent.

The Stone Flower was a *skazka* about the underground crystal world of the Urals, and it was accompanied with all the *skazka* trappings, including a little lizard that wore a crown. It was all that the American critics had said, a beautiful movie, beautifully done. The critics had been unable to understand why more movies like this did not come out of Russia, saying that it did more to create good feeling for the Russians than anything they had seen. Now, after living here for many months, it is very easy for me to understand why the picture is played down in Russia and difficult for me to understand how they ever let it be made at all, for it is completely out of key with everything one sees and experiences through the media of publicity. It is devoid of propaganda and does nothing to contribute to the power of the Bolshevik Party which is identical with the Soviet government. Beauty for its own sake has no place in the Soviet Union, but must be utilitarian. Utility means the power of the regime for good or ill, and there is a great deal of ill involved in the maintenance and exercise of that power.

There is a feeling of spring in the air, although it is much too early in the year for it to be authentic. Perhaps it comes from the sight of the gay balloons which an old man is selling in the plaza below. Yet even while I was watching him a horse passed by drawing a low sledge on which was a coffin. Three women were pushing the sledge to help the horse draw his burden across the icy square.

I have been making my usual round of the bookshops and

came back with a fisherman's handbook. There is a vast literature here of "how to do it" books ranging from how to build your own radio set to how to make your own soap. They are clearly written and practical, and often very well done indeed. This book for fishermen was no exception, for it is filled with details of fishing rigs that are completely new to me, and there is much curious information on the habits of fish, particularly in the wintertime.

There is an association of amateur fishermen in Russia. If its existence had been known to me on my arrival I would probably have tried to become a member, but now it is clear that the atmosphere is such that the effort would be certain to end up only in embarrassment both to me and to other members of the sporting fraternity. It is not that I am just giving up, but rather that one comes to sense what one can and cannot do. Moreover, there is no feeling of frustration. Although there are many things here that are different from what I expected, not much was expected, and I feel that I am just beginning to learn what Russia is really like, or at least what a foreigner can find out about it.

7. THE INFORMER

ONCE MORE MY KNOWLEDGE OF THE LANGUAGE has paid off and I have found out for myself that the dark side of the Soviet Union is not only very black but very pervasive. At a reception last night at one of the satellite embassies I met a fine-grained, gracious Russian woman, neither beautiful nor plain. She did not speak any English since her foreign connections are in eastern Europe. We talked for a long time, and she flattered me by saying that she thought there were few foreigners who have as much sympathetic feeling for purely Russian things. At last she began to tell me about herself.

She had been a student in a Leningrad university when her mother, who was all she had in the world, suddenly disappeared. There was no reason for it, as they had lived a quiet, inoffensive life. Her mother had been employed as a sewing woman in one of the shops of the dressmaking trust and had been content with her lot, particularly since her daughter was doing well in the university. Nevertheless the girl suspected that her mother had been arrested for some unknown reason, and she became more sure when she reported the disappearance to the police and found that they showed only the most perfunctory interest in her report.

Not long afterwards, the worried girl was called before the authorities of the university and told that she must leave because her mother had been found to be an enemy of the people. She was much more disturbed about her mother than about herself, for she could sew and type, and both those skills were in demand. She went to the police again to find out what had happened to her mother, but they would tell her nothing. Then she started hunting for a job.

Everywhere she went it was the same story. The employment manager would say that they were in need of typists or seamstresses and that they were delighted to have someone like her. Then she would be given the usual forms to be filled out and told to report for work the following morning. But when she would show up, she would be told that the position they had in mind had just been filled, or that the establishment had suddenly been given unexpected orders to cut down on its force, or was to be closed for repairs. Perhaps in a few months they might have a place for her, but as for the moment there were always excuses and evasions.

At first she thought that all this was just hard luck, but it eventually became clear to her that the real reason was because she had filled in the forms truthfully, saying that she did not know where her mother was or what she was doing. Her money soon ran out and she became actually hungry and desperate, so, the next place she tried, she put on the forms that her mother had died when she was a child. This time she was promptly employed as a typist.

Several years went by, and, although disappointed to have had her education terminated and still worried about her mother, she was afraid to pursue the matter further for fear of losing the livelihood that had been so difficult for her to get. One day she received a letter from her mother from a town in Siberia, saying that she had completed her prison term and been released, but would never be permitted to leave that Siberian town, and asking her to come to see her if she possibly could. So, when her vacation came, she went to Siberia, and there she found her mother.

Tears began to roll down the cheeks of this fine, delicate Russian woman as she told me this. We were in a quiet corner of one of the rooms, and I stood between her and the chattering guests so that they could not see her tears.

Varya, as I shall call her, told me that her mother was so completely broken that she hardly recognized her. Her mother told her again and again that she did not know what she had done. "Perhaps I did do something terrible. Perhaps I even committed a murder. I do not know, for I am confused and cannot remember things clearly. The only thing I do remember is that I had repeated some political anecdotes about Stalin which had made me laugh when I heard them. I told them that, but they kept asking me day after day, night after night, what else I had done. They would give me salted fish to eat, with no water to drink. And then, while they were questioning me, they would pour themselves water from a cold pitcher, and give me none. I became so confused that I did not know what I was doing. I know I signed something to get it over with, but I do not know what it was."

Soon after Varya's return to Leningrad, the police sent for her. "We notice," they said, "that you have been to Siberia to see your mother. We also notice that in your application for your present position you said that your mother was dead. Please explain that."

"I lied," said Varya. "I had to lie to keep alive. It was your system that made me lie."

"Why did you not come to us when you were first in trouble? That is what the police are for — to help people in trouble."

Varya told them truthfully that she had never thought of doing that. They said that they could understand this, but that now she had committed a serious crime in lying. Still, they had no reason to believe that she was not a loyal Soviet citizen. She could prove her loyalty by doing something for the state. All she had to do was to report to them on certain things in which they were interested, and which affected the safety of the state. "Otherwise," and they shrugged their shoulders, "we can only believe that you are a traitor as well as a liar, and it will go hard with you."

By this time, although I still stood so as to shield her from anyone who might pass by, Varya had composed herself. Out of the corner of my eye I saw an embassy attaché hovering about. Varya had seen him also. "Please do not think badly of me," she whispered, and then, as she held out her hand to me to say good-by, she added, for the benefit of the approaching attaché, "Nevertheless, I am sure you do not understand what the Soviet Union is really trying to do. Your ideas and mine are so far apart that I do not think we should talk with each other again."

All of this is of course an old story. The tale of the forced informer has been told over and over again in books on Soviet Russia, but its very stereotyped familiarity is what makes it so terrible to me now. Although all Americans here are continually aware of the possibility of provocation and plants, no motive for such deviousness seems possible in either this case or that of Petrov who told me that the Russian people was so ripe for a new revolution. And because of the very fact that my opportunities to talk with Russians have been so very limited, such experiences convince me that the appraisal of the regime which they imply is not due to isolated cases, but is a common condition and a real force.

There is a vast difference between reading about such things in a book or hearing of them at second or third hand and experiencing them directly yourself. Things which one accepts intellectually become much more real when they become emotionally part of one's own self.

A murder mystery may be exciting, but it is not pleasant when one actually lives it. I am learning what I came to Russia to find out for myself. And although it holds the attention, it is hard on the nerves. The emotional experience of trying to shield this weeping woman from observation as she told me her story will not soon be forgotten.

8. THE DARK PEOPLE

For some time the Soviet press has been attacking what they call "formalism" in music. Shostakovich seems to have seen the light, but they are still having trouble with Prokofiev and Khachaturian. Although, like Stalin, I much prefer Tchaikovsky and the old Russian folk tunes to modern dissonant music, it is easy to concede that other people have other and perhaps more educated tastes. It was difficult to see where ideology came into the matter, and until I talked with Senta it did not make sense to me to persecute composers because of a difference in taste.

"Senta," I said, "why are your Soviet composers in trouble? I cannot see that they have done anything wrong in trying to write modern music, although I myself do not like it."

"You must remember," she replied, "that everything anyone has in the Soviet Union is possible only because of the state, and so everyone owes a debt to the state and to the party which made our Revolution possible. Why should any composer just follow his own whims? After all, he could not compose if it were not for the state. How could he live? Where would he get his paper and his ink? Why shouldn't he write music that makes people patriotic and happy, rather than those gruesome noises that just fill people with unrest?"

Goncharov's *Oblomov* is an old book but full of insights into Russian character which are accepted by many Russians as still true. "Oblomovism" is to this day a word for the vague indolence and indecisiveness which have been so marked in the Russian character and which brought Goncharov's great central character to his eventual disintegration. Although the Russian intelligentsia have been well aware of it ever since Goncharov's time, no particular change took place until after the Revolution. The Soviet regime still has to cope with it, though in somewhat lesser degree. There is much reason to believe that the deep, dark mass of Russian countryfolk, particularly those who live out of the beaten track

— and there are few beaten tracks in Russia — are still much closer to their fathers and grandfathers than they are to the modern conception of Soviet man. That mass used to be called the Dark People, and it is incredible that the Dark People do not still exist, for there has not been enough time nor enough facilities for them to have changed very much.

There is a lovely passage in *Oblomov* which attempts to explain how Oblomov got that way:

Now it begins to grow dark. In the kitchen the fire again crackles, again is heard the intermittent tap of knives. Supper is being prepared. The servants and retainers have gathered at the gates. There is heard a balalaika, laughter. People are playing catch with a ball.

The sun has already gone down beyond the woods, casting a few rays that are barely warm, but which cut through the whole wood in fiery shafts, brightly bathing the tops of the pines with gold. Then the rays go out, one after another. The last ray has remained for a long time, piercing the forest of branches like a fine needle, but even it has died out.

Objects have lost their form, everything has flowed together into a mass that is at first gray, then dark. The song of the birds has gradually weakened; soon they have become completely silent, except for some sort of a lone stubborn one who, in spite of all amidst the general silence, chirps monotonously at intervals, but always less and less often, and even he has whistled weakly, faintly, for the last time, shaken himself, lightly rustling the leaves around him — and gone to sleep.

Everything has become silent. Only the crickets chirp more loudly, one after another. White vapors rise from the earth and spread along the meadow and the river. The river has also become very peaceful; just now something has suddenly splashed again in it for the last time and the stream is motionless.

It smells damp. Everything has become darker and darker. The trees have grouped themselves into some sort of monsters; it has become terrifying in the woods; there something suddenly begins to creak, as if one of the monsters goes from his own place to another and a dry twig, perhaps, is crunching under its foot. In the sky the first little star shines like a living eye, and in the windows of the house lights are twinkling.

The time of the universal, solemn silence of nature has come, those minutes when the creative mind works more strongly, poetic thoughts boil more briskly, when passion flames hotter in the heart or yearning aches more painfully, when in the cruel heart the seed of a criminal thought ripens more coolly and strongly, and when — in Oblomovtown everyone sleeps so soundly and so peacefully.

"Come, mother,' says Ilyusha, "let's go out and run around."

"God be with you! What are you saying!" she answers. "It's damp, your feet will get wet and cold. And it is terrible; the forest-demon is going about now in the woods, he carries small children away."

"Where does he carry them? What sort of thing is he? Where does he live?" asks the child.

And his mother lets her own unbridled fantasy run free.

The child listens to her, opening and closing his eyes, until at last sleep completely overcomes him. The nurse comes and, taking him from his mother's knees, carries him asleep to bed, with his head hanging across her shoulder.

"So the day has come, and glory be to God!" say the Oblomovists, lying in their beds, groaning and crossing themselves. "We have lived safely through yesterday; God grant that tomorrow be the same. Glory be to you, oh Lord! Glory be!"

After this gentle peaceful atmosphere, there follows a description of the *skazki* that the young Oblomov heard from his nurse, stressing both their attractive beauty and their unreality, and telling always of how the lazy, inoffensive younger son ends up by being richly fed and dressed in some miraculous way, and marries some sort of Militrisa Kirbityevna, a princess of unheard-of beauty — all through magic and through no genuine efforts of his own. Then the tales that are told shift to the Russian demonology, to monsters, the dead alive and werewolves. In vivid and beautiful language it is shown that the origins of the superstitions of the countryside lie in the conditions of its life and in mistaking coincidence for cause. This long passage of several pages ends thus:

Hearing from his nurse tales of the Firebird, which is our own Golden Fleece, and about the obstacles and secret passages of the enchanted castle, the boy now grew bold, with the prickles running up and down his spine as he imagined himself the hero of the deed, now suffered through the misfortunes of the valiant. Story flowed after story. The nurse spoke with fire, picturesquely, attractively, even inspired in places, because she herself half believed the tales. The eyes of the old woman flashed with fire, her head trembled with agitation, and her voice rose to an unaccustomed note. The child, seized by an unknown horror, pressed close to her with tears in his eyes. . . .

The imagination of the boy becomes peopled with strange specters, fear and melancholy have been planted for a long time, perhaps forever, in his soul. He looks sadly around and always sees harm and disaster in life, he is ever dreaming of that magic land where there is no evil, no fuss, no sorrows, where Militrisa Kirbityevna lives, and where they eat so well and are given clothes.

It is not only over the children in Oblomovtown, but also over the grownups that the *skazka* keeps its power to the end of life. Everyone in the house and in the village, from the nobleman and his wife to Tarasa the stalwart smith — all are afraid of something in the dark evening, every tree is then transformed into a giant, every bush into a robbers' den. The rattling of the shutters and the howling of the wind in the chimney make men, women and children turn pale. On Epiphany Day, no one goes beyond the gates after ten o'clock at night, on Easter Eve everyone is afraid to go into the stable, afraid that there they will meet the goblin.

In Oblomovtown they believe in everything — in werewolves, and in revenants. If they are told that a rick of hay is strolling around the field, they do not think about it, but believe; if some sort of rumor goes around that that thing there is not a sheep, but something else, or that such and such a Martha or Stepanida is a witch, they will fear both the sheep and Martha; it does not come into their heads to ask how the sheep came to be not a sheep, or how Martha became a witch, and they also turn on anyone who might have thought to doubt it. So strong is faith in the miraculous in Oblomovtown!

Ilya Ilyich Oblomov understands later that the world is constructed simply, that the dead do not rise up from their graves, that giants, as soon as they are found, are put straightway into side shows, and robbers into prison, but if the belief in ghosts itself vanishes, there still remains some sort of sediment of fear and vague apprehension.

.   .   .

This is the classical argument against fairy tales for children, put forth with eloquence not as an argument, but as a statement to explain the Oblomov psychology. I cannot subscribe to any general application of that philosophy, for many of the most admirable, decisive and courageous people I know were brought up on fairy tales. Still, the Russian *skazki* may be stronger stuff, or perhaps the Russians are more vulnerable.

In any case it is interesting to know that this theory was put forth by Goncharov in 1858, and that the early attempts of the Soviet regime to do away with the *skazki* may have been rooted in this old attempt to explain certain deficiencies in the Russian character. It would be still more interesting to know just why the Soviets abandoned that attempt — if it set up a clash with deep-rooted nationalistic instincts which they wished to exploit, or if a certain amount of Oblomovism in the people might not be advantageous to the power of the regime. It is hard to believe that they abandoned it just because it didn't seem practicable, for they continue to make strenuous efforts to foster other ideas which seem much less practicable.

9. "HE WHO IS NOT FOR ME IS AGAINST ME"

A BLOND, SMILING SOUL from the Czech Embassy gave us tickets to hear Sophronitsky play Chopin at the Grand Conservatory Hall. The Czech himself couldn't go because of the presence of a Finnish delegation, sent to Moscow by request to discuss a treaty of alleged friendship. Where the Czechs came in wasn't clear. They have been through the wringer already — their gentle, scholarly Ambassador and his accomplished wife left for Prague a few days ago for good.

Every seat was taken in the Grand Hall, with its majestic hangings and curtains of crushed old-gold velvet, its tremendous pipe organ with ninety-five pipes (I wonder if that is a standard number), two thirds of them all battered and dented. Now why are those pipes so battered? Perhaps scenery had been used there once, and had been handled roughly, although the stage is obviously not designed for a theater. The pipes were set into a massive wooden series of frames, plainly carved, but with classic lintels, arches and cornices like the ancient rock dwellings of Petra and the pictures from Doughty's *Arabia Deserta*.

The balcony was cut much farther back than it would have been in America, with a certain loss in seating capacity and a probable gain in acoustics. Above it, running almost the full length of the Hall, on each side, was a great row of great portraits of great musicians — Tchaikovsky and Glinka next the stage (Glinka with his puffed cravat and red fez covered with gold embroidery), and tailing off through the German great to Gluck and Borodin. The names of the last two couldn't be seen from the parterre, so I asked the little old lady doorkeepers if they knew who they were. They seemed pleasantly embarrassed because they didn't know, but one of them said she would ask and find out for me. When the evening was over, she was waiting to tell me. The ceiling was inset with several big clusters of lights, instead of a chandelier. Only the central cluster was lit, and it looked like a string of pearls surrounding six pools of light around a central fountain. Between the pools of light were six gilded personages with long slim trumpets, like the holy bean blowers of Boston. The ladies of the audience for the most part wore muffs and plain, badly designed and badly cut day dresses. During the intermission, as customary, the piano tuner came out and worked on the enormous handsome Bechstein, which had its legs tied together with pinned struts.

Sophronitsky was tall, with a gray unsmiling face, a little cadaverous, and a bit of a sourpuss. But he could play the piano. In the lyrical part of the funeral march — which is the third movement of the Sonata Opus 35 — his touch was so magical that the piano ceased to be a percussion instrument and was something liquid and coaxing. He played the great Polonaise in A *dur,* and one of the waltzes that Nell plays so well. At the end, no one in the audience made a move to leave, and they worked hard to get him back for five encores.

Then Nell and I got our wraps from the cloakroom. As usual, I was in civilian clothes, and the little gray-mustached attendant, who would not give us a claim number but repeated to my protest that he would remember us, came out from behind the counter and insisted upon helping us on with our coats while the long line waited patiently. We walked home over icy pavements in the fresh, cold air, past low, square, pink-washed and yellow buildings.

One degree above freezing, with the streets flooded with half-frozen slush, giving a chill, springlike effect mostly supported by the floods of sunlight. No sooner had we left the Embassy in the blue car than Nell saw a peasant woman with big bundles of pussy willows. After minor difficulties due to having to turn around in the traffic and to the ever-present police, who insisted that such things could not be sold on the streets but should be confined to the markets, we bought some. Valodya herded the woman, bundles and all, to the car in order to make the sale, relying partly on our diplomatic immunity and partly on the fact that the police scold rather than act in such cases.

Then over the Kamyenny Most — the Stone Bridge — to leave a note at the British Embassy. For some reason, the golden onion-shaped cupolas and domes of the Kremlin churches looked dull and tarnished in the sunlight. Valodya said that pussy willows were favorite decorations for graves, and that they were also much in evidence in the Russian churches at Easter services. We hesitantly left another note at the Czech Embassy, thanking our friend for last night's Chopin tickets — hesitant because it is quite certain that the note will never reach the addressee without being read by others, and we have no wish to embarrass anyone by advertising any kindnesses to Americans.

Then to the Balashovsky Market, reached through narrow muddy alleys. The faces and the padded clothing of the rows of women behind the stalls were much more interesting than the things they sold. Sly, shrewd, pleasant faces with narrow, smiling eyes, big, rosy-cheeked, high-cheekboned faces, dour faces, but all of them full of character and curiosity about what was going on around them. Potatoes, cabbages, mangel-wurzels, sticks of horseradish, strings of dried mushrooms, chopped-up salads, frozen fish like smelts, washcloths made of strings of dried grass, and crowded rows of milk cans with milk slopping everywhere and everyone drinking out of the glasses in which the milk was measured. Russians are always eating, in the theaters, at football games, on the street. Here they were eating raw carrots, raw cabbage leaves, even bits of raw tallow from the chunks and quarters of raw beef. For some reason, cuts of meat in Moscow bear no resemblance to those in America, but are only enigmatic lumps and gobbets.

From there we drove to the commission shops at the lower end of Stolyeshnikov Lane and sent Valodya home with the car to take Natasha shopping, leaving us to walk home. The commission shops, which are state-operated antique or secondhand stores, were all closed from three to four for lunch — further evidence that the competitive system serves the customer better than beaurocracy — so we walked up the hill to Gorky Street blinded by the blaze of sunlight reflected in the pools of slush and water everywhere. Bags and bundles of all shapes and sizes, red fox coats, fur caps and hats of all shapes and sizes.

Valyenki always seem the most exotic of footgear — they look like huge animal paws on people's feet — although some of them can be quite handsome, such as those made from spotted ponyhide, which are really not *valyenki,* since *valyenki* are made from felt.

Boots trimmed with mink or fox, black *valyenki,* gray *valyenki,* white *valyenki* — usually worn with black rubbers — soft black Russian leather boots. Five men in blue overcoats with black astrakhan *kubankas* on their heads, looking as though they were sent to do a particularly grim and gruesome job. And through every archway and at the end of every side alley was a scene of crumbling, molding, decaying buildings which gives Moscow much of its atmosphere of age.

I turned on the radio in the cozy little room opposite the Kremlin and listened to the programs in honor of some sort of anniversary in connection with Maxim Gorky. Never a week passes that is not crowded with anniversaries of all sorts. One of the programs was a visit to the Gorky Museum. As usual, it was very well done — one could hear the crowds of visitors talking, and the museum attendants described the various exhibits as they always do to the crowds. It was a children's program, and one old man took the microphone to tell of how Gorky had been kind to him when they were both young. Gorky's love for the people and for children in particular was well brought out.

Then someone described Gorky's visit to America. Whenever America is mentioned, one always braces oneself for the slap, and sure enough, it came. Gorky's impression of America was that it was a civilization of Stones and Things, without soul, heart, feeling, or kindliness — the natural result of a capitalist order, and such a contrast to the warmhearted, child-loving Soviet world of True Democracy.

Nothing here is ever dished up on its own merits — there must be purpose, meaning, and planning in everything. Skiing and skating are not to be done because one likes to ski or skate, but because they are good for you. The old plays, Chekhov and Ostrovsky in particular, are immeasurably superior to contemporary drama in the theaters, but even they must have revolutionary significance — which Chekhov has in an amazing way that I did not realize until coming here — or else they must portray the evils and follies of bourgeois life, particularly the greed and selfishness that is pro-

voked by money and property under the capitalist order. Even
music must now make a positive contribution to ideology.

Neutrality in the class struggle is a crime, and "He who is not
for me is against me" is a conception which forms the great sea
of life, all of whose manifestations are only waves on the surface
of that struggle. It is difficult to think of any human activity which
does not fit into that pattern, and it seems to me that the classical
ballet and some, but not all, of the endless variations of the charming, urgent *chastushki* songs — folk songs in the making — are
the only things that are not made to conform and direct their
energies to serve. Even these are so characteristically and traditionally Russian that they strengthen the thread of nationalist pride
and feeling, which also serves the state.

Valodya found a place which would cut a new lens for Nell's
cat-shaped, high-priced long-distance glasses, much to her delight.
According to Valodya, it was unusually expensive — twenty rubles,
or two dollars and a half at this new murderous diplomatic exchange rate — because of the fact that the cat shape made special
cutting necessary. They would have cost much more in America,
and Nell remarked on the fact that one is able to find such excellent skills among personal workmen, whereas any sort of production article, such as an ordinary handkerchief, cannot be had at
all, or else is fantastically expensive.

Nell and Valodya between them have succeeded in getting a
leather zipper-bag repaired which was completely beyond the capacity of both Washington and London, for both cities were can-
vassed well in an attempt to get the zippers fixed. And Nell got
some frames put on some other glasses in less time and for less
money than the job could have been done in Washington. The
individual Russian workman seems capable of better things than
his state production system achieves. But in general the old Russian handicraft, honest and often striking and picturesque but
seldom fine, has disappeared, to be replaced by sleazy, shoddy machinemade things which are cheap only in their quality.

We went to see Gogol's *Dead Souls* at the Moscow Art Theater for the second time. I wore uniform because we were going on afterwards to Spasso House for the monthly American Club party, and we were objects of very frank curiosity from Russians of all classes (in this classless society) in the parade that circles through the promenade and waiting rooms before the play and during the intermissions. Bearded generals and booted railway workers and their ladies stopped and stared at us more than they did at the pictures of past and present artists and shows that line those rooms.

The cast was practically unchanged from what it was when we saw it several months before, with Livanov as the roaring, drunken boyar-like Nozdrev in kaftan, wide trousers and boots, and with fantastic whiskers on his florid, popeyed face, while Byelokurov, with his sly eyes and smooth hypocrisy, was a perfect, scoundrelly Chichikov — Pavel Ivanich — and what unction can be put into those Russian syllables! Byelokurov is the best scoundrel I have ever seen. It is so hard to imagine him in any other than a rascal's part that it came as something of a shock when we saw him once boyishly speak a patriotic poem in a special evening of MXAT artists at the Grand Hall.

There are two scenes from *Dead Souls* that should live forever. One is Chichikov's visit to the flamboyant Nozdrev's house (never forget the brother-in-law, with his drooping mustaches, unbelievably drunk and inoffensive, but always in the way), with its unforgettable game of checkers where each tries to cheat his suspicious opponent in the midst of uproar and confusion. The other is the scene of barefaced flattery when Chichikov admires the Governor's hand embroidery — "No! it *can't* be *you* who has wrought this wonder!" There are half a dozen scenes of the same caliber as those two, and the entire play is uproariously funny — one of the very best things on the Moscow stage this season, where I estimate that around three hundred different shows are played every year, fifty-five of which we have seen already, many of them more than once.

There was the usual trouble getting through the pack and jam around the cloakrooms after the show — these people really love to crowd and push, it's sort of friendly and democratic — and the usual saving in time and patience to see Valodya on the edge of the crowd with our coats all ready for us. We have about decided to have Valodya stop this bit of service, though, because it certainly attracts attention, and attention is usually not apt to be very healthy for Soviet citizens like Valodya. But now we were already very late to the Spasso party, and didn't want to seem rude or indifferent to the Americans at the party.

PART III. SPRING COMES EVER

1. THE WESTERN EASTER

TODAY WAS EASTER SUNDAY — the Easter of the Western world, and not yet that of the Russian Orthodox Church. Paper-thin Russian pancakes — *blini* — for breakfast, a usual Sunday custom, and Natasha telling Nellie, *"Panamayu, panamayu* (I understand, I understand)" — before Nellie had even opened her mouth to talk. Some gorgeous tulips and a touching note from our Czech friend.

Father Laberge's Easter services at noon were packed and crowded — largely by Russians.* It was gloomy, and a fine cold rain, half rain and half sleet, was falling. Even the enclosure around the church was jammed with crowds of Russians, so that we could not drive to the entrance, but had to push our way through. Two or three rows in front had been saved, and we

* The only Roman Catholic church in Moscow that has been open in recent years is the old French Church of St. Louis, and its availability was due to the Litvinov Agreement, made when the United States established diplomatic relations with the Soviet Union. Two priests, one American and one French, officiated. Father Laberge, the American, later came home on a round-trip visa given him by the Soviet government, only to have the return portion of his visa canceled by the Soviets while he was in the United States. While I was still in Moscow, the two priests were forbidden by the Soviets to minister to anyone other than foreign diplomatic personnel. Eventually Father Thomas and Father Laberge's successor were denied the use of the church itself, which was taken over by a strange and ambiguous Polish "priest" in full sympathy with the regime.

finally made our way there. Roman Catholic churches always put me in a solemn and sympathetic mood, and this one was no exception, with the crowded gold of its candlesticks and little shrines around the altar, its pots of pink and blue phlox around the separate shrines, its fretted brass lamps hanging from above with an occasional drip of crystal, its great patterned candles, the tablet of Tsar Nicholas nearby, and its heavy oppressive smell of crowded people. One little old lady was on her knees in front, leaning patiently against the wall near the altar as if tired, covered with a great open-knitted white shawl tied around her throat. Every bit of space was packed with standing people.

Immediately in front was Madame Catroux, the wife of the French Ambassador, and the Ambassador himself, very grave and dignified, with his high scarlet and gold general's cap and his gloves in front of him. She was busy taking charge of the situation with reference to her own French people, and she called some of them from Ambassador Smith's pew into her own. It was probably just as well, for it made room for General Smith, who came in later.

Father LaBerge held his services in French, then English, and finally in Russian, quite an admirable accomplishment. He looked every inch a priest, with his bright little black eyes and his scholarly spectacles. So did Father Thomas, but his great bushy black beard and his red lips and his full, jolly face seemed to put him in a different, more medieval background. There were good voices in the choir, made up from the diplomatic colony, led by Madame Colonna-Cesari, the pink-faced, red-haired Bulgarian married to a Corsican. The faces in the Russian congregation were wonderful to watch — shawled and kerchiefed women and bearded, strong-faced men. One such woman nearby read continuously and devoutly from her prayer book, moving her lips slowly as she read, and another kissed her book throughout the service, never taking it from her lips, while others fingered their rosaries. An old, mild-eyed woman starts to blunder into the pew ahead, but is stopped by Madame Catroux, by whose side are the only empty places in the church.

The communion at the end was particularly affecting. Never before have I seen women kneel and place their foreheads on the floor in an Eastern gesture of submission, nor have I seen them come through the aisles to the altar on their knees. And when we finally went out through the rows of poor people at the door — it is not correct or proper to call them beggars — I felt soft lips on my hand. *"Batyushka! Mama! Matushka!"* Gentle, musical long-drawn-out Russian words that caught at one's throat.

I walked back to Mokhavaya House along Okhotny Row — Hunter's Row — at least there was a sign that said it was Okhotny Row, although I had thought that that famous street was farther out. One can never be very sure about such things without maps for authenticity, and besides, the Soviets are forever changing the names of their streets and squares and places in general. The people call places by their old names as often as by their new ones, often refusing to give up the old pre-Revolution names. Serpukhovskaya Square, which has one of the common bars that I like so much, has been renamed for years, but it is still Serpukhovskaya Square. All of which doesn't help in trying to find one's way around.

On the way I bought a handful of steppe grass, fluffy and delicate as ostrich feathers, dyed scarlet, green, or yellow, or blue, for Nell for Easter. When among the Russian crowds, one thinks that the most interesting thing about them is their hats — no, perhaps their boots — well, their clothes in general. And then one starts to notice faces, and decides that they are even more interesting. Eyes that don't quite match up, strangely shaped heads, amazing and enigmatic scars, pride, cruelty, sweetness, slyness, Tatar slant-eyes. I saw a woman waddling down the street with a face like a mask of Jenghiz Khan — enormous slanted eyes, high cheek-bones colored bright red, huge hooked beak of a nose, and a wide mouth like that of Greek Tragedy, turned far down at the corners. And I passed an olive-skinned, aesthetic, slim young man, exquisitely dressed in riding breeches and beautiful soft black boots, but with a faded, short, quilted, padded cotton jacket of the same material and cut as Navy life jackets. And on his noble young head was a flying helmet of the sort that children buy in the dime stores in America, with the flaps flapping in the breeze.

.   .   .

For several days the newspapers have noted a new edition of *Anna Karenina* for sixteen rubles. I have tried to buy a copy for months with no success. I have also tried in a half dozen shops for this newly announced edition, also with no success. Today an old copy was in a used-book shop window. I went in to buy it, but came out without it, for the price was two hundred rubles — twenty-five dollars. And it wasn't even a first edition.

There is some sort of mystery about this lack of correspondence between the published word and the facts. Perhaps it's a taint of some sort, a punishment for propaganda. There is a weekly radio paper, which can be bought in all the kiosks — never on the same day of the week, of course, but sometimes early and sometimes late — which lists all of the Moscow broadcasts for the entire week. A dramatization of Gorky's *Mother* was scheduled for 1.30 today. Not only did it not appear at 1.30 as scheduled, but none of the three listed Moscow stations had anything faintly resembling the published programs, nor did the two or three other stations which for some reason are not included in the weekly paper. As in many other instances, though, there was somehow no bad faith, for late in the afternoon I succeeded in tuning in on the closing words of a dramatization, and heard the announcement "You have been listening to Gorky's *Mother.*"

While I have been writing this, the weather has changed. The fine rain has stopped, and the vague sky is very black in some quarters, as if there were thunderstorms about. The sun struggles to come out, but even as it tries, large white flakes of snow drift and swirl in front of the Kremlin. The corner tower opposite our windows is surrounded with level after level of scaffolding, so that it looks like a fantastic Chinese pagoda against the sky. But the entire top of the ancient tower has disappeared! One can see right through the scaffolding, and the tall conical steeple is gone. The shape is still there, outlined by thin battens of new wood, but the old slates and stones and little projecting windows that have looked out over this secret city for hundreds of years, perhaps since the days of Ivan the Terrible, have completely vanished. The thought comes to me that when the steeple reappears, it will probably have the same outlines, but that a careful look will show that it has been given a new, utilitarian, and democratic significance.

I turned on the radio today to see if there was anything of interest, and found myself in the middle of a Russian broadcast of Shaw's *Pygmalion.* I have kept away from it on the stage, where it is now showing, because two or three people had told me it was terrible, and because it did not seem possible to translate a thing that is so dependent on peculiarly English speech and English prejudices into a language and a background as foreign as Russian. One or two Russians appreciated the difficulties when I talked with them about it, but said that it might be interesting to me in any case to study the attempt.

Over the radio, however, it was delightful, and the problems involved were solved most successfully. The exquisite clarification of Liza's speech under her tutor was beautifully done. The Russian language, which can be so typically peasant, still lends itself well to a delicate, birdlike sort of affectation, and the quaintnesses of "meestyer" and "ser" and English names with a Russian accent have become so familiar that they are seldom noticed. Indeed it might be better over the radio than on the stage, because Russian faces, figures, and types can easily go far afield from what they are trying to portray. Perhaps those who told me it was terrible did not have a precise appreciation of the two languages involved. Here one becomes sensitive to overtones of class significance which are hardly noticed elsewhere, and those overtones were there — enough to justify its being played in Moscow — but there was no mayhem with it, and it was really charming.

"Natasha, do you suppose that most of the people in that long queue moving slowly to see Lenin in his tomb — three or four abreast, and four or five blocks long, so that it extends so far down this side of the Kremlin that it reaches the old Tsar's riding hall — do you suppose that most of them are seeing it for the first time?"

"Who knows? There are very many people in Russia, and all of them want to see it. And why not? There is nothing like it in all the world. He is the only man that has ever been kept in that way, and since there has never been anything like it, multitudes of people stand in line every day for hours to see it."

Monday we had a dinner party in our apartment, and our Zoya

and Natasha, helped by the Carters' Zoya and that ox of a Valya who now sulks with someone else, were busy all day. Dumpy Natasha stumped around in her stocking feet, and those stockings were really long, heavy skiing socks of gray and red wool that didn't reach to her knees and sagged disgracefully. Her grim face wrinkled up in a big laugh when I told her that the season for winter sports was over.

When breakfast was done, Nell got me to look at the hazel-hens (that is the only word that the dictionaries give for the famous *ryabchiki*), and to prevent all argument by telling Natasha that I myself wanted them served whole, one to a person, with half birds for a second helping, and that therefore she was to find five more birds somewhere, and get them ready. Natasha just looked grim and didn't argue, but Nell said she came back from the market with six birds and a bottle of vodka which wasn't needed. There is always an undercurrent of excitement among the servants when a party is coming up, and Natasha's excitement is apt to take the form of a buying spree. And a huge pheasant showed up in the icebox, which no one had suggested.

Fortunately the elevator was working, which is no small consideration even for ourselves, to say nothing of portly ambassadors. The lift carries a big sign which forbids it to carry more than three people, so Sir Maurice Peterson, canny, dour, with his big Scotch nose, the tall, dark, shy but rather definite Lady Peterson, and the bright-blonde Mrs. Schnyder, the wife of the Swiss Chargé d'Affaires, with her thick glasses and her blue eyes, came up in the lift, while Schnyder arrived out of breath from the long climb up the stairs.

Nell's dinner was lovely. All the glass and silver and flowers were multiplied in the many mirrors on the table, the fish in the big shells was good, the *ryabchiki* — dark meat, gamey, and larger than quail — and the nine dollars' worth of frozen peas were delicious, and the Russian ice cream, all studded with little frozen cream flowers, was wonderful. It almost took a rehearsal with Valodya to be sure that he got the ice cream in time, but it was there, there was plenty of it, it was lovely to look at, and it was as smooth and delicious as any in the world.

Zoya and Lena, Sergei's big blonde sister, waited on table. When they bring in wine they always wait a moment outside the door so they can swish in dramatically in a simultaneous entrance. Willie Edenberg has kept us supplied with aquavit, and he roared out the time-honored Swedish drinking song when we had it at dinner. Sir Maurice said he didn't sing, but would be glad to participate by drinking in the pauses, and he did. And then we had something that I have been hunting for for nearly fifteen years, and never was able to find. The Schnyders sent to Switzerland for it for us when doubt was expressed if it really existed, and it was flown in with their trade delegation. *Metralie de Clavoz — l'Étoile de la Vallée!* After asking for it through Switzerland and half of Europe, I had almost reached the regretful conclusion that it was only to be had in fairy tales. It is quite true — the bubbles really form a star in any sort of glass, and it is a light, delicious wine as well.

During coffee. AMBASSADOR SMITH: "I note that the British were beaten in the International Fly-Casting Championships in Paris. And by the French, of all peoples! I didn't know that Britain had really reached such a low ebb. I thought that the Scotch, at least, were real fishermen, Sir Maurice!"

SIR MAURICE: "Eh, there were no Scotsmen in Paris — they would not pay the fare to get there! They were busy in Scotland, catching fish!"

After dinner, bridge. The last Metro had gone by the time the guests left, and Zoya and Natasha, at their own earlier suggestion, stayed the night. Valodya had acted out the suggestion to Nellie by resting his somewhat shaggy head against his clasped hands.

In the morning all the roofs and streets of Moscow were covered with beautiful, clean white snow. Russia is much more attractive in winter than in summer, even when the snow is old and grimy — along the railroads on the edge of town it looks like coal — because so much that is drab and bedraggled and dingy is covered up. And when there is a fresh fall, it is magnificent. In answer to a question as to how she had slept, Natasha said "Magnificently! So much sunlight and air!" And the Russian words for magnificent, triumphant, and such majestic ideas are themselves so very magnificent and triumphant.

For the first time, the French window in the Kremlin opposite, which has always been open in every sort of weather, was closed. I wonder what that signifies!

2. THE LENIN HILLS

I AM WEARY, AND THOROUGHLY DEPRESSED. There is always some sort of crisis in the making here, usually due to someone either actually or potentially putting themselves in the power of the Russian state, which is very apt to be merciless in using that power. Here Americans cannot afford to do things which would be perfectly normal anywhere else in the world. For another thing, we are about to lose Bob Dreher. His time is up, and his exit visa has been requested. His experience in Odessa has been invaluable, and he will be missed very much. The Navy has told me that it would be a long time before they could send a relief for Dreher, because of a shortage of Russian-speaking officers, and it becomes increasingly evident to me that none but Russian-speaking ones should be sent.

There was another dinner party at home tonight. Nila Magidov was there, in a lacy black dress, trying with only minor success to smile through her depression, for they were all packed up and closed out in order to leave early in the morning, only to be told by the Foreign Office that she could have no visa for this Friday. Perhaps some Friday, but not now. And after the way she was watched and followed when Bob Magidov was out of Russia recently, with all communication stopped with her own relatives here in Russia, Bob will not himself go and leave her alone here again. Never an explanation — only the mystery and silence and fear, leaving people to guess as best they can. And Nila is an American citizen, by official permission of the Soviets.

It's late, and it's too dark to see if the mysterious window in the Kremlin is still closed. Perhaps that is what brings the trouble. At any rate, the huge ruby stars over the Kremlin are turned full towards us, and glowing bloodily and balefully.

Since long before my arrival, no service attachés have been permitted by the Soviets to travel in Russia, except for one trip to Leningrad made by Willie Edenberg. Nevertheless, I got off a long, careful letter making a try. It is no mean task to compose a request for permission to travel which might have some chance of being even looked at by this suspicious government, and the ground for this one has been in process of preparation for months. I asked for permission to visit Kiev, which has some of the most famous and glorious churches and monasteries of all the Russias, or Kazan, the capital of the Tatar Republic, or Samarkand, where Tamerlane is buried, or the ancient Khorazm which was laid waste by Jenghiz Khan and which is studded with little-known archeological remains. My honest personal reasons for wanting to visit any of these places were given plainly, but it is probable that there will be no answer other than a long burst of silence.

My visa for Berlin, however, came back exactly as it had been requested, for travel both ways by either airplane or train. The last time I went out, an effort was made to get that sort of visa, but it did not come through until a few hours before my departure, and then for airplane only. By that time it was too late to do anything about it. Most of the foreigners believe that train travel, even to Berlin, is deliberately discouraged by the Soviets in order to isolate foreigners as much as possible from the people. It is worth remembering how effective a little bit of considerate treatment can be, for now it is very easy to wonder if, after all, it wasn't just some stupid mistake that failed to get such a visa before.

I usually get my hair cut at the skillful hands of a strapping, gray-eyed, black-haired lady barber at the National Hotel next door to the Embassy. She would be almost handsome if it were not for a large, dimplelike scar.

A fairly recent book I have been reading, in describing the way foreigners are isolated in Moscow, says that foreign envoys and newspapermen alike are not supposed to enter a barber shop, but must make special arrangements when in need of a barber. So I walked far up Gorky Street in the pleasant spring weather, without an overcoat for the first time since last October, and picked out a barber shop that was obviously frequented only by Russians. Although it was a long time before my turn came, it was not a bad wait, for the ubiquitous loud-speaker was playing Beethoven's *Emperor Concerto* instead of propaganda. The barber did not smell as good as my lady friend, but I got a satisfactory haircut with no difficulty. As a matter of fact, it is almost impossible to say what is permitted and what is not permitted without actually giving it a try, and the pattern changes from time to time.

This morning, while everyone was helping Nell search for one of her pearl earrings — Natasha at last found it under a pedal of the piano — I told Valodya to try to get tickets at the Bolshoy for Tchaikovsky's *Cheryevichki — The Little Slippers of the Tsarina.* It is one of the many operas that have been made from Gogol's wonderful *Evenings on a Farm* and *Mirgorod.*

"But that," said Valodya, "is Ukrainian, with many words that no one but the Ukrainians can understand."

"I know, but I can understand enough," I replied, and gave some demonstrations.

"Strange people, those Ukrainians," said Valodya. "Hard to make them out. We Russians say to them *khokhol,* which is a word for a Ukrainian; it means 'topknot,' and offends them very much. They answer by calling us *katsap,* which means a Russian, a 'goat beard.' And that does not offend us at all."

NELL (with a doubtful, timid look towards the lovely white and gray but temporarily barrel-shaped cat): "Natasha, when will there be little cats by Koshka?"

NATASHA: "Don't know. Koshka didn't tell me."

Such playful remarks are always unexpected from grim-faced old Natasha.

General Wang, the Chinese military attaché, prim, thin, straight and scholarly in his appearance, brought Lieutenant Colonel Tan, his new aviator assistant, to call. Tan was very heavily Chinese, his face giving a sort of three-dimensional reality to his Chineseness, with square white teeth, liquid black eyes, and a shock of blue-black hair. He had just come in over the Trans-Sib railroad. He speaks good Russian, and, like all of the Chinese, is far from dumb. Mac, Dreher, Levy and Ensign Goloway, our new self-contained graduate of the Navy language school and the wearer of size thirteen shoes, came in, and we sat for an hour over coffee and whiskey, which is a pleasant local custom for formal official calls. I still remember the unusual, tall conical glasses in which the Chinese served champagne on the occasion of my initial call.

We hear that the Russians have started to organize air-raid precautions in every block in Moscow after the pattern of the last war. That could be disturbing, or it could be only the sensible, normal prudence of a highly regimented nation which believes its own teachings — that the final, imperialistic stage of capitalism, in which they say the Western world is now mired, is sooner or

later forced by its own nature and by the greed of its ruling monopolists into foreign wars in order to make a last desperate attempt to maintain its capitalist order against the righteous indignation of the oppressed and exploited masses.

When I got home from the office, the blessed event had occurred. Koshka blinked her big Russian cat's eyes in a box which Natasha had fixed for her, and three scrawny little balls of velvet fur, with almost batlike hands or paws, wriggled after their food. And Koshka is little more than a kitten herself. As Senta said, "Why, that isn't done! It's a criminal offense!"

This is the ninth month now without any liquor or wine except Soviet wines and vodka and what other foreigners have been good enough to share with us. Our own is still in the customs warehouse, entangled in the endless wrangle about our customs. What hasn't frozen should be well aged.

Nell and I went to see Fletcher's *Taming of the Tamer* at the Yermolov Theater. Nearly always I have been in the first or second row, close enough to the stage to be able to see the really old and beautiful laces and the brocades — things which one seldom sees except in museums or collections.

My idea of the Russians before coming here was that they were robust and bawdy people, and I expected those qualities to be reflected in their theater. They are in actual fact almost Victorian in their propriety — at least in public. The theater, the parks and entertainments, and even the crowds in the street seem especially designed for bringing up small children in strict properness. Sometimes, when some line in a show has been just a very slight shade towards some suggestiveness, I have heard the audience gasp and laugh nervously at its audacity. This Fletcher play was bolder in some of its lines and situations than anything I have yet seen here. It is probably true that some things which are suggestive in English completely lose that quality when translated into Russian, unless the translation is deliberately coarse, but if my ear really caught what it seemed to catch, one of the women — a nurse sort of type, like Juliet's nurse — used a Russian word when she flipped up her skirts that nice Russians do not use.

Occasionally one sees a really pretty woman or a handsome man in the audience, and once in a while there is someone who is just breath-takingly lovely, but for the most part the faces of the grown people look strange, squinched up, almost deformed, either physically or mentally. This seems due not only to long hardship and malnutrition, but to the virtual elimination of the higher classes as such and their replacement from the lowest levels of society.

The Russian figure is as different from ours as their cats, their fish, swine, or other beasties. Pushkin did Russia a great injustice in his lines in *Eugene Onegin* when he said that in all Russia you could hardly find three pairs of lovely women's legs. That is completely untrue, and I cannot believe that my opinion is due either to a change in taste or to evolution over only a hundred years or so. One of the sights of Russia is the combination of *valyenki,* or boots, and short skirts, with the interval between more often than not filled with clean, shapely strength, and even grace. The hip bones have a peculiar close-coupled sort of squareness — I don't yet know just what it is — but the breasts of Russia are a marvel and a real mystery. They are frequently placed unusually high, but that isn't all. One wonders what they can possibly wear or do to themselves that makes them push out in the remarkable way that they do.

On the way home we saw a girl, poorly dressed with a shawl over her head, but with an amazing pair of flesh-pink Russian boots to make her gay. And two nice-looking young soldiers, with soft black boots, and light plum-colored overcoats reaching to their very heels, woolly caps to match, and scarlet shoulder marks, tenderly held the arms of their buxom girl friends as they walked along Gorky Street.

When we came into Mokhavaya House, we were mystified to notice a little cross set up in the narrow grassy space in front of the building. We stopped, and asked the broad-faced, evil-looking MVD guard what it was for. His scarred face wrinkled into a grin as he said that it marked the grave of a little Easter chicken, buried by Durbrow's small son, Bruce.

In the afternoon we drove south and west to the Lenin Hills. On the way, we passed the French Embassy, a rococo but handsome old brick building. One of our Embassy's Russian employees has told me that it stood empty for many years — empty of people, but full of furniture, pictures, rugs, and devils. That, of course, was why it stood empty for so long. Of course, too, there couldn't have been devils, because all that time a caretaker lived there, which he wouldn't have done otherwise, but the reason they thought there were devils was because they would hear knockings and noises at night, and in the mornings all the furniture would be moved around. It was a regular poltergeist story. When we passed the place, I told Valodya that there were rumors that there had been devils there — I did not want to implicate the source in repeating such unideological deceptions — one really has to be careful about such things, and careful as well in repeating them — and asked him if it were true.

"*What!*" said Valodya.

"Devils."

"Devils?"

"Yes, Devils!"

Valodya could hardly believe his ears. "Of course not. They always say that about empty houses. If I heard that people would not live in a house because of devils, I would hurry to try to get there to live in it myself."

The Lenin Hills were the Sparrow Hills before the Revolution, and although Sergei, who used to drive for me, had never heard of it, it was from those hills that Napoleon surveyed Moscow and waited for the surrender of the city, which never came. From them there is a fine panorama of the wide bends of the river, with the pale trunks of birch trees rising below on this side of the river, and broad flats on the other side, covered with a squalid wilderness of shacks and sheds and empty mud. To right and left and in the background, as far as one can see, are the strangely big buildings of Moscow, interspersed among the usual sort of architecture of such a city as, say, Cleveland. But from the middle foreground, the bud-shaped domes of some old church rise gracefully from tall towers against the sky, and beside it is a whole cluster of strange Byzantine niches and arches. And in the far distance, the golden domes of the Kremlin twinkle in the spring haze.

In the Sparrow Hills are many old wooden *izbas,* the usual wooden homes of the villages, which are found in abundance, with variations in size and style, throughout Moscow. Such houses are made from whole logs, tightly fitted together. I have seen new ones being built, and the seams are packed with moss or bast. The windows, the gables and the eaves are ornate with carved fretwork. Frequently they are painted a bright blue, or only the carved parts are painted, or some strange and unaesthetic color is used in part or in whole. The carving is often very elaborate, not in detail, which is almost always geometric, but in amount and in effectiveness. And on the roofs are sometimes similarly carved structures, usually of no conceivable use, and of the oddest shapes and proportions. Doorposts and lintels are often carved in sections sometimes square, sometimes round, sometimes diamond-shaped or tapered, so that they look like bits of St. Basil's itself.

We drove on between walls of muddy snow, past ugly, tall dull gray apartment houses, so thin that they have a two-dimensional effect or an aspect of being starved by the hunger which is often too close in Russia. And everywhere there were factories or institutions of some sort or industrial areas all mixed up with the rest of the city. Someone like Pennell could do wonders in putting Moscow into pen and ink. Pennell did get into Russia once, but not as far as Moscow. His account of his difficulties in the nineties reads like today.

We crossed the city and went along Komsomolskaya Square, where there are three great railway stations — the Leningrad, the Kazan, and the Yaroslavsky Stations. Of these, the last is amazing, with its bits of painted designs here and there, its areas of what looks like glazed colored tiles, some made into mosaic work, its broad roof arched in a way that no Western building would ever be arched, and its tremendous buttresses that are either wrong side up or in the wrong places. It is all put together wrong, but charming and effective in some strange way. From it the trains run to Siberia. I have tried to go into the Yaroslavsky Station, tried entrance after entrance, and have been turned away from every door by armed guards asking for my tickets on the Trans-Sib. One can go freely into Moscow stations, but not that one — except for one isolated part of it, which leads to local trains.

A company of MVD swinging down the street in their long dark blue overcoats with red shoulder marks and black fur caps. Men and women indiscriminately in its ranks, the women with big masses of the dark reddish hair that is so characteristically Russian. Two soldiers in some uniform I have never seen before — there is never any end to the strange uniforms and costumes. These two wore light fawn-colored shaggy overcoats, shaggy fur boots, hats to match, and bright red shoulder marks.

Through the birches and tall pines of Sokolniki Park, over some bad roads past seas of mud, and home through Dzherzhinsky Square — named for the Polish zealot who organized the Cheka. There is where the old Lubyanka Prison stood, and there the new one stands as part of MVD headquarters, for I finally found a Russian who knew all about such things. He had been there, and not pleasantly. And at every door and entrance to MVD headquarters stands a sentry in his long overcoat, carrying a rifle with its long, sharp, narrow bayonet ready-fixed in place.

3. BERLIN SPRING

EARLY IN THE MORNING Nell drove out with me to Vnukovo Airport to see me off for Berlin. In the settled country, the roads are strung out with people, going or coming from somewhere on foot, seated on the tops of loads in open trucks, or in low sleighs drawn by unkempt little horses with big stiff wooden bows arching over their necks. In the city there were fewer people up and about than on these country roads.

On the edges of Moscow loom big buildings — usually apartment houses or institutions of some sort — with a strange sort of architecture. It is utilitarian, but succeeds somehow in being vaguely improbable and inconvenient without even the faint touch of sleekness that might make it "modernistic." They are too thin, or too drab, and almost always in just plain bad taste without any use of the really Russian sort of decoration that could make them charming — or, say, less uncharming. One I remember — a tall, gaunt structure of a cherry-pink color, whose upper parts and eaves were so styled that it gave a very remarkable effect of deep perspective, and made it look even larger than it was. It was like camouflage, but with no evident purpose, ending up by merely looking disturbingly queer. The groves of silver birches were, however, lovely as always, and soon we were in the main airport terminal, which is reminiscent of some sort of minor resort hotel.

The big waiting room, with its gigantic map of all the Russias, with the air routes marked in straight silver lines, all out of proportion, was crowded, but there were none of the silk-trousered Asiatic women among the patient, waiting, sleeping people who sometimes make the place interesting.

This time it was possible, but only with difficulty, to hang onto my *laissez-passer* which frees one from customs inspection and is particularly desirable when entering Russia. If they hadn't been told very definitely that not only was it needed in case I did not return through Vnukovo but that I myself could take care of it more easily than they could mail it to me somewhere, they would have had it away from me. As often as not, they are really trying to be helpful. Sometimes it seems to me that the average Russian attendant tries to do some thinking for you. I'm quite sure that their first thought, when a question is asked them, is "Now, just why does he want to know that?" For example, when my luggage was weighed, the attendant said that everything was in order.

"How much does it weigh?" I asked.

"There's no charge on it."

"Yes, but how much does it weigh?"

"Oh, everything's all right. It's within the limit, so there is no excess to pay."

"But I want to know exactly how much it weighs, so that I will know how much I can bring with me extra, without charge, when I come back."

And then a light dawns on the expressive Slavic face.

I told Nell good-by — she looked very gay and lovely in her gray Persian lamb coat and cap — and the Douglas C-47, or the Russian version thereof, taxied away. One can tell without a map when one is over Russia, at least in these parts. Everywhere, as far as one's vision reaches, are snow-covered expanses, heavily broken by large patches of dark woods and forest. Even the woods, with their black, conical, heavily foreshortened fir trees, are broken by wispy lines and misty patches of birch.

But the one distinguishing mark of Great Russia is the utter and complete lack of farmhouses or farm buildings. The Russians do not live on separate farms, but cluster into villages, where the huts and houses are snugly strung along a single street, as close together as in an Indiana or a Nebraska small town. There is not even a separate word in the Russian language that means "the country" — one says "in the village" instead.

We were over Byelorussia before the unending expanses of white snow began to thin out to white crusts around the edges of the woods and ponds, although the Dnepr was still full of ice. There were fewer forests, less wasteland, and the countryside looked less shaggy from the air. Then through some thick white snow flurries which drove briefly past in horizontal sheets, and then between pale gray and slate-colored layers of cloud above and beneath, sometimes breaking to blue above, but with the ground out of sight so that one felt free to read.

I had with me Kaverin's *Two Captains,* which is difficult to put down. Senta lent it to me, because of my wearying of the labored propaganda points that are required in everything contemporary, and because of the lack of contemporary language in the classics. There are not many Russian books like her *Two Captains,* for it has many points of view and attitudes which are usually smothered in propaganda. It is a straight adventure story, but it has many interesting sidelights on Russian life, as seen through the eyes of one of the homeless children left from the Revolution. Senta said that the author "strangely enough" was a Jew. Jews are not popular in Russia, which prides itself, however, on its equitable treatment of minorities — in the press.

Germany seemed very fresh and neat, with its shining, rain-washed streets. Everywhere the yellow forsythia was in bloom, and the lilacs were breaking out with small, vivid green leaves. For the first time, the English and French on the trilingual signs at the edges of the various zones of Berlin seemed more outlandish to me than the Russian.

Most people forget something whenever they go a-traveling, and this time I had forgotten to take anything to eat with me on leaving Moscow. Since it was midafternoon, Admiral Schuirmann's aide and I stopped at the snack restaurant at Tempelhof, and my first hamburger sandwich in nearly a year was very welcome. Had three of them — and a chocolate milk shake with two scoops of ice cream.

Pinky Schuirmann's house in Wannsee seemed extraordinarily restful, pleasant and hospitable, although we greatly missed Jinny. She had been on a week-end visit to Bremen when the Russians got sticky about the railroads. Goods could now come into Berlin by rail, but could not move out, and all passenger traffic was at a standstill except by air, and of course that was on an urgent priority basis. So Jinny was stuck outside Berlin with nothing but an overnight bag. Rather than wait it out in the Enclave, she intended to go to Switzerland.

The grove of big white birches on the lawn back of that peaceful house was particularly beautiful, though the only signs of spring were occasional little bursts of heart-shaped lilac leaves and the brown-green of willows reflected in the still water. The coloring was such that it looked more like late autumn than like spring.

Schuirmann was pink-cheeked and solemnly but heartily cordial, and we sat in utter peace over a bottle of Old Something-or-other in the late afternoon. And then the radio told us that a Russian fighter had collided with a British passenger plane, and that everyone in both planes was killed. It was on the edge of Berlin, within sight of where I had landed a few minutes before. We ate the caviar which I had brought the Schuirmanns and talked it over. And every few minutes the telephone would ring, bringing more details and developments, such as the fact that both the British and the Americans had ordered out their fighters to escort all transports from then on.

The next morning was a gray, misty, rainy day, with the freshness of early spring in the air. Although the fighter escorts were canceled, the situation remained very tense. I drove out through the jagged, staring ruins and the great neat heaps of bricks of the city to Tempelhof. Pinky's plane was in check, but Wilbur Hall, its bright-eyed curly-haired pilot, had borrowed General Clay's C-47 for us, and we took off for Frankfurt-am-Main — held up for forty minutes by Hardy, Pinky's blue-eyed daughter, who arrived with clothes and shoes for us to leave at Frankfort for Jinny to pick up on her way to Switzerland. Everywhere, of course, there were crowds of people waiting for air transportation, so we took a full load of passengers with us both to and from Frankfort.

We were in the overcast most of the way and picked up not a little rime ice, but it was pleasant enough to be at the controls again. The Air Force was running its traffic efficiently. We were tracked by radar all the way, and now and then we would hear "Plane number so-and-so, alter course five degrees to the left," or "two degrees to the right." Once when we were thoroughly lost in some heavy snow that clopped against the windshield somewhere in the vicinity of Gotha, we asked for our position, and received no answer — only continued coaching from the radar track. They told us on the field at Frankfort that there was a Russian fighter formation on the radar screen in our vicinity at that time.

There was business to be transacted in Frankfort which required privacy. It was not until the officer with whom I had to talk showed some mild surprise that I realized how natural it was to me to take him out into the open air for our conversation, where there could be no prying ears, human or mechanical.

All the way back we were flying through snow and ice. Over Berlin everything was a dark gray, and Wilbur brought us in on a Ground Control Approach that lasted nearly forty minutes, for we were quite high. It grew so dark during the approach that we had to put on the lights, but when we broke out into a gray drizzle of rain, right over the honeycombed ruins, there were the lights of the runway right in front of us, and Wilbur scarcely touched the controls until he pulled back for the final landing. Even the GCA told him over the radio that it was a perfect approach.

Cold spring rain on the long drive to Wannsee, and twice there were hooded figures beneath the corner lights that made me think of "Lili Marlene," and all the way that sad, lovely song was in my head.

Again a drink, caviar and a pleasant dinner — cold chicken, with some stuffing that was just simply and wonderfully *pâté de foie gras* — and again the fabulous bed in the quiet guesthouse, with the sad rain dripping outside in the darkness.

Always half my mind is in Russia, even when in Germany. So I remembered this conversation:

"What is the Russian name for this sort of bread, or bun?"

"Bread."

"Of course, but what special sort of bread?"

"Bread made from dough."

"I know, I know. Most bread is made from dough. But it must have some special name. Is it *krendyely?*"

"Oh, no. Just dough-bread. But you should have seen *krendyely,* when it could be had."

"Yes, the old writers frequently mention it. Was it crisp?"

"Oh, no — it was soft — and hot — and oh, so fragrant! There used to be a great market, by the river in Moscow, and on winter mornings whole loads of *krendyely* would be brought into the market by horses. When the lids of the baskets were opened, what a fragrance would fill the air!"

"Can't one get it now?"

"No. No one has seen it for many years. It was private enterprise that brought it to the people. But oh, how delicious and fragrant it was!"

The following day, Wilbur and I flew to Munich. It was a dull day, but at seven or eight thousand feet we broke out of the overcast between towering clouds, and from there all the way through the corridor to Frankfort we were once again in the blue and silver paradise that I remembered so well from a year and a half of flying over the Pacific during the war. Between the high clouds, the white floor was almost level, and it looked like an Antarctic waste of ice. Around Frankfort, the clouds started to break, and we came down low and went a bit out of our course, in order to take a look at Heidelberg and Stuttgart — two enchanting cities in my memory. But the clouds were thick and close.

We went up to the main airport building in Munich, all pockmarked with bomb fragments and machine-gun bullets, and I was met by the commanding officer of the field. During lunch — hamburgers again — in the lounge he told me that General LeMay was running them ragged. "He's not going to get caught with his pants down. We're on the alert all day and all night. It would be a relief to go to war and get this over." Eighty per cent of the fighter pilots have had combat experience, and in the European theater.

That night in Berlin, General Clay had a very large sit-down dinner at Harneck House, the luxurious ex-German club which is now used for social affairs as well as for housing very senior transient officers. Being Schuirmann's house guest, I was invited. The very tops of the American, British, and French governments were there; Koenig, the soldierly-looking Robertson and Clay himself, with a hospitable smile on his otherwise rather severe, almost morose face. I had a grand time with the food, which impressed my Moscow taste more than anything else, and with my dinner companions, neither of whose names, to my regret, I remember, although one of them was a blue-eyed, dark-haired, high-colored beauty. After dinner, we danced. According to his wife, Pinky, like me, always grumbles about having to go out evenings, but always has a wonderful time when he gets there, and this evening was no exception.

I spent the next morning in driving back and forth between the various places where one can buy things: the post exchange at Onkel Tom's Hutte; the commissary at Andrew's Barracks — grim, burned-out red brick buildings that were once the Adolf Hitler Barracks which had housed the storm troopers; the Telefunken complex, which was the only place that would let me have a couple of bottles of liquor; and the cable office, from which I sent a reminder to son Stevie in New York to be good. I came away with sugar, flour, a ham, some butter, candy and other groceries, a silver wrist-watch strap for Zoya, some comfortable house slippers for Natasha, some shoes for Valodya and for his wife, French perfumes and such, all of which do not exist in Moscow or are so sky-high in price that they are practically unobtainable. Imagine coming from one European capital to another in peacetime with sugar, flour and butter!

Since intelligence officers always have something they want to show me, I went to the Navy office after lunch. And then, with all my flight time in and all my chores of every sort completed, I drove out to Wannsee and that night slept soundly and beautifully in that fabulous bed.

4. RUMORS OF WAR

IN THE MORNING I PACKED ALL MY GROCERIES, including the big box of sandwiches and such which the plump Prussian-looking young maid put up for me. Soon I was on my way with a brand-new and inexperienced driver, but with Shultz, the snub-nosed, competent Marine orderly who knows practically everything about Berlin, between the fantastic, high, ruined walls of empty roofless buildings, once more into the Russian Zone and the Curtain. When we crossed the bridge over the Spree that marks the beginning of the Russian Zone, it was very noticeable how empty the streets suddenly became. People seemed to keep off the streets there, for some reason.

There were no porters at the Silesia Station, but plenty of volunteer helpers. Shultz was wary of them, so he and the driver helped me with all my parachute bags and boxes, including my "topee-case." The British taught me to travel with a topee-case. Their hard, tropical sun helmets, or topees, are so awkward to carry that they stuff them in a laundry bag, together with all the other overflow of packing.

As soon as I was in the red sleeping wagon which always constitutes the best accommodations on this train for Brest-Litovsk, I was left alone, the only foreigner on a long, long train which literally swarmed with Russian troops. My wagon was filled with senior Russian army officers, most of them from tank divisions, going home on leave or on transfer, accompanied in a few cases by wives and children. The *nachalnik,* or head man, of the wagon — he has more authority than a porter in America, but includes a porter's duties in his responsibilities — seemed a little bewildered when he took me to my compartment to find that it was already full of Russians, so he picked another compartment at random, and soon my parachute bags and bundles were stowed in the big boxlike space under the lower berth.

While the last package was being put away, a tank officer came in with some enormous suitcases and more bundles, which made the stowage in our double compartment a bit complicated, but not impossible. He was on the far side of middle age, with sandy gray hair and a slightly angular, convex aspect to his face that was vaguely reminiscent of one of the flat corners of a large nut. Sometimes he looked surprisingly young, and at other times old and worn. His hands were big workman's hands. He had come to Berlin with the conquering army in 1945, and, except for his annual leave, which he had received regularly, had been there ever since. His family had been with him for a while, but had gone back to his home in Leningrad, and his name was Vassily. But of course all that came later. My initial conversation with him began before the train left Berlin, when we were both trying to fight our way through the passage out onto the platform against a tide of people, big suitcases wrapped in canvas or sometimes in Oriental rugs, and big bundles.

"Lots of people," I said to him, using the word *narod,* which means plain people en masse, instead of the word *lyudi,* which means individuals.

He bristled perceptibly. "Fine people," he said combatively.

"Certainly, certainly. The Russians are fine people." I had had no intention of being critical, and besides, the more I see of Russia, the more I believe that they really are a splendid *narod.*

We paced separate ends of the platform until the train was finally ready to leave, and then sat in our compartment in silence, watching the staring shells of houses blink slowly past the windows. He wandered off, and I started to read my *Two Captains.* But not for long. A couple of small, fat children, with liquid brown eyes, came in to investigate me. I put up my book, and permitted myself to be questioned and investigated in the way that children have the world over. I suppose the little girl, who was the older, became a little jealous because I took her brother on my knee, for, unlike most Russian children, she turned out to be a regular brat. She deliberately strewed the contents of the ashtray all over the place, and then looked at me, warily defiant. Then she snatched a box of matches from my hand, and threw them about with a big gesture. The argument as to who should pick them up was still unsettled when the mother, a sensitive-looking but healthy and energetic young woman, came in, beamed on all of us, and dotingly took them away, leaving me to gather matches and cigarette ends.

Soon Vassily came back. He was interested in my book, and we started to talk.

I said, "Didn't your wife like Berlin?"

"It's not Russia. It's too beaten up. I would like her to come back to Berlin again, but living conditions are so much worse in Germany. Food is hard to get. We owned our own house in Leningrad, but it was destroyed in the siege. Now she lives in a *dacha* with the children, and is much happier. Russia is a wonderful place."

And so we talked, off and on, through the end of the afternoon. He slipped out for a nip of vodka with someone. Soon after he returned, a handsome young colonel with a healthy red face and fair, wavy hair, and a broad chest covered with medals, came in and said to Vassily, "Let's eat." The train to Brest still carries no restaurant car, and there was no water on board, not even for washing or flushing. The new arrival was not so reserved as Vassily.

"Who's that?" he asked, jerking a thumb towards me.

"American. He's going to Moscow."

"Would he drink with us?"

"Ask him and see."

Then Nikolai, the bemedaled newcomer, addressed himself to me. "Why are you going to Moscow?"

"I work there."

"What sort of work?"

"In the American Embassy. I'm the American naval attaché."

"Ah, spy!" His face lit up with sudden spite.

"What do you mean 'spy'? Look at this uniform! How can one be a spy, when it is clear to everyone who I am? Everyone in Moscow who knows me knows that I am an American and knows that I am not a spy."

His spite died down. "Will you drink vodka with us?"

So we wrestled with the bags to bring out food and drink. Nikolai went out and brought back an unopened bottle of vodka, some food, and some large plastic tumblers. He couldn't knock the cork out, so he pushed it in with a powerful finger. I poured myself a large drink, and passed the bottle back. Neither would take it. "More! More!" they said. And they simply sat there, hanging their heads and looking sad and sorrowful, refusing to pour themselves a drop, until at last I filled my tumbler to the brim. Then they brightened up and did likewise, and we drank to each other's health.

Did you ever chew on a half-inch strip of raw bacon? Fortunately, the bacon wasn't quite as obligatory as the vodka, and my Swiss cheese went well with their black bread. It was pleasant enough, with food in plenty. Nikolai, who had commanded an artillery regiment, must have counted my ribbons a dozen times. I think I had one or two more than he, which filled him with great respect. Russians, even the Soviets, have a tremendous veneration for rank, and when the meaning of my broad stripes was explained, he bowed to the floor, with two fingers extended in the formal Eastern gesture of sweeping, outturned palm.

We ate and drank and talked, not about politics, which, though difficult to avoid, is apt to be dangerous for all concerned, but mostly about the war. Both were very proud of their Soviet Union, its accomplishments, and its aims, and during all the time I talked with them gave not the slightest indication of disaffection. But all of us had seen enough of war, and we all agreed that war was a bad thing.

"Nevertheless, there will be war," Nikolai said, suddenly and somberly.

"Perhaps," I replied. "It would be too bad."

"Yes, too bad. But *budyet* (it will come). And soon."

I scoffed. "Neither your country nor mine wants war."

"Lock the door, Vassily." He lowered his voice and said, intensely and emphatically, *"Budyet! Budyet!"*

I still protested, but Vassily backed him up. *"Budyet! Budyet voina!"*

I told them that not only did my country genuinely not want war, but that under our form of government it was impossible for us to start one. I told them that the continual blare in the Russian press about capitalist warmongering was not founded on fact, and was dangerous. Every time our voices rose a bit, one of them would put up a hand to caution quiet. Someone knocked on the door.

"Don't let him in," said Nikolai, and after a few more raps whoever it was passed on.

"Budyet! And soon — very soon!"

"How soon?"

"Three months!" and Nikolai held up three fingers.

Again I scoffed. "But why? Why are you so sure?"

Another rap on the door. "Tell them they can't come in. *Nyelzya* (forbidden)."

"But why? My country will never start a war," I said in a lowered voice.

Nikolai fished in his inside pocket. "Show him your party card, Vassily."

And they both showed me their red booklets of membership in the Communist Party of Bolsheviks — the fundamental requisite of all power and influence, the mark of the modern aristocracy. I looked the cards over, and handed them back.

"*Budyet voina! Boo-oo-oodyet!*" and again the three fingers. "*Boo-ooodyet!* And it will be not your doing, but the will of Moscow!"

A strange creep went down my back. But by this time the door was thundering and voices were shouting outside. "Let them in!" I said, suddenly realizing that the train had been stopped for some time. "It's the Polish frontier!"

We hunted for our documents. The hawk-nosed, proud-looking Polish officer, with his strange mortarboard cap and his attendants, looked at the tumblers and the fragments of food, and did not view us with undue suspicion.

After they had gone and the train was again under way, we talked for a long time. They said that, although there was no doubt but that America and England would lose the war, it was unnecessary and a great mistake, but — *boo-oodyet!* They asked me if I had a family.

"Yes — a wife and a son."

"Where are they? In America?"

"The son is in New York. My wife is in Moscow."

Nikolai winced and put his hands over his face. "That is a bad place to have your wife."

He was on his way to somewhere in the south, but he was a native Muscovite. If by any chance he should come to Moscow, I could go underground, and he would help me and be like a son to me. And so on into the night. But it was eerie, to see their intent, earnest faces in the dim, smoke-filled compartment, and to have the future laid on the line for me with so much conviction. I shall long hear that *"Boo-oodyet!"* in my ears. For three months, at least.

The next morning, I was awakened by Vassily's long legs descending from the upper berth. I watched him wrap them in heavy cloths before putting on his boots, and was conscious of being very, very thirsty. The oranges which Schuirmann's German maid had put up for me saved our lives. I didn't run across Nikolai until midafternoon, when I gave him the usual Russian greeting.

"How are you feeling?"

"Very, very bad!"

It was easy to tell one was in Poland because of the little shrines to be seen by the roadside, sometimes painted a bright blue, sometimes draped in faded flowers. The train stopped for a long time at Siedlce, to take on water, among other things. That helped the flushing situation, which was in need of help, but there was still no water to drink, nor was there even tea. I got some beer at the station buffet and then walked the platform. Polish soldiers and guards, some of whose uniforms were incredibly dirty, were in evidence, together with a few officers in their square caps. Mostly there were Russians from the train, stretching their legs. One very handsome young officer in a belted Russian shirt, with a warm, ruddy-olive complexion but with something eroded about the shape of his nose, came up to me, apologized, but would I please be good enough to tell him just what I was?

Outside the station fence of barbed wire and a few old boards stood three or four old battered open barouches, with the heads of their horses completely lost in enormous nose bags. Women were trying to trade bacon, chickens and other food for vodka through the barbed wire, and tried to catch my eye or call to me. The Polish guards carried peculiarly evil-looking bare, drum-fed light machine guns across their backs, and there were plenty of them. Nevertheless, there were two or three deals being put across through the fence. One sandy-blonde girl with a very brown pretty face was almost caught, and was chased away by a guard who reached for his gun as he ran towards her. She took doubtful sanctuary in the "ladies' room" of an adjoining toilet building, but in two or three minutes she was back at the barbed wire again. The business couldn't have been very serious, for I smiled at her, and she answered with a quick, broad smile that showed her fine white teeth, and her eyes sparkled and danced with excitement. A comely woman water-tender, in black military jacket, black skirt, high black boots, and the usual brown stockings, showed an expanse of amazingly white leg as she swarmed up on top of the car to uncouple the water connection, and then the train moved on across Poland.

I had been trying to make up my mind about the significance of the evening before. Remembering Pearl Harbor, I knew that I must make no mistake. I appraised it as an outgrowth of the genuine camaraderie that exists everywhere between military people, who are not the makers of wars but the ones who fight them. Almost always there is a certain respect for the professional soldier or sailor of the other side, although not for the policies which he carries out. I also decided that it was most probable that my friends had no real inside information, but were reflecting the current talk of the Red Army and the Party. After that I felt better — but not much. *"Boo-oo-oodyet"* still whispered in my ears.

It was late in the afternoon when we reached the Russian border. The Bug was in flood, but the wrecked spans of the old bridge and the half-drowned locomotive were still to be seen. The spans of the bridge were diminished considerably since last summer, doubtless for scrap, as all the way to Moscow long trainloads of scrap iron were to be seen, heading east towards the industrial areas. It was a chilly gray day, with a thin light fog in places, but the prevailing grayness made the new green meadows on the edges of the flood waters more vividly green. As before, we stopped for a long time at the actual frontier just beyond the river. Gone were the German war prisoners, and the roadbed was clean and neatly sanded. This time, the windows of the train were not locked, but no one got off to stretch his legs, and there were scores of railroad and frontier troops who thoroughly checked the corners and crevices and rods of all the wagons of the long train to insure that there were no clandestine entries into the promised land.

The slogans to Stalin and the garlands and wreaths were still bedecking the entrance to the frontier guard's camp, but the green had long since withered to brittle brown. These entrance bowers are to be seen all over Russia. I thought they were a product of the Revolution and the present regime until I saw exactly the same thing in an old book on Sakhalin, printed in 1903. Instead of looking gay, even when the green is fresh and new, they always seem a bit bedraggled, and almost pitiful, as though children had tried very hard to make something effective which hadn't quite come off.

The station at Brest-Litovsk was crowded. As before, I was met on board the train and escorted alone to the comfortable Intourist lounge before anyone else was let off the train. When the porter strapped my heavy parachute bags together and hoisted my topee-case on his back, I was horrified to see a great stain of blood covering half of the topee-case. Fortunately, the cause was soon evident — five pounds of freshly ground hamburger from the Berlin commissary, which had been stowed with the overflow, had begun to ooze.

I made straight through the crowds for the restaurant in the station and drank glass after glass of tea, brought me by a very pretty, neat, high-breasted waitress. Even the tea didn't satisfy my American thirst for cold water, so, on her assurances that it was good to drink, I had a whole carafe of brownish-colored but delicious water, the first unboiled water that I have ever knowingly had in Russia. Maybe this was boiled. At any rate, it didn't harm me, somewhat to my surprise.

The restaurant was crowded and gay, with the never-ending fascination and variety of the Russian *narod*. An orchestra played, and played as if it enjoyed it — trumpet, clarinet, drums, two jolly accordions, and a marvelous, sobbing violin. There were great, lovely paintings on the walls of Russian fairy tales, in tender, light colors. But (I hate to be always saying "but," and God knows there is plenty to criticize which is not worth mentioning, and of that which seems to me to be worth mentioning I try to pick out what seems to be interesting or strange) — but the largest and loveliest of the paintings, the Swan Princesses being transformed in the forest glade, was three-quarters blocked out by a big bar, with shelves full of vodka and wines, placed squarely in front of it. Utility, doubtless — and beauty seldom has a chance with utility. The restaurant was so full of music and chatter that it must have made many Russians like Vassily and Nikolai feel that they were really home again in Russia.

I went back up to the Intourist lounge and settled down to a couple of hours of reading the Byelorussian papers. They were not too far from Russian for me to be able to make out. As I sat there in the quiet room, a peculiar, very slight, but disturbing odor began to intrude itself. It made me think of the shock an American officer received when he went into a Russian-held port at the end of the war to serve on the commission which was dividing up the captured German shipping. He was billeted in quarters usually occupied by a Russian admiral. What he found in the bathtub made him at first think that he had stumbled on a murder mystery, but it turned out to be only a supply of fresh beef. I gave the porter who at last carried my luggage to the broad-gauge train five pounds of beautiful hamburger, warning him that it had been off the ice for more than a day and should be eaten fast.

5. FUNDAMENTAL FREEDOMS

IN THE LOUNGE AT THE STATION I had noticed with approval a big, honest-looking man with a handsome, sensitive face. He was better dressed than anyone I had seen for many months, in excellent taste, and completely at ease. I had heard him talking with someone, and because of his easy and natural speech I had put him down for one of the very top Russian engineers who might have been returning from a long detail abroad, although I had never yet seen a Soviet citizen as gracious in appearance and manner as he. It was pleasing to find that he was to share my compartment.

"This is a fine train," I said to the pale-eyed, hard-looking, jolly, flat-faced *nachalnik* as he stowed our luggage in the compartment.

"Yes, a fine train. It's as fine as drinking vodka!" he answered, philosophically. So I broke out one of my bottles of liquor.

Instead of being Russian, my companion was from one of the satellite countries. He was an engineer, and had been working in the Soviet Union off and on for several years. His name was Gregorev, and he was an educated man, broad-minded and gentle, with some understanding of and interest in anything we might talk about. He knew nothing at first hand of the world outside his own country and Russia, but hoped mightily to be sent to Washington some day. We sat over the Scotch until long after two o'clock in the morning, and I told him what seems to me to be the true nature of the quarrel between Russia and America.

It is not one of social issues between communism and capitalism, but a question of fundamental freedoms. And as Elyena, the little Komsomolka, and I had at last agreed, the Russian and the American words for "freedom" ought not to be equated to each other in the dictionaries. Regardless of all ideologies, there are only two things which make any real difference. They are the American Bill of Rights, which protects the individual against an all-powerful state, and the multiparty system. The suppression of all competing political parties makes it impossible in all communist countries for any sort of minority — or majority, for that matter, so long as they are not of the Party — to exert any effect whatsoever upon the state, no matter what other democratic forms it may exhibit, and turns that state into a naked power complex. I told Gregorev that with the Bill of Rights and freedom from the one-party system, no country need fear anything from within except the elimination of those two things.

Gregorev believed that communism was the logical solution to the world's economic and social ills. But there are other ills, with which ideology as such has little to do. The Bolshevik Party, which is communism throughout the world, is itself convinced that it cannot continue to exist without the single-party system, the police state, and the suppression of liberalism, which it has often branded as its number one enemy.

The next morning I woke late, just before we pulled into Minsk. We went very slowly past a wreck. There were four or five sleepers, including at least one like ours, lying on their backs and propped with crutches at odd angles to keep them from rolling down the steep embankment. The roadbed seemed to have given way, for it looked loose and sandy and ragged, and there were no rails at all to be seen for part of the space under the wreck. It was obviously something that had just happened, from the position and condition of the cars.

"Good God! When did that happen?" I asked Yakob, the *nachalnik.*

"Long, long ago," he said, with a sly smile.

"War damage, no doubt," I said, skeptically.

"Yes, of course. It happened during the war." And Yakob walked off with an air of finality.

Minsk is much more built up than it was when I went through last, and no longer gives the impression of being primarily a blasted, war-torn city. Completely gone were the hundreds and hundreds of the hungry. Of course, the large stations, like Minsk and Smolensk, are fenced off better than they were then, and it would be easier to keep people from the train. However, it was not due to that, for the fences were open enough to slip through, and one could always see that there were no hungry crowds beyond them. And above all, at the unscheduled stops in the country, and in the smaller towns where there were no fences, there were no signs of the hunger which before was so affecting.

Gregorev dropped a paper bag with his remaining food into the hands of an old man who was passing, and I went to dig out the rest of my sandwiches for the same purpose. And then I couldn't find anyone to whom to give them. We started to the restaurant car, when I saw a small boy on the off side of the train who wasn't asking for anything, but who said, Sure, he'd like something to eat to take home. So I went back and got the food and left it with the beaming, polite youngster, who shouted thanks after me.

Three fried eggs with bits of ham chopped up in them, served sizzling in the skillets in which they were cooked, some black Russian bread and a glass of hot cocoa made a grand breakfast. And I'm sufficiently used to the prices that the thought of what it cost didn't choke me.

In the usual promenade on the platform, I said good morning to Vassily, who was in a soft sleeper for this part of the journey. There were the usual Russian strollers; a woman with fine face and eyes, wearing a dress with an integral fur-edged hood that looked like a woodcut from the last century; a pompous, eagle-beaked, bald old general wearing blue breeches with broad red stripes down the sides.

All day long, and far into that night, Gregorev and I talked. He told me, and I am sure sincerely — one comes to distrust everyone in Russia — that it had been a wonderful thing for him to talk with an individual who, like himself, tried to figure out what was behind the propaganda on both sides and who said in plain terms what he really believed. It helped him to orient his own ideas. He was impressed with the fact that last year, while out of Russia on a trip, he had had the opportunity of talking with another non-political American, and I was confirming the things that he had said, but with a different background, and in other words. He was particularly impressed by my saying that my mother was a widow, with nothing but three small children, and that I had become an admiral in the United States Navy with no other background or help than that which American life provided everyone. It was still hard for him to realize that many things I had told him were so, for they were so unlike anything he had ever seen in his native land or in Russia, but he knew objectively that they must be true. More than ever, he felt that he must go to America to really incorporate them into his faith and viewpoint towards life. His breathing showed that he was frequently under some emotional stress and saying things that were new to him.

But our talk wasn't entirely of such things. He told me much about his own land, and about Russia as well, while the ragged fields and the woods of birch and fir went by. He laughed long when I told him how Nell fell through a bridge in the Florida Everglades in excitement when I was hooking a tarpon in a narrow stream, and how I had to choose between wife and fish.

And he told me of how he had been to a great cavern in the Urals, near Kongur, and all its wonders. Fish without eyes, of course, but he gave a wonderful description of lakes so still and clear that it was impossible to escape the illusion that the boats were floating in mid-air. The place was endless, and parts of it were stacked and lined with great colored crystals.

There was an old and famous scientist who lived for that place alone. He was ragged and incredibly poor, but he wanted nothing else in life. He had a special breed of dog, from Switzerland or somewhere in western Europe, which could be specially trained to eat only a part of the ration which they carried with them, and so could live for many days where there was no food. (Saint Bernards, I thought to myself.) He had sent these dogs into the caverns, to have them emerge from some other opening twenty or thirty kilometers away, after several days. Against the opposition of the old scientist, someone from the Academy of Science had attempted to drill through from the surface above, in order to establish the scientific data surrounding a peculiar drip from the roof of one part of the caverns. In spite of all their surveys and measurements and blasting, they could never come through into his caves, much to his delight. They even poured red dye down their drill holes, powerful dyes that would color a whole lake with only a few drops, in the hope that they could trace its course to the cave. But nothing came of all this, and finally the Academicians gave up and went back to Moscow. Long after their departure, the peculiar drip from the ceiling suddenly turned to blood, and there was much consternation until the scarlet dye was suddenly remembered.

Then the old scientist said, "I'm going to put the lamps out, and let you literally see darkness!" He turned out all the hand lamps, and Gregorev felt the physical pressure of the unbelievable blackness all around him. And suddenly the old man, in a wonderfully moving and dramatic voice, began to declaim some famous passage from Russian literature about darkness. The goose prickles ran all up and down Gregorev's back, and he said that it was worth going all the way to the Urals just to hear that weird declamation. The old man is dead now, but before he died Gregorev had seen him once more — on the stage of the Bolshoy Theater in Moscow, where he had been brought to give that very declamation.

Meanwhile, the woods became fewer, and gave way to rolling prairies, which were beginning to be plowed for the spring wheat. In the middle distance could be seen the village groups of low houses, snuggling together in a hollow, thatch-roofed and made from solid, unpainted logs, rooted halfway to their shaggy roofs in the soil.

The restaurant car was crowded all day with Russian Army files drinking beer, but the full-lipped, fine-eyed, coarsely handsome waitress offered to bring us our meals in our compartment. Russian soup of almost any variety except bortsch is always good, and there were veal steaks smothered in onions, and fried potatoes. In the evening, late, the beer on the train gave out at last, so our waitress sent for us and turned out some beef strogonov that would have made the reputation of any restaurant in the Western world.

Most of the day we had a running argument with Yakob over keeping our window open. The heat was on in the rest of the train, and it just wasn't economical to have windows open. Nothing happened when we didn't close it, except that Yakob would be back soon to see about it again.

"What a pleasant job you have, Yakob," I said. "Nothing to do but ride back and forth on one of the best trains in Europe."

"Yes, it is a nice job. Only it's hard to believe how difficult it is to get any vodka!" And every time I poured out some Scotch for him, he was unhappy until his cup was full. "Yes, I know that this isn't vodka, and that it's very strong. After the last drink, my face was all numb for half an hour. But you see there are two of us. I have an assistant."

Gregorev was not a communist, but a member of one of the two or three other parties that still existed in his homeland. There was much talk of merging the Communist Party with one of the other parties, but they would still be able to develop the possibilities of a multiparty state — or so he thought. The next morning, he asked me to send him some copies of *Amerika*, the Russian-language American publication which is permitted here by the Soviet government, saying that copies were difficult for him to get.* He was trying to learn some English, so could I also send him any American magazines or periodicals that I might have?

"Have you definitely made up your mind that you want to go to Washington?" I asked.

"Absolutely. I've long wanted to go there, and after all the things you have told me, it's now a necessity for me."

"If you really want to go there, perhaps the surest way to bring it about is not to have me send you American magazines."

He looked startled. "What do you mean?"

"It may not be healthy for you to have much to do with Americans. I fully intend to ask you and your wife to my house in Moscow, and you know that I would be very happy to see you there. But when I do so, you will have thought things over a bit, and if you decide that you had better not come, I shall understand completely. Perhaps that way we shall be surer of seeing each other sometime in Washington."

Gregorev was visibly shaken. "That's a very unpleasant thought," he said.

"I know that's hard to believe," I added, "but things change

---

* The permit for *Amerika* was withdrawn by the Soviet government in 1952 on the grounds that there was insufficient demand for the magazine. These grounds were obviously false, but inasmuch as the distribution and sales were in the hands of the Soviets the falsehood could not be statistically disproved. The American government thereupon forbade a generally comparable publication distributed in the United States by the Soviet Embassy in Washington. In this case the retaliation was desirable but ineffective, as the vast American press is not controlled.

rapidly in the People's Republics. I've had good friends, who once came freely to my house, ask me please not to call them on the telephone, and not to try to acknowledge appreciation of things they have done or might do for us."

He was quiet and somber the rest of the way. Every now and then he would interrupt our conversation on other subjects by saying "Unpleasant — unpleasant!"

Trainloads of fresh lumber, headed for Moscow for construction, clogged the railroad. When we crossed a river, it was free of ice. I was sorry that I had missed seeing the "strange ice" in the Moskva River. Valodya had told me that after "our own ice" went out of the river, the strange, or foreign, ice came grinding and piling down through Moscow, and that it was a sight worth seeing. Drifts of snow were still left in the hollows and in the woods. Mozhaisk was a sea of mud.

"There is perhaps a good reason why Russia is so muddy," I said. "In Germany, England, and even Poland, the grass does not die in the winter. But the Russian winters are so severe that the grass dies, and until the new grass comes up in the late spring there is no turf to cover the soil."

Then Gregorev thanked me for having the decency to warn him — thanked me warmly, and said much about what our many hours of talk had done for him. It seems to me that he was very representative of the many fine people throughout Europe who have not — yet — felt personally the hand of the secret police. Of course he knew that there was such a thing — he could not help but know — but somehow it was the sort of thing that "can't happen here," even in his own captive country at this late, late date. And there is so much of vision in the communist dream!

"Do you still want the magazines?" I asked.

"Send them along. You've given me some unpleasant things to think about, but I want very much to have them."

Yet it was a new surprise to him when I pointed to the houses on the edge of Moscow, dingy, squalid, tilted at odd angles, and told him that millions of American Negroes, even in the Deep South, actually live in better quarters than those.

I saw Nell and Mac waiting for me on the platform at the

Byelorussian Station, full of smiles, and felt as though I had been gone for months instead of days. We all swirled with the crowd towards the gates, only to see those gates for some reason forced shut against the struggling crowd ahead of us. The guard at the gates spotted us as foreigners among the crowding people, and beckoned to us over their heads. Russians, except for the policy-makers and perhaps those who directly enforce some of their policies, are extremely considerate of foreigners — more so than the people of any country I have seen. This is one of the reasons why it is so easy to get a false idea of Russia on a short visit when the policymakers themselves desire that a good impression be created. We forced our way through, followed by our porters, past the tall, jet-black heroic busts of Lenin and Stalin on their high black pedestals of Ural granite to the familiar blue car outside. Gregorev took a smart, luxurious new Zees taxi, which takes its name from the initials of the Stalin factory where it is made.

It was very pleasant to be home. Nell had obviously done a great deal in my absence, for the apartment was really livable and beautiful, and for once the upstairs bedroom seemed spacious and un-cluttered. She had also, for the first time in her life, been in the embarrassing and undignified, but legal and to us necessary, old-clothes business, and had five hundred rubles from a commission store to supplement my pay and allowances.

The gifts I brought back were well received, particularly the shoes for Valodya and his wife, which fit them both "right now." I can never pass up the round-faced, smiling Sergei. He has always been so puzzled since I demoted him as my own chauffeur. When given a box of candy for his wife, he was so surprised and pleased that he shook hands with me enthusiastically.

6. HOW TO LOSE FRIENDS

GENERAL WANG, THE SHY, FRAGILE little Chinese military attaché, had a party at the Grand Hotel. There the big-nosed Norwegian military attaché told me that there will be no war. Colonel Hjelle says Norway is in a position where it has to know, and that it is his business to find out, and he is sure.

At the party, the wife of another Scandinavian told me that she had wanted so much to be particularly nice to Nell during my absence, but that her household had been in too much of an uproar. Their wonderful old Russian servant, who had worked practically all her life for the Scandinavians, and who looks exactly like a Russian peasant doll, had been sent for daily by the secret police, and told daily that she must quit. She is too old to do any other sort of work, and has a little girl, the apple of her eye, who is completely dependent on her. She doesn't dare to stay and she doesn't dare to quit, and is in tears all the time — as is her mistress.

Colonel Shepherd, the wise-faced, punctilious Annapolis graduate who is one of our assistant military attachés and who has been expecting to leave for the States, told me that he does not yet have his exit visa. A few months ago his car brushed against a Soviet boy. Shep stopped and talked with the boy, who seemed completely unharmed, and went on his way without any worry. And now he is confronted with a demand for some fifteen hundred rubles for doctor's bills for the boy. Perhaps there is some connection with the delay in his visa.

And one handsome and distinguished-looking ambassador's wife, looking unusually well in her stately evening gown, but nevertheless disturbed about something, called Nell aside. Probably another crisis blowing up somewhere.

However, Serayev was quite cordial. So was Pasco, the pale-faced, contained, pleasantly courteous Ukrainian naval officer from Serayev's office. Although he never goes beyond the bounds of proper Soviet decorum, he and Nell always have a grand time together. Tonight she said, "Do please be sure to let me know two or three days before any war begins, so I can get out of here."

"There isn't going to be any war, unless your country starts it."

"Then there isn't going to be any war. But if you're wrong, please don't forget to tip me off. Don't you think you might be promoted for that?"

And Pasco laughs in real amusement.

We walked home, past the enormous grayish bulk of the Moskva Hotel and across the equally enormous width of Gorky Street to our quiet apartment.

. The next day one of the crises arrived. Someone came into the office asking if I had a copy of *Izvestia*. Of course ours hadn't come — it has been a puzzle as to why our office is never able to get its daily newspapers until long after everyone else — but I heard the reason for all the interest and soon had a paper to read myself. It carried in headlines a long letter from Magidov's American-born, Soviet-naturalized secretary, saying that while searching for some necessary correspondence when Magidov was not in the office she had chanced to come across some of his letters which she had never before seen. These letters explained so much to her, including his recent intimacy with the American naval attaché and military attaché, with whom he had nothing in common, that she considered it her duty to inform the proper Soviet authorities. She had found copies of questionnaires sent Magidov by his company asking for information about the effectiveness of underground installations, what was being done in atomic energy, air transport and such, and Magidov had been criminally doing the dirty work of the American capitalists in espionage against the Soviet Union, using the privileged diplomatic mails of the American Embassy for receiving and transmitting his correspondence. He had married a Russian woman, and so had become acquainted with the Soviet people, who received him widely and gladly. The years that the secretary herself had spent in the USSR and her close acquaintanceship with Russian people and Soviet activities had convinced her that only in the Soviet Union nowadays could simple people live freely, and that only here could a person regard their future without alarm.

It can be no coincidence that these last remarks were almost identical, even in their phrasing, with those of Miss Bucar, the Czech-born employee who also turned against us. It seems to be one of the recognition marks of Soviet propaganda that it lacks the skill and attention to detail which would make it much more plausible to those who are accustomed to it. When seeing its effectiveness, Westerners are apt to mistake for skill its single-minded intentness of purpose. It is not that the Soviets are not interested in working on those who are familiar with their propaganda, but rather that they rely on repetition to create habits of thought, simultaneously excluding competing thoughts, as they exclude competing parties.

Ambassador Smith's press statement was a clear statement of the truth. He dictated it in front of the foreign reporters and issued it as dictated, with a copy to the Soviet Foreign Office. Magidov had never received or transmitted any information or stories through the diplomatic post, but had used the open mails. Obviously, he had close relations with Embassy personnel, including the naval and military attachés, because, through no fault of our own, the few Americans in Moscow were forced to associate entirely with the foreign colony. Moreover, those relations were entirely of a social nature. The Ambassador had given strict and direct orders to the naval and military attachés, and had insured that they were carried out, that their information was to be obtained only from open and aboveboard sources. Magidov could not be held responsible for any questionnaires sent him by his company, and in any case, those questionnaires consisted of subjects which everywhere else are considered legitimate matters of public information.

The potentialities of the case are really distressing. The Magidovs have no diplomatic immunity, and consequently can be arrested, imprisoned and brought to trial in the same manner as Russians. God knows what the uncurbed power of this state will do to them if they are in for a typical espionage trial. This denouement accounts for the weeks of waiting for visas, and for all the shadowing and terror. If the Soviets only knew it, they have — or had — few more understanding friends than the two of them. Poor Nila has told me of the brightness of the dream she held when she was a Soviet girl. The whole case against them does not have the slightest foundation in actual truth, but is the fruit of an almost psychopathic suspicion.

The Magidovs have not yet been arrested. The Ambassador offered them asylum in the Embassy, but they refused to accept it. Their consciences were clear, and they decided to fight it out. The whole affair gave me a feeling of sickness because of the evil of the policies that commit such basic and dangerous injustices. There is almost an uncanny touch about it, a very disturbing, shocking element, as though we are dealing with alien minds. It seems possible to me that those minds may have been warped and scarred into something really alien by their past experiences of oppression and injustice, for so many of them spent so much of their early youth underground and in prison as professional revolutionaries and, until they achieved power, they had always looked on the seamy side of life, from below. They take pride in saying that they use the processes of human logic, but it is logic without morality or pity, with no heritage or background except cruelty, resentment, oppression and hate, and directed towards the pursuit and maintenance of power. In any case, it seems a strange and medieval survival of bigotry and refined brutality, all the stranger because it is set in this world of today.

When Nila told me that it was dangerous to write things like my Russian sonnets it was a bit hard to believe — then. Perhaps that was because our own American ideas of freedom are too familiar to us for us really to grasp the difference that can exist elsewhere. Freedom is like the air we breathe. We are so accustomed to it that we never think of it, and it is difficult to imagine the nature of forms of life without it. When she had been worried because she had had those sonnets in her house and had asked me to destroy them, I had put it down to Russian temperament on her part, but now it is possible to see more clearly what was bothering her.

Senta amused me today by saying that I had a "colossal" Russian vocabulary. "There is not another foreigner in Moscow who knows as much Russian as you." She is usually very businesslike, and not given to such overstatements. She is one of the only two remaining teachers who work for Americans. Last summer there were plenty of them, but they have all disappeared or quit, usually with extraordinary and unexpected abruptness and without warning. Some have managed to send word that they had been told they could no longer work for Americans. One would think that their reports to the police would be of enough value to make teachers available. Perhaps isolation of Americans from all Russians is at the moment more important than receiving reports on them. Perhaps it's all imagination. At any rate, it is one of the many mysteries in this enigmatic place.

When Senta had gone, Nell told me that the Ambassador's wife — not our own, but the one of the party the evening before — had been to see her while I was talking with Senta, and had left Nell with another crisis on her hands. One more case of the effects of arm-twisting on the part of our neighbors across the street in the Kremlin.

The cheering word came that Magidov had been sent for, and told that they must leave Russia within seventy-two hours. Everyone feels much lighter-hearted because the Magidovs' arms were not twisted. They were only shown how easy it would be to do so. Nila will be missed, but it is a relief to know that soon they will be safely out of Russia, and also that they probably will not be permitted to return. Otherwise Nila would be sure to try to come back, since this is her homeland, her *rodina* — a word with which the Russian can forgive anything.

Late in the evening we went to the Byelorussian Station to say good-by to the Shepherds. Shep had sent a dispatch to the War Department yesterday asking for cash to pay the claim against him, and had received a prompt affirmative answer. The money was sent to the Foreign Office, and the Shepherds' exit visas came through immediately.

There was a large turnout of Americans and foreigners at the train, including Pasco, whom I saw laughing at something or other which Nell had told him. Mrs. Shepherd filled the whole doorway of the wagon when the train finally left, and all the foreigners sang "Jolly Good Fellow," "Auld Lang Syne," the Swedish drinking songs, and others that were not so familiar. The custom of seeing other foreigners off when they leave for good is widespread and graceful.

The Magidovs were there, she in a big soft brown suède coat and he in some bright checks, more full of smiles — genuine ones, that is — than they have been for a long time.

"When they called me in to tell us to get out of Russia," Bob Magidov told me, "they were actually embarrassed. They know that although I'm not a communist or fellow traveler — perhaps I might have been that, once — I'm not an enemy nor a spy. They actually stood up to shake hands with me, but never looked me in the eye once."

When the train had gone, we drifted out of the station, passing an extraordinarily well dressed Russian woman. She had a gay, enameled chamber pot strapped to the outside of her neat suitcase.

The day was often interrupted by military aircraft, including plenty of jets and Soviet versions of the B-29, flying over the house, practicing for the May Day parade. It was sunny and warm, and the population has begun to throw off some of the wrappings of the winter, and some of their picturesqueness with it. It is less like a foreign land to see brown cotton or rayon stockings on all the women's legs instead of boots and *valyenki*.

It is very agreeable to step out on the balcony after a long day on Americana in the office. To watch the crowds on the streets below is to step suddenly back into Russia from a desk in the Navy Department. The low sun of evening floods the Kremlin walls and towers with a warm, rosy light and flashes from its golden domes and the tall sharp spears that crown the Historical Museum. Like many Russian public buildings of the Tsar's time, that one looks as if it was made up from a vast collection of complicated children's building blocks — when I was very little, children used to play with the duplicates of many of its elements — and in the evening light it glows as if it were made of dull, burned-out rubies.

Nell and I went in the evening to the Theater of Drama and Comedy, a small place on Chkalova Street far beyond the river. It was still light as we drove through Red Square, and the dull colors of St. Basil's fantastic twisted domes were soft and lovely. The play was a very old one, *Kashirskaya Starina,* which might be translated "Long Ago in Kashir." We went because Senta had said it was worth seeing, since it showed the old Russia and had a Russian quality to it which was genuine and charming.

She was completely right. But there was a gigantic plaster bust of Stanislavsky in the promenade. Although the head was pleasant enough, plaster pince-nez two feet high seemed somehow incongruous. Come to think of it, I don't remember seeing Lenin and Stalin there. Now that is either unusual or due to the fact that one gets so conditioned to them that they aren't noticed. In spite of the two narrow seats (no, it wasn't I, for my midshipman's overcoat still fits), which were made of thin veneer, like folding chairs which can be hired in quantity in America, and which sloped uncomfortably towards the stage, and in spite of the drabness and general discomfort of the theater, the play was a delight. Every gesture was planned and stylized, and the costumes and settings were wonderful. A flat, angular wooden arch, with sloping sides, framed the stage. From the costumes, it was obvious that the time was before the reforms of Peter the Great. The story was a tragic one of frustrated love, and the lovely Russian language lends itself well to varying moods and intonations.

One scene was unique, even to the Russian audience. The women in the play wore very full, stiff, heavy gowns, hanging down from their high boosies to the very floor, hiding their booted feet. All the costumes, particularly those almost shapeless but stately gowns, were very colorful and rich, of silk or embroidered wool, brocaded, frogged, and, although completely Russian, there were always suggestions of the bordering lands, something Swedish, Persian, Turkish, and above all Chinese. And this group of maidens dressed in that fashion danced without ever the slightest movement of anything but their feet, which were completely hidden by the long gowns. The effect was startling. It was as though the stage were moving, or as though they were carried along by some unseen force. The audience gasped and showed its appreciation by nervous, excited, delighted laughter.

Another scene, that of a classical *svad'ba,* or wedding, was also splendid in its picturesque formality and its Russian charm. The bride is about to marry the wrong man, and she and her women await the bridegroom.

"Who knocks?"

"A hunter, tired and weary from the chase."

"What does he seek?"

"A beautiful woman."

"There is none such here." And the maidens all laugh.

"But I have been riding hard to follow her, and I saw her enter here."

"Come in, and see if you can find her."

Then the bridegroom comes in and bargains for the bride with purses of gold of increasing size, against the pretended scorn and contempt of the household. And all the time the dejected, unhappy bride, who loves another, sits with downcast head, and the malicious, stylized gossips, who know that this is so, crowd the doorway.

The next morning, Senta told me that perhaps the play was not quite as well done as when she had seen it recently, as the artistic director of the theater had just died. I told her of the Western tradition that "the play must go on," and how more than one play had been built on that idea, with a clown continuing to put forth his merriment when he had just received word that his little daughter was dead.

"What a barbarous custom!" she said, and shuddered.

When Nell and I were home again, and she raided the icebox, she remarked that her belief in whether or not there was going to be a war seemed to be connected with whether or not she was hungry. Right then she was quite sure that everything was all right.

Although it was a Sunday, the alarm was set for six thirty, my usual time on weekdays in Washington. One of the great compensations of duty in Moscow is that customarily there is no need for an accursed alarm clock, but this morning the Magidovs were leaving. Soon we were on our way to the Vnukovo Airport, past the strange, high buildings, past the signboard showing Lenin and Engels (for a change) in black and white stone mosaic, into the open country. Along the road were herds of goats, and far across the empty, rolling fields was a tall, pink church, thrusting up its lily bulbs to the sky, with a humble village at its feet.

In spite of the early hour on a Sunday morning, there were many people to see the Magidovs off, including our own Ambassador. But it's not all over yet for them. When they got their passports back from the Foreign Office, they were stamped for exit from Russia at Minsk alone. Ordinarily the visa says Vnukovo, and it is a matter of chance whether one has the usual nonstop flight to Berlin, or, as sometimes happens with adverse winds or very heavy loads, whether one has to stop at Minsk to refuel. This time it was prearranged and planned that the Magidovs should go by Minsk. Into everyone's mind came the inescapable thought that they would go through the Soviet customs at Minsk rather than at Vnukovo, and that there they would be completely cut off, with no witnesses to see what might happen. It is a shame to Russia that foreigners have come to believe in and fear the possibility of planted evidence — or of no evidence at all. But soon they were on their way, for whatever might be awaiting them.

7. SPRING ON THE CANAL BANKS

Natasha had put up some sandwiches for us, made from her tender, cakelike new bread. We headed out for an all-day drive to the Volga, where it flows out of the big lakes and reservoirs. The radius of our drive was limited only by the gasoline we could carry with us. It was soon apparent that Valodya, with characteristic Russian vagueness about geography, had started on the wrong road, for we headed steadily towards the west, and the Moscow-Volga Canal, which I wanted to follow, runs towards the east of north. In the vicinity of any other modern city there would have been some sort of road or highway by which we could have cut across to another road. Perhaps there is in Moscow, but Valodya didn't know of it, and there were no side roads to be seen that looked even passable. So we had to come back almost to the center of town, and then start over again, this time out the Leningrad Chaussée.

By now, people were beginning to throng the streets, for there was a warm sun and a very blue sky, across which raced small white clouds, driven by a strong, chilly wind. Everyone was wearing topcoats or quilted jackets, but only the babies were still bundled up tight. If they were old enough to walk, they looked like little toddling bears, and, if still in arms, like Indian papooses. There is a sort of reddish-blue long trousers, gathered at the ankle like ski pants, that thousands of little girls wear under their short little skirts. Pink-cheeked, white-coated women, muffled in shawls over their heads, hurry across the broad streets with little blue wagons from which they sell ice cream, sandwiches, or cakes. It is a common sight to see the police stopping people on the streets, as traffic policemen stop motorists, asking to see their documents, and to see the people unbuttoning their coats and searching through their pockets to find them. It is not all mental background — the Russian police really do look sinister. The bread stores were not yet open, and outside every such shop were

patient, block-long queues of people, standing in line in the hope
that all would not be sold before their turn arrived.

A very attractive modern building near the race track, with
its entire sides covered with elaborately fretted stone which might
have been marble, and with old, spirited statues of horses near its
entrance. Buildings of red brick, with all the windows and doors
fancifully picked out in white brick. A palace of one of the Tsar's
princes, with the building-block effect. Troops, standing crowded
in small, open trucks, such as are used for taxis. Troops in covered
lorries, troops with guns, searchlights, field pieces — practicing for
the May Day Parade. The Suvorov Academy cadets were ranged
up in parade formation in trim blue uniforms, with the tall boys
in the front ranks and the others diminishing in size through rank
after rank until the very little ones brought up the rear.

A plain, poor-looking pink stucco church, with its towers
crowned with porcelain bulbs of a beautiful, rich, deep blue,
dotted with golden stars and surmounted with golden crosses. A
traffic policeman, this time not sinister, but very young and fair-
haired, stops Valodya for making fifteen kilometers in a ten-kilo-
meter zone near a school. Valodya quotes to him the proverb
which says that the more gently you travel, the farther you will
be. And then the outskirts again, with log houses capped with
decorative structures that are both utterly without use and un-
graceful and disproportioned to contemplate, but which give them
a fantastic, unreal character — little cupolas, towers, things shaped
like boats, like bathtubs, like big seeds. And a profusion of carving around the windows and foaming from the eaves — carving
that is not fine, but which is very decorative, making the houses look
like old lace valentines. Blue glass in the windowpanes, red glass like
the colored chimneys around the candles in a church, or no glass at
all. And, as proof that Moscow is really part of this world, on
one fence was chalked "VANYA PLUS NINA EQUALS LOVE!"

It was I who had decided on the Leningrad road, from my
memory of a wartime map, which came from Germany, not Russia.
But either my memory or the German aerial cameras must have
been at fault, for when we reached the Moscow-Volga Canal there
was no road forking off to follow it. Or rather, the road that turned

off there ran bewilderingly through a couple of small villages and then petered out in the open fields. Most roads in Russia, except for the main *chaussées,* do just that. No matter — all day ahead of us, and we not going anywhere that matters whether we get there or not. So we turned around and went back, again into the outskirts of Moscow. This time Valodya knew a crossroad. Part asphalt, part cobbled, part atrocious, it twisted between factories which were themselves small towns, camps with khaki army tents patched like some of the Russian trousers, ponds, goats, and groups of soldiers and sailors. Always sailors in odd places the world over. At last we jolted out onto the Dmitrov Chaussée, hoping that it was the road we sought which would follow the canal.

Past a small, polygonal church jutting onto the road, with walls whitewashed in places, and in other places showing old, faded, but quite fine mural paintings which somehow survived the winter snows and the weather better than does most of the architecture itself. A woman on a ladder, painting a road sign. Women really make Russia go. One sees them everywhere, doing any and all sorts of man's work, no matter how heavy or how skilled. The country villages become larger, but farther apart, with always many of their low log houses leaning and tilted at strange angles. Valodya and I tried to decide why they leaned so oddly. He was inclined to put it down entirely to improvidence on the part of the inhabitants, but we finally agreed that also the Russian soil must not be very firm.

Sometimes there were pictures of Stalin on the houses — not in the windows, the way election posters used to be shown in America, but on the outside, permanently installed. If the country folk could possibly have any superstition left in them in this Soviet reign of reason, it might be that those pictures were like good luck charms. Perhaps they are, in any case. There were wells of all sorts, some with huge wooden wheels set on edge, which were turned to raise the water buckets, others with long counterweighted poles, still others with overhead pulleys. There were women with yokes across their shoulders, with splashing buckets hanging from the ends of the yokes. And everywhere, the peasant women sit in the warm sun in the doorways, rocking their babies, or just sit. If they are working, they are working furiously, and if they are sitting, they are sitting intently.

Dmitrov, a city of some twenty or thirty thousand people, was swarming, doubtless because of the Sunday morning market. It was difficult to drive through because of the crowds and the local traffic, which was mostly horse-drawn, with a few bullock carts to be seen. Whatever the occasion, it was a social one for the *narod,* who sat around everywhere in great good nature. The big church here was topped with battered, dull, iron-gray domes.

Beyond Dmitrov, the countryside was much less settled, and soon there were no more tomblike churches to be seen rearing their domes and towers among the low hills on the horizon. There were groves of still bare trees, thick with crows' nests in their tops which looked like mistletoe in the Virginia and Carolina woods. There were groups of cattle grazing in the meadows, always attended. Sometimes, counting the children, there were more herders than cattle. And always women doing the work, bent under great loads of brushwood, or digging energetically to plant new trees. All along the road there were many old, rusted tank barriers to be seen, moved off to the sides of the road, made from lengths of railroad rails welded together with fishplates.

Most of the way the road ran along the Moscow-Volga Canal, but the canal was seldom to be seen because of the high grassy dikes along its sides. The stacks and masts of an occasional ship seemed very strange, seen above the fields and trees. Occasionally there were fishermen, with ten-foot dip nets suspended from an iron ring, working the little estuaries that flow into the canal. The occasional bridges were guarded at both ends by soldiers with bare bayonets, and their approaches were studded with signs which forbade stopping. The canal lighthouses rose incongruously from the fields in tall wooden structures that frequently were unsymmetrical because of a staircase which had been enclosed within the whole for protection from the weather. Sometimes, when they catch the light of the sun, they look like tall sails. At one place on the canal, surmounting some locks, there was a pair of full-rigged, high-pooped old frigates or caravels, riding proudly on tall columns, made, sails and all, from bronze or some such material. They were almost half the size of real ships.

About a hundred kilometers from Moscow, and for the last thirty kilometers or so before reaching the Volga, the villages disappeared completely, and there was nothing to be seen to the east but endless flat swamp country, thickly wooded with pine, birch and pussy willows. We gathered an armload of pussy willows, and they are very nice, with furry buds much larger than those in America. We stopped and had our sandwiches on the canal dike, sheltered from the strong wind by a grassy hillock. Valodya, like Russian help generally, was very self-conscious about eating with us. After a single sandwich, he said he had already had two breakfasts and wasn't very hungry. He went to put some benzine into the car from the spare tank which we carried and to make sure that we could get back onto the road without getting stuck in the bottomless mud.

There came several stretches where the road had given way and had been covered with a corduroy of brush, and a couple of times there was some doubt if we could continue. The swamp birches were lovely, their slender, thickly growing white trunks looking like silver rain, or like light trapped among the trees. And the woods made a great rushing sound in the wind. At last the canal took a turn away from the road, and in the distance, across the swamps, we saw two gigantic dark statues, looming above the flat bright wilderness — Lenin and Stalin, marking the end of the canal.

We came to Bolshaya Volga, a sprawling town of unpainted log houses, and saw a crude sign which said that a pass was necessary to go farther along any road. We wanted actually to see the Volga, so we hunted up the house of the *nachalnik*. He was not to be found on this bright Sunday afternoon. The deputy was an untidy young lady in military blouse and skirt, but she refused to take any responsibility, preferring to start a search for the *nachalnik* himself. Although we waited for the better part of an hour, he still wasn't to be found, so we turned around and went home. Although still without a license, I drove on the way back, and talked with Valodya about life in Russia, which in many ways is the same as it is everywhere in the world.

"Papa" — that word, particularly in its diminutive or affectionate form of *Papasha* which Valodya used, seemed out of place from such a rugged-looking middle-aged man — "Papa used to go off into the woods for the night with a couple of comrades, to gather mushrooms. They would all get drunk. Next morning, when it was time to come home, they would realize that they didn't have any mushrooms, so they would stop in the market and buy some. Everyone at home would tell Papa how much nicer these fresh-picked mushrooms were than the ones in the market. But Mama, having several mouths to feed, was very tight about money, and she would soon find out that the mushrooms he had brought had actually cost much more than the market price because of the vodka they had drunk. And then she would think that perhaps he had been out with some strange woman, and would swear at him and not let him go again for a long time."

"Do Russian wives swear at their husbands for getting drunk?" asked Nell, from the back seat.

"That depends on who holds the power in the family. If a man does not seize the power when he first marries, he is apt to have a tough time of it."

We stopped on the canal banks for an hour or so, and I rigged a casting rod and fished in the high wind. Just before quitting, I came up to three or four small boys who were bottom-fishing, gave them the cigarettes for which they asked, and found out that they weren't doing any better than I.

When we finally came home, past Pushkin Square, where the ornate little booths were being freshly painted for the May Day Parade, it was beneath regular shoals of clouds, herded together by the wind and bright with sunset.

I asked a passer-by why the crowds of people around the October Hall of the Home of the Soviet Union. It was because of the world's championship chess matches, now just finishing. The Russian Botvinnik is far ahead. It would be interesting to see, but the business of getting tickets would probably become a Project before it was done. There is too much here to see and do, and too little time.

Today was full of showers, with bursts of warm sunshine between. McMillan and Dreher went with me to return the call of the Chinese military attaché and his new assistant. We sat in straight, high-backed Chinese chairs, that somehow resembled lodge furniture back home, and drank champagne, brandy, green tea, and ate candy.

Bob Dreher likes Tan, the new Chinese, and has taken him to a Russian public dance, given by one of the clubs of the police — of all people! He says that Tan had a great deal of trouble in getting any Russian girls to dance with him. In spite of the large number of Mongolian types that are seen here, and of the racial equality of which the Soviets are so proud, the girls said that it was because of his appearance. That, since he is a normal, present-able, neatly dressed Chinese, is strange.

The long-opened window in the Kremlin opposite has been closed now for a long time. I put my glasses on it from my own windows, and saw three pigeons fly from one of its broken panes of glass.

Dreher is very sorry to be leaving, and his loss will be felt. He has been paying a good deal of attention to one of the attractive young ladies in the foreign colony. Bob's date was at Spiro the other night for dinner, and was looking at the rows of books, ask-ing what was good to read. Bob asked her if she had ever read Kravchenko's *I Chose Freedom.* She replied that she wouldn't dream of reading such trash. But then, the girl has only been here a short time.

Dreher had read it before coming to Russia, and, like most people, didn't think very much about it one way or another, as-suming that there was some truth in it, but that it had probably been written by someone with an ax to grind, and that much of it was susceptible to other explanations. In his year of isolated duty in Odessa, Bob came to realize vividly that the book was really Russia — the Russia of all his friends and acquaintances. He had first been reasonably sympathetic with the Great Experiment, in spite of its dark side, thinking that if that was what the Russians wanted, why, let them have it. But Russia itself, its people and his unsought experiences with them, convinced him that that was not what Russia wanted, but that they were bitterly unhappy under the Party's regime, and deserved something far better. Bob's experiences are very characteristic of those that happen to people who have any real access — if one can call it access — to Russia.

Last night we saw *Ivan the Terrible* at MXAT. It is a great spectacle, but a damned dull play. Few people seem to know that Aleksei Tolstoy's great epic is in two parts. This was the second part — *Difficult Years* — and nobody seems to know if the other part is ever played. The settings were imaginative, and the costumes were themselves worth going to see. They were rich beyond belief, and sitting in the second row I found it easy to appraise them. Some of them must have come from the great museums, lent for such purposes, although they say that there is a central storehouse of costumes in Moscow, from which all the theaters draw.

There was a profusion of furs, mink and sable, old and rich, broad collars, *shubas,* hats and caps, and in the throne scene Ivan Grozny himself wears a deep, full gown of cloth of gold, sewn with pearls and bordered with rubies, emeralds and semiprecious stones. Perhaps the rubies and emeralds and pearls were not real, but the cloth of gold and the furs and the glowing brocades were. And always the frogging and the Chinese cast to the design — and to the eyes of some of the actors.

In the audience were two men who were obviously visitors to the big city. They wore blue uniforms with bell-bottomed trousers like sailors, and with enormous gold chevrons on the sleeves of their roll-collar jackets. Slantwise on their collars was a big row of stars and insignia, which I could not make out but which were new to me. One of them, a huge man, carried a heavy brief case tightly clutched in his hands. He never let loose of it, but carried it with him while strolling in the promenade during the intermissions. Nell and I had some ice cream cones, at a dollar sixty-five our money. But the ice cream is good, even though one can easily break a tooth on the cone part.

8. SHOOTING IN THE VOLGA SWAMPS

IT WAS PROBABLY GENERAL GUILLAUME, the French military attaché, who was responsible for a surprising Soviet venture in large-scale farm and forestry management. He loved to hunt, and all the years he was in Moscow he made needling, insulting remarks on every possible occasion to all the Soviet officials whom he met, pointing out that in all civilized and uncivilized countries, except Russia, foreign diplomats had opportunity to engage in that healthful and ancient pastime. He was caustic on this theme even when, on the occasion of his final departure for France, he had opportunity to talk with powers far above the level of OVS.

It may be that the Soviets could not think of any convincing arguments to rebut Guillaume's sharp tongue, and realized that they were vulnerable. At any rate, a large area of swampland along the Dubna River, a short tributary of the Volga, was turned over to Burobin, the office which deals with the housekeeping of foreign missions in Russia, and the announcement was made that foreigners could now shoot and fish in this region. The seasonal fees seemed exorbitant, but few knew that Burobin had been cannily required to make these lands at least break even financially. The twenty-five thousand hectares — over sixty thousand acres — of swamp and peat were dotted with occasional small villages for whose management Burobin became suddenly responsible, and fees from foreigners would be only a drop in the bucket in keeping out of trouble.

The foreigners reacted disappointingly. Very few of them knew enough about fishing and hunting to be willing to pay the stiff fees, and many of them were unable to do so. Two or three drove to take a look at the place, but were unable to get near it because there were no roads over which an ordinary automobile could possibly travel. The only ones who had succeeded in penetrating the area were a couple of my enlisted men in a jeep, and they had had to abandon their jeep in the mud and walk for the last four or five kilometers. There was much cynical comment in the embassies to the effect that the Soviets had probably built a luxurious lodge with which to impress foreigners, and that any sucker who bit would be sure to be followed and kept as isolated from the real country as if he were in Moscow. The report of my enlisted men did not bear this out, so I borrowed some shotgun shells from Ambassador Smith, all of mine being still tied up in customs, and prepared to give it a try. The olive-drab, powerful weapons-carrier, because of its big balloon tires and its high road clearance, should be able to get through where even a jeep couldn't travel.

Volkov and Kiril from the pool of Navy chauffeurs both wanted to drive for me because both of them like to shoot. My own driver Valodya is not a huntsman, and was perfectly willing to step aside in favor of one of the other drivers in case I decided to take any-one and not drive myself, but his wife told him that he ought to be ashamed of himself — I had done so much for them, and now, when it looked like a little rough going, he was too lazy to take care of me the way he should. They were unable to settle among themselves who should go, so I flipped a coin and ended up with Valodya.

After many delays, we started about noon, carrying two extra twenty-liter tanks of fuel. Especially for the departure, I put on an old but striking white-and-black Irish tweed jacket over a dark blue woolen Chief's shirt, and my gay yellow tie, embroidered with trout flies. As Kidder, my red-haired, smooth, sharp-looking chief yeoman, said, I certainly looked sharp.

We stopped at Burobin to pick up the manager of their new estate, Aleksei Mikhailovich Ivlyev. He was a tall, rather dignified man in his late forties, with gray hair, a big nose, and deep, but not unkindly lines around his mouth, with boots, knapsack, and double-barreled shotgun. On the way it developed that he was a Siberian and had shot and fished all through the taiga and Central Asia. He had done a hitch as a petty officer in the Baltic Fleet, and then, when the war broke out, had gone in the Red Army as an artillery officer.

On the way through Moscow we saw, for a change, a woman holding a chisel while a man swung the sledge. It's almost always the other way around. There was a strong, cold wind blowing out

of the north, so I concealed my bright raiment beneath a heavy,
fleece-lined khaki jacket and wrapped the rest of me in a wind-
breaker. On the edge of Moscow we were stopped by the police,
but after the single word "diplomatic" from Valodya they waved
us on.

"And why did they stop us?" I asked.

"They asked for our pass, but of course a diplomatic car doesn't
need a pass."

"Why a pass?" Apparently the American touring cars in which
we usually rode had been easily recognizable as diplomatic.

"Oh, everyone has to have a pass to get out of Moscow. That's
to keep anyone from going out into the country on private business
of his own. It's no trouble getting a pass, if you have legitimate
reason, from the factory or office where you work. But if you don't
have a pass, the militiaman says, 'Aha, I thought so!' "

"And then what happens?"

"A fine!"

"Yes," added Aleksei, "a militiaman fined me five rubles just
the other day for walking across the street after he had blown the
whistle to change the traffic."

"The militiaman fined you? Didn't you have to go to court?"

"Oh, no. They fine you right on the spot. They are obliged to
give you a receipt for your fine. I wouldn't wait for my receipt,
and started to walk off, but he called me back and was ready to
fine me again for not taking my receipt."

When we were out in the country I took over the driving, having
noticed that the driver was not only sheltered from the wind by
a big spare wheel and tire, but was also on the sunny side of the
road. It was the same road we had traveled not long before to
almost within sight of the Volga, strung with little villages of low,
thatched, unpainted log *izbas*. If any paint is ever used, it is only
on the carved window frames, and then usually a bright blue or a
Chinese red. Sometimes the thatch sprouts grass and crops, making
the houses look bearded.

Once, along a long stretch of uninhabited country, we saw a
crowd of people, plodding thick together along the road far ahead
of us. I guessed what it was before the others, and sure enough,
it was a funeral. We took off our hats as we passed. The coffin

was wrapped in white, carried on an open horse-drawn cart and covered with a few bright paper flowers. A bearded priest, with his robes and staff, brought up the rear, with a sly, jolly face straight out of the Middle Ages.

"Russian people do not drink much at funerals," said Valodya. "Only at weddings and on holidays, and other special occasions. Of course, there is always a special occasion, but funerals are not included. Maybe just a tumblerful or two of vodka, for when a Russian gets drunk he always wants to sing and dance, and of course that is not becoming at a funeral."

When we got into the swamp country around the Volga, we turned off the highway along a road cobbled with round wooden blocks, in a disreputable state of repair. There were holes in it as big as our car, and it was high-crowned, with deep ditches full of moss and watercress on each side. There was a long village strung out on this street for three or four kilometers, with a glass factory at one side, and the street was liberally strewn with broken glass. There were piles of glass from time to time beside the road as big as industrial coal dumps. Not only was it hard to hold the bumping, jolting, clattering weapons-carrier on the road, but every time I threw out the clutch for a big chuckhole the engine died. "The next time that happens," I said to Valodya, "I'll let you drive." And soon he was driving, with the choke half out to keep the engine going.

Long since, we had noticed that Aleksei was blue with the cold in the back seat, so we had brought him up in front with us, but by now we had another Russian bumping and shivering in the back. Fyodr Petrovich, a *yegor,* or huntsman, had been waiting all day long for us where the side road turned off from the highway. He was a little, wizened, shrewd-looking fellow, snaggle-toothed and sunburned to the color of leather, born and raised in the village of Glini on the Dubna River where we were heading. As he told me later, he had been a soldier of the Tsar and had been badly shot up at Tannenberg, too badly ever to serve in the army again. But during the Great Fatherland War, they had sent him to work in the Ural mines, and that was much worse than any war. He didn't complain, only the war in the mines was all hard work and no fun.

Finally we turned off our road, which had lost its wooden blocks and become a deeply rutted sea of black mud, reputed to be even worse ahead, into the open fields, and came out on a vast, grassy, abandoned airfield. How it was ever used, except in frozen or very dry weather, was a mystery. Wagon tracks and truck tracks laced across it, with frequent black wallows, filled with branches from trees, where cars or wagons had been bogged down earlier. We came up to two light trucks, half out of sight in the soft earth.

"How long have you been standing here?" asked Valodya.

"Four days."

Valodya shook his head deprecatingly, but smiled. That couldn't happen to our American reconnaissance car. And straightway we, too, were bogged. All four wheels just spun in the thick, sticky mud, and we couldn't move forward or back. We scattered to gather brush out of the scars of similar past catastrophes. It began to be clear why shovels and axes were necessary car equipment, and why all the Russian drivers had not been entirely self-interested when they had urged me not to try to drive alone through the countryside. We dug out the mud ahead and astern, and literally built us a road with brushwood. At every step, the whole earth quaked and shook for several feet around. We pulled out of that hole, and then stopped on firmer ground. Ahead was a bright green ribbon of mossy stream bed which we must cross.

"It would be better if the rest of you walked, and left me to drive the car alone," said Valodya. "Then I could gallop across some of these places without any fear of you flying out."

We tramped on across the mossy, peaty field and, with considerable admiration, watched Valodya roaring, sliding and jumping along, turning like a polo pony. Several times all four wheels were clear of the ground, and only once more on that field did we have to dig him out and build us a road.

"What a machine!" said one of the truck drivers who had been there for four days. Russian drivers don't mind bogging down. Time means nothing to their half-Asiatic minds. They always have with them bread and a bit of sausage, and it is pleasant enough to curl up and sleep until things dry up.

After that, we came to a village, where we rejoined our muddy country road. There were birch woods and soft plowed fields on all sides, so we had to keep to the road through the village. There were stretches of bright, new, green grass here and there along the sides, but they were cut up with water-filled ditches that were too deep and steep for even our wonderful machine, and Valodya was forced into the black, rutted road. Again we walked and watched Valodya do acrobatics with the car, but soon he was stuck fast, with worse going ahead. This was where the enlisted men had abandoned their jeep a week before.

The entire village turned out to watch and help, but a dozen men couldn't move that car. Horses were scarce in that country. There was some talk about getting a tractor, but there was much doubt if a tractor would be any better off. Meanwhile we kept on working, trying various schemes, but the car just dug in deeper until even the transmissions were completely buried and it was resting in the mud on its frame and body with the big balloon wheels almost out of sight. It was a little discouraging to see that sticky mud swallow big logs of wood, one on top of another. Fyodr, the little *yegor,* had disappeared in the woods, but finally he showed up, carrying on his shoulder a pine tree, twenty feet long and eight or ten inches thick, which he had cut and trimmed with the axe he carried with him at all times. We built a fulcrum from logs of firewood from the village and stuck one sharpened end of the pine tree under the car. Eight or nine men swung onto the other end of the tree, in order to pry the car up. Nothing happened. They swung harder, and then, with a snap, the tree broke, dropping a couple of our helpers and me into the bordering ditch. Everyone laughed, and soon Fyodr was back with a bigger tree. This time it worked, and when the car started to heave, Valodya set the wheels spinning while we fed everything we could find into the ruts behind all four wheels until the car crawled back onto a firmer place.

All the rest of the way to our own village of Glini we walked, scouting ahead, picking the most possible places, laying brush, and wondering if Valodya wasn't getting too filled with pride when he would grin at our head-shakings in front of some broad ditch, say *"Ni-i-ichevo!"* — back off, and leap across it with the horizon showing beneath all four wheels at once. The sun had set when we tramped and clattered into Glini — eight o'clock, and we had left Moscow around noon — a drive of only some hundred and twenty-five kilometers.

Glini was a village of about twenty or twenty-five *izbas,* indistinguishable from all the other villages but for the wide, swift river that cut through it. Our *izba* was right on the river bank. I took one look through the door, sat down, took off my muddy Marine shoes, and, against protests, went on in in my socks. Never have I seen such a clean, scrubbed house. The bare floors and the heavy logs that made the walls were worn and weathered with scrubbing. They were not only spotless, they fairly glowed and shone with a soft, white splendor. Pavel Dmitrovich, whose house it was, was far more untidy, with his scrubby beard, scrubby hair, and wide smile. Ephrosinya Vladimirovna, our hostess, was kerchiefed and booted with *valyenki,* and she had a smooth, unlined pink face, with shoebutton eyes. It was surprising to learn that she was fifty-eight years old. She attributed her young appearance to the fact that she was childless.

There were three cots in the main room of the house, which was turned over to Aleksei Mikhailovich, Valodya, and me. Burobin had sent down a half dozen thick, long-haired woolen Russian blankets, woven with two shades of green into a leafy pattern, two or three Bokhara rugs for the floor, and some straight-backed chairs. It was plain that they came from Burobin, for the price tags were still on the blankets — nine hundred rubles each, or $112.50 at even the diplomatic rate of exchange — and there were tags on the rugs. Otherwise, the house was like every Russian *izba* in the vicinity — bare and poor of furnishings. There was a throaty radio, probably also Burobin's. The house was deliciously warm, for the inner partitions were formed by the famous Russian stoves, which are fired with charcoal. This gives a tremendous radiating surface, which is kept so that it is hot to the touch.

Ephrosinya busied herself with eggs for me, and soon we were sitting around the samovar in our room. Everyone broke out their own food, for food in Russia, beyond potatoes and *shchi,* or cabbage soup, is such a problem that everyone carries their own. Eggs, milk, meat and the sort of thing that one thinks of peasants as constantly enjoying, are mostly taken by the state. What is left beyond coarse vegetables is too expensive to eat, and is sold to the markets. Perhaps the *kolkhozes,* or collective farms, are different, but I doubt it. At least that is the way the people of this Volga swamp country live, where there is not sufficient agriculture to form a regular *kolkhoz.* I always paid for my eggs and my milk, except once, in another house and at another time, when they had some milk which they relished as though it were a great luxury. There was some gin in my bag, and one by one the host and hostess and Fyodr were invited in to join us. No Russian ever drinks anything but a large glass full of vodka, and that all in one draught. I warned them that this was *dzhin* and not vodka, but one round finished the bottle.

"It's a good life in the country here," I said. "I think that if I were a Russian, I would much rather live in the villages than in the city."

"Not I," said Ephrosinya. "My husband has been promising me every year for many years now that we would move to the city. It's much more exciting and interesting in Moscow than here. I know, for I have been there."

"Maybe so," said Pavel, noncommitally. "And it isn't always a good life in the villages. Suppose your cow or your goat falls ill, and dies? Then you and your family may die too."

The margin between life and death is always close in Russia. Pavel Dmitrovich was a cabinetmaker, who walked ten kilometers each way to his work in some small factory. Perhaps Ephrosinya Vladimirovna will yet get to Moscow.

A choice was offered me between getting up at half past three in the morning for ducks, or setting some lines yet that night for *nalim,* the big fish that live on bottom of the river. Since it was already late, we obviously couldn't do both. I chose the fishing, and for an hour the two hunters, Aleksei and Fyodr, were busy rigging lines. They twist them along short rods and wind them around forked sticks like slingshots. I was too sleepy to try to become familiar with the elaborate rig, but rigged my own casting rod and went out on the riverbank with them while they set their lines.

The moon was veiled with clouds, but it was a full moon, and it was light enough for me to cast without too much difficulty. It was peaceful and lovely, with the slender birch trees ghostly in the soft light. From the bridge down the river came the sound of an accordion, and laughter, and the rhythmic stamp of the sort of dancing that the Russian people love. Some of the lads saw me casting, and drifted down to the river's edge to watch me and to ask questions. They could not be seen distinctly in the moonlight, even when they were close, but their big furry caps and their long kaftan-like coats made them seem very outlandish. And their Russian speech was very soft.

They didn't waken me in the morning to watch them bring in the lines, and when I finally rolled out of my green blankets the reason was plain. They shamefacedly showed me two tiny three-inch fish — the total catch.

I've wondered long how the people of the *izbas* manage, for there are never any privies to be seen in the villages, and now I learned. The barn or shed for the chickens, cow or goat, is always built integral with the house. It is floored with straw or hay, and is very convenient.

The day was raw and cold, with low clouds driven by the strong, bitter wind, which whipped the wide, swift river into foam. The water was brown, but a clear brown, so, accompanied by Aleksei, I fished downstream all morning. There were clumps of willows and copses of birch and pine along the banks, but everywhere bits of fat, greening meadow, close cropped by goats, came down to the water's edge, and it was very easy to fish, although too wide to cast even to the middle. The river was deep, and there were many ideal places for fish, but never a strike. After four or five kilometers, followed by a stretch of real forest, we came to our objective, where once there had been some sort of mill and a dam, now washed out. The water thundered wide and tumultuous. It was too heavy to fish, but there were great, deep, brush-lined backwaters and pools where one could fish all day, and in the middle was a great *omut* — a deep pit, where the river made a big whirlpool, and which was said to be full of fish. It was probably full of devils as well, for the Russians have a proverb, "Devils lurk in *omuts*," which means that still waters run deep.

During the war, the Red Army had thrown a pontoon bridge across the old dam, but the bridge had carried away, loaded with troops and equipment. A great many of them had drowned, and to this day skeletons and machine guns are occasionally washed out of the *omut* by the whirlpool. In many of the pools and backwaters were *lyulki* — cradles — which are big flat dip nets suspended on one end of a long pole. The pole is pivoted in the middle, and on the other end is a counterweight. No bait is used, but the nets are kept in the water, and occasionally someone — whoever may be passing — bears down on the counterweight and raises the net to entangle whatever may be passing at the moment.

Sabin, my chief electrician's mate — "Gospodin Elektrik," — who was here with the enlisted men of last week, said that he saw some enormous fish brought out by the *lyulki*, but now the weather and wind were too bad for fish. Yet I saw them raise one nice *shchuka,* about thirty inches long. The translation of *shchuka* in the dictionaries is "pike," but, except for their teeth, they were quite unlike our pike, being spoon-billed, and covered with big white spots. Nearly all Russian beasties are definitely different. Their swine are big and coarse, with different ears and heads from ours, and their cats have enormous eyes, large heads, and much thicker, longer fur.

Before I had begun to cover the water, the base of my reel carried away. Perhaps it was just as well, for it was already lunch time. We cut through the mossy woods towards home, and on the way met a fine, clean-looking, clear-eyed lad in a black astrakhan cap and a black short overcoat lined and trimmed with white sheepskin. With him were two wild-looking Siberian dogs, which they use for hunting elk. From their description of their *losi,* which the dictionaries call elk, they must be very like moose, for they are about the size of a big horse, with palm-shaped antlers, great hooked noses, and beards. The lad was Vassily Fedorovich, the son of my *yegor* Fyodr Petrovich. Aleksei told me that he was indeed a fine boy — very respectful towards his father.

Valodya told me that since he was just a lad it was better to address him as Vassily rather than as Vassily Fedorovich. The etiquette of addressing Russians is subtle, and the use of both names, although not always acceptable, is a stage halfway between stiff formality and intimacy. I noticed that Valodya always called Aleksei, Aleksei Mikhailovich. There is a trick in pronouncing these long Russian middle names which makes it really possible to handle them. It consists of leaving out some of the syllables, so that Ivanovich becomes Ivanich and Vladimirovna, Vladimira.

Vassily said that we would get no game or fish in this sort of weather, and that there was worse weather to come. The hares in the forest were still snow-white, showing that winter was not yet over, and the ducks, which too knew the seasons, were drifting in only in very small number. It is so far north here that it is the end of the journey for ducks. One would have thought that they would be plentiful in the breeding grounds, but by the time they get here the flocks have broken up and there are only singles and doubles to be had.

After lunch I lay on the bed and read while Valodya, who loves to tinker, did a neat job of lashing up my broken reel. When he had finished, Aleksei and I went through the woods again to the dam, leaving Valodya to his favorite pastime of sleep. We were beaten by a fine, powdery hail, which lay white on the green moss. In a few minutes of casting, Valodya's lash-up on the reel had carried away. This is the second reel that has gone bad on me in Russia with very little use. If they had been Russian reels, I would probably have had a harsh opinion of Russian ineptness in making such things, but these were American reels. Because of the war, no doubt. Instead of fishing, we warmed our hands at a fire that two or three bearded fishermen had built.

We went back home, and sat around and talked. Aleksei had had such a bad case of bronchial asthma when he was mustered out of the Baltic Fleet that the doctors had told him he must go somewhere to the mountains, where the climate was very dry. "But how was that possible for me? And then came the war, and where should I fall for service but the Caucasus! My asthma soon went away, and has never come back." He told me much about the Caucasus, its wild scenery and its wilder tribesmen. More than Central Asia, the Caucasus is the land of romance to the Russian.

Fyodr joined us in the late afternoon, and the three of us tramped for miles across the fields and through the woods until we came to a suitable place for *tyaga,* which is the shooting of *waldshnaip* against the evening sky during their brief nightly flight from the sort of woods which they like during the day to their nests in the more open, brushy glades. We cut some pine boughs and sat on them until it should start to darken.

The sun had gone down, and we were in an open space surrounded by the forest. There was a silver splendor from the rising moon behind the barriers of dark cloud in the east. It was very peaceful, and very cold, with the wind moaning through the trees. Things began to grow dim and formless, and the slim white birches shone like thin ghosts among the dark firs. Suddenly Aleksei jumped up. "There they come!" he whispered, and we all scattered. I stood alone in the dusk, shaking and shivering with cold, looking in all directions, but there was nothing to be seen. Suddenly, right over my head, so low I could almost touch it, was a big *waldshnaip*, skimming and skittering through the air like a black, silent ghost. By the time I could bring up my gun, it was gone.

I stopped shivering and kept my gun ready, my head turning round and round like an owl's. Another one, and the roar of my gun echoed through the woods. Missed. Something had gone wrong with the magazine of my automatic. In the cold and half-darkness I could not see to remedy it and so could have only single shots. A long wait, and another chance. But it was at a very long range, so another miss. Afterward they told me that it would have been well to have thrown my cap up in the air to lure the bird closer, for the *waldshnaip* hens rocket up from their nests to show the way home.

Then there was a shot in the distance, from Fyodr's direction. Another wait, and two quick shots from the other direction. Against the pale sky, I saw Aleksei's bird fall. Suddenly two more birds, braiding their ghostly flight together, but so low that I could not get them against the sky. I shot, and then saw only one. I was still groping in the blackness for the possible bird when Fyodr came up. He had missed his one shot, and Aleksei was unable to find his in the dark.

On the way home, we debated the desirability of next time bringing leashed dogs to find the birds. Dogs in springtime are against the law, for they are apt to destroy the nests. As we tramped in the dim moonlight, we again and again passed square pits of water, shining pale in the blackness.

"Fyodr Petrich, what are those pits?" I asked.

"During the war," he answered, "the Germans came as far as the Moscow-Volga Canal. Those pits are where our guns were placed."

When we got home, we drank the vodka that I had had Valodya buy at the village *chainaya,* and I fixed the magazine of my gun. Although Aleksei had once been the champion trapshooter of all the USSR, he was completely unfamiliar with automatics. Everyone remarked pleasedly when I remembered the full names of our host and hostess to drink to their health.

As I dropped off to sleep towards midnight, warm and tired, I heard young people singing softly as they passed the house on their way home.

9. WHITE FLIES IN SPRING

ALEKSEI WAS TO WAKEN ME if there was any possibility of ducks. I woke up by myself when Fyodr came in with the news that everything but the river was frozen solid. There was an outside chance that we might find some ducks, but I refused to move and went back to sleep.

All morning we sat in the *izba* and overhauled fishing gear, talking and listening to the throaty radio snarl out its propaganda, while through the steamy windows we could see big flakes of snow whirl past in the wind.

"One cold afternoon," said Aleksei, as he was wrapping a rod, "I was shooting with a comrade in a small, narrow boat on a big Siberian lake. We had our boat in a clump of reeds, but there was no land there, and the water was ten or twelve feet deep. The wind was rising all the time, and in the evening, when it was time to go home, we found the lake covered with such waves that we nearly swamped, and had to put back into the reeds where we had a little shelter. All we could do was to sit and wait for the wind to go down. At last the boat gave a tremendous lurch, and we nearly swamped again. My comrade had dropped off to sleep, and slumped over to one side. The boat was so narrow that we could only sit upright, and we didn't dare go to sleep after that. So all through the night, we sang songs to keep awake, until the wind died down the next day."

"You must have known a great many songs, Aleksei Mikhailich."

"Of course, every Russian knows enough songs to last the night through. And many of the Siberian songs take a full hour to sing from beginning to end.

"And once," he went on, "I shot the most beautiful wolf I have ever seen. It was winter, and there was snow everywhere. When I shot him, he came towards me before he dropped, walking on his hind legs like a man, with his arms held out in supplication. It made my hair stand on end. He was taller than a man, for after he was dead we could not raise him high enough from the ground so that his tail would not all still drag on the snow. There were fifteen of us together, but the only other thing we shot during the whole day was one hare. When we came into the village that night, we sold the wolf for his hide, and got a hundred and fifty rubles for it. That was before the war, when vodka was cheap, and we bought ten liters of vodka for our hundred and fifty rubles. Then we made soup out of the one hare. The one hare and the ten liters of vodka were enough for fifteen men, and we sang songs all that night too.

"And in Kazakhstan there is a bird called the *drof,* which is very like an ostrich, only smaller, very good to eat. I have hunted them on horses with the Kazakhs. It takes a very swift horse to keep up with the *drof.* We killed them with long whips, ten meters long, with a lead ball on the end of the whip. The lash would wrap around their necks, and then the lead ball would whang them on their heads."

I have never yet heard a Russian tell a tale who did not tell it with much drama, gesticulating to show exactly how everything happened, raising and lowering his voice, changing his tenses, and pausing suddenly before the final climax.

We decided that there was only one possibility of any ducks, and that was to go some fifteen or twenty kilometers to where there was much water. The road would be much worse than that by which we had come to Glini, so we filled our pockets with shells, packed up a little food, put on warm clothes and started out, stopping at an *izba* across the river to pick up Fyodr, and leaving Valodya to sleep, which he had been doing ever since we arrived.

Fyodr Petrovich was asleep on top of the stove. He climbed down from the stove, barefooted, in long woolen drawers, and grinned brightly at us. Vassily said that an NKVD jeep had been over that road in the morning, and that it was well frozen, and consequently passable.

While Vassily went back to rouse Valodya and help him crank up the weapons-carrier, and while Aleksei and Fyodr puttered around getting ready, I sat on a box and talked with Mariya, Fyodr's grown daughter. She was grave and self-contained, neither shy nor forward, and as handsome in her high-cheekboned way as her young

brother. Her little fat baby — another Valodya, and also sleeping
— was curled up on the floor in a nest of old quilts, and a brindled,
furry Russian cat was curled up asleep beside him. Mariya wore a
khaki blouse and skirt, with bare legs showing above her *valyenki*.

"Were you in the army during the war?" I asked.

"Yes," she said proudly, "I was a chauffeur with the Red Army."

Like country youth the world over who have seen a bit of the
world, she was dissatisfied with the villages and wanted to go to
Moscow.

When we first entered Fyodr's house, it was like entering an

empty, abandoned place where people just happened to be camping.
They have so very little. There is no furniture, no rugs, no pictures
— only bare floors and walls. But those were scrubbed as snowily
white as at Ephrosinya's.

"How clean your house is, Mariya," I said.

"It ought to be. We scrub it hard enough," she answered gravely.
"With sand, and then with soap. But for real cleanliness, you should
see the houses in the Ukraine!"

Even the things that these people own — a big chest or two,
folded full of women's finery and treasures, a sewing machine, a
bare stool or trestle on which to sit — are never arranged in any
orderly fashion as they would be anywhere else, but are put out
in the middle of the floor at odd angles.

At last the car came, and then we were bumping along the

frozen country roads, stopping frequently to go ahead to scout for the best passages, or to let Valodya leap a ditch alone. After ten or twelve kilometers, the road went through a big village where stakes were set up to keep such travelers as we out of the front yards, and then it died in a big plowed field. We unloaded our things and kept on on foot towards a distant edging of forest. Just before we reached the trees, we could see a white swirl of snow coming towards us, and by the time we were in the forest, the ground was white everywhere.

Fyodr led the way. The ears of his cap flapped in the cold wind. He wore quilted, padded trousers, and hanging on one arm was an enormous woven basket in which two live female mallard decoys were complaining and talking. All he lacked was a little short skirt to make him look exactly like a little old *babushka*.

We came to a little group of three or four *izbas,* where we were to spend the night, and went into one of them. It was scrubbed just as clean as the others in which we had been, and was just as bare, poor, and unoccupied-looking. No one was home but a young girl with fine eyes who was swinging a fat baby in her arms. She was the sister of our new host, and everyone else had gone off to some village for something or other. Fyodr pulled out a big *shchuka* from somewhere in his belongings, and the girl put the baby in a criblike cradle in order to take it for our eventual supper. Fyodr looked so *khitry* — so sly — that I asked him where he got the fish, but he only wrinkled up his face, grinned, and looked more cunning than ever. "Out of some neighbor's *lyulka,*" I said, and he laughed. Each person builds a *lyulka,* but the rules that govern the ownership of the fish that come from it were never clear, to me at least.

We left our food there, and followed a road for what seemed endless kilometers through the forest, then across some open, swampy country, where stood a good-sized village. We passed an occasional person in the village, but it was noteworthy that there was no exchange of greetings, but an air of almost mutual distrust. The tall stacks of some sort of little factory at the end of the village rose dark against the sky. Beyond the village was more swamp, and then a very large area of old peat cuttings, filled in now with water, and forming an irregular area of hundreds and hundreds of little ponds, bordered with thick peat moss and scrub birch and fir. We circled and twisted endlessly between these little lakes that shone against the dark earth, with the cold north wind chilling us thoroughly and Fyodr's big basket bobbing along ahead of us.

At last we found the sort of place which incoming ducks might like, bordered with ice but reasonably cleared in the middle by the waves which were whipped up by the cold wind. There were many traces of elk around, with their droppings looking like caches of Texas pecans. Fyodr turned to with his ax, and in a very few minutes had built me a *shalash* — a wigwam out of young birches and fir boughs to serve as a blind. He moored one of the live ducks in the water, and then I crawled into my *shalash* while the other two disappeared to find their own places.

My duck had apparently acquired a tremendous appetite from the journey, for she ate — just ate — noisily, steadily, and voraciously, sticking her head under water to reach what was on the bottom and then coming up to enjoy it gurglingly. But never one word did she say — not one quack or call. The wind shrilled through the boughs of the *shalash* and I sat and shivered, but never another duck was there to be seen, nor did any gunshots echo in the distance. When the sun had gone down and the cold light began to be gathered up from the earth into the sky, my companions came up.

"Our duck also was silent," they said. "She simply ate and was silent."

We left Fyodr to gather our live decoys into the basket, and on the way home turned out of the peat beds into the forest until we found the sort of open glade where the *waldshnaip* nest. There we stood, out of sight of one another, while the silver birches misted into blackness, but there was no ghostly fluttering against the sky. At last Fyodr started to call, "A-oo-oo-oo! A-oo-oo-oo!" I passed the call along, and we plodded back through the peat bogs, the big unfriendly village and the endless straight road through the forest. My coat, with its weight of shotgun shells, was very heavy on my shoulders by the time we saw the light of our *izba* twinkling in the distance.

Our host, Vassily Fyodorovich Bakhalyev, poured a cup of icy water over my hands for me to wash. He was bright-eyed, with a ruddy, high-cheekboned, handsome face. Quiet, soft-spoken, dignified, and completely at ease, he appeared wholly unconscious of the artificial arm that replaced the one he had lost in the war. He was a forester, and his wife had the same extraordinarily fine eyes as her young sister. There was also a small, smiling, well-behaved young brother.

The women rushed around in their *valyenki* and poor cotton skirts, putting charcoal in the samovar, which was soon bubbling on the table, and bringing in enormous dill pickles and a big bowl of potatoes boiled with something which made them very good. Fyodr's *shchuka* was cut crosswise into convenient pieces which we ate with our fingers. It tasted almost like swordfish. There were no plates, and we all dipped into the common bowl of potatoes. The good-natured, fat baby was brought in for us to admire. Fortunately, I had a few chocolate bars and some vodka, and we drank to everyone's health.

There was no electricity in the *izba,* and the dim "smoker" made a strange light. I had thought "Oh-oh!" when I saw two anti-American posters on the walls — a little Uncle Sam snarling against a heroic Soviet soldier, and Churchill with some cigar-smoking American generals lighting the fires of another war — but I soon realized that those posters were simply used as wallpaper, piecing in some patchwork of newspapers and varied bits of real wallpaper. I believe that Vassily and his family were completely unconscious of them. There was a small lithograph of Repin's "Reply to the Sultan" with its savage, shaven-headed Cossacks thoroughly enjoying their joke, and high in the corner hung an ikon. These people were as much at ease and as gentle and hospitable as one could find anywhere in America. Vassily had a worn and much-prized copy of one of the excellent Russian *sputniks,* or how-to-do-it books, on dogs and hunting, and the hunters thumbed and admired and discussed it for a long time.

Then they laid a couple of bare boards on a pair of trestles to make a bed for me. I would have liked to have slept on the stove, but that was Fyodr's place. He took off his jacket, shoes and quilted trousers and swung out of sight, while Aleksei Mikhailovich lay down on the floor beside my trestles.

Low voices and the sound of the bubbling samovar wakened

me. It was very dark at half past three in the morning, but the whole family was up to get us on our way. They thought that my desire for cold water to drink was very unhealthy and bad for the stomach, so they insisted that I drink hot milk as well, including the crusted cream, which was regarded as its major tidbit. After several cups of tea from the samovar, we were plodding through the long forest road once more to the peat lakes.

When we got there, the little lakes were frozen solid with a half inch of ice. It was with difficulty that we beat out enough ice to make a place for the live decoy, but as it grew light I was again in the *shalash,* shivering in the rising north wind. In fifteen minutes the duck was also shivering on the bank and the places we had beaten out in the water were again frozen. From time to time I crawled out again to beat the fast freezing ice away, and between times dozed and froze in the wind. After an hour or so of this, Fyodr appeared, his teeth also chattering, so we gathered up twigs and moss, gnarled roots, brushwood and some white birch logs, and built us a fire. It was very wonderful to lie on the moss and thaw out beside that fragrant, smoky fire. Aleksei, attracted by the smoke, came up, and we sat around and talked and toasted the last chunks of the fish over the embers. I found out how to eat their raw bacon or fatback — *salo.* It is delicious and tender, fried on a forked stick until it is brown and dripping, and laid between two chunks of black bread. The last of the vodka helped to warm us, and we lay for a time beside the fire.

"Now let's see what sort of shot you are with your American gun," said Aleksei, picking up the empty vodka bottle and walking away.

"Oh-oh!" I thought, as he walked further and further away. "Here's where my reputation goes!"

At last Aleksei stopped and threw the empty bottle high in the air. But I was lucky, and blew it completely to bits with a clean hit. They were pleased.

"And now," said Fyodr, taking off his worn cap-with-ears, "let's see if you can hit my cap." He hung it on a shrub, and Aleksei took me with him, pacing off eighty long steps through the peat moss. When we turned, the cap was hard to see in the distance through the brush. I aimed high and well into the wind, and when we went back we found two new little holes squarely through the middle.

"Now you try, with your double-barreled Russian guns," I said.

"Here's where one of our triple-barreled guns would be better," said the champion skeet shooter of all Russia. "The third barrel takes rifle cartridges."

We could not find any holes after his shot, nor after Fyodr's attempt. Since their ammunition costs about a ruble a shell, we didn't try any more. I gave Fyodr a handful of shells, and we gathered up our decoys and started back once more, this time along a different road through the swamp. It started to snow hard.

"White flies," said Aleksei, "little white flies. That's what we call the snowflakes."

My heavy rubber boots were getting very heavy, and from the weight on my shoulders I could have wished that we had shot up all our ammunition.

"And so this hunter searched and searched," said Aleksei, "but he couldn't find his lost watch. Next year he was hunting in the same place, and all at once he saw the watch. He picked it up with a shout, and held it to his ear. 'I told you it was a fine watch!' he said. 'It's still running!'" And that led to still taller tales.

We could scarcely make out the houses through the swirling snow as we came through the big swamp village. And yet we could dimly make out one woman on the road, who modestly stopped in the storm to pull down her skirts, blown about by the wind, over her shapeless dark blue bloomers.

We stopped at our own *izba,* gathered up our things, had more tea and potatoes and black bread, said good-by to that dignified, smiling, simple family, left a few rubles on the table, and went wearily through the woods back to the open fields. And there was Valodya and the weapons-carrier, bouncing across the plowed land to meet us. It would have been better to have turned over in the car than to walk farther, so I rode all the way back, poised to jump if necessary.

When we got back to Glini, Ephrosinya insisted upon still another breakfast — the third that morning. Afterwards I lay on the green blankets and went to sleep while trying to read. The others noticed that I was asleep, for from time to time I was half wakened by their endless gossip, now carried on in emphatic whispers. When we finally packed and left for Moscow, Ephrosinya Vladimirovna and Pavel Dmitrovich told me many times that I must come back to them, soon and often.

The sun came out between snow squalls, and although the surface of the mud was slippery it was frozen underneath. We were only stuck twice, and then not badly. We knew that we were very short of gas, but it lasted us until we were well back on the high-road, and there the car rolled to a stop. The first car that came along was a big truck, and the driver, induced by a package of cigarettes and fifty rubles, doubtfully consented to let us have twenty liters of benzine, which would get us at least as far as Dmitrov. There we found the postoffice down a side street, from which Valodya telephoned to Spirodonovka House for the duty driver to come to meet us on the road with fifty liters more, for nowhere in Russia are there stations along the road where one can buy gas.

Since we had too much time on our hands, we hunted up a *chainaya* where we could leave our car underneath a window so we could keep an eye on it. After the four meals of that day I was not hungry, but still managed a big bowl of *shchi,* made from pickled cabbage. Valodya and Aleksei ate heartily, and the latter insisted that the only thing that would warm us up was the Russian equivalent of a boiler-maker — vodka followed by a mug of beer. It being Sunday and a market day, the *chainaya* was crowded with people, all laughing and talking vivaciously. Many brought their own little packages of food and only ordered something to drink. Aleksei and Valodya disapproved of women who came to a *chainaya* unaccompanied, although the only such who were in evidence were wrinkled old peasant women. We amused ourselves by guessing at the origins and jobs of various people.

"See that old man with the little goat's beard and long mustaches, with his fur cap pulled down over his eyes," said Aleksei. "He must be a Tatar. He's probably up to no good."

"You have to see his eyes to be sure he's a Tatar," answered Valodya. He got up and walked around the bearded man's table a couple of times, trying to peer under his cap, but when the old man suddenly looked sharply at him Valodya turned up his coat collar and hurried back to us. At last the old man pushed back his fur cap.

"Russian!" they both said at once.

"But still not up to any good," added Aleksei.

When well on our way out of Dmitrov, we met Pyotr, the duty driver, in a closed car. He was very much worried about the possible inconvenience to us because of the lack of fuel, particularly since he was the one who had worked on the weapons-carrier to be sure it was in good shape. His big pale face was all wrinkled up, but I reassured him. He was still not sure he was not out of favor, though, because of my refusal to go with him in the warm closed car. I had started in the weapons-carrier and intended to return in it.

The rest of the way we chattered about everything from borzoi hunting dogs to why the Moscow architects did not use the decorativeness of the *izba* in their public buildings. As we came into Moscow, Valodya said, "See how all the militiamen stare at us. They think we are villagers, and not used to Moscow. And the militiamen do not like villagers and dirty cars in Moscow."

Against the protests of Aleksei Mikhailovich, we drove him almost home. I have never yet seen a Russian in Moscow who will permit you to bring him all the way to his actual doorstep, and even the manager of an estate of over a hundred square miles was no exception. We left him at the nearest street corner.

The house seemed empty when I came in, and, since it was Sunday night, it was to be assumed that Nell was at the movies at Spasso House. She was upstairs, however, and partly because I had assumed she was gone and partly for unfathomable feminine reasons that seem connected with fishing and hunting trips, she was noticeably cool for a day or so.

10. ANOTHER CRISIS

IN MY OFFICE ON MONDAY MORNING McMillan and Dreher were waiting for me with worried faces. When things blow up, they usually do so when one is away. What it was this time was soon clear. Friday night a new automobile for the Embassy had arrived in Moscow. It had been shipped in from America by way of Odessa. The Port Director of Odessa, who was a friend of Dreher's, had arranged to accompany the car to Moscow to see that it arrived safely and without damage. He called Dreher from the Customs House and asked him to come there. Dreher, thinking nothing of it, since it is standard practice that Embassy shipments be guarded by someone and there had been previous conversations to the effect that his friend would try to wangle some way of getting to Moscow to see him, went to the Customs House. While the two were talking, the secret police moved in on them. (Time out to drink a glass of *kvass* which Natasha has just brought me while I write. It is a brown, nonalcoholic drink which she is always making from bread crusts and raisins, and not bad.)

To make a long story short, Dreher was caught talking with a Russian about the sort of things that went on in Odessa that were common knowledge there, and which would be considered unusual only in Russia. There had been a bit of a scuffle, Pasco was sent for from OVS, and Dreher was held for about four hours until he finally got in touch with the Ambassador by telephone. The State Department people here were naturally rather resentful of an extra, unpleasant, and conceivably avoidable chore that was being put upon them. To insure keeping out of trouble, one must stay in America. Nothing to do now but wait and see what capital the Soviets will make of the incident.

Dreher had already been waiting an undue length of time for his final exit visa when this thing took place, and he was very low and worried. I assured him that he had done all right and that no one had any legitimate complaints to make. Then Vishinsky sent for the Ambassador, who showed him his own dispatch to the State Department saying that the Soviets, obviously intending to use the matter for propaganda purposes, had set a trap into which a child should not have fallen. Vishinsky said that Dreher was, of course, *persona non grata* and must leave the country. That was exactly what Dreher had been trying to do for some time, but not exactly under those circumstances.

I made an appointment to see General Serayev. Five minutes before I left for OVS to keep my appointment, Dreher's passport arrived, with a visa for air, ominously via Minsk. We had originally applied for an exit visa via Odessa, but from the beginning did not expect to receive one through the Black Sea area. The Magidovs had been minutely searched at Minsk, and every letter, every book, every scrap of paper had been taken away from them.

Serayev and Pasco received me alone in one of the dark, chilly reception rooms of OVS. Serayev started off by saying that Dreher had admitted his guilt.

"Guilt of what?" I asked.

"Why, espionage, of course."

"No, he was not guilty of espionage, nor did he admit to that. He had received information from a Russian citizen, who admitted it, as did Dreher. But that information passes currently in Odessa and was given him freely. That is what I wanted to talk with you about. When I first came to Moscow, I told you that I and everyone in my office considered ourselves as guests in Russia, and that we would conduct ourselves as guests. When one is a guest in a house, and the host has some locked rooms or locked chests, one does not try to break into them. We have no intention of going into closed rooms or prohibited areas, but we will not shut our eyes to the pictures on the walls, the books in the bookshelves, and the things that are lying on the tables. Like guests, we will not suborn your servants, nor will we pay them in any way for information. But if a Soviet citizen, of his own free will, tries to tell us something, we will first warn him that it may go hard with him with his own government, and then, if he persists, we will not put our hands over our ears."

"But how about the bribes he gave?"

"What bribes?"

"Tins of food."

"An occasional tin of food is not a bribe. He gave food to many people in Odessa. A tin of food is like a pack of cigarettes. He had plenty, so why should he not share it with friends?"

"But how about the fact that he was taking notes when he was caught?"

"Serayev, it is exactly as though right here and now, you yourself told me something interesting or curious about Russia. I would not put my fingers in my ears to keep from hearing, but you know very well that that does not make me a spy. What difference if I make a note of it now, or wait a few minutes later, until I return to my office?"

"Yes. Yes, I understand your viewpoint."

Pasco said that it was very unpleasant for him to have been mixed up in it, particularly since my office was involved, which he had not expected, ever. I thanked him for his courteous conduct at the time of the incident. Both Serayev and Pasco were quite decent. It was obvious that this sort of thing was not handled by them at all, but "over there." There was a wave in the general direction of the Kremlin and the Lubyanka Prison. There was nothing they could do, nor did I expect them to do anything — they could not afford to, even if they had really wanted to. And after all, they are Russians. But my point of view was abundantly clear when I left them. Ambassador Smith had used it in his interview with Vishinsky. Under Russian law, every scrap of information that is not officially released constitutes a criminal offense, yet the things Dreher had been discussing that day would have been normally published in the papers in America. At least, if I or any of my people get in similar trouble again, some of the Soviets will know that we are living up to our own standards, and that those standards are higher than theirs.

What a country, where such a value can be set on basic food! Dreher's supplies were not delicacies, but plain meat and vegetables. And here it is the normal thing to think that the director of a port that compares to New Orleans or Baltimore could be bribed to treason with an occasional tin of food. I realize more and more that the Russians think in terms of values that are very different from ours, and that one must live here a long time to begin to understand them.

Nell and I went to dinner at the Emmerson's, who live in a separate house well out of the center of town. On the way we picked up some others, including the owlishly pleasant Hooker, a visitor from the State Department. We stopped at Spiro House for a drink, since Dreher had to leave for good the following morning. Spiro was orderly and pleasant, with its long low bookcases full of books, and Levy had made some good hot cheese *canapés*. It was a blue, misty evening as we drove out from there, with Moscow mysteriously lovely in the twilight.

General Wang was there, seeming a bit alone, so I spent most of the evening asking him questions about China. The thought kept coming to me that if he had been Russian instead of Chinese he would have been risking his neck to answer even such questions. He gave me a vivid picture of the little Chinese village in Hupei Province from which he comes, and promised to play the two-stringed Chinese violin for me some time.

John Emmerson put on his two famous acts at the piano — the competition in various styles of various sexes, ages and nationalities playing "When You and I Were Young, Maggie," which ends with the small-boy half of a duet taking his absent sister's part with his feet, and also the song of the hunter and the rabbit in English, French and Japanese. John was in good form. He always has to put on those piano acts at every party, no matter where, and, since he is of completely professional caliber, one never gets tired of hearing and seeing them. He actually looks like a Japanese when he is impersonating one. His attractive and admirable wife, although she must have heard them hundreds of times, seemed as fascinated as the rest of us.

Up very early the next morning to go to the airport to see Dreher off. Although Spiro cars have always been followed, this time they had an MVD escort in front and behind, all the way to the airport. And in the station, who should come up to Bob and greet him with every sign of friendliness but one of the assistants of the Odessa man who had either done Bob in, or, much more probably, had been done in together with Bob by the secret police. And there was nothing Bob could do to stop his dangerous friendliness. Yet perhaps it would not be dangerous to him. Perhaps his presence in Moscow can be explained by his having been the doer-in.

All of us wanted to do something for Bob. A *laissez-passer* was refused him by the Soviets, but we had a courier on the same plane, so Bob went as guard for the courier mail. That meant that if he were held at Minsk, the courier would also have to stay there and we would know the story. For me, the proverb of the ill wind held good, for he had given me his dress aiguillettes, my own being fit to wear only on the darkest of dark nights.

Few foreigners have left Moscow in recent times more regretfully, or with more sympathy for the Russian people than he. Among his many Russian friends was one intellectual girl in Moscow whom he saw infrequently. When they had first become acquainted she was violently pro-Soviet, remarking on how Americans hated the Russians, with all the propaganda arguments at her tongue's tip. But later, all the underlying doubts and questions came out. She had telephoned to try to see Bob several times after his trouble, but he told her flatly that it would only get her in difficulties, and so was out of the question. But when his car left Spiro for the airport, early in the morning, with the police in front and behind — there she was, standing on the sidewalk across the way, risking the MVD just to wave good-by to him.

As the plane for Minsk taxied out to the runway, Bob waved good-by to us all from his window, and it seemed to me that it was rather a wistful gesture.

Russian invitations always come at the very last possible minute. I can imagine them brooding for days over the problem of invitations, unable to make up their minds, until at last the pressure of time forces a decision. In the middle of the afternoon all of the diplomatic list received invitations to a special showing of a Soviet movie, *The Third Blow,* at the House of the Kino, beginning at seven that same evening. Nell and I have missed all of the other special showings of movies because we were always booked for previous engagements. This evening happened to be free, so we were pleased to go.

The Dom Kino has a rather elegant auditorium, but it also has rather hard seats. It was hung at the windows with crushed-orange velvet hangings, which, when the setting sun shone through, blazed gloriously to a hot flame color. The movie was an account of how the Germans were finally thrown out of the Crimea. It was spectacular, and, like most Russian historical movies, was well done, but towards the end it was hard to keep my eyes open from being up so early in the morning.

Nell tells me that one day during my absence the whole Embassy was startled by a rumble which crescendoed into a great crash, followed by silence. At first she thought it was an earthquake, or a plane that had crashed in the streets. She rushed out on the balcony, and saw everyone at the windows. People were running past the corner of the Kremlin wall, and she thought that perhaps the plane had crashed in a part of Red Square that she could not see. Then the activity centered on the Kremlin tower opposite our apartment, and she realized that the scaffolding which had surrounded it for many weeks had collapsed like a drinking cup. There were no ambulances, so it is to be assumed that no one was hurt. Even if dozens had been killed, there would have been no mention in the newspapers. No accidents or crimes are ever reported in the press, nor any of the multiform happenings that make up the news. The meager pages of the Soviet papers are completely free of such bourgeois interests.

Now the reconditioning of our Kremlin tower is all finished, and the re-erected scaffolding is gone for good. The upper part of the tower shines all new as though lacquered, with its red fresh bricks in violent contrast with the rosy mellowness of those of the untouched lower part and the crenelated walls. Before the Revolution it was topped with a double-headed eagle, but it now has a shining gold cap and ball, above which is a small, golden, stiff metal flag. The first flag that was put up on it was white, but that was the day after the Italian elections, when the Communists suffered their first important setback since the war, and for some reason the white flag was taken down at once. The pen-and-ink sketch I once made of our tower has been mislaid, so there is no way of telling if there are any changes other than the manifest newness.

·   ,   ·

Valodya has always looked very Russian and very disgraceful in his khaki coveralls and civilian cap. Now he has a new blue uniform, peculiarly suitable for an admiral's chauffeur since it was converted from an old one of mine. Mrs. Smith told Nell that they had plenty of chauffeur's caps at Spasso which would go very well with the new splendor. Valodya returned from Spasso saying that they didn't have one to fit him. Nell, being sure that he was either unduly fond of the old civilian cap or was being given the runaround by the Spasso servants, took charge of the situation and took Valodya back to Spasso in person.

While he was below, going over the caps again, she sat in the Spasso kitchen while Norah Smith made a special custard for the Ambassador. Valodya came into the kitchen, his long, sandy hair falling over his eyes, and made a long speech in Russian. Nell didn't get a single word of it, and asked him to say it again. Again she didn't understand a word. Tiny Bruce Durbrow, some six or seven years old, was there. When Nell and Norah continued to look blankly at Valodya, Bruce intervened.

"He says," he announced importantly, "he says — that there just isn't a cap there that will fit him, but that he can take one of them to a tailor, who will alter it to fit for very little money!"

I had sent a bundle of American magazines to Gregorev, my friend of the train, together with an invitation to dinner, as promised. Days and days went by, and no acknowledgment. Finally the day for the dinner approached so closely that Nell had to know whether or not he and his wife were coming. I called up the address he had given me and was told immediately that Gospodin Gregorev had gone home! One of the magazines I had sent him was a copy of *Time*. It had on its cover a keyhole through which Beria, the head of the secret police, was peering. I hope it had nothing to do with his sudden return to his homeland.

11. MAY DAY

ALL OVER MOSCOW THE SCARLET BANNERS and the enormous pictures of Lenin, Stalin, and the Politburo are going up in preparation for the May Day Parade. The whole front of the Historical Museum at the entrance to Red Square is covered with scaffolding, and there is a gigantic frame for the usual full-length picture of Stalin which appears there.

"I wonder whose picture they will put there this year," I said innocently to a chance Russian acquaintance in the Alexandrovsky Gardens.

"*Ekh,* who knows?" was the equally innocent answer. "Maybe it will be mine!"

When I came home from the office I found Alan Little, our Scottish-born, erudite press attaché, and the puckish Tom Ireland, also from the State Department side, sitting pleasantly with Nell over a drink. We lingered in the little room across from the Kremlin until Nell and I were almost late for our dinner party at Edmund Stevens's. He has recently succeeded in getting Nina, his fair-haired wife, back to Russia from Berlin. Though now an American, she is a double Cossack, for her father was a Poltava Cossack and her mother a Ural Cossack. It is remarkable that such people as she would want to put their heads in the lion's mouth again after once being safely out of the country. She wore a light, beautifully embroidered Russian blouse and a very full dark skirt, and was attractive in a light, almost delicate sort of way with the marked slant of her blue eyes to give her an exotic touch.

At dinner I sat between Norah Smith and the earthy, full, handsome Hungarian wife of Navarinni, the Italian First Secretary. Both of my dinner companions were fun, and it is always enjoyable to talk Russian with Mrs. Sohlman, the aristocratic Petersburg-born wife of the Swedish Ambassador. Her Russian is so precise and beautiful that it is a delight to listen to her. The Leningradtsy are still the aristocrats of Great Russia, and to this day the Muscovites have a certain inferiority complex towards them. General Smith was in good form, and it was a merry dinner party.

When we left, the Navarinnis asked if they could follow us, as he was driving his own car and did not know that part of Moscow. I kept an eye on their car to be sure we did not leave them behind. It was fortunate that I did, for I saw them stop. We turned back to find out what was the trouble. They were completely out of gas, so Valodya siphoned a few small tobacco-tins-full from our car, for which they were quite grateful. The difficulties they would have had in finding a telephone and eventually getting gas at that time of night, had we not been with them, would have been unbelievable. Even at two o'clock in the morning the roads were all blocked with troops and equipment practicing for the parade, and we had to take a very roundabout way through the old city, but finally brought them home.

On the way back, we came through Pushkin Square. The fair there has been all done over in spring greens and tender pastel colors. The big cat that at Christmas crept up on the cuckoo clock is gone, and in its place is a revolving circle of fuzzy yellow Easter chickens, with a glowing firebird ready to pounce on them. The Communications Building up Gorky Street looked like Times Square itself, with a flowing fountain of red and emerald lights. We drove through Red Square, which was illuminated with festoons of lights distortedly reflected in the dark, polished marble sides of Lenin's tomb, which is set in a live grove of dark fir trees against the high walls and bizarre gates of the Kremlin.

The May Day Parade was on Saturday, and we did not receive our invitations until the night before. Apparently the unpleasantness connected with the invitations to the American military for the November Parade on Revolution Day was forgotten, so perhaps Washington has given some more thought to the technique of retaliation. All day Friday the red banners and flags were breaking out all over the city and the loud-speakers had begun to broadcast music in the streets.

Traffic for cars in this part of the city was shut off at seven in the morning, but Natasha and Zoya, who have never failed us, were on hand. Zoya had brought Irochka, her lovely and beautifully behaved little niece. We left the house in the hands of Tom Ireland, who had stayed all night with us to avoid early rising, and whoever from Spiro and American House and elsewhere might wish to watch the parade from our balconies, and, taking the slim attractive Eileen Carter with us, walked across to Red Square.

Some time during the night Manezhny Place in front of the Embassy had filled with battery after battery of mechanized guns, their crews strolling back and forth waiting their turn to enter their places in the parade. Many of the battalions wore the blue caps of the MVD, the genuine army of police that exists here side by side with the Red Army itself. One of the sights of the day was the Durbrow child Bruce, out in the middle of the plaza with a big pair of binoculars around his neck, waving an American flag.

Lines of MVD troops were drawn up on foot across the entrance to Red Square, and through each of three separate lines we had to show not only our invitations but our regular diplomatic documents, while the hard-eyed troopers looked at our photographs and then at our faces to be sure that there was no funny business. I left Nell and Eileen in the diplomatic stand near the shining dull-red marble of Lenin's tomb, and went on to my own place in the enclosure for service attachés just beyond the tomb but forward in close proximity to the parade itself.

Serayev and Pasco seemed to go out of their way to be pleasant and cordial with me. Every attaché, as he arrived, was introduced to the eight or ten Russian officers in the enclosure, and then shook hands with all of the other foreign attachés as though he had never seen them before. Duncan Hill and I wore service with white caps, white gloves and dress aiguillettes, but Willy Edenberg, the tall Swede, came in his cocked hat with shiny chin strap and epaulets, and Henrik Madsen, the Dane, also wore his cocked hat, and had his epaulets on his scarlet-collared frock coat. The Russian officers were in their summer parade uniform, which is a long jacket of a peculiar bluish-green color, known to them as "gendarme green," belted with gold, breeches with the stripes of their particular service down the side, and dazzlingly shiny boots. Beside us, away from the tomb, was a larger enclosure crowded with Russian flag officers and general officers, among whom could be seen a marshal or two. The dress uniforms of the Russian naval officers were thick with gold, covered with rows and rows of medals. Taken altogether, that enclosure was on the fat and elderly side, but their faces were generally hard, dignified, and competent.

Everywhere were rigid lines of the MVD, and every half hour throughout the day they were accurately replaced by new lines moving in, with never a word of command to be heard. Over the Kremlin gate behind the tomb was a great old colored stone painting or carving, with wonderful winged, ikonlike angels that could barely be distinguished. I asked Pasco where it was that people — like John Reed and many Russian revolutionary figures — were buried under and even in the Kremlin walls. He took me back and showed me the black and gold markers in the walls behind Lenin's tomb and the graves between Lenin's tomb and the walls themselves.

In front of us were two or three big military bands, displaying their outlandish insignia which come straight from Tatar times — tall standards of heavy brass or silver, hung with long streaming horses' tails which were white or dyed scarlet, and dripping with tiny bells which made strange music as the bands passed by.

And then Stalin and the entire Politburo, with a dozen or so high-ranking military, climbed up to the top of Lenin's tomb. A long line of buglers filed out, sounded a fanfare, and the May Day Parade of the Workers and Their Armed Strength began. It was an impressive show. The military academies and schools, from the little Suvorov lads to the middle-aged staff officers of the Frunze War College, came near the head, followed by all branches of the regular services. Motorized guns of all descriptions, mortars, field pieces, machine guns, antitank guns, big, complicated rocket projectors, huge guns like naval rifles, howitzers, giant mortars, and troops of all sorts moved past with precision. The jowls of the foot troops shook with each stamp of their goose step as they went by.

The naval troops, with fixed bayonets, were particularly smart, and all the Soviet generals and admirals turned to look when the foreign naval attachés clapped and cheered as they came along. There were hundreds and hundreds of paratroopers, who looked

particularly tough and murderous with their sunburned faces outlined by their helmets. When a long line of horse artillery, with
beautiful, prancing, cream-colored horses went by, old long-mustached Budenny on top of the tomb put on his own demonstration of clapping and cheering, for the horses are of course his
favorites.

About three hundred airplanes thundered low overhead, a third
of them jets. And then came the swiftly crawling, lizardlike tanks,
seeming like antediluvian monsters. There was never a man in
sight, for their drivers were hidden somewhere within their bowels.
"Pleasant enough in winter, but plenty hot in summer," said Pasco,
wiping his forehead. Dozens and scores of them rumbled past, of
all varieties, ending up with fifty of the new Josef Stalins, which
all the military attachés say is the best tank the world has yet
produced, with their flattened turrets like big, neckless, reptilian
heads.

I had brought a pair of field glasses — the only ones in sight —
but we were so close to the parade that they were of use only to get
a still closer look at Stalin and the Politburo — Stalin with his
dark pock-marked Georgian face, the heavy, good-natured face
of Beria in animated conversation with the impassive, strange-
looking, deadpan Malenkov in his high-necked worker's blouse,
and the rest of the Soviet power looking like well-dressed civilians,
but with some sort of uncanny conspiratorial touch about most
of them. Or perhaps it was just imagination. They played their
parts well, continually waving and acknowledging cheers, and always on the job. Once or twice Stalin dropped out for a few
minutes for a rest, but soon he was back again, waving and pointing emphatically to some slogan or emblem in the parade that
particularly pleased him.

The "popular demonstration," or civilian part of the parade that
followed the military portion, was essentially monotonous throughout, but infinite in its variations. Somewhere between one and
two million people took part in it, channeled between MVD troops
in four parallel columns, each column surging fifteen or eighteen
abreast, filling the broad Red Square to the brim, shouting and
cheering, sweating and smiling, with no pretense to any military
order but always moving and flowing like a great river — the

representatives of factories, bureaus, institutions, trades. As far as one could see in both directions, hour after hour, was a great sea of scarlet flags, banners, big portraits of Lenin, Marx, Stalin and the Politburo, slogans of Russian words white against red backgrounds, emblems, hand-borne floats, fantastic spiral streamers, and sprays of paper flowers that at times made the place seem like a spring orchard of dogwood trees or cherry blossoms. Many of the flowers, emblems and floats were cheap and crude, but the mass effect was overwhelming.

There was almost a total absence of acid slogans and posters, for a change. For some reason the whole tone of this May Day celebration was not provocative, even to the speech which preceded it. Is it possible that, as a result of a whole string of events such as the Marshall Plan, our firmness in Berlin, and the Italian elections, they have started to take their classical step back after their two long steps forward?

From the walls of the Kremlin came great voices over the loud speakers — "Glory to our great Stalin! *Slava! Ur-r-r-rah!*" And the crowds marching past in the square would shout *"Slava! Ur-r-r-rah!"* and beam and smile. Sometimes there would be a sea of upraised, clapping hands, little and big. Every conceivable person and acceptable idea was cheered and echoed by the great voices and the great crowd, until the catechizing voices would grow hoarse and would be replaced with other great voices. There were many pictures of famous Stakhanovites carried aloft, and once the man who was carrying the picture was the man himself, unmistakable from his portrait above, grinning at the stands. Loud speakers blared music, and people among the marchers played on their accordions.

Sometimes there would be groups of people in national costumes — colorful, kerchiefed Byelorussians or Ukrainians. They would catch my eye as they went past, close aboard, and I would clap all by myself, to have them bow and laugh and wave acknowledgment and afterwards to go dancing off. Uniformed groups from the sports clubs went past, with effective sweater girls — and a Russian girl in a sweater can indeed be most effective. And everywhere in the parade were small children, carried on the shoulders of their sweating fathers, standing high above the colorful, stream-

ing crowd, often with little skirts spread out over father's bald
head to protect him from the May sun. They were all so thrilled
and delighted to have seen Stalin, to have had him wave at them
personally, that they fairly beamed as they passed us, looking
curiously at the strange uniforms and the great mass of generals,
and shouting "Glory to our Red Army!" — at which the generals
would smile dignifiedly, and themselves wave back. And always,
high overhead, were small colored balloons, adrift from somewhere
in the watching or marching multitude.

Now, as many foreigners believe, this may have been all a
planned, staged, perhaps forced demonstration. It is true that it
was not "spontaneous," in that it *was* planned and staged, and
not prepared on the spur of the moment, but it is doubtful if
much of it was "forced," except insofar as no important organization or factory would dare to boycott participation. It is the only
chance that most of the people ever have to see the living great
of Russia. They cannot even see the parade without participating
in it, for that part of Moscow where it takes place is closed by
the police to all but invited guests, and the parade breaks up after
passing through Red Square. We were so close to the marchers that
I could have reached out and touched them, and there was no
doubt from the hundreds of thousands of faces that went by that
they were thoroughly enjoying it all. They were a part in a great
show — actors before Stalin himself.

Through the stands went white-jacketed women with big baskets, selling fruit and soft drinks, ice cream and such. After a
few hours, many of the old generals grew a bit tired, and dropped
back into the stands to rest their feet. Every foreign attaché except
those from the satellite countries, the Finns and me, left almost
immediately after the military part was over. I was determined to
stick it out to the end, and although there was no place for me
to sit down and I grew wearier than for many a month, there
was a reason for staying. Not only was I genuinely interested in
aspects of Russia other than the military ones but it seemed desirable that the Russians should know that this was so.

When at last the Red Square was empty, except for the long
rigid bordering lines of MVD, a civilian massed band of a thousand
pieces, closely packed at one end of the Square, went by. They

were followed by a thick forest of tall red banners, and it was all over. Stalin and the power came down the marble steps from the top of Lenin's tomb, disappeared within it — perhaps to commune with Lenin, but more probably because there may be an underground way from it to within the Kremlin — and I picked my way wearily back to Mokhavaya House. Nellie saw me limping across the plaza, and was down on the street to meet me, good as gold. The dispatch that was sent to Washington said: STALIN AND STEVENS STUCK OUT SIX HOUR PARADE UNTIL END FORMER APPEARING HEARTY AND UNTIRED.

After a belated lunch and a drink, I took the weight off my weary feet — it was nearly five o'clock by then — to be awakened in the evening by the blare of the loud-speakers and the noise of the crowds in the plaza below. It was dark, and only the ruby stars shone over the Kremlin, trimming themselves into the wind. Red Square itself was lit to a bluish white by searchlights turned on the milling crowd, and the Head Place looked like a distant crimson fountain with its close-packed mass of rippling red flags, bordered with great urns of paper flowers.

At the end of the plaza towards the Tsar's riding hall had been built an open-air red-draped stage, and Manezhny Place was packed thick with people watching the show. An act was under way with what seems to be a standard Russian comic type — a booted man in conventional clothes except for a long Russian shirt that hangs well below his coat and waistcoat. It may be a peasant type from somewhere in the southwest. I have seen the type at the Gypsy Theater and elsewhere in Moscow, and it is always a rather loutish young chap with a heavy watch chain, a sort of Russian version of the zoot-suiter. In the packed and surging crowds around the stage, the white hats of sailors and the blue hats of the MVD made mosaics of pattern.

And then, suddenly, began the glorious Russian fireworks. The display was short, however, and the Kremlin was dark, not picked out with strings of lights as it was at the time of Moscow's eight hundredth anniversary. Nor were the crowds as great as then, but this May Day was still what the papers said it was, a *narodnoye gulyaniye* — a walking about of the people.

12. CHRIST IS RISEN

ALTHOUGH MY FEET WERE STILL TIRED and Nellie was too
weary to stir, Tom Ireland and I drove out to Novodevichi Monastery about ten thirty in the evening. Not only was it May Day,
but it was also the eve of *Paskha,* Easter Sunday. There were many
people on the streets, but there was no difficulty in getting through
the crowds when we were once clear of Manezhny Place.

We left Valodya outside with the car and walked through a
long, deep arch straight through a great wall like that of the
Kremlin, with the same sort of cleft crenelations with archers'
slits in each tooth, and out in the soft spring darkness into the
enormous inner enclosure, covered with scattered buildings, tall
domed churches, and big, tree-studded, grassy places. Inside the
walls, against them and even forming a part of them, were populous houses with all their windows alight, and the tops of the
savage walls and their massive towers were jagged and dark against
the night sky.

Everywhere were groups of people, sitting on the grass or strolling about. There were crowds around open-air counters where
one could buy thin candles, or around long tables covered with
kulichi, or Easter cakes — Natasha had baked one for Nell and
me, one for Valodya, and one for herself — studded with burning
candles, being blessed and sprinkled with holy water every now
and then by a passing priest. Everywhere were kerchiefed women,
piously crossing themselves, mysterious in the darkness.

The Easter mass begins at midnight, so it was still early, and
we had little difficulty in making our way into the *Khram,* or main
church, which was lighted and in use this Easter Eve. Once inside, we went up a couple of broad flights of steps to the level of
the nave. On both sides of the steps, in the window embrasures,
everywhere except in the very middle of the stairs, were patient
crowds of people, sitting or lying. Many were sleeping. And everywhere the kerchiefed women. Pale young acolytes, with long, flowing brown beards, went softly through the crowds.

We passed into the nave through a big archway, between twisted columns covered with clusters of grapes in high relief. It was packed and jammed with people, most of them poorly dressed, many of them in rags, but with a good sprinkling of rather well-dressed ones among them. There was even an occasional army or navy officer. And everywhere, the kerchiefs and the crossing one-self and the quick bobbing of respect. The church was completely bare of impeding pews so that the people stood so close they could scarcely move, but through the center of the dense crowd was a twisting line of bodies elbowing their way to and from the altar. We joined in the twisting line, and soon, with no effort on our part since we were being pushed from behind, we were in front of the very altar. It was lit with lamps and enormous candles, and about it were priests in brocaded robes going to and fro on their mysterious business. Back of the altar was a great ikon screen, thickly set with ikons, and on the wall to one side was a flat picture of the Crucifixion, garlanded with flowers, and with Christ draped in actual garments. We listened to the drone of the priests and the low conversation of the multitude for a while, and then wormed our way back out.

The air was heavy with so many people, and it was not easy to breathe. Just as we came down the flights of steps to leave the Khram, one of the youthful, bearded attendants, with ample help from the bystanders, was busy forcing the doors shut against the gathering crowd outside, so we had to stay. Not a window was open, and the air was drowsy. Now and then the sleeping crowds on the stairs stirred and moved. The crowd outside began to knock on the door, and then thundered against it for admission. The pale, bearded young acolyte brought some heavy braces and shored the doors against the assault of the multitude seeking to get in.

"It's impossible!" he shouted to them through the heavy door. "The Khram is already too crowded. You can't come in." But still they knocked and thundered at the door.

Low singing began from behind the altar, and we drifted back into the nave, watching the thick crowds of people, many of them with lighted candles in their hands, and all of them acting very naturally and at home, talking freely among themselves, but con-tinually interrupting their talk to cross themselves. At last the pale attendant, who reminded me of the pictures of Rasputin, opened the door, because a sufficient crowd of those who wished to leave had gathered. We were swept out with the crowd into the densely packed mass outside, in the soft, clean, sweet night air.

We worked ourselves free from the crowd and strolled around the grounds, wondering at the strange Byzantine arches of the churches which seemed to have no architectural plan, and looking at the bulbous domes outlined against the sky. Once we found ourselves between a long line of soft-voiced seekers for alms. Remembering our own earlier Easter, I had brought a whole pocketful of ruble notes, and left a long string of blessings following me in the darkness.

We wandered to the deep arch through which we had entered the monastery — and there discovered that we could scarcely get out. Through the arch was swiftly pouring a regular river of people, hurrying, hurrying for the midnight mass. It was such an urgent, incessant stream that we paused and watched in sheer wonder. The Khram was already jammed to the doors, and outside it was a great crowd, but here were thousands upon thousands, still pouring in through the big arch. We stood in an embrasure in the wall in which, on a floor littered with straw, was a strange combination of a muzzle-loading cannon and a khaki-colored motor truck, and watched. And always the crowd poured in, hurrying, hurrying, shoulder to shoulder, tens of thousands of them. Occasionally I saw a man who was obviously drunk, but in every such case he was accompanied by an old mother or a woman of some sort who urged him along, and although drunk he always seemed to be trying obediently, only to stagger off in the darkness — probably the results of the May Day holiday rather than of the approaching Easter.

I asked a waiting woman why so many people kept pouring in, when there were more people there already than could possibly get near the Khram. Simultaneously with my words came the realization that it was a foolish question, requiring a complicated answer from anyone, let alone a strange woman in a land like Russia, where the Church is still openly attacked in the Komsomol and Party papers and exists only on dubious sufferance. And still the tens of thousands kept crowding in.

It is certainly true that religion is not dead in Russia. The Orthodox Church, which was useful during the war, has made many public statements of subservient agreement to the Bolshevik regime, which must be the only way by which it can continue to exist. Yet only the other day one of the dignitaries of the Church was reported in the Soviet-controlled press, without adverse comment, as saying that although the Church could not agree with the materialistic philosophy that underlies communism, it was still in agreement with the practical results. Never in the past has the Party brooked any sort of competition, and it would be surprising indeed if they would really permit any competition of thought at the very roots of their philosophy. As Tom said, at least we are not apt to see any new churches built with public funds under the Five Year Plans.

There was no slackening of the tide of people. Suddenly a great bell began to boom from the tall, fantastic, separate bell tower. It was a beautiful bell, deep and rich, and it boomed and rolled, not slowly, like a toll, but like a great drum. Then it was joined with other bells, high but sweet. They were not tuned, at least not to any of our intervals, but somehow they all blended strangely, with the wild high bells, which must have come straight out of Tartary, chiming against that rich, booming background. The midnight Easter mass had begun.

We drifted back towards the Khram, over some old, grassy graves and between dark and mournful monuments until we could look out over the great multitude. From the Khram came liturgic singing, and through the crowd twinkled the lights of thousands and thousands of candles, carefully shielded with bits of paper by all who carried them.

And then we suddenly realized that there was just as strong and wide a current of people hurrying away as that which had brought them all in. We let ourselves be carried out through the arch by the ebbing tide, and found Valodya in the car, asleep as usual. When we had waked him, the car wouldn't start. With a dozen willing Russians to help us, we pushed it through the crowd until the engine took, and then came home through thicker and thicker crowds until we finally reached the Embassy.

. . .

This morning, when I awoke, the streets were washed and swept as clean as if there had been no millions of people crowding them the night before. At each plate at breakfast was an Easter egg, dyed purple or red. Eggs have come down now, to forty cents each, our money. We ate our *kulichi,* and I told Natasha about the Novodevichi Monastery of the night before.

"And did the priests, in all their robes, go around through the crowds and bless the people, and say 'Christ is risen'?" she asked. "Perhaps not. Many things change through the years. But oh, Gospodin Admiral, you should have been here in the old days, and seen the priest go down into the Moskva River to baptize the ikons! He would dip them right into the river, and then a dove would fly down from the sky!"

In the afternoon we drove slowly through the city, studded everywhere with red flags, out to Sokolniki Park, where there is another Easter fair like that in Pushkin Square, with little fairy-tale booths where things are sold — by the state — all decorated in spring colors with figures of butterflies and little *skazka* beast-ies. There is a big church at Sokolniki, with part of its brickwork colored a deep blue, and with a central dome of gold, around which clusters a group of slender domes of dove-colored porcelain. It was a beautiful warm Easter Sunday, and the streets were crowded with people, already without topcoats. In the sky were big fleecy summer clouds, thickening up here and there to spring showers.

Women were wearing brightly colored print dresses, and it seemed to me that I have never seen such short skirts. They were usually well above the knee. But then, perhaps the skirts are really not so short, for most of the women fill them up so completely that there isn't much of the skirts left to hang down. The spring breeze whipped them around their long legs, but most of the girls managed to remain quite modest, because of their long brown cotton or rayon stockings and their dark little bloomers beneath their skirts.

We drove back through Kirov Street, which, except for the extraordinarily wide boulevards, is the stateliest street in Moscow. It is lined with buildings that look more like Europe than most of Moscow, and was hung with red flags, singly and in effective, clustered masses. Then we went past the Kremlin and along the river, past the Mongolian Embassy with its exterior of fantastic colored tile, over the Krimsky Most or Crimean Bridge to the Gorky Park of Culture and Rest. Everywhere were crowds of people, who had suddenly burst forth in bright colors, and women selling balloons from great colored bundles of purple and red.

When we came home, there was a tremendous throng in Manezhny Place outside the Embassy, crowded around the open-air stage, but they were soon driven to cover by a quick shower. Then the sun came out again, and the endless show went on with its singers, dancers, boxers, actors, wrestlers and bands. Big trucks were pulled up in the plaza, from which were sold ice cream and things to eat. There were occasional little groups of people in provincial costumes, with bright kerchiefs on the women's heads, and everywhere in the crowds were little and big groups dancing in the streets. More often than not, girls danced with girls, and boys with boys. But I think this means nothing here, other than a general shyness and awkwardness. Most of them are nice kids, even if they sometimes are strange-looking. At times the crowd would make space for someone who felt like doing some solo dancing, and would watch gravely, whether or not the dancing was well done.

Outside it is now night. The loud-speakers still play their music and the show still goes on on the outdoor stage. The crowds fill the great plazas and squares, and red and blue colored army search-lights play back and forth across them. All the sounds of the crowds come up like the roar of the sea. The whole side of the Moscow Hotel across Gorky Street is covered with moving electric lights, making bubbling fountains and the semblance of rockets that always rise and burst and rise again. Too much to see, too much to do. But a dispatch came in from Berlin today, saying that Dreher arrived there safely, with no customs examination at all in Minsk. And still no propaganda publicity in the Moscow papers. Strange people — and yet sometimes it seems that they can be figured out. The Kremlin plays its hand very carefully, and very thoughtfully.

Next morning there were some more hard-boiled Easter eggs for breakfast, hand-painted by Natasha's grown daughter, with flowers and "*Khristos voskres!*" (Christ is risen!). She is married to a sculptor, and consequently well off, by Soviet standards. Natasha is always turning out some new Russian dish, and today she produced *pilmeni*, little dumplings stuffed with meat. They looked exactly like a dish of oysters, but were quite good.

Zoya had gotten herself a permanent wave for the May Day *prazdnik*, and her hair is still frizzy and tight. Her husband works in a big factory, and she was very proud of the fact that he had been among those selected to take part in the parade. She herself, although she has lived all her life in Moscow, has never laid eyes on Stalin.

A Russian woman told me that when she came home from the *prazdnik* late at night, the stairways of her apartment house were littered with citizens who had had a drop too much, and couldn't quite make the grade all the way home.

"All men in decent black!" she said.

Valodya has been wearing his new neat blue uniform. He looks much smaller and frailer and thinner now that all his bulky khaki and windproofs are put away. This evening, while driving through Pushkin Square on our way to a movie, he suddenly slowed down and shouted to a very small little girl standing in the edge of the street, "You ought not to try to cross the street alone!"

The fat little thing shouted something back which I couldn't hear. Valodya stopped the car dead in the middle of the traffic, got out, took the child by the hand, and led her all the way across the wide pavement to the other side. When he got back in the car, he said, "She had run away from home and was all alone! It was necessary to help her."

The lobby of this movie theater, the Forum, had large portraits of Lenin and Stalin, but they were better done than any I remember having seen before. They were on canvas, and appeared to be done with separate strokes of a fine brush with a technique almost like pen and ink, but in colors, and the effect was extraordinarily good. The eyes were particularly soft and vivid, and when examined closely there seemed to be a sort of bubble superimposed on the pupils.

While waiting for the movie to begin, Nell and I went to one of the rooms for waiting people. There a big soprano was singing, and when she was finished the master of ceremonies announced a new invention — the electric piano, which could play in the fashion of any instrument. And it could, very well indeed. We heard it play a most realistic violin with piano accompaniment, and a clarinet and piano arrangement. It was definitely not an organ, and although I think there may be something of the sort in America, it would have to be good to compare with this one.

Last night we went to MXAT's Filial, and saw Ostrovsky's *Talents and Admirers.* This year is some sort of anniversary of Ostrovsky, I think the hundred and twenty-fifth anniversary of his birth, and, although there is soon to be a special week for him in all the theaters, he probably has been played more extensively than usual as a result. Ostrovsky is not as well known outside Russia as he should be, but here I have seen a half dozen or more of his plays and have just finished reading his *Thunderstorm.* His characterizations are marvelous, and marvelously played here, his plots are complicated and ingenious, and he combines much humor with tenderness and tragedy, sometimes getting some exciting dramatic effects.

The social significance of Ostrovsky's plays is noticeable when one sees them in Soviet Russia, for one of his favorite themes is the effect of money, and the wanting of money, on people. Ostrovsky's contemporary, Dobrolyubov, in his two long essays on the *Kingdom of Darkness,* points out the deep Russian universality of his work. The rich merchant class in the provinces, the minor nobility, and the *chinovniks,* those numerous uniformed assistants and petty officials, governmental and private, that are swarming over Russia even today, give him his backgrounds. His drunken people are always extremely well done and amusing, and they usually abound in his plays. In this play, one pair of them wandered throughout all the action — an old tragedian who had outlived his days on the stage, and a wealthy young chap. Their companionship lay in their regard for nobility of character and of talent, always with another bottle of champagne to drink to its manifestations.

Tarasova, regarded as one of the great actresses of Russia, played the lead. She is a fine, competent actress, with a great deal of character. But the play was to me particularly delightful because the two people I like best of all on the Russian stage were also in the cast — Androvskaya, who can be so aristocratically immoral, so fashionable, exquisite and femininely earthy, and Ershov, so big, so dignified, so perfectly stylized and finished in every gesture and intonation. He played the part of a very wealthy man, but wore one of the little military-type caps which one still sees in Russia on an occasional civilian. The play ended up rather indefinitely, more like one of Chekhov's than the usual closely-knit Ostrovsky. Considering the rich volume of Ostrovsky's work and the diversity of genuine character that he gets so economically, he seems to me to be a very great playwright who has been neglected in the West.

We walked home down Pushkin Street to Sverdlovsk Square, and then along Okhotny Row to Mokhavaya, behind some buxom girls who were out strolling with their sailor boys. The Russian sailors are good-looking lads, big, strong, and bold. They have a great tradition of shore fighting behind them, from Sevastopol in the Crimean War to the later revolutions, the *Aurora,* the relief of Moscow, and the Black Sea, Leningrad, and Baltic actions of the Great Fatherland War. Their wide-bottomed trousers, their buckled belts, their blue-and-white striped shirts under their jumpers, and the long ribbons streaming from their flat hats set them off well.

Here and there we saw someone in a Russian blouse without a coat, sometimes the true Russian *kosovorotka* which buttons up the side and sometimes the Ukrainian type which buttons normally up the front, but both always edged with embroidery. The trees that were planted along the way last fall are beginning to bud out with new green, and there is not one dead one among them.

Natasha's one remaining tooth has to be pulled. "I'm very much afraid," she said. "I don't like it at all. I'm afraid of what the tooth-doctor will do."

"Why, Natasha," I said, "you're as bad as Valodya. Once when I was fishing on the Moskva River, I caught a frog and asked him to hold it for me while I found a hook for it. Valodya was scared to death of it. He said that he wasn't afraid of Germans in the war, but that he was very much scared of mice, worms, and particularly frogs."

"I don't mind mice, but I, too, am very much afraid of frogs—and tooth-doctors."

Now perhaps here is a discovery. Never in my life have I seen an American, man or woman, who was afraid of frogs. Perhaps spiders, worms, and all sorts of creeping and crawling things, but never frogs. And yet here are two Russians in my household who view them with horror. I'll have to think that one over, and see if I can find out what it is in the dark history of the Slavs that causes that particular peculiarity.

Today there were little white puffs of summer cloud floating in the blue sky. The skies of Russia are in actual fact different from those in England or America or elsewhere in the world, just as the skies of the Western Pacific are different from those of Honolulu. For one thing, the sky is not as blue in Russia as it is elsewhere. There is an unusual wideness to it, and the clouds seem lower. It seldom has much color, and its sunsets are more on the diffused Turner type, with the colors, however, concentrated into smaller, harder spots.

Recently, the tender blue of American skies after a spring rain has been coming before my eyes, or the gray clouds shoaling out from the sides of the Blue Ridge. And sudden waves of a sort of homesickness come over me for all the loveliness of those mountains, and for the breath of the wild honeysuckle and the sound of rain in the Shenandoah Valley. Lurid evenings after rain—wisps of fog at night. And here, in Moscow, the background of mood and atmosphere that comes from weather does not seem to exist. Things are either flat and dull, like a Whistler nocturne, or they have a sort of commonplace disorder. After these remarks, there will probably be a really spectacular sunset soon.

I suppose it was because of this half-dissatisfied mood that the following came out:

> *I am lord of a marvelous town,*
> *Moated and walled and strong,*
> *With gabled roofs that go sloping down*
> *And spires that rise like a song.*

Lord of the seasons and sun and rain,
I call them forth at will,
And bid the hawthorn blossom again,
Or say to the wind, Be still!

I spread the fields with covers of snow,
And veil the walls with mist,
I watch the people come and go,
But cause what I wish to exist.

Tonight we went to the ballet at the Stanislavsky — *Doctor Aibolit,* which has just won one of the season's Stalin Prizes. I read about it in *Ogonyok,* the Soviet illustrated magazine, in an article which made me want to see it. The ballet is for children, and so began at six o'clock.

The Stanislavsky Theater is of the modern Soviet design, with the back part of the house sloping upwards, and a shallow balcony, set rather far back. The huge curtain was of dark velvet, and the chairs were covered with the same material, making them look soft, although in actual fact they were as hard as the chairs in most Moscow theaters. Overhead is a glory of a chandelier, just a limpid cluster of dripping crystal, with almost no brass or other structure showing. Moscow's chandeliers are among the beautiful sights of the world, with those of Spasso House leading them all.

Nearly half of the audience were children, all dressed up and on their very best behavior. And how these Russians love their children! In the May Day Parade, when so many hot, sweating fathers, carrying the children on their shoulders, would have begun to be tired and irritated anywhere else, more than one reached up to pull a little face down to be kissed.

The ballet was an enchantment, with settings and costumes that were out of this world. It was one of Chukovsky's fairy tales, about an old doctor who cures all the beasts and birds of the vicinity, and who goes to the tropics because word has come that the monkeys there are ailing, leaving his place to the tender mercies of a wicked housekeeper and a flashy animal trainer. Monkeys, alligators, dogs, cats, elephants, giraffes, a stork, bear, cat, owl, swallow, lynx — all sorts of birds and beasts, with two lovely white rabbits, danced and cavorted. For some reason, a woman's face, when cowled closely, is always much purer and lovelier than with any other arrangement of costume. Perhaps it seems so because of associations with nuns, sisters, or Madonnas, but there is also something else for which I have not found words. And every dance step and every gesture was delightfully and wonderfully in character.

There was a marvelous rooster, who strutted and acted thoroughly as a rooster should act, and a pretty, slant-eyed, bushy-tailed fox whom any man could love. The bear was bumbling and stupid, but goodhearted, which is conventional for Russian bears. The monkeys were amusingly random, filling the stage with byplay like a three-ringed circus, even when the leading dancer was doing her solo. One ceased to think of them as people, they were so much the way *skazka* animals should be. And when the band of robbers came snarling in with their big daggers for melodrama, a beautiful curly-haired child next to me buried his head in his father's coat and refused to look, while children all over the house ran to cover.

PART IV. SUMMER HEAT

1. A FISH·FOR NELL

I TOLD AMBASSADOR SMITH that I was going up to the Volga swamps again. "You're a bear for punishment," he said. "Tell your people to stay at home while you are gone, and not to put their noses out of their quarters. I'll shoot the next person who gets in trouble!" And he laughed.

By the time I got all my gear together, Nell said, "You take more things when you go anywhere than anyone I know, and I think you just do it to impress people." Even at that, necessary things are always left behind. In the back seat of the weapons-carrier with all the gear rode Bruce Sabin, my thin-faced, slight Chief Electrician's Mate who is known to the Russians as "Gospodin Elektrik," and Ilyin, a big, square-chinned, strong-faced Russian who works in the commissary. Although it is much more desirable to be alone when going among the Russians, the weapons-carrier was the only transportation that could hope to travel off the main roads, and I did not have the heart to refuse their wistful hopes that they might be taken along. Ilyin was still grateful to Nell for some spectacles she had given him months before, when she found him wearing a pair with one lens gone, tied over one ear with string.

The grass was very green in the countryside, the pussy willows had fluffed out into polleny flower, and all the trees were beginning to burst into green. It was warm and pleasant that first day. Most of the women were now barefoot, padding down the roads carrying their burdens or hauling them on little platforms on tiny rollers smaller than the wheels on roller skates, or scrubbing clothes in the ponds and streams. In the canal were some grown boys, swimming naked, but, as Valodya said, boys will swim while the ice is still floating, if you let them.

Once we passed a train, with its green locomotive running on bright red wheels. The most foreign thing about European trains is the open wheels on the coaches. When silhouetted against the sky, those wheels, together with the shortness of the wagons, make the trains look like toys. Where we turned off the hard road, there were now great heaps of boards, thrown off the trains in disorder like jackstraws and doubtless just as hard to untangle, and long rows of piled-up white tile, all for some new construction job. The material was guarded by soldiers with needlelike bayonets on their guns, and the scene was swarming with women who were doing all the work.

The road into Glini had dried out considerably, although it could never be passed by cars with normal road clearance, and we were stalled only briefly before we reached the village. Ephrosinya Vladimirovna and Pavel Dmitrovich seemed glad to see us. No, no other foreigners had ever been there, nor had they heard of any others who were coming.

As the sun was setting, Fyodr Petrovich showed up, and we took our guns and started out. As we passed Fyodr's house, Mariya, his handsome brown daughter, came out to say hello, all dressed up in a dark red silk blouse and skirt. The calm self-possession of these Russian peasants is remarkable. They are neither shy nor forward, but reserved, calm and dignified.

We left the car and walked down into the edge of a swamp, where Fyodr called for ducks for some time. None appeared, but as we started away for the higher ground and clearings where the evening flight of the *waldshnaip* takes place, something rustled through the trees. Before I could see what it was, Sabin had fired twice and a nice little teal hurtled slantwise down to the ground. Then we separated for the *tyaga,* Fyodr going with me. As the shadows gathered, it started to grow cold. All around were thick dark trees, with only an occasional birch to lighten them. The hemlocks drooped their branches sadly, as though they were hung thick with drowned seaweed, but through their tops burned the evening star, as bright as a tiny moon.

At last Fyodr came up and started to gather some dry bark and moss with which to start a fire. "The birds like it when the smoke goes up in a straight column," he said, but just why they should like it was never clear. At any rate, I liked it, although the whole seat out of my trousers split while helping with the fire. A moment later, there was a sudden pang — my Navy class ring was gone. It is strange how immediately one notices the absence of something that is so familiar one is seldom conscious of it, and it was evident that it must have slipped off while I was breaking some branches. We had hunted for it only a minute or two in the gathering darkness when Fyodr stepped on it, giving it to me with a wide, snaggle-toothed grin. When I told him what it was, how Nell had worked in a store for enough money to get it for me, how it was useful in cashing checks all over the world, and how much I valued it, I am sure he expected at least a new gun as a reward for having found it. He got a package of cigarettes on account.

We waited until it was dark. Somewhere not far away a cuckoo was calling loudly, and all around was the noise of birds, chirping, singing and whistling. But never a *waldshnaip* did we see, although once there was the ghostly croaking of one not far away. At last we walked back to join the others, with the puddles in the trail reflecting the pale ashes-of-roses of the sky.

When we got home, there were no lights. The local power station had had a transformer failure. The station was in the hostile-seeming village on the edge of the great peat bog, and was what I had thought before to be some sort of small factory. We put a candle in an empty bottle, but it seemed to be the only candle in the house. Supper was a confused affair, because no one knew exactly where even their bags were, let alone what might be in them. The bottle of gin on which I stumbled while groping in the darkness did little to clear up the confusion.

It was nearly midnight before we got to sleep, and we were up again at two thirty, Fyodr rapping on the windows to tell us it was high time. It seemed almost as cold as it had been when I was there before, but at least there was no ice this time, and the roads were sufficiently dry for Valodya to take us through the strange village and to the verge of the peat bog, where we left him mired in the mud while we continued on foot.

All the way, although the sky was lightening, it had been black enough for the headlights to show brilliantly, but by now there was enough steely light for us to pick our way easily between the little peat lakes. Ilyin had stayed comfortably and sensibly in bed. We left Sabin in my old *shalash,* and I went on, finally stopping in a broad ditch covered on all sides by a thick growth of white birches. But again our decoys were silent, doing nothing but eat. Fyodr could be heard calling skillfully off to one side, and once or twice a duck answered from somewhere, but not a word out of our two hungry mallards.

After the sun was well up we went back to the car. Valodya had extricated himself from the bog, turned the car around, and gone to sleep, wrapped up in a blanket. As we bumped home along the country roads, we passed herds of cattle being driven to pasture. Trailing from the shoulder of every cowherd was a terrible *bich,* a thirty-foot blacksnake whip, braided from rope and leather, as thick as your arm at one end. Goats, cattle, horses, all were herded with it. Still cold, Sabin and I went straight to bed when we got home, but first Ephrosinya took my trousers to stitch up on her machine. In spite of all the luggage, there was not one spare pair of trousers, although plenty of everything else.

When I finally wakened in the early afternoon, Ilyin was quite disconsolate. He had left his rod on the river's edge for a while and had returned to find it gone. There is no doubt that the Russians are a thievish lot where anyone other than their own household is concerned. The last time we were here, a spare can of oil was stolen from the car, and a shovel, which jolted out on the way, disappeared before we could get back to pick it up. They have so little, and what they have is so primitive, that the minor belongings of someone from outside must create a great temptation. Also it is apparent from the precautions they themselves take that they steal between villages, and sometimes even between households.

In the latter part of the afternoon, Valodya drove Fyodr and me down to the dam. "See, I'm going to try some spinning myself!" said Fyodr, proudly showing me his rod. It was a thick, long pole, cut from the branch of a tree, with a few gentle bends in it and a couple of rings for guides to a line the thickness of a small clothesline. The reel was made from a couple of big plywood disks, turning in a brass bushing on an iron pin. All of it he had made himself. It took two hands to swing it, but Fyodr could cast with it almost as far as one could with my light gear. No one was catching any fish. We blamed it on the chilly wind.

Towards sunset, Valodya, still sleepy-eyed from his pleasant sojourn on the stove, came and got us. We picked up Sabin and Ilyin, and went on to still another place on *tyaga.* Here there were more birches than firs, the tops of the birches a rosy gold in the last rays of the sun. We built our fire early, for it was quite cold. As it darkened, the birches seemed like light shadows against the few heavy firs, and their tops made a marvelous lacy pattern against the sky, like tapered strips of Milan lace, or like the dark tracery of little trefoils on the silvery skin of a Canadian lake trout. And, like the pattern on the fish, this delicate tracery soon faded to darkness. But for a time it seemed like the work of a skillful etcher who had paid heed to the old belief that every dark area should have in it a pattern of light, and every light area should have in it a pattern of black.

I wandered off on the edge of the big bush-covered glade, and finally came to the skeleton frame of some sort of shed, made from young birch trees, and wondered at it. Soon I heard the whispering croak of a *waldshnaip,* shot, and missed. Then another, and another miss. Fyodr came up.

"Fyodr Petrich, this is a strange sort of shed."

"Strange? Why?"

"But look! Everywhere at its base, it is all burned. The grass and the moss under it is burned, but only in a thin line, exactly outlining its shape. And the frame is all dry, and plaited here and there with old thatch and dry straw which catch fire easily, yet it is charred only for an inch or so at the very bottom. How could that have happened? And what were they trying to do?"

"I don't know. But why do you think that it is strange?"

I'm not sure that I myself knew why it seemed so queer to me, and was still trying to put it into words when there came the ghostly overhead croaking. I swung my gun up, and the black bird was directly overhead. I almost fell over backwards, turned, and fired. "Got him!" I said, as the *waldshnaip* dropped like a stone. But ten feet off the ground, in front of our very eyes, he suddenly stopped dropping and fluttered heavily off at a shallow angle into the thick woods. It was hopeless even to try to find him.

While we were warming ourselves over the embers of our fire in the sweet-smelling smoke, I said, "Fyodr Petrich, there seemed to me to be something strange about that village where the electric power station is."

"Yes, it is a strange village," he replied, rather unexpectedly.

"Why?" I asked.

"It's because the people there are mostly Chuvashi. There weren't enough people in these parts, and the Chuvashi came here from the east for wages. They don't like it here, so they keep to themselves, and we keep to ourselves too."

At least that is one mystery settled. The Chuvashi are one of the aboriginal peoples that were here before the Russians, and, although nominally Christians, in actual fact are said not to be, but to still hold to their ancient pagan worship.

When we joined the others, we found that Ilyin too had shot a bird which he couldn't find. But Gospodin Elektrik met us with a soft brownish-black, long-beaked *waldshnaip* in his hand and two more teal in his pockets.

When we were home for supper, we found Aleksei Mikhailovich there, arrived with three horses for the estate. He had tried to bring a boat, but had left it bogged somewhere in the road. He and Valodya slept in the hay of the lean-to where the animals were housed, and the rest of us were soon dead to the world under thick green blankets.

Having decided that the duck shooting was so thin and freakish that one place was as good as another, we avoided the long drive in the early morning to the great peat bog and went to a nearby swamp instead, just as the cold light was beginning to come over the green fields. It was beautifully still and calm, and the river was covered with thick white mist, as though a long, twisting cloud had dropped on it during the night and had not yet gone away. It was cold, but there was not a breath of wind to bite and burn. The others disappeared into the swamp, and I stood in the shelter of a *shalash* and watched the very tips of the tall birches begin to glow with the first light of the sun.

This time, my female mallard couldn't find too much to eat, so she began to talk. I couldn't help but think of the cynicism involved in the way such decoys act. Wild animals and birds are not dumb — they are amazingly astute and clever in so many ways. And surely that wild duck must have known, in some dim fashion, that for her own selfish ends she was calling one of her own kind to death. Ilyin had told me that one of the greatest insults that one could give a Russian was to call him a *chuchelo* — a stuffed animal or bird. Possibly the word has a more vivid connotation to the Russian than to other Europeans. Such thoughts were so heavy on me that when a big, beautiful male mallard suddenly slanted down, I didn't care much whether I shot him or not — at least at that moment. He cupped his wings to brake himself, wheeled, and circled out of there, and it wasn't until Gospodin Elektrik showed up with a lovely mallard and still another teal that I was sorry.

The thick white frost was all gone and the fog no longer clinging to the river when we got back, so I pulled on my boots, hurried in the car down to the dam and started to fish alone. At one of the *lyulki* was an old man with a long white beard who might have stepped right out of Tolstoy or Ostrovsky. He wore a tattered black astrakhan cap, and his long overcoat was completely and unbelievably made up of nothing but patches. And he talked with the half-whining, ingratiating peasant accent, slowly, and lingering over the stressed syllables. I offered him a cigarette, but he used only snuff. He was delighted to find that some people in America used snuff too. His favorite word was *chudyesny* — miraculous. "*Chudyesny* world," he said. "Every people has its own customs, and yet many of them are the same. *Chudyesno!*"

I showed him the lure I was using, the little wires that kept the hook from becoming entangled in the weeds, the spinner and the swivel that kept the whole lure from twisting in the water, and the bit of wire leader that kept sharp teeth from cutting the line. "*Chudyesnaya mashina!* (Miraculous machine!)" he said appreciatively, and called up some others to come and listen to him while he in turn explained how it all worked. Nobody was catching anything, not even in the *lyulki.* Across the river, two or three men were also casting.

I picked a brushy, difficult spot where the swift current flattened out over a hidden boulder, and cast just above it. I had no sooner started to retrieve the cast than something big shot out of the water, splashed and fluttered, and ran away with the line. I held onto him, scared to death for fear the line would slacken and he would be lost. A few more short, zigzag runs, and he jumped clear out of the water — some two and a half feet long, all green and silver, with big coarse scales. Finally he was on the bank. He looked very like a bass, with a little shiner blood mixed in. I called to my long-bearded friend in the patched and ragged overcoat. "*Dyedushka* (little grandfather), come and look!" He came running. "*Chudyesno!* Simply *chudyesno!*" he said, his face smiling into a thousand wrinkles.

"What is it?" I asked.

"That's a *sherespyor,*" he replied.

"Is it good to eat?"

"I should say it is! *Chudyesno!*"

The *sherespyor* isn't in any of the dictionaries, but this one weighed a good four pounds. I treasured it the rest of the morning, mooring it out on a line every fifty yards or so while moving down the river, so it could swim about and keep itself in prime condition. It was a Sunday morning, and there was no place along the next two or three kilometers of river where, on one bank or the other, one couldn't see at least two or three men or small boys still-fishing. Here and there the roofs of some little village showed up over the trees beyond the farther bank. From somewhere came the music of an accordion and the voices of both girls and boys singing — sometimes long, sad songs, and sometimes short, choppy, merry ones. But no one was catching any fish. In spite of another strike, there were no more to be had, but the one on my tether was enough.

Everyone who came past, man or boy or girl, would ask me if I had caught anything. I would appear negligent and indifferent, and tell them to go look at the end of my tether in the water. And all morning I was the hero of the day. One fine-looking boy in Red Army uniform, home in one of the villages on leave, asked me if he might take my picture holding my fish in one hand and casting with the other. I complied, and, after showing him how to work my reel, sat and rested while he struggled enthusiastically with backlashes. He learned fast, however. Later he came back, and presented me with a little piece of paper on which he had neatly written the date, the exact place, and the details of the fish, so I would not forget them. As if I could!

Late in the morning I worked all the way up the river, past the dam and the three or four kilometers more to home. There, near the bridge, a truckload-full of naked Red Army engineers were scrubbing clothes in the river. They all admired the fish. And all the bright-eyed barefoot women in the village admired it, and had something complimentary to say.

For lunch I had a can of corn — *kukuruza,* which, to the Great Russians, and probably to all Russians except the Ukrainians, is something to feed the pigs. Even Valodya, who always has at least one meal every day in our apartment, won't eat it. I had brought some before, but Ephrosinya didn't know how to cook it and left it untouched. I told her this time to just heat it with some milk. And for lunch it was ready, still standing in the can on my plate, well heated, with a glass of cold milk to go with it.

I had sent Valodya to bring in the boat during the morning by towing it on a cart with the weapons-carrier. In the afternoon Sabin and Ilyin paddled out in the stubby, high, unstable craft while I went down to the dam again. But the fishing that day had been so thin that the entire river was now deserted. Even the *lyulki* were untended. Valodya finally came to get me. The others had wanted to stay on until the following day, and I had promised them earlier that if I got a single bird or fish we would stay. But now there were great black clouds forming in the west, with every promise of rain. Remembering the roads, even Gospodin Elektrik, who already had six ducks and a *waldshnaip,* thought that it was a good idea to be on our way. I had told Fyodr that we would take his daughter Mariya to Moscow with us, so we stopped past his *izba* to tell her to pack up and be ready as soon as we could get our things together.

"Can I take a girl friend with me, who also wants to go to Moscow?"

"Sure — if you don't mind being crowded."

So we gave away what was left of our food and cigarettes, and six of us piled in the weapons-carrier and jolted off in the twilight. It was dark by the time we reached the hard road, and it was a long, cold ride to Moscow. But the lights of the car were splendid, so we made excellent time. For some unknown reason, while we had been away the main highway in several places had become so badly torn up that it was difficult to get through. We were also stopped by the occupants of several cars that were out of gas, broken down, or in the ditch. And often our lights picked out soldiers, strolling along the road with their girl friends. Once we passed a girl in uniform, with long overcoat and with long bayonet on her rifle, guarding something or other.

While we were still a long way from Moscow, we began to see dim red flashes far in the distance. After every flash there was a light glow reflected for several seconds against the distant clouds, which were now spitting a little rain.

"Gunfire," I said.

"Yes," said Sabin, "but why the glare afterwards?"

"Searchlights, maybe. But why after the gunfire instead of before?"

All the Russians ridiculed the idea of gunfire, but had no better explanation to offer than that perhaps it was lightning — which it certainly was not. Mariya and her girl friend chattered in the back seat until everyone grew too cold to chatter with anything but their teeth.

Towards midnight we reached Moscow, took the two girls to their destination through endless twisting, cobbled streets, and let Ilyin out near his home (never at the door). When we reached Red Square and saw the colored searchlights playing over the crowd, we remembered that this was Victory Day, which explained the distant gunfire and the glare of fireworks.

We let Sabin crawl stiffly and wearily out at American House on the banks of the Moskva River, and finally brought all my gear up to my apartment. Nell was still up, with all the news of what had been going on while I was away, particularly about a birthday party she had given for Tom Ireland, where everyone was in costume, and about Stevie's call from New York because of Mother's Day. There was a little difficulty in convincing her that I had brought her for Mother's Day a dozen fresh eggs, some milk, and a *sherespyor.*

The next day the fish fed the entire family. It was delicious, with fine, dense white meat, more like trout than bass.

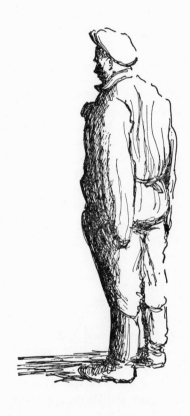

2. ALLILUYEVA'S GRAVE

TO CELEBRATE THE EXPEDITION, Sabin invited Nell and me to a duck and *waldshnaip* dinner. The doctor and the dentist, Captain Vaughn and Commander Cosby, turned over their apartment for the occasion. Besides those two, he invited a couple of other Navy Chiefs and his girl friend, Darya.

Darya is only twenty, married to a British officer who has long since left Russia. She is now a British subject and working at their Embassy, but unable to get an exit visa to leave Russia to join her husband. Why those cases occur — and there are many of them — nobody knows. The usual theory is that the Soviet government is unwilling to let any of the "little people" who really know the difficult way of life of the Russian little people leave the country because of the truths that they might tell, and because it would be difficult to explain away such truths by the claim that such people might be malcontents. Another theory is that the Soviets are reserving such action until it may fit in with a general policy of seeming to be co-operative. Perhaps there is some other reason, but, if so, it should be an important one, to pay for the hardship and unhappiness that it causes. There is, of course, a darker theory, and I have seen it working. The possession of such a hostage can give a strong leverage over the foreign husband.

Whatever the circumstances may be, Darya was self-possessed and simple, with an attractive voice and manner. She was very fair, with deep-set blue eyes, more like a Balt than a Great Russian, although a true Muscovite. It was a good dinner. Dr. Vaughn, blunt-nosed, broad-faced, and wise in fact as well as in manner and appearance, mixed the drinks, and there was champagne, the famous Russian cherry brandy, and two kinds of vodka, one being a brown variety known as "hunting vodka."

This morning Ambassador Smith left in his plane, brought in for the occasion, for some leave. He is going fishing in Normandy. I would envy him if it were not that the Russians on my own fish-

ing expeditions seem more interesting even than fish. The alarm
was set, Natasha came early to get us some breakfast, and Nell and
I drove in the chilly morning air to the airport. But this time it was
not Vnukovo, but the Central Airport, well within the limits of
Moscow, a great green field surrounded with houses and apartments.
It was necessary the evening before to notify the Foreign Office of
the license number of my car and the names of the driver and all
the occupants, and we were well checked at the gates. Nobody
knows why Vnukovo, which is far out of the city and most inconvenient, is normally used when there is such an ideal airport right
in the city. Of course, the Central Airport is a military field, but
there is an abundance of military fields around Moscow.

Two Russians, one a radio operator and the other a navigator,
must accompany the Ambassador's plane in and out of the country.
When the American pilot brought the plane in a day or so ago, he
did not know until he was near Moscow that he was to go to
Central, so the people who were waiting for him at Vnukovo with
transportation did not know it until after he had landed at Central.
Perhaps the Soviets are really beginning to be nice to us, for a
change. There were half a dozen propellered Yak fighters on the
field, but the area was so vast that little could be seen beyond the
fact that there were many buildings fading off in the distance, including a proper airport terminal building.

All of the senior people in the Embassy were there to see the
Ambassador off, in spite of his frequent past protestations that that
sort of thing was unnecessary. Exactly at the scheduled hour of
seven thirty, a car with some Russian officers pulled up. They asked
why the plane hadn't left, and were told that General Smith hadn't
yet arrived. Just then his car came up. When he was safely aboard
and the plane had finally taxied almost out of sight on the far
corner of the field for the take-off, Marion, the Ambassador's valet,
made a gesture of despair.

"My God!" he said, "we forgot to put his fishing rods in the
plane!"

He and Morris, the expediter, jumped in the big Lincoln with a
leather case full of rods, and took off across the grassy field at full
speed. After a moment of hesitation, a Russian car shot off after
them, full of MVD. Another few seconds, and another car started

out at full speed, this time full of frontier guards. Marion and Morris caught the plane in time, but they were nervous wrecks for the rest of the day.

"What did the general say?" we asked, evilly.

"We didn't stay to find out," one of them replied, "we just shoved the bag in the plane and got out of there as fast as we could."

When I got back to the office, my *Pravda* was early for once. Spread out in it was an account of the Ambassador's recent conversations with Molotov, giving the impression that the Americans were so thoroughly disturbed by the increasing dangers of the "cold war" that they were suggesting some bilateral conversations with the Soviet government. The Soviet reply pointed out that of course America was at fault, but that they themselves, as always, were a peace-loving people and also hoped that something could be done about it. It was obvious from the internal evidence of the Russian text that important omissions had been made from our statement.

I went up to Durbrow's office and took a look at the entire correspondence. Any sixth-grade child who could have compared the actual text the Ambassador had given the Soviets with the version published in the Soviet press would see from the omissions how distorted the whole affair becomes, and could also get a fair idea of how the Soviet mind works. It is a perfect example of deliberate twisting of another's words for propaganda purposes, and should convince anyone of the fundamental dishonesty — to our way of thinking — of the Soviet government's statements and methods of approach.

The Museum of Eastern Cultures is not a large museum, but an interesting one. We had a bit of difficulty in finding it, for the name of the street it is on was changed after the Revolution, and Valodya, like most Russians, still calls the street by its prerevolutionary name. Not far from the museum was an empty, battered church, standing in the middle of the populous city streets, but with shrubs and bushes growing out of its roof. No doubt the regime is well aware of that symbolism.

Oriental art is so complex that it soon becomes bewildering.

Some of the things I remember there were the rugs, underfoot as well as on the walls, a whole roomful of Tibetan Buddhas in bronze, some beautiful illuminated Persian books from the Middle Ages, and many big pieces of oxblood ware. There were some exquisite ivory cups, elaborately and finely carved in full relief, that showed forests and people and towns. One such cup had dragons for handles. And there was some Uzbek jewelry, with earrings as big as your hand, crusted with rubies and turquoises and emeralds.

Nell and I picked up Hooker at Spasso House on the way to see what we could of the inside of Novodevichi Monastery by daylight. The grassy grounds within its Kremlin-like walls were dotted with tombs and gravestones, many of them in bad repair. Children played among them and climbed on top of them. Many people, mostly women and girls, lay around on the grass, resting or sleeping. Here and there from the towers and domes sprouted trees and bushes, and the great golden crosses above the bulbs leaned crazily in all directions. Many of the tombs were those of noblemen and princes. One, which was of black granite and well kept, was of that Davidov who led the partisans and guerrillas against Napoleon during the bitter retreat of the French in 1812. The houses and sheds against the mighty walls sagged and drooped picturesquely.

We went into the church, where I had been on Easter Eve. It looked bare and poor without its murmuring crowds and its candle-lit darkness, but we found a christening in process. The parents were very young, seeming to be still in their teens. There were two couples, the men obviously of the working class, mechanics of some sort, and the women wearing the very short skirts which are fashionable in Moscow today. The two babies were stripped to the buff and were seated, one after the other, in the font, which was a portable basin.

A young priest in a soiled white cotton or linen robe, with long flowing beard and with long uncut hair hanging down his back, read rapidly in a singsong monotone from his Bible or book of services, with his back to his audience. From time to time he would turn, to dab holy water or oil or something with a sponge on the forehead, eyes, lips, hands and feet of the red, squalling babies, who were hard to hold and who continually squirmed out of their wrappings. The priest cut some hair from each of their heads, and finally one of the young mothers took one of the babies and rocked it violently in her arms, her short skirts swishing high in time with her rocking. Then the priest held up a cross for everyone, including the babies, to kiss, the parents dressed their young in newly consecrated clothes, and everyone went away, grinning happily.

We wandered around the inside of the church. Once Nell breathed too close to a candle in front of a shrine, and to her distress the candle winked out. We could only hope that it was permissible for laymen to light candles, and Hooker and I formed a discreet screen while Nell relit this one. We left the church and walked around the grass. At last we found a big door ajar in an archway in the wall, and started to go through it. A woman stopped us and asked if we had any cameras. When I said no, she stood aside, and said *"Pazhaluista!"* — the Russian word of polite invitation.

We passed through the door into another enclosure which lay outside the grim wall. It was a tight-packed, well-kept cemetery, planted thick with trees and shrubs, and with clean-swept sandy paths. Many of the monuments had photographs embedded in them, and many of them were planted close with growing spring flowers. It was an interesting place, and I was struck by the high percentage of high-ranking army and navy officers who, having died during the Soviet regime, had found their last resting place in holy ground. The militant atheism of prewar days has been muted. Churchgoing, like so many things in Russia, is not directly forbidden, but it is continually made clear, in the press and otherwise, that it is inconsistent with Party membership. If one values his job or his position in life, he will not go. Even when one is dead, and beyond the reach of the long arm of the police, there remain the relatives who put up the monuments. Perhaps these relatives had little to lose.

One monument in the cemetery to Polikarpov, an aircraft constructor, was surmounted by a beautiful full-sized male figure, head down in the wings of death. In the monastery walls was a long, long row of niches, like those in the walls of the Moscow Kremlin itself, where people, or at least their ashes, were buried. The cemetery was a big place, and off in the distance was a new bier, literally buried in flowers. We would all like to have stayed much longer, but we had engagements, and time was running out.

I knew that Stalin's wife was buried somewhere in Novodevichi, so I asked someone where we could find her grave, and was told the direction to take.

Alliluyeva's grave was surrounded by a low rope. It was a plain, tall white shaft of stone, from the top of which was formed only a woman's head and hand. The face was strong, pensive and peaceful, not particularly beautiful, but satisfying. Nearby was a low stone which, from its dates and name, must have been that of Alliluyeva's father. It was strange to think of Stalin, the embodiment of power in his godless police state, coming to such a place alone in the evenings, as they say he has often done.

Zolushka is a beautiful ballet, studded with lovely faces, lavishly staged and beautifully done. The name is a feminine diminutive of the word for "ashes" — literally, Cinderella. Although Valodya had managed some tickets for us in the eighth row — by a little flattery and some candy for the girl at the office which sells tickets, since none but ambassadors are now on the Bolshoy's list for special reservations — I had a pair of navy binoculars which, although hard on the eyes in a theater, let me see that many of the faces of the dancers were really as lovely as they seemed.

There was one scene of the starry night, with the streaming stars and galaxies filling a three-dimensional space, done with a series of invisible nets, that was full of magic. In the deep backdrop of the ballroom scene was a gigantic scrolled mirror, and behind that glassless mirror was another real ballroom which gave the illusion of an actual reflection, duplicating the great colored lanterns hanging from above and the crowded dancers. Another scene was memorable for its hundreds of candles set one above the other in the heavy golden walls of the palace. Still another scene had a real fountain, on which played colored lights, while a panorama of fireworks filled the sky. And when Cinderella fled from the palace at midnight — each of the hours was a little dancer — the palace rooms rushed past her on a moving stage.

Semyonova, who danced the lead to Prokofiev's music, is a big, fair woman. At one place she slipped, and, although she finished that scene, she had obviously twisted her ankle. Her place was taken in the last act by the more exquisite Ulanova. Both of them are idols of the Soviet public, and it was apparent that the audience, although sorry for Semyonova's misfortune, considered themselves fortunate to have seen the two of them in the same evening.

It was warm, and during the entr'actes Nell and I walked outside between the big Greek columns. It was still light, and the foreign quality of our clothing brought stares and whispers from all sides. Nell has found a way to keep the stares from becoming supercilious and patronizing, as sometimes happens when a certain type of Russian woman eyes a foreign woman. She merely stares back, but at their shoes. Such women immediately become flushed and self-conscious and move hurriedly on.

We were importuned by a flower woman, who was constantly looking around for the police to suppress her particular effort at private enterprise. The police could not have avoided seeing her, but paid no attention. We bought several bunches of fragrant lilies of the valley from her for only three rubles a bunch.

Only one of the kittens is left — the one with a white chest and face and thick Persian-like fur, which Natasha calls Masha. Natasha has given the others away, and the other day she took the mother cat to her own home in a big shopping bag to help clear out the rats. Masha, although still unsteady on her feet, is beginning to play. But we all miss the rest of the family noticeably.

Somewhat to my surprise, my friend Gregorev called on the telephone and asked if he could come over to see me. We spent the entire afternoon in my apartment, talking, and he was just as friendly and just as interested in America as he had been on the train. He said he had made an unexpected but routine trip back home, thanked me for the magazines, including the copy of *Time* with its article on Beria, and said that he was confident he had nothing to fear in renewing our acquaintance. He also remarked that it was very impressive to him to see some of the personal views I had given him reflected in the recent statement of American interests in the Soviet press, and he seemed pleased to have the full and much more accurate text, which I gave him. Perhaps he is assigned to work on me, although he seems very sincere. In any event, it may work both ways.

Today the Embassy got word that everything which has been piling up in customs for the last eight or nine months must be cleared out within ten days or it will be confiscated. No one knows why, or what duty we will have to pay. Molichkov, the Foreign Office official with whom Durbrow deals in such matters, is "ill" and can't see him. For weeks we have been trying unsuccessfully to get Crawford, one of our men, into the warehouse to try to find out what was there. Yesterday the Russians suddenly let him in, and then he got locked in, and couldn't get out for several hours.

Today was a big day, for a big surface mail arrived, the first in several weeks.

We drove through scattered spring showers to the Filial of the Maly Theater, near Serpukhovskaya Square in the far southern part of the city. This theater is more like a high-school auditorium than a regular theater, the seats being hard chairs with that pronounced uncomfortable slope downwards and forwards which characterizes the seats in so many Russian theaters.

The play was Shakespeare's *Twelfth Night.* The horseplay in it between Malvolio and the household is inherently none too light-handed, but it was exaggerated to the point of burlesque in this Soviet version. Only the main ideas of the English text were taken, with no attempt to put the language into its Russian equivalent, and the entire play was freely adapted in many of its arrangements and details. Yet it is possible to make an excellent full translation of Shakespeare. *Othello,* at the Moscow Soviet Theater, is a magnificent and completely satisfying production, with every mood and shading of its complex speech accurately reflected in understandable Russian, retaining all its lecherous imagery, its intensity, and its beauty. That translation was by Moritz. But this translation of *Twelfth Night,* which is by someone else, did no such thing. It completely scamped the job, leaving the play just a slapstick collection of incidents around the rather thin central plot.

Mordvinov, who played the Moor in *Othello* at the Mossoviet, would be a great actor in any country. The Mossoviet's *Othello* was one of the very best Russian productions of anything I have seen. Both the Red Army Theater and the Maly suffer from experimentalism, done by uncertain hands, and Russians are often aware of it. At the Maly this night, a single actress played the part of both Viola and her twin brother up to the point where both of them have to appear on the stage at the same time, when a stand-in was used with disconcerting effect. The Maly usually goes in heavily for scenery of trees and shrubs made out of real foliage set in some sort of plastic, which is often effective.

The audience was more of a show than the play itself. In front of us were two women who just couldn't keep their eyes away from Nell at every opportunity. One was dark, with a typical dark Russian high-cheekboned face with very deep-set dark eyes — but those eyes most amazingly slanted in that face. The other was tow-headed, with hair combed straight back and braided, the ends tucked up like pigtails into the rest of her hair. She had china-blue eyes and very pink, tight skin which wrinkled when she smiled, so that it looked like the material from which the little old Russian peasant dolls are made. Her nose was long and flat and turned up at the end like a putty nose. Both of them wore shoulder pads under their blouses to give the current fashionable effect. Such shoulder pads are sold on the street corners, together with shoe laces. Nell obliged them by breaking out all the contents of her purse while they were watching, and giving a demonstration of how everything was used. She had a good audience.

3. TULA AND TOLSTOY

FRIDAY NIGHT NATASHA STAYED ALL NIGHT, for we were to get up bright and early in the morning to drive to Tolstoy's home at Yasnaya Polyana, some two hundred kilometers to the south beyond Tula. When we left to go out in the evening, she said, "Ah, tonight I shall sleep like a countess!" And she had a snack all laid out for us to eat when we got home.

There was light rain in the morning from low, confused clouds, but here and there a glimpse of clear sky showed blue. We took Alan Little with us, big, bald-headed and glibly Scottish, and also picked up the decorous Hooker at Spasso. The spring rain made the browns and creams of the older Moscow houses look rich and warm. In the country, the fruit trees were in blossom, and there were plenty of them, sometimes single trees, sometimes grouped in little orchards. Rain and wisps of fog hung like smoke beneath the dark clouds. Everywhere were bright yellow fields of wild mustard or its Russian equivalent.

One soon got a sense of the vastness of Russia as mile after mile went past and low hills spread out like the smooth ground swell of the sea. The Russian countryside could never look lovelier, except perhaps after a fresh, clean snowfall. The little villages strung out along the road seemed to be a part of the soil in their coloring and in the way they were crouched into the ground, and the thatched roofs were green and brown with rich moss and sprouting grass. Every *izba* has its little birdhouses, stuck up on the tops of tall poles if there are no trees alongside, otherwise hanging in the trees along with the crows' nests. Barefoot women, working, working.

All along the road, thicker and thicker the farther south we went, were German prisoners, at first an occasional little group, then dozens of them, then hundreds. We saw thousands and thousands of such prisoners during the day — three years after the end of the war, and still literally slaves — in their heavy German army boots, their short jackets, and their green or brown peaked German caps, with prisoners' marks on their sleeves. Along the highroad was many a prison camp for them, surrounded with barbed wire and guards, but the camps looked as comfortable as the usual Russian dwelling, and the prisoners themselves appeared sturdy and well fed. Sometimes they would be working without shirts, and unlike the prisoners on the railroad when we first came to Moscow last summer there were no ribs showing gaunt and thin. Most of them were working on the road, rebuilding bridges and putting up a standard type of brick or tile housing for future permanent Soviet road maintenance foremen. It was noticeable that they were used for the more skilled types of labor. They did not work hard, usually at the tempo of a slow-motion picture, and many of them seemed to be in positions of authority. But they were all guarded by Russian lads in uniform with guns and bayonets.

We passed churches with porcelain domes of dull blue or green, and everywhere were colts and calves, kids and lambs. And over the hills, rolling like the open sea, spilled the green forests broken by green fields of grain. Except for Podolsk, which is a big place with many mysterious industries not far from Moscow, the only city before Tula is Serpukhov, a hundred kilometers from Moscow. It is a pleasant place, with plane trees along its streets, and with at least two big, church-crowned enclosures that looked like fortified monasteries. On the edge of Serpukhov was the greatest assemblage of guns that I have ever seen, stowed thickly together as far as one could see, probably a reserve from the last war. The Oka, one of the main tributaries of the Volga, flows past Serpukhov, placid and calm and wide.

I took over the driving, but Nell, like womenfolk generally, moaned more than once that she would be much happier if Valodya would drive all the way. So when we came to Tula and had to stop because a crowd barred the road, I gave up and let him do so. The crowd was watching some sort of difficulty between the MVD and some wide-skirted, earringed gypsy women. We never found out the reason for the trouble, but the grimy gypsy wenches were far from cowed. They were still shrilling defiantly and giving black looks to the crowd as well as to the police when we had succeeded in honking our way through.

Tula is a very large city. It is difficult to estimate the size of

Russian cities because of the way Russians are crowded together in all sorts of structures, but Tula stretched as far as the eye could reach in every direction from its center, and the usual population figure is half a million. On the way into the city we had passed two or three flying fields, with scores of aircraft on each. Although there were the usual mysterious factories here and there in the distance, it seemed very much of a provincial town.

We caught a glimpse of a brown-red crenelated brick wall, exactly like that of our own Kremlin, so we turned aside to investigate it. Sure enough, it was an old fortress, a kremlin, completely enclosed by that massive, crumbling wall. We left Valodya in the car and went on foot through one of the great gates. There were two big churches in the center and a few isolated buildings here and there, most of them sheds and dwellings. One end of the enclosure was walled off with a board fence to make a grassy stadium — grandstand, pictures of Stalin and all — but the greater part of the space was just bare ground.

We went up to one of the tall churches and, since the little old attendant at the door made no objection, went inside. It had been turned into a storehouse, and was packed and crowded with bales and boxes of all descriptions. Part of it was used for issues, for there socks and clothing were heaped up on shelves and some women were being fitted out with what they needed. But the walls, the heavy tall columns and the vaulted roofs were painted solid, without a single break, with saints and prophets and cherubs and angels, all in gold and a rich, dull, dark blue. It must have been very magnificent at one time, and it was still in fair condition, with but a few places faded and discolored. The little old man told us that it was the Summer Church, and that the other church in the kremlin, which was also used as a storehouse, was the Winter Church. The Winter Church was closed and there was no one about, but we could peer through the cracks of the door and see that its walls and columns and roofs were also completely covered with painted figures like the first one, but this time, instead of being all in blue and gold, it was black and gold.

Nell went back to the car, but the rest of us wandered around inside the kremlin, across into a churchyard on another street, which was filled with sagging log buildings like a stage setting of the

Russian Middle Ages, and back into the kremlin. As we started to go out another gate, a red-headed militia girl asked us for our documents. In spite of their authenticity, she would not let us go farther. A dark-faced, pleasant ex-soldier, with a chestful of service ribbons on his civilian jacket instead of the usual medals, became interested, and told us that the museum, which lay beyond, was closed on Saturdays. Now Tula, ever since the Middle Ages and the Time of Troubles, has been the center of some sort of arms industry, varying throughout the centuries, but always of great importance to Russia. And this museum was the Arms Museum. The ex-soldier volunteered to help us try to get in, and, after a considerable amount of telephoning, led us to what corresponds to the City Hall.

There our friend dropped out of sight, and we were on our own. We showed our documents several times, telling our story each time and each time advancing one room further, until at last we were ushered into the presence of the president of the city soviet. He was a young, bright-looking man, with heavy jowls and a decisive manner. We told him that this would probably be our only opportunity ever to see the famous Arms Museum of Tula, and could it be arranged? He sent for an assistant and told him to get in touch with the director of the museum. While we were waiting, he told us how Tula had been completely surrounded by the German army for forty-five days towards the end of 1941, but, although subjected to daily artillery bombardment, had never been occupied by them. The director of the museum wasn't in. "Well, try to find him!"

The office was spacious and reasonably comfortable, and the president's desk was orderly. Once or twice the telephone rang. "That's your responsibility," he said, in answer to some question about local repairs or construction. "You think I should decide?" he went on, "all right, I'll decide, and right now. You go ahead and do it. Do everything that is in your power to see that it is done promptly and properly." Altogether, this Soviet administrator seemed effective and efficient. The director of the museum hadn't yet been located, but the suggestion was made that, since we had had no lunch, perhaps we could take care of that and then come back in an hour or so, by which time they would have found him.

When we emerged from the City Hall, Nell was waiting outside in the car, a bit worried for fear that we might be in there against our will. How she succeeded in taking charge and finding us is still something between her and Valodya. We had lunch at the hotel, a colorless sort of place. But two hundred grams of vodka, washed down with beer, and some well-seasoned *entrecôtes* and salad made an excellent lunch. Vodka is always sold by weight when one buys it by the drink. When we went back to the City Hall, we were told that the director of the museum couldn't be located at all, since it was his day of rest, and that consequently there was nothing that could be done for us. At any rate, it was a good effort, but, as we suspected at the time, we should never have gone away for lunch.

About twenty-five kilometers beyond Tula, after a very rough road under reconstruction by scores of German prisoners, and just beyond a big group of blast furnaces towering up in the leafy rural landscape, we came to the turnoff for Yasnaya Polyana, the "Bright Glade." We left the car at the gates, and a militiaman ran on ahead to carry the news that foreign visitors had arrived. We walked some distance along a road lined with tall dark cedars, and finally came to two broad low houses, set some distance apart in the trees.

There we were met by a young man with a strong but rather artistic face who was wearing a belted dark-patterned Russian blouse, and with him was a neat, reddish-haired girl in bobby socks. The man, Pyotr Mikhailovich, was born in Orel, and he spoke with a strong, rather affected accent which was certainly not Muscovite. He was some sort of kinsman of Turgenev, and had been specially trained for scientific work in connection with artistic and literary museums, serving in the art gallery at Kharkov until it was ruined by the Germans, after which he had come to Yasnaya Polyana. He not only knew his work, but was very much wrapped up in it. The girl, Vera Vasilyevna, would have been a fine, interesting and interested girl in any country. They were as good guides and companions as could be found anywhere.

The two broad separated houses were only the two wings of the original house, which had had thirty rooms, and which was said to have been sold at Tolstoy's order for the income from the sale of the material in it at the time he was in the army, in the Crimean War, when he was hard up. Beyond one wing was a large grove of extraordinarily tall linden trees, forming beautiful avenues, which

Tolstoy loved to frequent. His mother had died when he was only a year and a half old, and it was down one of those lanes that he used to fancy that he still saw her steps in the snow.

The wing in which Tolstoy had lived and in which he wrote *War and Peace* and *Anna Karenina* was kept in all its details with extraordinary care. The walls were very thick, and from every window could be seen nothing but great pines, firs, lindens and birches. It was a lovely, peaceful place, not luxurious, but comfortable.

The Germans had occupied it during the war. Surprised at the last minute and unable to carry its things away, they had set fire to each room and left a placard saying that the house was mined. In spite of the sign, the Russians had gone in and put the fire out without too much damage. Part of the damage had been repaired and part preserved, but always there were photographs to show what the Germans had done. They had littered the place with empty bottles (photographs) and had hung pornographic pictures on the walls (no photographs of them). There was still a hole in the upholstery of the divan on which Tolstoy himself and most of his children had been born, which Pyotr told us had been put there by the boot of a German doctor just in spite. And in the guest book were two or three pages of the names of Germans. At the end of that part of the guest book, the Russian officer who had liberated the place had written, "What a pity that these swine were able to leave on their own feet!"

Some Russians say that this is all only a fabrication of the regime to inspire patriotism and hatred of the Germans. The difficulty of learning the real truth about even recent events of importance is one of the snakelike fascinations of Russia.

Aided by everyone's simultaneous suggestions, I wrote in the guest book an appreciation of the sympathetic help of Pyotr Mikhailovich and Vera Vasilyevna. We all signed it. Our two Russians wanted to know what it said, as I had written in English. We translated it for them, and they seemed very pleased.

Meanwhile a group of Russian school children of high-school age had arrived. They asked Alan if he could not give them some message from the youth of Italy.

"Why from Italy?" asked Alan.

"Oh, aren't you the Italian Ambassador?"

"No, I'm an American."

"Then can't you give us some message from the youth of America?"

Alan did his best, which was very good indeed.

The last place we went was to Tolstoy's grave, set deep within a dreaming wood of birch and linden in the place where, when a child, he had searched for the "green stick" that would bring happiness for everyone. It was impressively simple. There was no headstone, no marker, only a sharp-cornered, coffin-shaped mound of grass, strangely small in size, as coffins always are, covered with grass and new-picked wild flowers. The gravel path was swept very clean, and the tall, dim trees were very peaceful and still. There had once been a cross there, but the Germans had used the place for a burial ground, and had put an inscription on the cross to those who had fallen for the greatness of Germany. Now there is neither cross nor Germans.

Pyotr Mikhailovich and Vera Vasilyevna walked with us all the way to the entrance gates where we had left Valodya and the car, past a still pond where youngsters were swimming and women beating out their wash with little paddles. On the way we passed a symbol of Russia — a horse-drawn cart on which was loaded a splashing barrel of water for the cattle, driven by a grave-faced woman who walked barefoot beside it.

Before we reached Tula on our way back, we drove off the road and stopped beside a big pond where one or two lazy fishermen slept in the late afternoon warmth. There are no roadside restaurants, stands or taverns in Russia, so for emergencies Natasha had packed some food and drink for us in the little coffer-shaped gay wicker basket I had once brought home from Portugal. A small boy and his still smaller sister, come to drive the cow home, sat nearby and eyed us. When we loaded them with food, the boy gave all of his to his sister, and most of it went into their pockets to take home. Although he said that he was eleven and his sister was five, they were no bigger than half that age. They were very frail and very ragged, not carelessly snagged and torn like country children generally, but completely and pitifully ragged.

Beyond Tula we stopped and picked great armloads of *chery-*

omukha, a fragrant, white-flowering shrub, to bring some spring-time into the Mokhavaya apartment. At Serpukhov we found a restaurant on the second floor of a cream-colored, thick-walled building, and there we sat and drank seven dollars' worth of beer, looking out the deep-set window while the green twilight faded from the rainy sky. A phonograph blared noisily all the time, and a few Russians at the tables around us pursued their usual provincial lives. Once there was a crash when one of them, who must have had a drop too much, morosely threw a glass through a closed window.

It rained hard the rest of the way home, and Valodya had to stop now and then to let the glaring lights of a car or truck go past. More often, as seems to be the custom in Russia, both we and the other car put our lights out, followed by an interval of darkness and a cautious approach, with only an occasional brief flashing of headlights to show the way. I drowsed in the front seat, for it was long after midnight when we finally reached home.

4. THE RED SHIRT

MONDAY MORNINGS USUALLY BRING BAD NEWS. This Monday it concerned one Staff Sergeant McMillan, a code clerk with the army. I do not recall him, but that is not surprising, since our Embassy personnel total about one hundred and twenty-five. After two years' duty here, the sergeant was due to leave by air yesterday for America. He did not show up, nor had he appeared in the military attaché's office to get his clearances the day before. Instead, he sent letters to Ambassador Smith and to the "Mayor of Moscow," saying that he had not realized until he had come to Russia that here at last was a system of government under which the simple people were not oppressed and robbed by the capitalist monopolists. Instead of returning to his own land, he was staying in the Soviet Union. That seems like rather an elaborate euphemism for jumping ship.

His letters said nothing about his having barely reached the mature age of twenty-one, nor that he had been living with the Soviet wife of another army enlisted man who had gone home a year or two before. And this boy was the son of an army officer. My own Navy men are good lads, and I hope I know what goes on in their minds well enough to be sure that that sort of thing won't happen. Pride, however, goeth before a fall, so I had better start talking with the newcomers the day they arrive, and try to insure that they at least come to me first with any sociological and political perplexities.

Natasha has lost her voice almost completely. Yesterday Nell told her to take the day off. Natasha's face fell.

"No, I must scrub and clean the house here."

"But you scrubbed and cleaned everything only a day or two ago," said Nell. "There's nothing to be done here."

"But here it is light and warm! And so peaceful!"

"Well, if you want to stay here, it's all right, of course. But it's

not necessary for you to work. Take a bath. Lie down. Listen to the
radio. Go to bed and rest, or look at magazines."

"Yes," interrupted Zoya to Natasha in her deep, husky voice,
"she speaks the truth!"

Perhaps Natasha did take a bath. At any rate, her voice was
almost gone today.

She saw me trying to memorize some passages from *Eugene
Onegin.* "Do you like *Onegin?*" she asked, and when I said yes, very
much, she went on in a piping, toothless whisper, "*Ai-ai-ai!* What
a life the nobles and the gentry lived in those days! Gospodin
Admiral, would you believe it — I have helped great ladies to
dress. I did not just help them, but put on them every stitch that
they wore, corsets, skirts, laced their high boots, while they stood
still for me to do it. And in the days of the serfs, they even had
serfs to scratch their heels for them!"

I told her that it didn't sound like a bad life. And when I gave
her aspirin to gargle, she whispered, "Gospodin Admiral, the world
lost a fine doctor in you."

Natasha is having some new teeth made, but the weeks and the
months go by and they are never ready. It speaks well for my
knowledge of Russian that I can understand her peasant speech
under the circumstances.

The Vakhtangova Theater, although old and famous, is even
more like a high-school auditorium than the Maly Filial. We went
there to see a light and amusing musical show, *Mademoiselle
Nitysh,* which had been well recommended by the Navy lads at
Spiro. Perhaps it was because of the sort of show, but whatever the
reason, the audience seemed even more Russian than usual. They
were not poor, but less pretentious. Tselikovskaya, who played the
lead, was an intriguing person with bad blue eyes, a willful red
mouth, and a deadpan face when she was in trouble, as she usually
was. When I saw her it was clear why the Spiro lads had gone so
often to see *Mademoiselle Nitysh.*

Most of the morning was taken up with the commissary committee, trying to decide what to do about our ultimatum on getting
everything out of customs, for if we should have to pay the maxi-

mum duty on everything that is there for the commissary, as seems probable, it will come to some $30,000. We need the food, but the commissary is jointly financed and run by the Americans attached to the Embassy, and not by our government. In any other country, supplies for diplomatic people are admitted duty free. In any other country they could live on what they could buy locally. But here the Soviet government has decreed that American money is worth only about one thirtieth of what it would bring on the open market. Durbrow's blood pressure is going up daily, for Molichkov, who has finally worn out the excuses of illness and out of town, has sent word that he himself is now so busy that he will be unable to see him for at least three days more.

Perhaps it's all just as well. It isn't good for one to eat out of tins too much.

One day when Nell wasn't feeling too well, Elyena had said to me, "What is the trouble?"

I gave the classical answer — "Something she ate, no doubt."

"Ah, I see! She has been having some of our lovely fresh vegetables. Since you Americans have never known what it is to live in any other way than out of cans, your systems are not used to fresh food!"

One of my enlisted men told me of a conversation with some of his Russian friends. They are tearful and apologetic ex-friends now, alas, since they have been told by the MVD never to see him again. The old grandmother of the family had said in all seriousness that in their apartment house lived a genuine witch, who frequently flew off to the Witch's Sabbath with all the other witches in this part of the country. Sometimes they held their Sabbath right in the Kremlin itself, for there lives the greatest witch of them all.

I told Natasha this story, omitting the name and dwelling place of the chief witch so as not to compromise her through having to listen to such blasphemy. When she laughed tolerantly, I asked, "Natasha, did you yourself ever really see a witch or devil, in the days before the Revolution, when they may have lived here in Russia?"

"No, Gospodin Admiral," she said, looking remarkably witch-like herself, since her nose and chin nearly meet over her toothless mouth. "No. But one time I did see something very strange, in the village near Nizhny Novgorod when I was a little girl. All of us children were picking berries on the side of a hill near home, when suddenly, across the sky, high over our heads, came flapping a great red shirt! Perhaps it was blown from somewhere by the wind, only there wasn't any wind, and it was much too big to belong to anyone. That great red shirt flapped across the sky, and we were so terrified that we ran crying into the hut. Our mother went out to look, but it had gone."

She could tell me nothing more, nor did she admit that she knew of any special significance to be attached to a red shirt. Now Gogol, who comes closer to skirting the creepy edges of genuine supernatural horror than any other Russian writer known to me, has a red shirt in his *Sorochinskaya Fair*. That fair was held on ground which carried with it a curse, and the reason the place was accursed was because the devil had once left a red shirt in pawn in a tavern there, and had been cheated out of his shirt by the tavern keeper. All through Gogol's story, bits of the red shirt appear, accompanied with manifestations of extreme terror far beyond what one usually finds in Russian literature.

There is a strange universality in the manifestations of witchcraft in which the lower, more unchanging levels of peoples who are close to the soil really believe, and what might be called those genuine manifestations often seem to have the same quality of childish irrelevance as the messages of mediums. Gogol's pig snout in that same story, and the images in the terrible church scene of his *Vii* and in Tatyana's dream in Pushkin's *Eugene Onegin,* are authentic both in their universality and in this eerie quality of irrelevance. It is the dealing with ancient, genuine convictions that makes such things as some of Goya's pictures, Bram Stoker's *Dracula* and some of the phenomena of the great witchcraft trials so chilling.

Nell and I drove out to the Botkin Hospital to see Mrs. Shaw, a British newswoman who is laid up there with rheumatic fever. A Russian who had worked in a hospital had told me that when Elliot Roosevelt once visited them they had worked for three days doing nothing but shine the place up, so this looked like a chance to see one of the leading Soviet hospitals under more normal circumstances.

At the place where we turned off from the Yaroslavl Chaussée was a distant church with a cluster of dull green domes surmounting its sliced-off tall and cream-colored sides. That church is unusual because it is one of the few that show the real architectural reason for all of the little arches that cluster under the domes like the petals of a flower — *kokoshniki,* women's headdresses, they are called — for each arch frames a painted saint which has not yet faded away.

The hospital was made up of many buildings set in a large area, and it seemed to be unusually livable, partly because of the profusion of green trees and shrubs outside the windows, and partly because it was neither too dirty nor, what would have been a bit out of character in Russia, too clean. It nevertheless had a sort of institutional air, probably because the many patients who sat around in the grounds, men and women alike, were dressed in blue or brown issue pajamas of wool or denim.

We had no trouble getting in, but at the entrance we had to put on white coats that were far from clean. It made no difference whether or not we actually put them on, but at least we had to drape them over our shoulders. Nell was undecided whether the protection was for us or for the patients. Mrs. Shaw, a big-faced woman with brown eyes, was in bed, and all bandaged up. She seemed to be thoroughly enjoying the hospital, and spoke highly of the care she received. Dr. Vaughn tells me that although some of the Russian doctors are skilled and highly intelligent there is a pitiful lack of equipment and materials. The lack of things of all sorts is always so apparent here that it seems as though all of the great voids could never be filled under a whole series of Five Year Plans.

We then drove out to the Ostankina Palace, set in one of the many Parks of Culture and Rest, but, as so often happens here, found that it was closed at that particular time or on that particular day. Close by was a church with a clustering of domes that, except for its uniform soft brown color, looked like a small version of St. Basil's, and a pond in which many children were swimming, some of them, boys and girls alike, mother naked.

In spite of all the fresh green leafage of spring, Moscow somehow remains drab. The people seem less picturesque than in winter, but there were touches of color from the red ties of all the Pioneers — the youngsters who are not old enough to belong to the Komsomol — for that day marked the end of the school year and the beginning of their summer camps or vacations.

That night Zoya took home the last kitten for her little niece Irochka. The next day we asked if Irochka had taken it to camp with her.

"Irochka wouldn't stay at the camp," Zoya replied. "She cried so much that I'm letting her come home every night instead."

We are having our first servant trouble in many months. Tomorrow is our day to get things at our commissary, and since we are freshly out of sugar, Nell told Natasha to use saccharine until we could buy sugar from the commissary. At lunch a bowl of Russian sugar appeared. When asked why she had bought Russian sugar, which is a dollar and a quarter a pound, Natasha said that Zoya and Valodya had demanded it. Both Zoya and Valodya denied any such thing, and said that Natasha wasn't telling the truth. They were probably right, but Nell told them that if they didn't like what they got to eat here, they could eat at home, and, since then, Valodya has been proudly doing just that. It is strange to be in a place where the simple problem of basic food is the key to most of life, and it is difficult to know what to do about it, particularly when there are definite limits to one's own resources.

We went to the Theater of Drama to see Arbuzov's *Tanya*. The theater was like a small, old-fashioned Western Opry House of a generation ago. Even the chandelier was sparse and poor, unlike the richness of the bigger theaters. The scenery and furnishings of the stage were modernly and deliberately fragmentary, and a big bleached blonde — a familiar Russian type — played the leading role. She overacted it badly. Many Westerners think that Russians always overact, but there is a great difference between the stylized emphasis of some of the theaters and the plain grimacing and gesturing of this one.

The play itself was a contemporary Soviet play. Although it was a complicated account of modern life in Siberia, it was completely lacking in drama and in talent of conception and construction. I have seen literally dozens of contemporary plays, and not one of them is even remotely comparable to those which were written before the Revolution. The best of them deal with prerevolutionary historical subjects, such as Aleksei Tolstoy's *Ivan Grozny* and *The Last Days of Pushkin* at MXAT, although I am not sure that even that last one is by a contemporary writer. Although the themes do not come off, the trouble seems to lie less in those themes than in the complete lack of any imagination or freshness. And in most of them, of course, everything is subservient to the Mission of glorifying the good life in the Promised Land. Surely there is ample evidence in every land, including Russia, that, contrary to Soviet conception, playwrighting does not have to teach a lesson or serve the ends of propaganda in order to be great. Yet even the blight of propaganda seems hardly enough to explain the low state to which Russian playwrighting has fallen under the Soviet regime.

We walked the few blocks home from the theater, and in the soft darkness Moscow lost some of its drabness and became filled with mystery instead.

The Edenbergs live in an apartment on Sadovaya Boulevard, and there is a little balcony outside the windows. From that balcony, and perhaps aided by Willy's good Swedish liquor at dinner, the mysterious night aspect of Moscow became almost theatric. My memory of the evening is of good food, of Tamara Gilmore all in white except for her black gloves, the fine, precise Russian spoken by Mrs. Sohlman, and the scene from the balcony of old low pastel-brown and cream-colored buildings, lit as if in the theater, with people around them making entrances and exits as if on a stage.

The next morning everyone felt bad, but one ray of lightness appeared when Durbrow finally managed to see someone from the Foreign Office and was told that perhaps there was some mistake about their customs being on the point of confiscating American property. If we would only continue to be patient, they would try to work something out, and nothing would be confiscated until then, at least.

·   ·   ·

Captain Madsen is a tall, serious-looking Dane. He, together with Edith, his sensitive wife, are friends indeed, for they have helped us out tremendously with Danish bacon, cheeses and butter. Edith, who has had some sort of training in psychology, is eager and interested, and it is a delight to talk with her. We went to their apartment for a luncheon.

They live in a new apartment house for foreign diplomatic personnel on Narodnaya Street, well down the river. Although the house is so new that construction is still going on on one wing, that which has been built is already sagging and falling to pieces. The entrance was bad, worse than that of a Western tenement, but the Madsens' apartment was very livable. From its windows, the surrounding part of Moscow looked like a frontier town, for there were big areas of wooden sheds and ramshackle shelters in all directions, with the Moskva River shining as it wound its broad way through them all.

A dozen or so women were busily shoveling dirt from the excavation for the unfinished wing of the house into a line of trucks, and just beyond them was an equally characteristic Soviet scene. It was difficult at first glance to pick out any sort of order from the jumble, but the eye could follow a double line of fencing which enclosed a large area full of sheds and temporary wooden buildings. On the corners of this irregular fence were little wooden booths, and in each booth was a guard with a rifle. It was a prison camp, this time for Soviet citizens.

We sang Swedish songs with the aquavit, and Mrs. Madsen made a sentimental and appreciative speech to the Hills, whose time in Russia is ending. She told Nell that when the Germans came into Denmark during the war she herself got out of Denmark for Sweden in a small boat. It was foggy and dark. On the way, a German motor torpedo boat passed within easy sound. And just then she dropped her handbag overboard, and watched it sink beneath the water. "That is how I too shall drown!" she thought.

What a world!

5. SAINT'S DAY

SUNDAY MORNING, IN SPITE OF SOME EXTRA SLEEP, I was for some reason a little jittery. I straightened out my fishing gear, and became well-nigh inextricably entangled in a new double-tapered fly line. Valodya finally showed up, an hour late because someone had forgotten to put oil in the weapons-carrier and gone off with the keys to the oil storage, which didn't add to my good temper. After a few days of sulking Valodya is now eating in our apartment as though nothing had happened. At last we got under way for Glini, but we had no sooner reached the outskirts of Moscow than I knew that the fishing would be no good, for the wind was laying the smoke flat along the thatched roofs of the *izbas* and tossing the leafy green trees wildly.

The countryside is now luxuriantly green, and great heavy heads of lilacs were blossoming around the village houses. The wind whipped the little short skirts of the peasant women high around their strong, shapely legs, in cotton stockings or bare and white — it is too close to winter for them to have sunburned. Beneath the first long bridge over the canal was a tremendous raft of logs, several hundred meters long, with little thatched huts built on it as if they had grown there naturally. I remarked to Valodya's disgust that that would be a pleasant way to live. "No!" he said decisively. "It would be very unpleasant to live in constant fear of the logs opening up to let you fall through and drown." He said that most Russians do not know how to swim, as only in very recent years has anyone regarded swimming as a form of sport.

On the far edge of Dmitrov a white, cold rain lashed down on us. "Valodya," I said, "let's stop and give some of these poor people a lift who are trudging on in all this rain."

"They're used to it," he said, without any sign of slowing up. "They'll soon get home and dry out on the stove. Besides, it's very dangerous to give strange people a lift in Russia. I never did it when I was driving a truck with the armies during the war. They might crack you on the back of the head."

"Sure, I know that. But these are simple country women, with bundles in their arms that they have obviously just bought at the market in town. They're not going to crack anyone over the head."

"Yes, that's true. But you never know which of them is a thief. If we didn't have all your fishing gear and bags in the back part of the car, it might not be too bad. But all the time we would have to keep looking around to see if they had put anything in their pockets."

And then he went on to tell me a long Russian *skazka* to illustrate his point, about a wolf who had followed some cunning advice and tried to catch fish with his tail by dangling it through a hole in the ice, only to have the ice freeze solid and catch him by the tail. When the farmer who had given him that advice came up to take him, the only way the wolf could get free was to leave his tail behind. I had heard that tale before, as it is in the literature of many lands, and began to wonder what was Valodya's point. He went on.

"So the wolf stole some fish instead of catching them. Then, when it grew dusk, he lay down in the snow by the side of the road and began to moan. Soon a sleigh came past. The old man driving the sleigh stopped to see what was moaning beside the road, just the way we might stop and give some of those people a lift. The wolf promised the old man his fine string of fish if the old man would take him home and let him warm himself beside the fire. So the old man told him to jump in the back of the sleigh. When he got home, the old man shouted to his wife to come out and see what he had brought home — not only all the things he had bought at the market, but a fine string of fish for a present! The old woman went out to the sleigh, looked in the back, and there was nothing there — no wolf, no present, not even the things her husband had bought at the market. So she swore at the old man for telling her lies, saying that he had probably spent all the market money for vodka!"

By the time Valodya had finished his story the sun was out, and the plodding peasant women were somewhere far behind us. We turned off the main *chaussée* and bumped along the unspeakable wooden paving of the glass-factory town. Even in that drab village there were notes of beauty — lilac bushes, in one place trimmed into tall trees, higher than the *izbas,* slender and stately, with their tops bowed down by the heavy reddish blue fruit of their blossoms. And there was a new house, with the wood still white and fresh as if it had been cut from the living wood that day, carved as beautifully and as elaborately as any *izba* in the land, showing that at least that art is still alive in Russia.

But the road was even worse than the first time we went over it. The Russians have a word *bezobrazny,* which means literally "shapeless." It also means "hideous" or "monstrous," but just in the last few days I have heard it used several times like current slang, and that word is very apt for our road. It is amazing how much a Russian country road can change in the course of a couple of weeks. The very nature of the road was different, and it went in different places than before, so that it was almost unrecognizable. New ditches were dug across it, for no apparent reason, and it wandered into new and different morasses.

Not far from Glini we passed a truck, stuck deep in the mud. They had been there for three days, so I told Valodya to tow them out. The weapons-carrier was really a marvelous machine, for we hooked their heavy wire cable onto the hooks on both cars — all Russian cars in the country have built-in hooks for towing — and pulled them out with ease. But Valodya, elated with success, kept on towing them. While I hung on with both hands to keep from being catapulted out and tried to make him hear that I was telling him to stop, the car would surge up against the towline with enough force to send me through the windshield if I hadn't been well braced, and soon we slithered to a forced stop, with the truck off the road in a worse position than it was before our help. After a couple of futile tries to move them again, Valodya threw off the towline and we left in the abrupt Russian fashion, without a word on either side, and with neither hard feelings for abandoning them nor appreciation for effort already expended.

I petted two beautiful white kids that were galloping about in Ephrosinya Vladimirovna's house, greeted her and Pavel Dmitrovich, and went alone straight to the dam to fish. My new tapered line cast nicely, although the high wind was a great hindrance. The river was as much altered as the roads, being now several feet lower, changing all the contours of its bed and uncovering all sorts of reed banks and rocks and shoals where before there had seemed to be deep water. It had even uncovered a lure I had once hooked on a sunken snag and which I was glad to have again. Probably the peasants thereabouts had not recognized it as a lure. I fished with dry flies until dark, with no success other than some trifling little fish that snapped greedily at the flies.

Just as it grew dusk, Fyodr Petrovich appeared. He used the expressive Russian word which means to make a guest of someone by regaling them with food or drink, and offered me a couple of buns. I bit into one of them, and found that it had been baked with a stuffing of eggs. On the way home in the dusk, he urged me to come to his house for supper. Knowing the importance of food to the Russian, and that when he makes up his mind to be hospitable he will completely clean himself out to make a good gesture of it, in traditional Russian fashion, I insisted that he have supper with us instead, and promised to go home with him afterwards to "drink tea."

During supper, Aleksei Mikhailovich showed up, having ridden in on horseback, and also a *yegor* from the place near the main *chaussée* where they have put up the few other foreign hunters or fishermen, mostly Poles, none of whom have ever been able to make it over the roads to Glini. The *yegor* from the other settlement had a bleak, weather-bitten face, with good gray eyes which had a thousand wrinkles around them. His name was Dmitry Petrovich. We put a good dent into a bottle of Willy's Swedish gin — big bottles they are, too, full liters — ate some baked beans from my supplies and some fried eggs. Then I took some gin, some cigarettes, candy, and a couple of tins of food, and went to Fyodr Petrovich's, taking the other guests with me.

There we all sat down around the table, and the first thing Fyodr did was to break out a couple of bottles of vodka, which we all drank Russian fashion, bottoms up without a breath. There were nearly a score of us there, all Russians but me, including the smoky-dark Mariya and several unidentified kinfolk or friends. And they were really hospitable. Fyodr Petrovich showed me snapshots of all the family in various stages of growth, including the world-wide naked baby pictures which are equally embarrassing throughout the world to those same babies when grown, and I was showered with food.

Every Russian village has its own saint, and the saint's day is always a local holiday for food and drink. Everybody gets drunk. The day before had been the Day of St. Nikolya, the local patron, and I profited by what was left from the celebration, including several things of which I have heard but never seen, such as *vatrushka,* a sort of cheese pie.

Fyodr's wife looked on and beamed, and Mariya's baby was as good as gold. They are a fine family. When I said so afterwards to Valodya, he said, "Yes, they are the Russian *khlebsol* — the bread and salt of Russia."

When the vodka and the gin ran out, we drank beer, which every villager makes for himself. They said that many villagers also make *samogon,* or moonshine vodka. I knew that *samogon* was against the law, so I told them that during prohibition days in America I had learned to make my own beer, and even what they probably would not have been able to tell from *samogon.*

"But wasn't that against the law?" asked Aleksei Mikhailovich.

"Yes, but many people made it anyhow. The probihition law was an unjust law, and my people are a free people who will not have unjust laws."

"Will they do the same thing about the Mundt Bill?" he asked. "That seems an unjust law."

So I had to explain that the Mundt Bill did not outlaw the Communist Party, but merely required them to register and show their hands in the open. Then Valodya, who has been rather officious ever since the trouble over the sugar at home, interrupted. "That is politics, and one shouldn't talk about politics. Let's talk about something else."

We did, but I had one thing more to say. "Something else which I wanted to point out before Valodya changed the subject is that the Soviet government has outlawed every party but its own. Please note that even the Communists are not outlawed in America."

"Ah, but here I have never heard of anyone wanting anything else but Communism," said Aleksei Mikhailovich, looking cunning.

I did not need to answer, for I saw a look of great disgust on more than one face.

All the next day the wind kept on. I rigged my fly rod, went to the dam, and wandered far downstream, casting as best the wind would let me. Here and there a girl or woman, with tucked-up skirts, was scrubbing out clothes at the water's edge. At one place was a village across the river, with a little red Soviet flag flying from a ragged roof. There a small boy shouted at me, "American! American! Americans are worse!" And then, although the river lay between us, he took to his heels, shouting still, "Americans are worse!" He didn't say what they were worse than, nor did I care to try to find out.

Around noon I gave up, went back to Glini, found some food, and packed up my things. Dmitry Petrovich, the new *yegor* from the other settlement, urged me to try the Moscow-Volga Canal. There the fish were undoubtedly ravenously hungry, because the banks were all of stone and there wasn't so much food for them. Also he wanted me to see his place. So we bumped over the shapeless road, nearly losing him out on many an occasion, to the paved *chaussée*. There was still the enormous heap of tiles and boards, still piled like jackstraws, but for the first time I realized that the guards were there not merely to protect the material from theft, for the scores of women who were working on the mountainous heaps were themselves prisoners under guard. Every soldier had a dark, un-Russian, Asiatic face.

"They're not Russian," I said. "What are they?"

"Tatar, or maybe Chuvashi," answered Dmitry, but I pointed out that their eyes were not slanted like those of Tatars. Valodya said that he thought they were "Natsmen." I did not know just what he meant by Natsmen. Valodya said that "Natsmen" were a small nation, but from where he did not know. At any rate, they looked like pictures from an old book with their fierce faces and their white teeth. And there was a barbed-wire enclosure for the women.

We turned there away from Moscow and went along the road towards Bolshaya Volga, passing more and more women, and I began to realize that more and more of them were prisoners. Everywhere were women, cutting peat in the bogs, working on the roads, building houses, driving steam rollers and tractors, with great gangs of them handling mountains of peat onto the ships along the canal.

A few hundred meters from the highway, at the end of a corduroy road into some swampland, was the other settlement, with a large, many-roomed barracks or house where Dmitry, the *yegor,* lived. It was obviously some sort of summer camp. We went in and sat down for a while. The rooms were lined with pipeclay, and there were three or four cots to a room, but otherwise they were quite bare and cheerless. The more prosperous *izbas,* such as those in a city like Dmitrov, have their windows crowded with potted plants, many of them flowering with something like varicolored geraniums, and all of them green and cheery. Even Ephrosinya Vladimirovna's house had a potted fig tree in it, but this place had only a pair of antlers on the wall. Dmitry's comrade came in, and was introduced — Boris Petrovich. He had tousled sandy hair, a hard face, and was apparently an ex-sailor, from his blue-and-white striped jersey. I asked him, and found that he was.

They told us of a marvelous place for fish, in one of the main sluices of the canal, only one had to have special permission to go there. They were quite sure that permission could be had to fish there, but when I suggested trying to get it on the spot, their faces fell. Even the simplest of formalities is usually a long-drawn-out process, but Dmitry was willing to give it a try, so we went back to the highway and farther almost to the Volga. We finally reached a great set of locks. Nearby was a big new village with much construction going on, all being done by women. I looked around and, sure enough, spotted the barbed-wire enclosure and the blockhouse booths that guarded them. We asked around, and finally some minor authority sent a businesslike young sailor to accompany us. We walked through some lovely grassy woods to the locks, and there were told firmly by the young sailor that it was forbidden to go farther, but that I might fish in the canal up to the beginning of the locks. I started to cast, and soon a soldier came out of the lock structure and watched. He, too, was not Russian by his face, but he was pleasant and accepted a cigarette. He said that it was only when the locks were opened that there were fish to be caught there, and he confirmed the story that it was marvelous sport at that time. Unfortunately, the locks were opened only at four o'clock in the morning. So we walked back, through the short green grass, studded with violets and little shoals of bright blue flowers that grew clustered on spikes. Snowflowers, they are called, because they blossom even before the snow is gone.

Dmitry took me to one more place on the canal, and there I fished while Valodya, worried about the Moscow militia, washed the very dirty car. When Valodya was done, I sent him to take the *yegor* home and kept on fishing. Here a considerable stream, as clear as vodka, flowed out of the canal, tunneling through the high dyke. In such a place the fishing was said to be superior. A few hundred yards farther there were streams flowing the other way, into the canal, but never a fish did I see.

The canal stretched absolutely straight, as far as one could see in both directions, and on both banks was swampy forest. In the distance a thunderstorm was building up, and there were vivid lightning flashes and almost a continual roll of thunder. Before Valodya got back, the storm had arrived. Suddenly the wind, which had been blowing steadily, stopped, and there was a great silence as the black clouds piled up overhead, writhing and boiling on their ragged edges. And then there was a sound, sad and distant, and far across the canal the distant treetops began to toss with the breath of the storm. The trees were a livid, unearthly green against the black sky, and the sound was the myriad voice of their leaves. The oncoming wind blackened the canal itself. Finally it reached me in a burst that effectively stopped my casting. Great drops of rain started to patter into the water, so I ran for cover under the little bridge that crossed an outflowing stream. I heard Valodya come thundering back, blowing his horn to call me from the canal side of the dyke. I let him shout for a while, until he started to get out in the pouring rain.

We stopped in Dmitrov at the same *chainaya* where we were once before, and there we had a very good steak. Steaks are always veal, at least those which I have managed to get, but this one brought with it some well-seasoned potatoes and sliced dill pickles. Even the beer seemed better than usual. After the storm, the wind had completely died down, so, although it was late and nearly sunset, we stopped once more along the canal for me to fish. Still no strikes, although once something jumped far out in the middle, as big as a Newfoundland dog.

And then, as the twilight came on, the whole scene took on a
real beauty — perhaps the first entire scene of real beauty, apart
from snow, that I have seen in Russia. The canal here was not rigid
and straight, but swept in a wide curve, and the high green banks
looked like Rhineland vineyards in the late light. There was a great
sense of space in the landscape, the water was mirror-still, and
everything seemed caught as if in a dream. Here and there was a
motionless fisherman, and in the distance some naked lads were
swimming from the banks. White mists began to form on the
marshy pools in the meadows, and there was a looming sense of
great distances in all directions. The countryside looked as Europe
should look, like part of France or England, and not like a half-
savage, primitive land.

Away off in the distance, on some heights, was a row of enormous
hills, but they were too regular not to be man-made. They looked
like old prehistoric British earth-castles, and yet they were too big
for even that. When I went back to the car I asked Valodya what
they were, remarking that they seemed artificial and not natural.

"It's hard to say," he answered. "These peasants are strange
people. They are always digging or doing something. If there is a
ravine, they are filling it in, and if there is a flat space, they are
building a hill on it."

Valodya had scraped off the rear number plate of the car somewhere on the shapeless road and he was very worried about the
police. In Dmitrov we had tried unsuccessfully in several places to
buy some chalk, and at last succeeded in getting some at the
chainaya, with which Valodya marked our license number on the
back of the car. Nevertheless he was worried, because the police
can make endless delay and difficulty. For that reason, he drove
fast so that we might slip into Moscow before it got dark enough
to turn on our lights, which would disclose our lack of a proper
license. The Russians never turn their lights on until it becomes
really dangerously dark, but in spite of this we bounced and jolted
through the villages without lights at headlong speed until well
beyond that time, blowing our horn continuously and hoping that
the dim crowds of strolling villagers would get out of our way in
time. We passed several new prison camps I had not noticed on
the way out, plain now because their floodlights outlined their

barbed-wire fencing. In Moscow, we were stopped only a couple of times, and then because the police were stopping all cars and not because of our license. I was so weary when I got home that I went to sleep in the bathtub.

6. THE DREAMING WOOD

SABIN'S TIME IS UP. He told me that the day after his exit visa was requested from the Soviet Foreign Office, his quiet, well-mannered Darya began to get into trouble. She now has to appear in court on a charge of hooliganism, brought by the *nachalnik* of her apartment house. There is no chance of Sabin's letting them use her as a lever over him, if that is what they are up to. Darya is too obviously quiet and well-behaved for them not to be up to something.

After long negotiations, the Embassy succeeded in chartering a neat, streamlined river diesel steamer for a picnic. The court of Mokhavaya House was crowded with people and various arrangements for transportation of them, their guests and gear to the Khimki river station, all of which brought a few gray hairs to Atkins, the sensible, sandy-haired American engineer who was in charge of such things, and who works for my office because he has a lovely Russian wife whom the Soviets will not let leave Russia.

There was plenty of cold beer on the boat, and it was very pleasant to be slipping silently and swiftly along between the high green banks of the canal, past the villages and settlements that looked as though they grew out of the ground. For a long time Tamara Gilmore sang — *"Steppe da Steppe,"* *"Stenka Razin"* and many another Russian song — in a soft, dramatic voice. The Danish guests whom we had brought seemed quite happy, so everything was fine.

After about three hours, before we came to the first lock, we moored to a large heavily wooded island and all went ashore. The Gilmores, the Eddie Stevenses, and we had arranged to pool our resources. Nell had brought some cool green cocktails, chicken, salad, and a big crock of baked beans, Nina Stevens had brought some Tulsky cookies and some little veal patties that her *babushka* had made, and there were the usual picnic things to eat and drink. Holiday was in the air, perhaps because everyone was out of Moscow, perhaps because of the way they were dressed. Tamara had a blue silk play suit, Nina wore a wide peasant skirt, and Nell was in pink gingham.

Eddy Gilmore started up his portable radio. The Gilmores' small, pretty daughter has china-blue eyes, and was wonderfully good-natured. She had once asked her father why he didn't have any hair, and he had told her that he had given it all to her. When he was away in Berlin recently, she cropped off all her hair herself to give it to him when he came back. So now she has to wear a kerchief on her head until it grows back in again.

During a dull moment, and to avoid the exertion of the inevitable baseball game, I slipped away into the woods and walked through them to the far side of the island. It was much bigger than I had thought, for it was a full half hour's walk each way. More than once I wondered if I would ever be able to find my way back to the boat. They were beautiful woods — what they call a *dremuchi les.* Always in *skazki* the woods are *dremuchi* — thick, impenetrable, but carrying with it the connotation of dreaming. That adjective is used only in connection with a forest, and there is a Russian proverb which says that strangers are such a wood.

The character of the wood would change within a few hundred yards, now nothing but thick, dark fir trees, with the trunks standing clear of underbrush but so thick that one could see no more than a few feet in any direction, now not a fir, but only a ghostly shimmer of tall white birches all around, and now a mixture of both, or a little open glade, or a lost, grassy road that began nowhere and went nowhere. And all around in the grass and moss were violets and spiky blue flowers growing thick, and a profusion of fragrant lilies of the valley.

At last I came out on the other side, where the island was tied to the mainland by a big dam. There was no road or means of access to the island except by boat or on foot across the long dam. Edenberg told me afterward that he too had tried to walk in that general direction along some sort of road, only to be turned back by a soldier who told him it was forbidden. As I came back through the edge of the dreaming wood, I suddenly came upon a soldier sitting in the grass. I think we were both equally startled, but it happened to be at a point where I had broken some twigs to guide

me back through a particularly confusing part of the wood, so I
faded away into the dark trees before he could gather his wits.

Three or four rowboats, filled with Russians out for the Sunday
afternoon, pulled up on the beach at our picnic place. Soon the
boats were full of American youngsters being taken for a boat ride
by the brawny young Russians.

On the river boat on the way back we ran into a black thunderstorm. There was blazing lightning and a downpour of cold rain,
but by that time everyone was drinking and singing, led by Eddie
Stevens playing a mouth organ. The storm cleared up before we
reached Khimki, and we kept on between the fresh-washed green
banks, which were more vivid than ever against the dark sky.

Sometimes the kerchiefed girls and the booted men along the
banks would wave back to us, and sometimes they would only look
at us. There is something childish about the way Russian people
wave, for there is no free gesture about it. They only timidly move
their hands up and down from the wrist. I have noticed it many
times, and it always seems like a small child who is being taught
how to do something of which he is not quite sure. Somehow a feeling of sadness came over me, a sort of it-never-can-happen-again
feeling, and, although there had been nothing outstanding about
the day, I was sorry to see it come to an end.

Valodya, with scores of other drivers, was waiting on the dock.
He caught our baskets and jugs as we passed them down from the
rail, and was very much pleased with himself when we were the
first people to leave the Khimki station.

It was almost night when we returned along the river from taking the Madsens home, and Moscow was all veiled in blue mist.
The long stretch of the ancient Chinese wall along the river was
magical and mysterious in the twilight.

It is too bad that Hollywood cannot see itself as foreigners see
it. Here in Moscow one can understand viewpoints that would seem
impossible in America. This week's American movie at Spasso
House was Somerset Maugham's *The Razor's Edge*. It was a complicated account of alcoholics and betrayals and mismarriages. It
was interesting enough, but I could not help but think of the
standard Soviet reaction to such a picture — how they would say:

"See, that is just what we have been telling you. Your Western freedom is only freedom to debauch and murder and betray. You are not fit for such freedom, and your movies, which of course reflect your lives, prove it."

The drama of the individual in search of his soul or faced with any sort of personal problem is unknown in Russia of today, for the only drama that is shown to the people is the drama of the state or its embodiment in people. And yet what grisly soul-searching and what lurid problems there must be to give drama to this world of spies and informers which substitutes for the Promised Land.

There is an entrance to the Alexandrovsky Gardens beyond the far end of the Tsar's riding hall near a sloping, medieval drawbridgelike entrance to the Kremlin itself. Inside, a huge round flower bed is gay with white tulips, with a deep border of scarlet tulips to set them off.

Today the gardens were crowded with well-behaved people — perhaps plenty of police and the proximity of the Kremlin had something to do with their behavior — walking around and sitting on the stiff benches or on the grass, many of them reading. I stopped to look at a tall, plain monument, like a shaft in a cemetery, and to read the long list of names of old revolutionists which is inscribed upon it. None of them are alive today.

The afternoon was hot and sunny. I left the Kremlin park and walked up Gertsina Street to Tverskoy Boulevard, and then through the gardens in the middle of that wide street that rings the central part of the city. Everywhere were crowds of people, and I sat on a hard bench for a long while and watched them, and wondered at the large proportion who carried perplexing deformities and scars. Many of those blemishes couldn't have come from the war, for they seemed to be equally distributed among all ages. Only a rare person seemed completely healthy, normal and comely, and these were usually much more smartly dressed than the others. It was noticeable that that kind of person was always alone or with someone else of the same sort. One such girl, with a golden-brown skin and violet eyes, wearing a blue bonnet that might have come from Paris, startled me by coming up to me and asking what time it was.

I talked today for a long time with a man who knows Russia well and is at last leaving it. His account checks in every way with so many others. It is a tale of fear and oppression and discontent, of incompetence and suspicion, laid on the backs of a fine people who deserve so much better. The whole picture is the familiar one which Kravchenko gives of a willing but primitive people driven by fanaticism, stupidity and mistrust to attempting things beyond their capabilities, and of refusing to recognize the truth when the results fall short. He said that from what he himself had seen he was confident that a great majority of the Russian people want something other than the government which they have — not the days of the Tsar back again, although many of them would even take that, but certainly not the days of Stalin.

He told me many examples and incidents from his own experience. They were particularly convincing because he had no emotional attachments, no ideology or politics, no ax to grind. His evidence for his beliefs will never be published to the world, for he is a professional man, and his interests lie entirely in his profession. He does not like publicity and its possible effects on his business. From talking with others like him, I believe that only a small part of such corroborating experience has been made available, but that that small part is very representative of the whole.

For some time I have been trying to find a satisfactory explanation of why the Russians love their *rodina*, their native land, so much when it is so harsh and cruel to them. Eddie Stevens says facetiously that perhaps it is because there is so much of it. There is something in that, for its very vastness and monotony is a little like that of the sea, exerting something of the same sort of fascination. But I have reached the conclusion that it is because the people are so close to the land.

Russia, in spite of its industrialization, is still primarily an agricultural country. Sowing and harvest take up much more space in the press than they do in even agricultural papers in the West. To a Russian, food is always a problem. It is not something that comes from the corner grocery, but life itself, that must be wrested directly from the land. Russian history is full of such a long series of invasions — Pechenegs, Polovtsi, Avars, Huns, Mongols, Livonians, Poles, Swedes, French, Germans — that the Russians are convinced that the land which gives them life is a cause for envy on the part of the rest of the world.

Also those who live close to the land develop a nostalgic affection for it which the congenital city dweller is not so apt to feel. Perhaps this is particularly true in a harsh climate, for there is something very appealing about being shut in snug and warm from the winter storms when those storms are only the thickness of the log walls away. Spring and summer are so brief that they do not have time to pall or be taken for granted, and the smell of autumn leaves and woodsmoke are not city smells.

The Gilmores' dark, vivid, positive maid, who was with us on the canal picnic, let Nell and me into their apartment. There we had a few drinks, surrounded by many attractive Soviet paintings, most of which Eddy said were given him in the days when it was possible to have an occasional Soviet friend or acquaintance. The Medvedeffs — he has recently arrived in Moscow for duty as our assistant military attaché — were also invited. Captain Medvedeff, like my own Lieutenant Levy, had a Russian mother.

Eddy took us for dinner to the famous Georgian restaurant, the Aragvi. The main room of the Aragvi is two floors high, and around the upper portion is a series of murals of the great Georgian epic of the weretiger. The snowy Caucasus peaks of those pictures made a cool setting for a warm summer evening. At one end on the upper level was a little balcony with the orchestra of accordion, balalaikas, and strange-looking Georgian instruments, and opposite it was a small private dining room where we were.

In our room was a huge carved wooden chest. Medvedeff repeated a story he had heard to the effect that the whole house had been built around that chest. Eddy pointed out that another fable was in the making, for he had been in the Aragvi when that chest had first arrived. He said that it was one of the first things to have been liberated from the Germans.

The food was splendid, with plenty of caviar, vodka and champagne, and shashlik — spitted meat — that tasted more like steak than any meat I've had in Russia. Tamara had on a slick, tight dress and looked very attractive, although no more so than Mrs. Medvedeff or Nell, who wore an equally slick and tight dress of dark green with spangles sewed all through it.

When I remarked on how disappointing it was not to have any real Russian friends, Tamara told me, simply and without complaining, that at least we had our own people, whereas she had nothing but Eddy and her little daughter. The Russians regarded her as untrustworthy because she had married an American, and the Americans and other foreigners regarded her with suspicion because she was a Russian, leaving her very much alone in the world. She told me to use the familiar form of speech with her, which pleased me not only because she has been always very kind and helpful, but because most Russian grammars and not a few Russians themselves have insisted that a foreigner can have no possible use for that form of speech. I use it sometimes with the servants when feeling particularly amiable with them, and have had many occasions to use it with children or with simple people, particularly when trying to be either a bit light-veined or deadly serious.

Some of the implications of the familiar form, usually translated awkwardly as "thou," are indicated in Goncharov's *The Precipice,* where Raisky is much attracted by his cousin:

> He finally succeeded in getting her to call him "brother" instead
> of "cousin," but she did not go as far as "thou," saying that "thou"

in itself, and without any right, authorizes much that one or the other sometimes does not wish, gives birth to intimacy, even sometimes embarrasses with a friendship which is unnecessary and often not shared by the other person.

It was breathlessly hot today, and late in the afternoon a black thunderstorm came up, with blazing lightning and lashing rain. I heard that much damage had been done by the storm in Moscow, with two or three people killed. One never reads about anything of that sort in the papers, but news travels fast in Moscow.

Nell has been in the dispensary for the last few days, helping Dr. Vaughn put up powders and filling capsules. When one of her earrings dropped off into a dish of powders for the second or third time, Dr. Vaughn said, "Why don't you let me pierce your ears?"

"What?'" she replied, "and let you go back and tell the Navy that all you did in Moscow was to pierce women's ears?"

The doctor laughed, but when he renewed the offer the next time an earring dropped, Nell, who has been losing earrings for years, agreed. She drew me a picture of the kind of gypsy earrings she wanted for her new ears, and after shopping all over Moscow I finally found a shop that had some big gold hoops such as she had drawn. Another customer, a little old peasant woman who herself had pierced ears, was a talkative and willing model while I made up my mind as to which sort looked best.

Having one's ears pierced is not as simple as it sounds. Nell's ears are still so sore that she has trouble in sleeping — particularly when she insists on wearing her new earrings while she sleeps.

We had a buffet supper in our apartment for some of the younger people. Among the guests was a sparkling-eyed, dark-haired girl who sang some purple songs about such subjects as the mountain girl who was married at the age of three and had still a long time to wait until she could be a grown-up girl of seven, and about how Pappy wasn't really her pappy — it was Uncle Bill! How horrified the Soviets would be at such goings-on!

Bouteillier, who served for many years with the French Foreign Legion, was there, together with his lush, handsome French-Algerian wife. Also there was Arthur Jansen from the Dutch Embassy, who is always amusing and interesting, particularly when he does his impersonations of various dignified diplomats and officials. His grandfather was Governor of Turkestan under the Tsars, for he is descended from the Dutch who were brought into Russia by Peter the Great and who came only on condition that they might always retain their Dutch citizenship.

Someone said that the very fair, blue-eyed Czech air attaché who was recalled to Prague immediately after the Czech coup had escaped to London, but a Czech who was with us either didn't know or couldn't afford to know. Altogether, it was a spirited and pleasant party, with all the windows wide open and the night breeze blowing through from the warm darkness. I particularly liked Mrs. Aldis, the South African. British colonials are more like Americans than any other foreigners, and we always have much in common, for we are all treated much the same by the English, as though Americans were colonials who had gone wrong, and we all react in much the same way to that treatment. Mrs. Aldis is young and strong, with good blue eyes and dark hair, and with energy and vivacity. Aldis, who is English, didn't quite know whether to be delighted or appalled when she broke forth in an authentic Zulu dance, chanting a refrain that was strangely like that of the great Maori war dance:

> *Ai ga da zumba, zumba, zumba,*
> *Ai ga da zumba, zumba zee!*

7. MOSKVA RIVER

TODAY WAS OPPRESSIVELY HOT. All the Russians say that Moscow air is not good, so Nell and I drove out in the country to get some good air. Right in the middle of Moscow, where the Mozhaisk Chaussée crosses the Moskva River, there is a little strip of gravelly beach, and it was as crowded with bathers as Coney Island on a Sunday afternoon. We were headed for Arkhangelsk, but found the road to that village blocked off for repairs and so kept on to Rublyovo instead.

Just before we got there, we went through a majestic pine wood, completely free from underbrush and carpeted everywhere with green, parklike grass. The pine trees were very big, and their lower parts were very dark. It seemed almost as though they had been burned by fire, but twenty or thirty feet up, the trunks became a light rosy red. There was a blue effect of distance through the dark woods, almost like smoke, and everything smelled delightfully of pines. And everywhere were people, lying on the grass, picnicking, playing, herding goats, or just lying. Nearly every girl and woman carried her shoes rather than wear them, going barefoot through the grass and the dust. It was not uncommon to see a girl so warm that she was carrying her blouse as well, striding unconcernedly along in short skirt and brassière.

Valodya obviously didn't want to keep on driving in the vicinity of Rublyovo — there are many military plants and factories on that side of Moscow — but I was adamant and kept denying his assertions that the road was about to come to an end. Although I was usually right at first, the roads we tried turned in unexpected directions, and in the long run we got nowhere, for every road eventually disappeared into high, boarded, barbed-wired gates, guarded by sentries with fixed bayonets.

The whole countryside was crowded with people, but the very nature of the terrain seemed secret. One could never see more than a few yards in any one direction. Now and then we could get glimpses of the river, with throngs in bathing and playing games and picnicking in the meadows, and everywhere in the fields were men and women — mostly women — working. Frequently the women working in the fields wore only brassières and panties in the breathless heat. I caught a glimpse of a big airfield once in the distance, but the road gave out into such violent ruts that we had to turn back.

On the way back through Moscow, the streets and pavements were everywhere being washed and cooled with hoses, played by barefoot women who were enjoying their jobs on such a hot day and who never let any passers-by interfere with the direction of the hose.

I found my handkerchiefs, shirts, and linen all smelling very strongly of fish. When I remarked on it, Zoya said that the supply of American soap had run out, and she had had to use Russian soap with which to launder my things. Whale oil, no doubt. At any rate, something has to be done about it, or I shall be followed by all the cats in Moscow.

We went to see Ostrovsky's *Forest* at MXAT. It has not been played for years in Moscow, and it is hard to see why MXAT waited until the very end of the season to put it on. It was an unbelievably hot evening and the theater was sweltering. When the curtain went up, it brought to the front rows a little breath of coolness together with the musty breath of grease paint and props, which Nell says is more like the breath of a livery stable than anything else. But the coolness didn't last long.

On the way home a gypsy street girl tried to sell us some peonies. I was trying to find out whether her price, which was unusually high, even for Moscow, was for single blossoms or for a bunch, when some Russian women came up. They joined the argument decisively by telling her that she ought to be ashamed of herself for trying to hold up honest people in such a fashion. We let the peonies go, but it was too bad, for the fragrance of peonies, as much as anything else, brings back my far childhood.

Some thirty or forty kilometers from Moscow a side road takes off from the Mozhaisk Chaussée for Zvenigorod, where there is

that serene stretch of the Moskva River by the high-arched bridge
which should have some fish in it, so Nell and I started out for it
early on a weekday afternoon, when it would not be apt to be
crowded with Russian picnickers. There comes a time when the
summer seems at its very height and when one knows that future
days will be on the downgrade towards autumn. This was that
sort of time, and there was a wealth of greenness everywhere,
sweltering in the heat, with heaped-up thunderstorms lying around
in every direction.

There was nothing that I recognized in the countryside, and even
the familiar Mozhaisk Chaussée itself seemed like an entirely new
and different road. It was not wholly due to the lush green that
veiled the villages and landmarks, but in large part because this is
a bewildering country, even a secret country. It has much variety
in detail, but a great monotony in general, and there is seldom
anything sufficiently outstanding or really different from anything
else to be readily recognizable. For hundreds of thousands of square
miles around Moscow there are no hills higher than the others,
from which one might be able to orient himself, and in such high
northern latitudes even the sun never seems to be in a well-defined
direction. There are few signposts at intersections, and even Russians get easily confused in their orientation.

We tried one side road after another, only to have them peter
out or end in nothing but high board fences, set deep in the woods
and guarded with bayonets. But along one of those bewildering
roads was the most wondrous wood that I have ever seen. It was a
grove of very tall birch trees, with no leaves or branches whatever
along their tall trunks until the fanning out of the light, feathery
green of their very tops. Those trees were so thick, so closely set,
that one could not see between them at all. They made a completely
solid wall, with no breaks or chinks through which the sky above
the horizon or even more distant trees could be seen. The silver
bark of the great vertical trunks was broken with the irregular
brown spots which are natural to birches, and whatever light
drifted down through the living green roof seemed to come from
the white trees themselves. It gave the effect of a solid tapestry of
brown and silver. It was an enchanted wood, so decorative that an
artist or stage director would not have dared to attempt it because

it was too exaggerated and unreal, a wood that was so thick it was gloomy and dark, and at the same time light and delicate because of all its whiteness.

Everywhere we went, and regardless of the fact that it was a normal working day, the pools and canals were filled with people of all ages swimming in the afternoon heat, occasionally naked, but more often in trunks or bloomers and brassières — obviously their normal underclothing, as could be seen when they were dressing or undressing on the grassy banks. In the villages, naked children played in the dust, usually lovely children, for Russian children are extraordinarily nice. Most of them remain attractive until they are grown, with clear eyes and bright, good faces.

We tried road after road until one, which seemed as unfamiliar as the others, brought us to the place we were seeking. I put on some khaki and some old Marine shoes and waded out into the cool, fast river.

It was too deep to wade everywhere, but comfortable enough to fish from about waist deep, with a gravelly bottom and bush-lined, grassy banks.

I fished slowly upstream from the bridge, and passed a middle-aged couple who were bathing, both wearing only trunks. The woman was a strong, brown, bright-eyed peasant. They watched me interestedly as I felt my way along the gravelly bottom, casting beneath the bushes and out into the middle of the river.

As far as one could see both up and down the river were groups of swimmers, with an occasional boat. I continued on upstream and came abreast three or four bare and shrieking little girls, pig-tails flying above the dark water. They were accompanied by their big-bosomed older sister. It was time for them to go, so the sister tried, none too determinedly, to herd the youngsters out of the water. Partially successful in that effort, she started to bathe herself before finally leaving. Unconcernedly she took off her brassière and used it as a washcloth. She was more modest about her shape-less blue bloomers, for they did not come off. She only pushed them up as far as possible, scrubbed, and then pushed them down to that same classic point. She was still scrubbing when I left her.

Ahead, a group of women and small girls had just arrived. They

started to take off their skirts. Then Nell appeared on the green
bank, telling me that about thirty German prisoners had been
brought down to the river for a swim near where the car was
parked. I didn't know that she had such a statistical mind, for she
said she had counted forty-two men so far, without clothes. There
didn't seem to be much chance to catch fish in that busy river, so
I walked back to the car with her.

There I rigged up a spinning reel, but gave it up as a bad job
and started to use a dry fly in a smooth, weed-bottomed stretch
below the bridge. The sun dropped below the horizon in a smother
of coppery gold, and it became very still and quiet along the river,
with the silence broken by the occasional shouts of swimmers on
the other bank. Now and then a fish would jump far out in the
stream, and I would change the dry fly for a casting rod. A little
below, on my side of the river, a well-dressed girl stood arm in arm
with a soldier. They stood for a long time watching the peaceful
scene, and then started slowly to take off their clothes, pausing
often to talk and look at the river.

Suddenly there was a tug on my streamer. Thinking that I had
hooked some weeds, I started to reel in. The girl was standing in
brassière and blue, short drawers, and her companion was already
in the water. As I reeled in closer, there was a flutter in the water,
and it was clear that I had a fish. Valodya, who was standing by
me, started to jump up and down with excitement. I landed it with
no trouble and found that it was a *shchuka,* with big yellowish-
white spots on its dark green sides and a spoonbill filled with long,
sharp teeth. It was not big, only about the size of a good trout, but
respectable enough, and it was very like a trout in its body. Downstream, the girl slipped off her blue bloomers and stepped slowly
down into the water.   .

While I was cleaning the fish, a whole family arrived beside us,
undressed completely, and slid into the water. It was late, time to
go home, but after the excitement of the lone *shchuka,* both Nell
and Valodya insisted that I try this and that. The soldier's girl came
out of the water and started to dress. It was growing dusk, and
soon it would be hard to unrig the rods, so we finally folded up and
left, a little reluctant to leave so idyllic a place. And one of the
most idyllic things about it was the complete lack of self-conscious-

ness, together with the complete modesty, with which these Russians undressed, went gleaming white into the dark river, came shining out of it, and again dressed themselves. There is no basic incompatibility between nakedness and modesty, and these people showed that they knew this instinctively.

It was nearly midnight when we reached the outskirts of Moscow. Although it was dark enough for lights to be lit, the evening sky was still white. One realizes the size of Moscow more at night than in the daytime, for in all directions for many, many miles were the lights of a great city, whereas in the daytime it would have seemed as though the city had already half faded out into the countryside.

As we came into the heart of the city, every light in every room in every house and apartment seemed to be burning. No blinds were ever drawn, but there was never any movement or anyone to be seen in all that myriad of lighted rooms. Most of the people were probably out on the streets because of the heat, but it was still somehow strange to see so many lights with so little evidence of those who were using them. Electricity and the electric lamp are still a wonder and a marvel to the ordinary Russian, so perhaps they had the lights on just so they could be admired.

On one or two occasions Valodya has taken it on himself to criticize Natasha and her ways, so it was necessary to call him into my office. I told him that our household had to be quiet, well-behaved and gentle, which excluded mutual criticism and gossip among the servants, and that Natasha and her lack of planning in the use of the car for marketing and such things were no concern of his. He was not overworked, and if he was required to drive back and forth to the Kremlin a dozen times for no apparent reason, or if Natasha went to the market a dozen times in preparing for a dinner party, it was not his business to question. So far, it seems to have been effective.

There are always exceptions to any broad statement but in general Russians do love to assert themselves over others, and are fond of assuming authority without too much responsibility. It seems necessary either to put one of them definitely in charge, or else to treat them with strict impartiality. They do not seem to have any intermediate relationship between one of complete equality and that of master over those who are subservient.

The King's Birthday is a national occasion, a sort of British Fourth of July without the fireworks, so the British Embassy had a very splendid party. Nell put on a trailing black evening dress and I, not without some assistance, solved the puzzle of how to hang my new decoration about my neck while wearing a white service uniform. The British Embassy is on the other side of the Kremlin, facing it from across the Moskva River. It was still broad daylight when we went there at half past nine. There is one place on the way from which some seventeen or eighteen of the golden domes within the Kremlin can be seen, all crowded together in one dreamlike fantastic group, and they were shining and splendorous in the clear evening air.

I talked mostly with the Russians and the Russian-speaking people who were there, including the brown, soft-spoken, pretty wife of the Czech Minister. Her husband did not seem very happy, but she showed no signs of trouble. Vishinsky came up and spoke to me, thrusting out an uncertain hand. Since I have never talked with him, he probably mistook me for one of the British hosts.

I sat out in the garden for a long time with Nell, John Emmerson, and Nina Stevens. I did not know before that Nina is a Wellesley graduate. She certainly knows what is going on, but is too Russian really to believe it, and so seems to hope for the best.

It was two o'clock in the morning when we came home. Already the sky was lightening with the dawn, the Kremlin domes now showing dark against the gathering whiteness.

Zoya cut her foot while tinkering about with a razor blade, and was hobbling around the house. "Zoya, don't do so much running around. Let Natasha do the moving around for you until your foot gets well," I said.

"Gospodin Admiral, *I've* got a bellyache!" said Natasha, owlishly.

"All right, Natasha. If you've still got your bellyache after Zoya's foot gets well, it will be her turn to wait on you then."

"That's right! You speak the truth!" they both said.

Tom Ireland and his current roommate, the dark, hard-looking, competent Winters, came in for a drink. Tom was full of all sorts of ideas about the world and the future. Rocky Winters, who gets his nickname from his origins in the Colorado mountains, is economic attaché, and he not only knows his economics, but is able to make them clear to others. We finally went on to the Leningrad Station to say good-by to a departing foreigner.

At first we went to the wrong train, and wandered around for some time before finding the Red Arrow. The station was crowded with people standing in pushing, surging crowds trying to get tickets to somewhere or other, never annoyed with the pushing unless it gets very rough indeed. Some of the cars that we passed had not yet been made up into trains but through the wide-open windows we saw that they were half-filled with shapeless huddles of humanity, patiently waiting. And down the middle of one such lantern-lit wagon came a blind boy, tapping ahead of him with a stick and shouting something long and complicated in a singsong voice like that of a prophet telling of his visions.

Sunday morning the band was playing in the Kremlin gardens. I agreed with Natasha that it was to give the Kremlin children a good send-off for their summer camp. Although we have never heard it before, Valodya insisted that it was a regular thing for the band to play there on Sundays — a typical Russian insistence on something that we can easily disprove with our own eyes and ears.

8. BORODINO

WE SET OFF ON A COLD, MISTY, rainy day for Borodino, some hundred and thirty kilometers in the direction of Minsk. In Russia one seldom experiences the effervescent feeling of being in a foreign country that comes to one so often in other lands. Perhaps it was because today was misty and cold, with the vague, mysterious loveliness that is associated more with islands and seacoasts, but at any rate this day I had the same feeling of excited expectation that I used to have in England. The bewitched quality which the Russian landscape can sometimes assume has something ominous and disturbing about it, but today's magic was buoyant and full·of promise.

We followed the Minsk Chaussée through miles and miles of forests and scrub, and finally stopped to get our shoes thoroughly wet in the dripping moss and fern while looking for wild strawberries. Everywhere was a sea of wild flowers, and it was so wet that we didn't seriously try for strawberries. Instead, when I was back in the car with my shoes and socks drying on the heater, we bought a whole jar full, three or four quarts, from some peasant women and children who came past. They had been out in the woods for berries since four o'clock in the morning.

Around noon we cut over from the Minsk Chaussée to Mozhaisk. They milk their goats and cattle here three times a day, and the noonday milking was going on among the herds all along the road. The sun came out from the clouds, and Mozhaisk was soon steaming from the rain. It is a sprawling country town, so sprawling that the damage done by the Germans, though extensive, is not too obvious. It seemed rather as though Mozhaisk had always been full of big empty spaces.

We hunted up a *chainaya* for lunch. The big dining room whose windows looked out on the streets was jammed with people. Valodya and the *nachalnik* tried to induce us to have our lunch alone in a dark, hot inside room. When we pointed out the disadvantages, the *nachalnik* promptly and without argument went to work and doubled people up until she had cleared a table for us. Although the beef strogonov was made from salted rather than fresh meat, the food was good and well seasoned, and our big glass mugs of beer went well.

A few of the people who were eating there looked just like nice American youngsters and parents who had come into town on a Saturday, but most of them looked as though they were made up for the stage, with their kerchiefs and their faded, shapeless, ragged clothing and their weather-beaten, often bearded, but almost always bright-eyed faces. Twice old women came up and asked for bread, and were hastily shooed away by the *nachalnik,* who was a busy, efficient woman. Some foreigners think that such solicitude on the part of the *nachalnik* would undoubtedly be due to a concerted and planned effort to conceal the fact that there are poor people and beggars in Russia, but it is probable that the same thing would have occurred with an important Russian customer. The poor and the beggars are so universal that it is a natural impulse to save strangers from a minor annoyance which the *nachalnik* can handle better.

After lunch we left Valodya to guard the car and went out into the crowds in the big market place. It was thick with *telyegi,* the long, narrow, country carts with sloping ricks for sides. Occasionally one sees them drawn by an ox or a cow, but usually by a small horse with a big solid bow arched over his neck. Between the carts the square was alive with pigs and calves and heaped with baskets and boxes full of rabbits and chickens. Rose geraniums planted in tin cans, and heaps of plain pottery and even plainer clothing and simple trinkets added to the confusion.

The blue-eyed, leathery-faced farm people were doing a brisk trade among themselves, an occasional drunken soldier or peasant weaved uncertainly and unremarked through the crowds, and an occasional woman unconcernedly gave her breast to her baby as she drove her bargains or chattered with the others. A chicken got loose, and went flying and squawking underfoot. Everyone tried to help catch it, women spreading their faded full skirts, and children diving for it. At last it was rounded up beneath a cart in which was a black and white calf solemnly watching the excitement and a young man who kept on playing a sad tune on his accordion as though nothing were taking place directly beneath him. And over the great, crowded square of that country market a white and rose

church, fantastically towered, looked down, but most of its towers
were shot away and the walls were all wrecked and open to the
weather.

The field of Borodino is an expanse of rolling meadows spotted
with clumps of woods, across which flow two or three shallow
creeks. The only building that is still standing which was in existence in 1812 is the church in the village of Borodino itself, and
even it was badly wrecked in this last war. Numerous monuments
dot the peaceful fields, practically all of them from the time of the
Tsars, as shown by their double-headed eagles with fiercely outstretched necks. Some of the monuments were surmounted by
golden crosses, always with three cross pieces, and always with the
lower one askew.

We went into the museum, a low, yellow stucco building. In it
was a large model of the battlefield, showing the disposition of the
troops. Although I had told the doorkeeper that we did not need
or desire a guide, the director of the museum soon came up and
started telling me about the battle. He looked and talked — as
much as one can in Russian — like a learned Will Rogers. He knew
his subject thoroughly, and was himself so interested in it that he
made it live again before my eyes, giving a long and fascinating
account of the leaders and their tactics on both sides.

Also in the museum were the actual captured French battle flags,
old cannon balls and cannon, a tremendous *baraban,* or drum,
which had been beaten during the battle, letters, documents, pictures and portraits, including some of Nick de Tolly's ancestor.
Most colorful of all were the cuirassiers' breastplates and helmets,
with their long, flowing horsetail plumes, and the bearskin hats
of Napoleon's Guards. There was also the old German wooden
cart and the big wooden coffin in which Kutuzov's body had been
hauled all the way from the German town where he died to St.
Petersburg for its last resting place. This must have happened in
the wintertime, for otherwise they would have been running out of
ice.

When we finally left the museum, the director, who had accompanied us throughout and been most courteous and helpful, asked
with whom he "had the honor" to have been talking. And then he
brought the big book for "special visitors" for me to sign, and even

the small charge for admission was pressed back into my hands.

We drove across the battlefield, through a little village with a rusty-red, ornate monastery, to the Great Redoubt which plays such a part in Tolstoy's description of Borodino in *War and Peace*. There Valodya, who had never before seen Borodino, and I waded across a wet field of deep alfalfa and climbed up on top of the redoubt. Although it looms high, like an ancient *kurgan,* or prehistoric barrow, it was surprisingly small when one was actually on it. There was a monument on top, and the old trenches were still to be seen, now grassy and peaceful.

On the way back to Moscow, we took the Mozhaisk Chaussée rather than the Minsk Chaussée. Valodya had talked against this, saying that it was a much worse road. At first I thought he had been unwilling to go that way because of the considerable number of prison camps that we passed outside Mozhaisk, but I soon found out that he was right.

I knew that Valodya's family was somewhere among the villages for a few weeks of summer, so I asked him just where they were.

"Not far from Serpukhov," he said. "You remember that we went through Serpukhov on the road to Tula. I went down there on the train after bringing you home from the King's Birthday at the British Embassy. I slept in the station for an hour or so until the train left at four in the morning, but I didn't mind, because at the British Embassy they had had a special dinner for all of the chauffeurs whose masters were at the party. Every week, on my day off, I'll go down to the village to take the children the sort of food that they like, and which they can't get there. There is a train back during the next night."

"Some day, if you like," I said, "we'll drive down to the village. I'll let you out there and take the car on by myself and fish somewhere in the Oka for a few hours, and then come back and take you back to Moscow."

"But that's impossible. You see, the road isn't passable for a car into the village. There are fourteen kilometers of road worse than that we went over when we went fishing up on the Dubna."

"How did you get there, then?"

"Oh, I walked."

"Both ways?"

"Yes. I can walk it from the station easily in an hour and three quarters. That's nothing. And it's only a three-hour ride on the train."

We turned off the highway onto the road to Zvenigorod, for I thought to do a bit of fishing below the high bridge where I caught the *shchuka* the other day. Not only was it too cold and windy for decent fishing, but there were two or three excursion busses parked below the bridge, and the banks were crowded with young people loaded down with spring flowers.

After a few desultory casts, I gave up, and we went on across the bridge to take a look at the town of Zvenigorod. I knew that there was some sort of monastery or church of note there, but the streets were too torn up with repairs to bother with locating it at such a late hour, so we turned back for home. Far off in the distance, though, we caught a glimpse of golden domes and towers which appeared worth another try.

When we got home, Nell scrambled some eggs that tasted better than all the Russian food in Moscow.

I've been trying to translate something I found in my Lermontov, and have decided that it is a vain effort to try to translate Russian poetry.

> *Farewell to you, unwashed Russia,*
> *Land of slaves and land of lords,*
> *And to you, uniforms of blue,*
> *And you, my people, submissive to them.*
>
> *Perhaps, beyond the crests of the Caucasus,*
> *I can hide from thy pashas,*
> *From their all-seeing eye*
> *And from their all-hearing ears.*

The music and rhythm might conceivably be managed, but the thing that makes it ultimately untranslatable is that, although terms of respect are used in connection with the blue uniforms, tender, familiar grammatical forms are used when it comes to Russia and its people. It's no good to use "you" and "thou." That just doesn't work in English, because our speech isn't built that way. Also, there is no English word for *narod,* which means people in the sense of the common, simple people, and yet embraces a whole nation. At any rate, that piece was written well over a hundred years ago, and already I've had two or three excellent opportunities to quote it in order to make some contemporary point with a Russian.

Nell and I went to see Oscar Wilde's *Ideal Husband* at the MXAT Filial for the fourth or fifth time. This play runs in Moscow because of the basic idea, even lightly handled as it is, that an English cabinet minister is susceptible to blackmail because of his financial dealings of the past. My two pet artists are usually in it, and it was probably their work in this play that has made them such favorites of mine. The stately Ershov played the ideal husband, and the wicked Androvskaya, who is always wicked with such an air, played Lady Cheevly, the blackmailer. The blonde Goshava, who is young and really pretty and who is already a great actress in her perfect speech and sincerity, was the daughter. The even blonder, but colder, Stepanova played the wife. In real life Stepanova is the wife of Fadeyev, who wrote *The Young Guard,* one of the very best Russian novels on the last war.

In this play MXAT makes effective use of the moving stage. As the action takes place, people actually remain before the audience, although they seem to move through a series of interiors of an English house with all its Wedgewood decorations and its stately staircases. At MXAT, champagne is always real champagne and the food is real food. Once, when Senta remarked on how meticulous their realism was, I had told her that it was a pity they did not have a good adviser on English evening clothes, for any Englishman would die sooner than appear as he is shown here in tails with his white weskit showing below his jacket. I also told her that I did not think that it was just period costuming, and that the only Moscow theater in which the men wore evening clothes properly was the Operetta Theater, which is not regarded as a great theater. And now, seeing *Ideal Husband* again, I began to wonder if Senta had reported back those remarks of mine, for suddenly their evening clothes were proper — until Ershov appeared. His weskit showed a broad strip of white just as it had always done before.

For some reason the audience was at first none too receptive, but the cast soon had them completely in their hands, until at the climax the audience clapped and cheered because everything was turning out all right in the end. Androvskaya is always wonderful. Her eyes and her smile can be so hard, or they can be so tender. When she came on in one scene with long green gloves and a marvelous green and gold evening dress, the audience rightfully cheered. Nell and I both thoroughly enjoy this play, for it is so remarkably well done. There's no doubt that there are queer Russian touches to it, certainly in their pronunciation of English names, but the acting is perfect, and we have seen so many Russian plays that we are no longer conscious of those minor queernesses.

Unless they flow naturally into the Russian language, most foreign words are not inflected until they have been used here for a very long time. Sometimes, like *menu, coffee, café* and such, they are never inflected. For some reason, however, the word "jeep" has been taken over as wholeheartedly as has the vehicle which it represents. It is amusing to hear it used in its different declensions — *jeep, jeepa, jeepy, jeep, jeepon, jeepye, jeepi, jeepov, jeepam, jeepi, jeepami, jeepakh.* There is no "*j*" sound in Russian, so it becomes *dzhip.* It was some time before I realized what was meant by a sign above a restaurant saying *dzhaz.*

PART V. THE WHITE NIGHTS

1. TSAR PETER'S CITY

ONE NIGHT LAST WEEK I left by train, the Red Arrow, for a few days in Leningrad. I had talked with Valodya once or twice about the possibility of getting to Leningrad by car, and he seemed surprised and a little disappointed that he wasn't driving me up. However, this is the first time that the Soviet government has formally let me go anywhere within Russia that involved staying overnight, and I had no desire to risk complicating that opportunity at this stage of the game by insisting on driving.

I told Valodya that we might yet try to drive to Gorky some time, though of course there was the problem of taking enough gasoline along, for it would be impossible to buy any on the way. "We might send another car as far as Vladimir," I said, "and have them leave some petrol there for us. That's about halfway to Gorky."

"No. Where would you leave it?" he replied.

"Perhaps we might leave it with the police."

"O, no! That would be the very worst place to leave it! There's a Russian proverb that says that goats are not good guards for hay."

Soon after the train pulled out for Leningrad, the Russian who shared my compartment wandered in and out a couple of times. He was fat, but light and graceful on his feet, and his head was completely shaved, as round as a billiard ball. He had hard gray eyes, and he carried himself with such an erect, military bearing that he definitely leaned backwards. A rich aroma of vodka accompanied him.

Soon he reappeared with a middle-aged friend, who, like most middle-class and upper-class Soviet citizens, looked like a mechanic in his Sunday clothes. The friend apologized for my roommate's condition, but I told him that such things happened in the best of society, and the two of us pushed and hoisted our fat friend into the upper bunk. He still kept a good-natured dignity, but was just too stiff to be able to help himself at all.

The roadbed was rough, and the train jolted and swayed. It being summer, there were no blankets on board, and although I got an extra linen spread from the *nachalnik,* it was uncomfortably cold. Worst of all was when the train started up after a stop. There was a great deal of lost motion somewhere in the couplings, for car after car would start separately, and by the time the middle of the train was reached, the engine was going so fast that those cars started with a jerk that would waken anyone — except my friend — from his sleep. At that, he was up ahead of me, brisk and bright.

After I had finished my breakfast of tea and good open sandwiches of ham and salamilike *kolbasa,* the fat one and his friend came in the compartment and sat down. Soon the girl from the buffet brought them a couple of bottles of beer. I held my peace, as always, and kept on with my reading, paying no attention to them, and sure enough, one of them asked me if I wouldn't like some beer. Another glass and bottle were brought. I told them that I was an American, and that their beer was more like English beer, whereas our beer was more like German. I ordered three more big bottles. They said that this began a working day for them, but didn't demur further. But they wouldn't let me pay for any of it. We talked generalities.

At last the fat one said suddenly, "Why is it that you Americans don't like the actions of Russia?"

This was such a sudden plunge into politics that I asked him to repeat his question to be sure that I understood it. Then I said, "That question has been answered many times. It seems as though all the world is out of step except Russia."

I wasn't sure that the metaphor would work in Russian, but it did. The fat one turned to his companion and said, "He understands, all right. And he speaks the truth."

But his companion said, very softly, "He said — *'it seems'!*"

When we reached Leningrad and before I could get off the train, I was met by a slim, competent peaches-and-cream young lady from Intourist. We got in a diminutive automobile, and drove down Nevsky Prospekt to the Astoria Hotel. It was eleven thirty in the morning, and the Nevsky Prospekt was bustling. Although a big block of buildings on one side of the street was being rebuilt, there was far less destruction than I had expected to see. At the far end of the street, ahead of us, gleamed a tall, needlelike golden spire. Somehow, already, the city seemed to have more of a Western atmosphere to it than Moscow, although the shops and signs were still much the same. Perhaps it was imagination, but there is one sound fact on which to base that impression — Leningrad houses and buildings do not have the air of great age about them that one feels in Moscow. Their corners are sharper, and they are not so much out of plumb.

There were three or four nice-looking girls in the Intourist office in the lobby of the Astoria, and they were very helpful indeed. They apparently are used to taking complete charge of foreigners, and were a little surprised when I refused to talk English with them and gave them some indications of having some ideas of my own as to what I wanted to do.

The Astoria was a bit run-down, but my room was comfortable enough. It was really a small suite, with the bed in a curtained-off alcove from the sitting room, and it had its own bath. One morning there was no water, but that might occur anywhere — or almost anywhere. Having encountered some zipper trouble on my newly Russian-repaired bag, I unpacked as best I could, and straightway set off for a bookshop on Nevsky Prospekt which has the reputation of being the best bookshop in Russia, where they would even try to find things for you that they didn't have on hand.

On the way I stopped in a combination restaurant and bar and had a cheese omelet and some beer. As might have been expected, I arrived at the bookshop just a few minutes after their luncheon closing hour began. Since it was too far to go back to the hotel, I killed time by wandering around that part of the city, along some canals and past a green park, and finally came back to the shop. They had nothing that interested me, but referred me to some other shops, a few blocks farther on, and told me to come back again before leaving Leningrad. There I found a whole nest of bookshops, and spent an hour or so in them, picking up a couple of books that Senta had told me were better than the usual run of Soviet literature for which I had been looking for a long time. One of them was a collection of Leskov which included *Lady Macbet [sic] of Mtsensk District,* the operatic version of which had once been slapped down for its ideology — or lack of it.

By that time it had begun to rain, and I got thoroughly soaked on the long walk back to the hotel. I dodged under a great semicircular colonnade to get out of the rain, in front of a big brown basilicalike building which carried the carved inscription of "ACADEMY OF SCIENCES OF THE USSR FOR THE HISTORY OF RELIGION." On the great bronze doors was a sign which said they were only open on the second and fourth Tuesdays of each month. A pink-cheeked, kerchiefed old lady told me that before the Revolution the building had been the Kazan Cathedral. Now it is shabby and run-down, with sheets of plywood covering great areas where once were windows.

By the time I reached the hotel I was thoroughly tired, and felt lousy besides, doubtless from all the beer that had served as an excuse for dodging in and out of the rain. I lay down on the couch for a while, and woke up laughing because of a dream in which I was still on the train, leaning out the window and listening to a conversation between the engineer and the brakeman.

"All clear — go ahead!" shouted the brakeman from the rear.

"Is the street completely blocked by the train?" asked the engineer.

"Yes, well blocked."

"And is all the traffic sufficiently in a snarl?"

"Yes, well snarled. And besides, it's getting dark, and we were due in the next town this morning!"

It was interesting to find that the dream characters spoke in Russian and not in English.

There was barely time to get something to eat before the theater for which I had booked. It was a hurried dinner under the big glass roof of the Astoria dining room, which was so like the roof of a well-remembered hotel in Manchester one night when the Germans came over during the blitz of 1940. It was late when dinner was over, so one of Intourist's cars took me to the Kirovsky Theater. Leningrad has bridges, streets, statues, squares, theaters, hospitals and all sorts of things named after the Kirov who was assassinated there in 1934. The death of that member of the Politburo touched off the Great Purge which eventually took in my friend Putna, who was Soviet military attaché in London at the time and whose loyalty to the regime had been to me impressive.

Next to me in the theater sat a little red-faced man who had also been met at the train by someone from Intourist. He startled me by telling me, in very broken English, that he was an American, a tobacco buyer. I was too weary to try to follow his difficult English.

The theater was very like the Bolshoy in Moscow, only smaller, and instead of being done in crimson and gold it was green and gold and white, with a great fountain of a chandelier overhead. The production was Glinka's opera *Ruslan and Ludmilla*. The magnificent music was beautifully sung and beautifully played by a large orchestra whose dress varied all the way from the white tie and tails of the leader through black ties and dinner jackets and ordinary street clothes down to one of the oboists who wore no tie at all. I was close enough to the orchestra to learn that bassoons are muted by stuffing a handful of cotton down their muzzles.

The costumes were as splendid as those of the Moscow theater, particularly the wedding costumes, which were heavy with ropes of pearls and wedding crowns of pearls. But of the whole thing, the stage settings were easily the best. The Russians get an effect of vastness on the stage by a very clever use of perspective, but over and above illusion, the beams of the roof of the house of the Kiev Grand Duke were actually about five feet thick. *Ruslan* is a barbaric *skazka*, a gorgeous fairy tale all done with *bunchugs*, or standards, of horses' tails and furs, foot-long waving mustaches and Russian Oriental splendor. One scene had a very effective use of the tall, half-carved stone Mongol idols, with skew-eyes and two or three great white teeth, that are called in Russian "stony peasant women." Another scene was the field of the dead after a battle, with an occasional bone lying about and shapeless ominous bundles that were pierced with great feathered arrows as big as a man. The arrows were all at the same angle, and the effect, beneath a gloomy, lurid sky, was terrific. Still another scene had a gigantic head rising from the ground, whose eyes and lips and facial muscles moved as it spoke. The use of animal ears in the costumes also helped the barbaric effect.

One of the dances was led by Balbina, who must be a great favorite, from the way the audience applauded and shouted her name when she appeared. Even the Muscovites admit that the Leningrad ballet is ahead of their own, and it may well be that the same is true of opera. It was a good show, but long before it was over I suddenly, with a start, was surprised to find myself in a theater and wondered if I had actually dropped off to sleep. This shocked me so that I did not stay longer, but went on home to the hotel.

It was after midnight, but the streets were still as light as day, for it is the time of the White Nights. The streets were alive with people, but I walked sleepily along a peaceful canal which led me almost to the Astoria.

It was nearly noon when I awoke. After a good breakfast of ham and eggs, served sizzling in the skillet in which they were cooked, chewy Russian toast with a huge slab of delicious butter, and coffee — well, it wasn't really coffee, but it was hot and there was plenty of sugar — I put myself in Intourist's hands and started off in a big Zees car with an auburn-haired lady with a nose like that of a Roman emperor. We started to tangle before we had passed the huge golden dome of the Isaak Cathedral across the square from the Astoria. She wanted to practice her English, and of course I wanted to practice my Russian. The customer won that bout.

We came out on the big square of the Winter Palace, with a great yellow semicircle of severe buildings facing the Palace and a tall monument in the center commemorating the victory over Napoleon.

"Has the Winter Palace always been of that green color?" I asked.

"What difference does it make?" she asked back.

"I've seen many a painting of the storming of the Winter Palace during the Revolution, and I don't remember any green in those pictures," I replied.

"Well," she answered, lamely, "it may have been some other color then. Perhaps rose. At any rate, this green is an authentic green, and it was a great favorite of the Russian Tsars, just as were also rose and a deep blue, which you will see in many places."

The next place we tangled was near the Petropavlosk Fortress — the great prison of Peter and Paul. Behind the fortress is a very beautiful mosque, with a gently pointed, fluted turquoise dome, flanked with two very tall, turquoise-tipped minarets. It was so exquisite that I asked her what its name was.

"It doesn't have any name," she said.

"Oh, come! Surely it has some sort of name to distinguish it from all other mosques."

"No. You see, it's not Russian, but Mohammedan, and we Russians don't give names to things that aren't our own, because we're not interested in them."

"But even a dog has a name, whether you're interested in him or not."

"Yes, but dogs belong to people. I'm telling you that that is a mosque, not a Russian church, and so it doesn't have any name. Perhaps you don't understand my Russian."

"I understand your Russian very well," said I, getting a little annoyed. "And I'm very much surprised that any Soviet citizen would talk in that fashion about their smaller peoples. After all, there are whole Soviet Republics that are Mohammedan, and I would have expected someone like you to have more respect for them."

She began to be apologetic. "Perhaps it does have a name. At any rate, I do not know what it is. And I'm very sorry."

We left the shining gold spindle of the cathedral that stood within the Fortress, which is so like the other gold spindle of the Admiralty that can be seen at the end of the Nevsky Prospekt, and drove past the Summer Garden. It was there that Eugene Onegin was taken when he was a child, as I took some pleasure in quoting to my guide. We went on to the Smolny Institute, the headquarters of the Bolsheviks during the October Revolution, and the Smolny Cathedral nearby, with its striking deep blue and white coloring, and then back past the Nakrovy Cathedral, which was built on the spot where Alexander II was assassinated. It has twisted domes very like those of St. Basil's in Moscow's Red Square, except that these are brilliantly colored instead of being soft and dull with age. Somewhere we saw a red flag over a dome, flying at half mast.

"Why is that flag at half mast?" I asked. "Is it a sign of mourning?"

"Oh, no. We use black flags for a sign of mourning. That flag always flies there."

"But why at half mast?"

"It always flies that way."

"It's an international custom to fly flags at half mast when someone dies. Perhaps Russia doesn't observe that custom."

"I assure you that Russia respects all international customs better than any other country."

I never did find out why the flag was at half mast. Probably they just stopped pulling it up a little too soon. But it was clear that we weren't getting anywhere, so I asked my girl friend if she were married, and when she said, "Yes. Why do you ask?" I told her that I was quite sure she was, because all attractive girls were married. After that, we began to get along better.

At my special request we drove out of the city, along a highway flanked with big narrow apartment houses very like those in Moscow, across long stretches of flat land filled with truck farms and little fields to a distant row of hills, beyond which lay Tsarskoe Selo, the place where Pushkin was brought up and a summer home of the Tsars. The fields were busy with workers, most of them women. Sometimes the peasants are quite ingenious, for once we saw an *izba* which had sagged down on one side being jacked up straight by the use of a long pole for a lever. On the end of the pole was lashed a tremendous collection of logs for a weight, and the entire family was heaving down on the end to add force to the lever.

When we got into the hills we were within the old German lines. Everywhere were conical concrete tank barriers, the familiar barriers made of railroad rails, and the snaggled fragments of buildings, completely shot away except for slivers and heaps. Pushkin's village, with its many lindens for shade, was pleasant enough, but the great Summer Palace of Catherine the Great was nothing but a rose and white burned-out shell. It was set in the midst of a half-wild park and it stretched out for an enormous distance. Through its walls the sky and trees showed starkly. Here and there was a broken row of caryatids, or a twisted wrought-iron balcony from which the double-headed eagles still screamed. Within was nothing but tumbled brick and plaster. All the richness was gone, together with the wonderful and famous room of amber.

We walked through the long grass of the landscaped park, beneath great lindens, to the edge of a large, dark green lake. On the lake were dotted little heavily timbered islands from whose green peeped little summerhouses. On the far bank were pleasure places, and some red, churchlike buildings which my companion said were there for nothing but scenery. Yet somehow, in the midst of all the desolation and the tangle of the long uncut grass of the park, there was a great feeling of power that had once held sway.

When the Revolution came in 1917, Tsar Nicholas was afraid to live in the great Summer Palace, so he occupied only three or four rooms of the much more modest Alexandrovsky Palace nearby. There he was finally arrested and sent, together with his family, on the long road to Ekaterinburg and death. The Alexandrovsky Palace was now almost hidden by a high board fence, behind which was going on some sort of reconstruction to make it presentable. Enough of it was to be seen to realize that, although far from being a modest, simple place, it had nothing of the endless vastness of Catherine's palace.

On the way back through the city my auburn-haired lady left me at the Russian Museum, a big yellow building with a city-square block of planted flowers in front, in which are all the Russian pictures in Leningrad. The galleries of the Hermitage now have only pictures from Western Europe. I had about half an hour or so until closing time, but the minutes could be spent to good advantage. They told me at the door where the Repins were, and I headed straight for them.

On the way was a whole series of pictures by Kuinzhe, who is also represented in the Tretyakovskaya Gallery in Moscow. He specializes in night scenes of Russian rivers, and there is nothing to compare with the impression some of his pictures give of the magic of a glint of moonlight on a stormy night over the Don or the Dnepr. Since the Revolution, Russian painters no longer paint as he could.

There was a whole room full of Surikovs, famous pictures, such as the one of Stenka Razin sitting in brooding Oriental splendor among his Cossacks in his boat on the Volga, and the great picture of Suvorov crossing the Alps. Suvorov's troopers are plunging with all their arms and equipment down an icy precipice, with joy in their eyes because they are doing so in his presence. There was still another well-known picture of a river battle between Ermak's Cossacks and the Tatars in the taking of Siberia.

And then there were the Repins, room after room full of them. The first one that I saw was the one for which I was seeking — the "Reply to the Sultan." A group of Zaparozhe Cossacks, barbaric, baggy-trousered, long-mustached, some with shaven heads and scalp-locks by which Allah might seize them to save them on Judgment Day, crowd gleefully around a scribe who is writing their answer to the Sultan's demands. Their letter begins, simply and literally, "Thou son of a bitch . . ." It has often seemed to me that except for the costumes and the haircuts this might well be a portrait of the Politburo composing a note to the United States or a speech for the United Nations.

Although every Repin is a delight to see there was one above all that kept me until the bells rang to clear the halls. That was a large picture of "Sadko," where a princess and her entourage, led by a sly mermaid, are walking in unconcerned glory beneath the sea. It has all the magic of the *skazki,* in an underwater atmosphere that is both dreamlike and realistic, filled with gaping fish and sea anemones, drifting bubbles and starry glints of light. A lovely thing to remember.

In the Astoria dining room that night was my fat friend of the train, erect and dignified as ever, sitting at a table with a middle-aged woman. We never gave a sign of having seen each other before, but, for that matter, there was no real occasion to do so without going out of one's way to seek it.

After dinner I set off on foot towards the Bolshaya Neva, past the huge dark bulk of the Isaak Cathedral, whose polished dark red columns of porphyry or granite were chipped with shrapnel, past the Admiralty and the Bronze Horseman, that huge figure of Peter the Great made famous by Pushkin, and down the left bank of the river. Below the Lieutenant Shmidt Bridge, which is the last bridge across the Bolshaya Neva, is a big bronze tablet which says that from that point the cruiser *Aurora* shelled the Winter Palace up the river. Across the Neva and a little lower down could be seen the *Aurora,* herself, with her three tall, slim, old-fashioned stacks standing out against the clear evening sky.

Everywhere were sailors, walking in the evening with their girl friends, and it was clear that Leningrad is as much a Navy town as Norfolk.

I went past a submarine, which was moored to the seawall and which had the usual guards with bayonets at the gangplank, and kept on until I was stopped by a high board fence where the Marti Shipyards began. I turned back, crossed the Lieutenant Shmidt Bridge, and went down the other bank of the river on Vassilevsky Island for a couple of miles, past the *Aurora* and many a tangle of tugs and trawlers, until I was again turned back, this time by the high board fences of the Baltic Shipyards.

All the way were crowds of sturdy, nice-looking sailors, with their long hat ribbons, their blue-and-white striped shirts under their jumpers, and their neat broad belts. They were clean-looking lads who carried themselves well and who, as far as I ever saw, never went beyond the tender stage with their strong-legged, blue-eyed, clear-faced girls. For the most part they were just respectfully awkward and young with them. On more than one ship alongside the docks were sailors dancing, and dancing well, to the lively music of accordions. In the stream was the hull of a tremendous new icebreaker, and across the river could be seen the Marti Yards, with several small submarines in various stages of completion and the sinister sections of some liberated German Type XXI submarines on the ways. Those last set up new and difficult problems in sea warfare.

I walked back the whole length of the waterfront to the very tip of Vassilevsky Island, where there are two tall columns which once served as lighthouses and out of which project the stone prows of ships. Along the far side of the island, my feet began to grow heavy, for the Astoria was many miles behind me. Across the next estuary was the shining needle of the Petropavlosk Cathedral, rising from the low, squat, sinister walls of the Fortress. The back side of the island was rather like a warehouse section, echoing and deserted, except for a rare pedestrian. Part of the way the waterfront was shut off by board fences, for no apparent reason except perhaps to safeguard material, for it was easy to see through the boards that there was nothing but heaps of junk beyond. There came a stretch of sidewalk made from the tombstones of some old churchyard, as was clear from the almost obliterated inscriptions. The only one that could be made out was that of an Orlov who had died in 1810.

It was getting on towards midnight, and it was rather eerie to be walking in the strange light over such a pavement in such a city, so, completely worn out, I cut across the island back to the Neva, through streets as busy as in the daytime. I sat down for a while beside the two stately granite sphinxes that were brought from Egypt in 1832, and looked at the powerful planes of their great paws and the savage peace of their faces. Nearly every passer-by stopped to read their inscriptions, for the whole city was abroad in unaccustomed places during these White Nights.

It grew imperceptibly a little darker, as though a cloud was passing by, but the sky remained clear and light. One could still read the fine print of a newspaper with ease. On the way back to the Astoria across the Shmidt Bridge, clouds of smoke from a couple of passing tugs made it still darker, but as I came out of the smoke everything had already begun to lighten with the dawn, paling the gibbous moon that hung low in the sky.

2. THE SHINING FOUNTAINS

I HAD TOLD INTOURIST that I wanted to see the other Summer Palace in Peterhof on the Gulf of Finland thirty or forty kilometers from Leningrad, and that I wanted to go there by boat. Although a British assistant attaché who was in Leningrad a month or so ago had said that Intourist denied any knowledge of any boat trips through the harbor, the girls told me promptly that the boat for Peterhof left at ten in the morning, and that they would provide a car to take me to the boat and someone to be sure I got a ticket.

All the way back from Tsarskoe Selo the girl with the Roman nose kept telling me what a mistake it was to go by boat when Intourist could so easily send me there by car. It would doubtless rain, and there probably was no boat back until evening, so one would sit in the rain all day long on a park bench with nothing to do. I had gone on board one of the River Fleet barges where they sold the boat tickets and had checked her predictions to the extent of finding out that there actually was no boat back from Peterhof until early evening.

When breakfast was over, a brown-faced, vivid, friendly young lady was waiting to see me safe on board. It did look a bit like rain. My companion berated me lightly because she had had to get up early to see me on the boat, for these days the Leningradtsy are up all night and sleep most of the day, if they can. I asked her if she couldn't arrange to send a car after lunch to bring me back from Peterhof.

"It is a long and very bad road," she said, "and it would be very expensive." I resigned myself, but she went on, "Why don't you come back on the train? They run every half hour."

She was really helpful, and she insisted on climbing with me across the intervening shipping to see me settled on the little *Turgenev.* A nice-looking, elderly man with a strong face and a close-trimmed little white beard sat on one of the benches on the open fo'c'sle, smoking a pipe and reading a paper-bound book in French.

"Ah, another foreigner," I said.

"Maybe not a foreigner," she replied. "Many Russians read French, or English, for that matter, as well as they do their own language."

She went away to catch up with her interrupted sleep. I became fascinated with the shipping as we slid down the Neva, past the tall *Aurora*, past two brand-new, uncompleted, red-leaded cruisers, the *Chkalov* and the *Chapayev*, the big bulk of the still unfinished ex-German *Lutzov*, which is now the *Petropavlovsk*, past the mysterious Baltic shipways. We slid on through a very long, narrow fairway bordered with breakwaters that were covered with trees and grass, and were in the midst of some big Russian merchant ships, when I was aware of someone speaking to me.

"Your tobacco is so fragrant — what is it?" It was the scholarly-looking little old man with the well-trimmed white beard. And from that moment on, I had a real friend, gentle and courtly, interesting and interested.

He knew the Continent well from before the Revolution, and it was as much of a delight to him to talk with someone from the outside world as it was to me to talk freely with an educated man within this country. Just as the Intourist girls had warned me, he had been warned by his wife that he would be bored and tired, and should never have gone on such an expedition, particularly alone and at his advanced age. But that came out later.

On the boat we talked about tobacco and pipes, but he would never put more than a pinch of my fragrant American tobacco into his absurdly small Russian pipe. Most Russians are extremely anxious to do more than their part in little generosities, in entertaining and in paying for mutual expenses, but very few of them are in a position to compete in those respects with any American. This embarrasses them, and many foreigners make a mistake in not sensing their embarrassment, insisting upon generosity until the Russian, in defense of his own self-respect, avoids them and ends up with feeling that the foreigner has perhaps been flaunting his comparative wealth deliberately. When we went alongside the little dock in the meadows of Peterhof, with the fortress island of Kronstadt dim in the distance across the water, my friend said that the hour-and-forty-minute trip had seemed to him only ten minutes, and it seemed the same to me.

We walked up the grassy hill, landscaped with lindens and hemlock, along the straight canal that led to the sea from Catherine's palace, and felt out each other's tastes a bit. At the top, in the distance, were big signboards with posters of the current Five Year Plan. From where we were, they almost completely screened the rosy, ruined walls of the palace. In front of the gaudy billboards and extending down to the canal past the dry fountains were scores and scores of statues. They were nearly life-size, and they were so newly and richly gilded that they shone like minted gold. I asked him what he thought of the statues, but all he could see was the atrocious incongruity of the billboards. We agreed that the statues must be of gilded bronze, because even the Soviet power would not gild marble lilies.

We walked slowly up to the top, and there talked with one of the strong, rosy-cheeked women who did everything at Peterhof. There was no complaint about her hard work or her hard life. She was only sorry that there were no longer in the world such great Italian masters to make more such statues and to build more such palaces. She said that almost every bit of the restoration, the statues, the water system, the buildings, and the fountains, had been done by women. There just were not enough women.

While we were talking the fountains were turned on, and we were able to turn our backs on the billboards and see the crowds of shining statues against a proper background of fantastic water and dark foliage. It was an extraordinarily beautiful sight — a half-savage Versailles with a somber and shining splendor that was Russia.

The main jets sprang thirty or forty feet in the air, and long lines of tall, delicate columns of water went far along both sides of the canal and to both right and left into the surrounding trees. When the water fell back, it boiled and surged over the skillfully wrought bases as the sea streams over coral. There was a gigantic golden Samson in the middle, wrestling with the lion, and golden lion cubs peeped out from the streaming caverns beneath. Behind him were two flying Mercuries, one on each side. The long, curving jet of water from the mouths of the serpents which were twined about their arms made perfect continuations of the curve of their bodies, so that there were two perfect semicircles of gold and crystal. Here and there among the golden figures were spouts and jets, and great fans of water gushed forth like huge seashells.

We must have sat on the parapet and watched and talked for hours. Still under the spell of the fountains, I asked my friend if he had ever heard or read of the strange experience which had happened at Versailles to two respectable, dull, middle-aged English schoolteachers, the Misses Moberly and Jourdain. He had not, so I told him of the curious affair, which is sufficiently well authenticated to constitute a real puzzle and to have its records kept in the Bodleian Library at Oxford. One day, while on a cultural visit to Versailles, these two unimaginative spinsters suddenly and simultaneously experienced an unpleasant depression and an unaccountable subtle change in the park around them. They found the place populated with people in the costumes of the days before the French Revolution and dotted with long-vanished landmarks. Years after this experience, convincing evidence, which could not possibly have been known to those ladies, was found showing that those landmarks had once actually existed there.

Then my friend told me that once in his life he had experienced something to remember. "I went to a certain small Swedish city for the first time," he said. "From the minute I entered the city, I had the feeling that I had been there before, and that it was all somehow very familiar to me."

"Yes," I said. "That feeling is not uncommon. There is even a special word for it in English, and there are two or three possible explanations."

"I know. This was quite different. For one thing, I could not shake off the strange feeling. I walked down one of the streets. There was a blind turn ahead where the street was blocked by a wall. The feeling of having been there before was so strong that I said to myself, 'When I turn this corner, I shall see in front of me a tower,' and I pictured to myself the arrangement of the turrets and the windows of the tower. When I turned that corner, my hair literally stood on end. There was that tower, its turrets, windows, and every detail as I had pictured it!"

Some dark women, untidy and dirty, wearing kerchiefs and wide, gay skirts and blouses, wandered around the fountains below. "Do you think that they go with this scene?" he asked.

"Perfectly," I answered. He chuckled and patted me on the arm.

What a place Peterhof must have been in Catherine's day, with the fountains lit with colored lights in the evening to give a background for an open-air ballet and for the fireworks which the Russians still love so much!

There was some talk about getting lunch somewhere as we strolled down through the park. "My wife always insists that I take a little something to eat with me," he said, "and I want to share it with you." He brought out a little packet of bread and veal. I ate a slice of bread and meat, and when he insisted that I take more, protesting that he wasn't hungry, I flatly refused until he finally promised to go to a restaurant with me and share a bottle of wine. Then I divided what was left equally in half. But he saw his story through and did not finish quite all of his half, keeping some to give to a passing child later on.

We walked along the waterfront, with the cathedral of Kronstadt bulking very dim in the distance like the upperworks of a ship almost hull down on the horizon. We came to the Chinese House of the Tsars. Its walls were still covered with green and white stripes of wartime camouflage to make it blend into the trees, and on its seaward side was still a big dugout, roofed with several thicknesses of whole logs and iron sheeting. Its windows were boarded up solid with plywood, but on the landward side were wonderful great beds of pansies. My friend raised pansies at home, and his wife, who was a very good woman, particularly loved them. When I told him that my own wife, who did not raise flowers but loved them, was also a very good woman, he smiled and again patted my arm.

It began to spit rain from the low dark clouds overhead, so we went into the one open wing of the Chinese House, which had a small exhibition. It contained little but more golden statues and a few stucco masks and decorations from the great palace. Then we wandered out and sat for a long time on a bench, sheltered from the intermittent rain by the thick leaves of the great lindens overhead. Opposite us was the Chessboard House, now well ruined. He told me that it was so named because it had once formed a series of huge, sloping chess boards, over which flowed the water from a group of fountains.

A brown-faced gypsy woman came up, shook her big hooped earrings, and asked me for some tobacco. She lighted one of the handful of cigarettes I gave her, and told me that I had had a full, happy life — interruptions of annoyance from my friend — and that it would be even fuller and happier in the future. I would have talked with her at length, but my friend took no stock in gypsy fortune-telling. Besides, he had some things he wanted to say himself.

"Have you ever heard the Russian nightingales?" he asked, when she had gone.

"No, but I have heard the English ones, many a time."

"You must hear them. I will take you to a garden I know, where they sing every night."

"But I am going back to Moscow tomorrow."

"No matter. You will come back again, and then I can take you. I want you to come to my home, and to get to know my wife. Also, I go to Moscow occasionally, and when I do, I shall call you at your Embassy. Perhaps we can see something of each other then."

We had kept away from politics until then, but at last the time had come when it was necessary to tell him what one has to tell all of the gentle people who are kind and hospitable in the countries under the Hammer and Sickle. I told him that nothing would please me better than to see him again, but it would only be asking for trouble for him. During the past year, there was not one Russian friend of any American who had not been told by the secret police that they must stop having anything to do with the Americans. People said that it had not always been so bad, and perhaps this last year marked a low point. Perhaps things would change a bit for the better, and then, when it was clear that it would not harm him, we could see each other often. Meanwhile, we had had this one lovely day. And I quoted him Lermontov's farewell to unwashed Russia.

"I know." He looked depressed. "I have never had any unpleasantness myself. But I am a Russian, and I know that what you say takes place — that you speak the truth. You are right. But I cannot tell you how much this one lovely day means to me."

We found a restaurant in a wing of the great, ruined, rose-colored palace, and there we took a table which was half outdoors on one of the little balconies but sufficiently sheltered to be clear of the occasional showers. There was no wine to be had, but we had some excellent big omelettes and some beer. He told me much of interest, for he knew all of the artists, actors, ballerinas, writers and scientists of Leningrad, and of most other places in Russia. All of the intelligentsia of Leningrad had been evacuated to the Urals during the siege, and he gave me a wise and understanding picture of Russian life.

I knew what would happen about the bill, so on the way in I had lingered behind and given one of the girls money to pay for whatever we might have. Sure enough, he tried to go back on his promise on the grounds that we had had no wine, but for once he was outwitted.

We might just as well have taken the boat back to Leningrad, for it was evening, but instead we caught a stubby little bus which took us to the railroad station. A nice-looking woman in the seat ahead of us was so obviously interested in our conversation that we both started talking for her especial benefit, and she was vastly amused. The railroad station was completely ruined and open to the sky, with only a long platform down one side.

Fortunately, the rain had stopped, and we did not have long to wait for our train. It was filled with holiday makers and children, all loaded down with wild flowers.

"At least you can call me on the telephone," said my friend.

I laughed indulgently. "Then everyone will know I have called."

"But I have my own private telephone. I am not on a switchboard."

"Since when has any Russian telephone been really private?" I asked.

"Yes. You are right," he sighed.

When we pulled into the Baltic Station, we took a streetcar. I know that both of us were genuinely sorry when we reached the general vicinity of the Astoria and it came time for me to get off. Perhaps we shall see each other again. One can never tell.

On a bright and windy morning I took an Intourist automobile, for there was a lot of ground to be covered, and went straight over the bridges to the Fortress of Peter and Paul. It does not give the impression of strength that some fortresses give, for its low, moated walls are of brick instead of stone. And there are dwellings and rooms within them. Those walls make up in thickness what they lack in height. We drove inside through a long tunnel. Like the medieval kremlins, the Petropavlovsk Fortress is really a walled town, with many buildings, trees and open spaces inside.

Although the prisons would have been interesting, there was one thing above all else that brought me there. We stopped at the doors of the *Sobor,* or Cathedral, and I went straight in. And there it was — a regular thicket of white tombs, packed close together in front of the altar screen and scattered all over the wide, empty floor. They were the tombs of all the Tsars from the founding of St. Petersburg to the fall of the Romanovs, excepting only Nicholas II, whose last resting place is known only to the Soviet power. Two great black flags of mourning hung across the tomb of Peter the Great.

It gave me a creepy, eerie feeling to read those names and to know that they were actually there — Peter I, Anna, Catherine the Great, the other Catherine, Elizabeth, the two other Peters, Paul, who had made his mother's lovers stand watch over her body and that of his long-dead father. Russia has always been more or less inaccessible, always secret and mysterious, and the violent, fearful lives of those rulers of all the Russias seem so remote and legendary that it was hard to believe this evidence of reality and of mortality. With only two exceptions, every tomb is a plain white marble rectangular coffin, with no decorations other than the name of the inhabitant and a flat golden cross, with the one skewed crossbar, on the top. The wives and children, the Grand Dukes and Grand Duchesses, are there also.

The two exceptions are the green jasper of the tomb of Alexander II and the rose quartz of that of Marie, his Tsaritsa. They are gorgeous pieces of stone. But there is a placard beside them, which says in the characteristically bilious Soviet fashion that the reasons for those two tombs being different were fear and deception. Nicholas II, terrified by the rising temper of the people after the 1905 Revolution, caused them to be made in order to build up the legend of Alexander II, the emancipator of the serfs, as Liberator of the People. Perhaps that may contain a grain of truth, which is doubtful, but even a loyal Party member must weary sometimes of the endless effort to grind every grain of grist in the propaganda mill. If it is in a Russian to appreciate the effectiveness of restraint, which seems often doubtful, the regime should be able to improve their propaganda from the viewpoint of their own interests. Still, no one can accuse them of not knowing what they are doing, and it is probable that those who are offended by their heavy-handed hammering are less numerous and less important to them than those they persuade. Intolerance stands high among their defects, and yet intolerance seems to be a peculiarly Russian characteristic.

The massive gold iconostas before the altar must have weighed many tons. It ascended far into the blue dome from which springs the golden needle of the spire that can be seen from so far away. The chandeliers, hanging low from the high roof above, are of blue porcelain, giving a characteristic Byzantine or Eastern touch. Apart from the tombs, the general effect of the Cathedral is one of lack of artistic taste, which is, however, compensated by its lavish richness.

There were several Russians in the Cathedral, all there to see the tombs and the church itself. Most of them were unconcerned and unmoved, but in two or three cases, including one Red Army officer, their deep reverence before their officially discredited former masters was remarkable. It would be easy for one who does not live in Russia to mistake such open respect for a sign of tolerance on the part of the regime. Just because the regime does not lay violent hands upon all who do not conform does not mean that it is not efficient in removing all competition. At best, the Red Army officer who was so moved at the sight of the Tsars' tombs would be regarded as politically undeveloped, and those who are politically undeveloped have no future unless they mend their ways.

3. THE WINTER PALACE

WHEN WE CAME BACK across the Kirovsky Bridge, the fresh breeze was blowing and the sun was sparkling on the water in the way that it does only where the sea runs in. There was a brisk feeling in the air which made Leningrad seem more of a seaport than it had seemed even when I was on my way to Peterhof through all the shipping.

At the end of the bridge is a statue of Suvorov, Catherine's great general, who fought his way so spectacularly through Switzerland with his Russian army when surrounded and unsupported. Leaning against the base of the statue sat a patient, weary, kerchiefed, booted working woman, dusty and tired, but with fine blue eyes. She seemed as symbolic of the Soviets as Suvorov was of the great Romanovs.

I let the car go at the Naval Museum, which is on Vassilevsky Island by the two old lighthouses. Only once before during my time in Russia has anyone from our Navy been in Leningrad, and then Intourist told McMillan and Goloway that there was no such thing as a naval museum. Perhaps it wasn't open then — in any event Intourist denied to them its very existence. It is one of the largest and most important buildings on the island, and it is undoubtedly one of the great naval museums of the world.

A great central room was packed and jammed with models of sailing ships, extending back through the days of the frigates to those of the galleys, and there was even a dugout canoe from the Ukraine from three thousand years ago. There was an unbelievable twelve-man oar from an old galley, and the oar was either twelve or twenty meters long — by the time I left the place my head was so jammed with other figures that I am not sure which. There was a model of the *Orlov,* the six-screwed, circular coast-defense monitor which was an imaginative effort even though she proved to be unmanageable.

The place was filled with all sorts of things of intrinsic as well as historic interest, as is every naval museum everywhere. The faces of the tsarist naval officers in the old photographs were extremely

interesting. The Tsars' navy had been officered by well-born men
and whatever their professional capabilities, which were, for the
most part, reasonably high, they were distinctive personalities.
Someone could do a good job on their biographies. For that matter,
the time that John Paul Jones spent in the service of Catherine the
Great after our own Revolution would make an interesting subject
for research if anyone could crack the nut of how to get at the
material which must be in this country. It might even have a few
touches of Casanova. For one thing we know that he was framed.

For some reason, the Russian navy has always been a focal point
of revolution, from the days of the Dekabrists in the early part of
the last century through the Odessa Mutiny and Lieutenant Shmidt
in the 1905 Revolution (the Shmidt for whom the bridge across
the Bolshaya Neva is named) to the cruiser *Aurora* and the
marine relief of Moscow in the 1917 Revolution. The naval base
of Kronstadt played a leading part in the Red Revolution. It re-
volted not only against the Tsar, but also against the Bolsheviks.
Another subject for research.

Another thing of interest in the museum was the realization it
brought of the tremendous extent to which the navy operated
throughout all the inland waterways of Russia during the Civil
War. That is not surprising when one realizes the importance of
those waterways to Russia and the fact that they have always been
and still are a prime method of movement and communication
throughout its vast and still primitive expanses. The dots and
crosses on one map which showed where naval craft had been
in action were thick enough to outline most of the many waterways.

All around the large central room of the museum was a series
of smaller rooms filled with models of power-operated ships and
equipment down to and including the war which has just ended.
Some of the ship models were very fine, and all were interesting.

I walked a roundabout way along cool green canals with many
little bridges and narrow sidewalks between the water and the
houses and palaces. Either the Russians or their Italian architects
have tried to bring something of Venice to this northern land. Once
I saw a footbridge whose suspension cables were held at each end
in the teeth of two huge bronze lions with great golden wings. The

beasts were so closely spaced that one could just squeeze through between them.

The Winter Palace is now a part of the Hermitage Museum. There are many bridges and passages between the two vast buildings of the Winter Palace and the old Hermitage, with its huge caryatids at the door. It was in the plaza in front that the massacre of "Bloody Sunday" took place in the 1905 Revolution, and it was from this affair that Nicholas II won the name of "Bloody Nicholas." That is a doubtfully deserved name, for the whole business is clouded in a tangle of provocation and deception which is typically Russian. I skirted the plaza and entered what may well be the greatest treasure house in the world.

There are some twelve hundred rooms in the Winter Palace and the old Hermitage, and for four hours I walked briskly through the place, stopping only for a moment here and there when something particularly caught my eye. The extraordinary thing about the Hermitage is that with all its vastness, there is little or no junk in it. Everything that one sees is at least fine, and often it is great. I must have missed many parts of it in hurrying through that endless maze of interconnecting great rooms and corridors, with its many courts and passages, and sections, such as the rooms devoted to French pictures, were closed at the time for one reason or another. It is no way to see a great gallery, nor is it a way that favors the impression one receives. Nevertheless, the Hermitage overwhelmed me.

The ground floor was filled with room after room of ancient and prehistoric things. From the mysterious barrows and mounds of Russia had been brought the actual bodies of horses — hide, mane, tail and all. There was a whole room full of the most amazing masks for horses from Scythian times, masks golden and feathered and plumed, some with branching reindeer horns. Bridles and saddles beyond end, jeweled and barbaric. Countless little bronze figures, some of them either obscene or sacred, depending on one's viewpoint. Breath-taking vistas of ancient statuary, most of it Roman but much of it Greek. I do not believe that there was a single cast in the whole wilderness. It was just an endless majesty of marble. Often the marble statues and busts were decorated with other materials, but, in accordance with my Peterhof friend's ideas, they were never gilded. There were the originals of so many well-known statues of emperors and gods that it seemed as though I was wandering through the pages of some boyhood schoolbook.

On the upper floors was room after room of Rubenses, others of Rembrandts alone, still other rooms with many Titians, Murillos, Tiepolos, on through the great list of masters. There was one big room with nothing but huge canvases of food, most of them Snyders, but a few by other Dutch or Flemish artists. No market was ever so lavish in fish and game. I missed many of the most famous pictures in the Hermitage, but it was hopeless to try to find individual pictures unless one had days at one's disposal. It was strange that, in spite of all the wealth of pictures, I did not see a single Goya or El Greco in the entire place, nor were there any Turners — those three being almost the only artists whose work I can usually recognize without looking for their names.

Through all those halls of great painting, however, there were many other things of interest which were not paintings. The floor in every one of the hundreds and hundreds of rooms is elaborately parqueted. Perhaps there would be a string of three or four rooms which seemed ordinary enough, and then you would come into a room which would take your breath away with the richness of its walls, its ceilings, perhaps its own native mural decorations, or a crystal forest of chandeliers overhead. In one room was an enormous map of Russia which Nell says was at the World's Fair in New York towards the beginning of the war. It was made entirely from precious and semiprecious stones from the Urals, and it was one of the few Soviet things that are now in the Hermitage.

There were corridors full of Della Robbias, and others of comparatively modern statuary. Everywhere were gigantic urns and basins of malachite, lapis lazuli, onyx, huge Sèvres jars, sets of china of the Tsars, tables inlaid with semiprecious stones, wonderful French clocks, period furniture at its greatest perfection, mosaics so fine that the separate stones could scarcely be seen with the naked eye. If the Hermitage is not the greatest treasure house of the world, it is certainly near the top of any listing of the concentrations of richness and beauty.

That night, after a good dinner of pheasant and ice cream, the tall, blonde, peaches-and-cream Intourist girl who had met me at the pale-green Moskovsky Station took me back to the same station and put me on the Red Arrow for Moscow. I shared a room on the train with a man whom I had seen once or twice at the Astoria and who I thought was a Russian. He had some jerky, nervous mannerisms, but was quiet, highly intelligent and thoroughly civilized when I once got to know him a bit. He was not Russian, but a Finn who had lived for many years in Leningrad before the Russo-Finnish war, when the border was more open than it has ever been since. Like most of the Finns of my acquaintance, he was a stout fellow who was not afraid of the Russian Bear, but who had no illusions about it or its intentions. We talked and watched the ragged fields and forests go past the windows, drinking glass after glass of tea, until I looked at my watch and was surprised to find that it was nearly morning. The White Nights are no time to catch up on one's sleep.

We both woke up late on Sunday morning and continued our talk while looking out of the window, after a breakfast of tea with juicy, fresh red caviar on slabs of bread. It was much warmer near Moscow, and the streams and ponds we passed were already well frequented with picnic parties and swimmers, the latter naked as often as not. Nell was on the station platform to meet me, looking very vivid in a dress of Chinese red, and it was very nice to see her.

It seemed as though I had been gone for a month, and it was very pleasant to come into our apartment, high and light, with a cool breeze blowing through it on such a warm day. I asked Valodya if everything was in order, and he replied, "Everything is in order, even the servants." That must have been his way of acknowledging that he had taken to heart my last talk to him.

Natasha was tremendously interested in everything I had seen in Leningrad, and I had to tell her all about it at great length. At the end, she said, "Leningrad is indeed a wonderful city. They say that once they had a rain of stars there. They all plunged into the sea, and it was a wonderful sight." After I had assured myself that I had heard correctly, she went on, "Yes, and once they had a great earthquake in the Crimea. The earth opened in great cracks in front of people, and it was very terrible." I felt that I had failed her a bit in not having seen at least a sea serpent in Leningrad. I'll have to remember that the next time I am away.

4. RUSSIAN MYSTERIES

A STRANGE RUSSIAN GENTLEMAN dropped in to the Embassy the other day. He told one of our people that the Tsarevich Aleksei was not dead, but had escaped the slaughter of the royal family at Ekaterinburg and had lived for many years in a monastery in the Urals. Then he produced a picture and asked his listener to look closely at the picture and then at him. "Do you see any resemblance?" he said. "Yes? Then I think we understand each other!" And he went on out.

Some one should try to make a serious study of the imposters of Russia, the *samozvantsy*. They are threaded through all of Russian history, and their enigmatic story cannot help but throw some light on the depths of the Russian *dusha*, that mysterious soul that seems so hard to understand. Some of them genuinely believed that they were the rightful heirs to power. Others have been subjects of much controversy within Russia, and to this day no one knows the truth of just who they were. I have made a list of thirty-nine of these claimants to position and power, beginning with the False Dmitry of the Time of Troubles (1598–1613), and there must have been many others, both before and after that time.

Martha, the widow of Ivan the Terrible, accepted the False Dmitry as her son, only to deny him at his death and then to accept another imposter as her son. Marina, who had married the False Dmitry, also accepted this new impostor as the true Tsar, marrying him and bearing him a son. The great Russian historian Karamzin says that many even in his day, the early part of the nineteenth century, believed that the False Dmitry was still the true one. Karamzin also says that there were stories that, even before the False Dmitry came to the throne, Boris Godunov, frightened by the successes of the claimant, did not really die in Russia but had a man who resembled him poisoned and buried in his place, and himself fled to England as a merchant.

During and after the Time of Troubles there was a swarm of impostors, sometimes several at one time, and so much violence and conspiracy surrounded the Russian court that there was always plausible reason for them to appear as long as there was a court in Russia. Stenka Razin was a *samozvanyets,* and Pugachev, the leader of the great revolt in Catherine's time, was another, issuing titles of nobility and having a court of his own. One of the most interesting of them all was Fyodr Kozmich, an aristocratic old man who died in Siberia in 1864, leaving behind him the story that he was in reality Alexander I who had supposedly died in the Crimea in 1825. There are many curious circumstances surrounding this case, such as the fact that Alexander's body was never exhibited in public as was normally the custom and the testimony of an English doctor who had attended the Tsar — so many curious circumstances that the argument as to the truth has continued into the present century, even members of the royal family writing pamphlets on the subject.

The last encyclopedia published before the Revolution says that "even today, impostors of a nonpolitical character are widespread in Russia." It goes on to give examples — priests, miracle workers, monks, ambassadors from the patriarchate of Jerusalem and other foreigners, judges, princes, doctors, lawyers, surveyors, government officials, inspectors, secret police agents. Russian literature is full of them, and there is no doubt that they still plague the Soviet regime today.

Why does Russia have such a peculiar affinity for the impostor? The chronic absence of a free press is one answer, for here there is no news as such, only rumor, and the press was never completely free even in tsarist times. Many of the political impostors were pawns in international intrigue, the Poles having done more than their share in this respect. Political ambitions of the Cossacks were responsible for others, for the strongest barrier to the ambition of a usurper was his illegitimacy. Yet there remain depths which cannot be explained on grounds of self-seeking (which itself has its Russian peculiarities), for many of these cases show a genuine change of personality, and many others may well have not been impostors at all.

I told Valodya to find some road that would cross the Moskva River below Moscow rather than above, where we usually went for an afternoon's drive. It was Trinity Sunday, hot, hazy and windy, and everywhere on the edge of the city were crowds of people bringing back armfuls of green birch branches. I remembered that I had once asked Valodya why they didn't plant birch trees in the city, since they were lovelier than any other Russian trees. He had told me that, if they were to do that, the trees would all be stripped bare to provide branches with which to decorate their homes on Trinity Sunday.

We passed a big old red brick church, and through the open windows of its upper parts could be seen someone's wash, hanging to dry on long clotheslines. Most of these numerous churches, which are perhaps the most picturesque things in Russia, are ruined and dilapidated. They serve as storehouses for all sorts of things, but are usually inhabited by several families as well. On the flats in the distance spread Moscow, with its southeastern part dominated by some old cathedral of Ivan the Terrible. Once we passed a milk wagon which was exactly like a small tank truck for gasoline, with the milk put out through a hose.

We came to a turnoff which went to Tsaritsino, for in the distance could be seen the toothed battlements of the palace. Valodya slowed down and wanted to know if we didn't want to go to Tsaritsino. I had been there skiing during the winter, and besides we might still be able to reach the river, so I told him to keep on.

We passed a pond, covered with myriads of white domestic ducks, and again Valodya wanted to know if we didn't want to stop — there was some water. He definitely didn't want to keep on on that road, and every few minutes he would ask if we weren't ready to turn around and go back. Perhaps one reason for his reluctance was a mysterious sight that soon showed up — a regular forest of literally hundreds of radio masts that stretched for a couple of miles beyond some small woods. Also in the distance was some strange sort of factory, looking very big with the deceptive loom that buildings have in this land, surmounted with a series of towers like miniature skyscrapers.

Some thirty kilometers out of Moscow we came to a well-paved side fork leading in the general direction of the river. A statue of Lenin stood among the fields and trees, brooding over the fork. We took the side road and went for a little distance along a beautiful alley of birches. However, Valodya stopped the first person we encountered, a red-faced, slant-eyed peasant woman, asking her where the road went and if we could get back to Moscow that way. She said that the road didn't go anywhere, which was surprising, as there are few such well-paved roads around the countryside. Valodya muttered something about the woman being a Tatar and therefore unable to understand good Russian. We passed an agricultural experimental station, and then the countryside became quite wild, with no traffic at all on that excellent road. We went for a few miles through a fairyland of thick, ghostly white birches, interspersed with glades of wild flowers and an occasional field of fresh-cut hay.

All at once Valodya pulled up short. The Tatar woman was right, in a sense at least. Although the fine road kept on without interruption, over it hung a sign saying "FORBIDDEN ZONE." On one side of the road was a high board fence, and as we backed and filled to turn around, we could see between the boards of the fence that beyond it were a few good-sized buildings. They were apparently not shops of any sort. There were several strange little enclosures no more than a few square yards in area, each surrounded by its own high board fence with plenty of barbed wire on top. Most curious of all, there were trees and green growing things within each of those independent secret places. A strange land. Perhaps one fancies things here. Perhaps the separate fences were only to keep the goats from eating the green within, and the barbed wire was to keep the children from climbing over. At any rate, a splendid road going nowhere in a land of bad roads, the forbidding signs, and Valodya's earlier reluctance were food for the imagination.

At the main corner of Gorky Street near the Embassy I saw a strange thing. A man, as limp as if he were dead, was being carried along the sidewalk by a militiaman and a couple of civilians at his head and feet. The man was ragged and hatless, his head sagging to one side. He had on brown socks, but no shoes. He might have been dead, the victim of an accident or illness, or merely completely drunk. But where were his shoes? And the strange, almost eerie thing about it was that, although it was broad daylight and the streets were crowded with people, not one of all those crowds of passers-by paid the slightest attention to the scene. They not only did not turn to look, but did not even glance at it as they passed. They were as completely unseeing as if the militiamen and his helpers and the limp body were invisible. Perhaps they were, to everyone but me. It does not pay a Russian to be curious.

The Durbrow apartment is all full of packing boxes. There must be a great feeling of finality about leaving Russia. Not that Derby cares, though, for after three tours of duty here he has had enough. He says that 1937, the time of the Great Purge, was once regarded as the worst year for foreigners in Russia, but that this past year far surpasses it. Now 1937 seems like the golden days of freedom in comparison with what foreigners have here today.

Natasha put up a picnic lunch and we took her and Zoya out in the country after wild strawberries. Zoya looked fresh and summery in her starched checked gingham dress. We let the servants decide where to go, and they picked the beautiful birch woods that we had seen on the edge of the Forbidden Zone on the well-paved side road off the Kashirskaya Chaussée, because Valodya had told them they were so wonderful.

We tried two or three different places in those woods, and they were indeed lovely, with a great sound of wind rushing through the tops of the birches. They were thick with moss and fern and clouds of baby's breath and forget-me-nots. There are almost no weeds of any sort in these Russian woods, no poison ivy or nettles. Here and there were huge swarming antheaps, as big as an office desk — a natural comparison for one who has done fourteen years off and on in Washington. Valodya said that the peasants fill big jars with ants and then put the jars on the stove. The resulting brew is a sort of spirits which is an excellent liniment for practically any ailment.

In an hour or so we had a full quart of tiny, fragrant, sweet wild strawberries. Since Nell has finally succeeded in showing Natasha how to make it, we have been having strawberry shortcake ever since. Natasha, in spite of her peasant childhood, seemed a little uneasy in the woods and would never wander far from the car. As Nell remarked, her childhood woods were probably full of wolves and God knows what else.

It was still windy and hot, and we came home early so that Valodya could get away early for his weekly journey to the village. We went past fields that were as white with daisies as if they were covered with snow. Once we passed a group of German prisoners who were working on the road. The Russian soldier who was guarding them was playing an accordion and wearing a wreath of purple flowers instead of a cap.

"Drunk as a shoemaker!" I said.

"Gospodin Admiral," said Valodya, " I know that that is a common Russian expression, but it is a slander on shoemakers. I know a shoemaker who never gets drunk. Sometimes they say drunk as a tailor, or as a smith. Other people besides working people get drunk in Russia."

I did not argue, but replied, "Perhaps so. In English-speaking countries they sometimes say 'Drunk as a lord.' "

There was a look of triumph on Valodya's face.

On the edge of the city we passed an open truck from which a high-cheekboned, high-bosomed girl, who had been sun bathing in brassière and panties as the truck rolled along, waved at us as she started to slip her dress on over her head.

Henrik Madsen is about to leave for a few weeks at home in Denmark, and he was all hot and distraught with his difficulties in trying to get his car out of Russia. A strike in London has tied up some of the Leningrad shipping, and although Henrik has been sweating it out for days, he is leaving without any knowledge as to whether his car will go to Helsinki or Stockholm, or when. Meanwhile, it is piling up two hundred rubles a day for charges on the Leningrad docks.

Edith told Nell that she had been to the bank. Just as she was getting out of the car a militiaman came up and told her that she couldn't park the car there.

"Couldn't I stay for just one minute, while I go in the bank?" she asked.

"Are you an American?" he countered.

"No, I'm Danish."

"Oh, *pazhaluista* — please stay!"

5. THE VELVETEEN GLOVE

THE SOVIETS ARE ALWAYS VAGUE about what one can do and what is not permitted. This vagueness has so many advantages for them that it can be nothing but intentional. It permits them to make broad propaganda claims to liberalness which cannot be specifically disproved, and above all they always retain freedom of action. A Russian cog in the vast bureaucracy does not like to commit himself if he can possibly avoid doing so, even though when committed he can always rely on excuses for not seeing it through. Official Embassy requests for information as to whether or not the use of a camera is permitted go unanswered, and as a result the Soviets are free to close in on anyone with a camera at any time and place that they choose. Nobody knows just what he can or cannot do with an automobile.

We have long tried to find out if there were any limitations on automobile travel beyond the normal difficulties of roads and total absence of places where one can buy fuel and oil. The only reply anyone has ever received was from Serayev, the head of OVS, who told me that I had the same freedom of movement as all the rest of the diplomatic people here — whatever that means. In order to be open and aboveboard with the Soviets, I had told Serayev that his office would be notified if I went anywhere by car for an overnight trip and that it was assumed he wasn't interested in shorter drives around the countryside as long as we kept out of areas that were posted as prohibited.

In accordance with this understanding, Levy called OVS to say that Nell and I were going to drive through Zagorsk and Rostov to Yaroslavl, some two hundred and sixty kilometers away, and would stay overnight in Yaroslavl if we could get accommodations there. If we could not find a place to stay, we would turn around and drive back to Moscow that same night. Pasco, with whom Levy talked, said that it would be necessary to write a letter for permission to visit Yaroslavl. This is the first time that anyone in this embassy has heard that letters of request were required if one didn't need help in some way, such as in buying railroad tickets or getting hotel rooms, which are usually refused to foreigners unless they have some sort of papers of authorization. Levy told Pasco that I wasn't asking for permission to go and needed no assistance, but was carrying out our agreement to notify OVS if we intended to be away overnight. Pasco got General Serayev on the telephone. Serayev said, for the first time, that written permission was necessary to visit any city other than Moscow.

Levy and I went over to OVS to talk in person with Serayev. It was a pleasant enough conversation, but ended up as might have been expected. The only thing that Serayev would or could say definitely was that letters were required for all cities but that it was all right to visit a *dacha* in the vicinity of Moscow. He didn't know about just driving in the country, or picking berries in the woods, or trying to do a bit of fishing in the Moskva River. I told him that since we had recently been to Tula and Mozhaisk without a letter or informing him, I intended to keep on doing so, whether or not I returned the same day, and that my previous agreement to keep him informed was at an end. I also told him that of course I would not try to go to Yaroslavl, about which he had been specific, without a letter. I asked him if Zagorsk, which is about seventy kilometers from Moscow and which was occasionally visited by foreigners because of its monastery, was considered a city. He replied that Zagorsk had little but the monastery and that he wasn't concerned about it.

When rising to leave, I said, "After a year in Russia I do not feel as free as even — "

Pasco finished the sentence for me: " — even as you thought you were!"

We all laughed, but it was clear to me that in spite of any legitimate effort that can be made, we are regarded as enemies by definition and not as friends.

We left for Zagorsk in the morning, and for the first time since we have been in Russia I knew that I was followed. I told Valodya to turn down a side street, and sure enough, before we could turn out of that street, another car turned into the side street to follow us.

There was a strong, warm wind that blew the dust in a yellow
fog, and created difficulties for the short-skirted women with their
arms full of their morning shopping. Beyond the truck gardens on
the edge of the city, where there were only woods and pastures
and ripening wheat, the dust largely disappeared, but the trees
bent and swayed heavily, the birches showing the light underside of
their leaves and the draped hemlocks tossing their branches.

The following car stayed far behind, taking continual advantage
of curves and wooded cover, but it was always there, no matter
what our rate of speed. Once when we jolted over a heavy bump,
Valodya stopped and got out to see if any of the spare gasoline in
the back, which had never been removed when the Yaroslavl trip
was called off, had spilled. The following car, far behind, stopped
and pretended to be turning around.

The Troitse-Sergieva Monastery dominates the town of Zagorsk.
It was built in Tatar times, and served as a strong point and a place
of refuge throughout all of Russia's stormy history. Its wealth is
indicated by the fact that in the time of Catherine the Great it
owned more than a hundred thousand serfs. Like most Russian
monasteries, it is really a walled town, filled with dwellings and
churches. Of its eleven churches, the main one has a great, high,
golden onion-shaped dome, clustered about with lower, but equally
big, domes. The lower domes are very blue, but with a slight greenish cast to them, and they are studded with golden stars. With their
big golden crosses, stayed with heavy chains, they look like something out of a fairy tale.

A peculiarly Chinese flavor was given to the place by the big
areas of green roof, which sloped at steep angles like the roofs of a
pagoda. The Oriental effect was heightened by a palacelike building that was elaborately painted and decorated. It looked as though
its walls were made of studded, projecting stones, whereas they
were actually flat and smooth. There was a tall bell tower standing
separate, built in layers like a high wedding cake, with a heavily
scrolled bright golden top. The churches, shrines and buildings
were all enclosed within a thick fortified wall without crenelations,
but with frequent towers that might have come from the Moscow
Kremlin itself if it were not for the fact that the tiles of their steep

slopes were sometimes made of bright green porcelain, looking like the scales of a Chinese fish. Sometimes green or turquoise-blue stones and decorations replaced the tiles.

We drove straight through the wall into the big inner square, and Nell and I left Valodya to sleep in the car, parked under some big leafy trees. In front of us was a towering shrine made of twisted columns heavy with clusters of grapes, all of a peculiar blue-green color. Inside was a golden cross from which continually flowed water, the gold looking cool and lovely as it glittered beneath the stream. The interior of the shrine was lavishly covered with paintings.

A woman was sobbing some sort of long, troubled woe to a heavily bearded priest. We could not help but hear, so, being ourselves troubled by such obvious sorrow, we went on out. Walking through the grounds were many monks, several of them quite young, all with beards if they were old enough to have them, all with long, uncut locks, wearing slim black kaftans down to their heels, black velvet skullcaps or church bonnets like Easter buns, and with enormous silver crosses hung about their necks by heavy chains. Their appearance was a strange combination of unkempt wildness, meekness, piety, and humility.

There was a long double line of pious, mild-faced seekers of alms at the main entrance to the cathedral, so we were soon out of rubles. It was a big cathedral, and within there was not one inch of its tall square columns, the vaults and domes of its roof, or its great walls and thick window embrasures which was not covered with paintings, all in gold and deep blue and rose. All across one end was a tremendous, complicated mural of the Last Judgment. I must have stared at it for twenty minutes. It showed the rising up of the dead, the Beasts of the Apocalypse, the weighing of the souls in the balance, the furnaces of hell where scores of the damned were frying, and writhing across the whole wall was the Great Serpent with a human head, with numerous devils sliding and frisking on its back. Over all were the saints and the saved and the heavenly choir, in a blaze of blue and golden glory. The details were endless, and very curious, well worth study. In one place was a transparent, ghostly figure, lashed with its arms about a post, and many other things with whose meaning I was completely unfamiliar. The whole thing was not heavy, but had a sort of *skazka,* fairy-tale air to it like one of the little lacquered Palyekh boxes, in so far as this was possible on a mural of such tremendous size.

A service was going on, and there were many people crowded around the priest. From somewhere, in the half-chant, half-singing of the service, came some rich, deep, Russian voices with a music that was thrilling. Long lines of people, mostly peasant women in their kerchiefs, but with a scattering of men and well-dressed women, went past the bearded, ecstatic priest to kiss the silver cross that he held out, and often to kiss his hand as well. Nearly all of them put something in a big collection tray, and there Nell and I got enough ruble notes in change to take care of the long lines of pious poor when we should go out.

We stayed there a long, long time, and could hardly tear ourselves away when we finally left the cathedral. The altar screen was impressive, all heavy with gilded carving and solid gold, rising high in five tiers of painted saints of more than life size, fifteen pictures to the row, extending all the way across the church. The paintings were very rich, and belonged to a much earlier age than those of Tsar Peter's Cathedral in Leningrad.

Here and there were the silver and gold traceries of portable ikons, carried on long staffs, and there were several reliquaries and ikons in stands that were richly painted or wrought of massive silver, with glass covers dim and smudged from the kisses of the pious. Many of them were framed with row on row of turquoises, emeralds and rubies. And the stones were not glass, but real. I myself know real emeralds when I see them, and Nell, who is very skillful in that sort of knowledge, spoke for the other stones. With the single exception of the Hermitage, Zagorsk was the most impressive display that I have seen in Russia, but there must be many other places in Russia that rival it in richness and interest.

At one corner of the fortified walls was what was called the museum. Actually it was an office where one could get tickets for its three departments. The first part was another church, smaller and older than the main cathedral, but also remarkable in its own fashion.

Its pictures were duller and smokier, but most of them dated from about 1422, when the Italian Renaissance was just getting under way. Parts of the walls had been chipped, laying bare still earlier paintings, showing that some wonderful things can well come out of the restoration of that church. Perhaps most amazing of all, across the altar screen, between the dark old paintings, ran a series of large, petaled flowers, ten of them in all, and the center of each flower was made up of seven large diamonds, each two or three carats in size. They were full of the piercing, dazzling colored fire that is peculiar to diamonds, although they were cut in some very old-fashioned manner which could not give them their full brilliance.

Somewhere within the maze of the fortified walls was the second part of the museum, room after room filled with sections of the carving from old peasant *izbas*, Russian peasant lace, lacquered boxes, including many Palyekhs, and peasant clothing, rich and gay of all sorts. It was a collection of *narodny* art, the art of the people, and it was good. There were carved walrus tusks and wood carvings of all sorts. Some of the carving was unbelievably smooth and delicate, showing scene after scene from the old *skazki*. Best of all were some of the wedding crowns and headgear, sewn solid with rough but real pearls until they looked as though they, too, were out of the old tales.

The last part of the museum was reached by a long climb through staircases in the walls. We were mixed up with several Russians by then. We all got lost and helped each other find the way, until at last we came into one of the towers which contained an historical exhibition of the sieges of the Polish and Livonian wars. The slits in the walls through which molten lead could be poured down on the attackers and other such medieval details were generally evident throughout the entire monastery, but here they were kept functioning. And all the time, from somewhere just outside the walls, was intermittent pistol fire, for no apparent reason.

When, after several hours in the monastery, we pulled out of it, we saw our followers parked outside the walls. We turned to go on through Zagorsk, looking for a place to get some lunch, as it was late. Our shadowers came along, far behind. We stopped in a *chainaya* which was cleaner than usual. As Valodya remarked, it would have been better if it had been less clean and the food more tasty. There I decided to drive on a bit farther, in the hope of coming on some stream where I could do a little fishing. At Rostov there is another monastery, and a lake as well.

After we were clear of the town, I didn't see our followers behind us. I had no doubt that they were there, but I was mistaken. They had done their work, and we didn't see them again. No more than four or five kilometers beyond Zagorsk the road crossed a small bridge, and there a sallow, sharp-faced MVD officer was standing waiting for us. I was driving, and I could see him for a considerable distance. Other traffic went past him, but he held up his hand and stopped us.

Where was our permit? And where was my driver's license? And what was Valodya doing letting me drive when I didn't have a driver's license? Valodya's papers were all in order and he handled his part neatly, pointing out that it was my car, not his, and that, although he worked for me, he could not very well tell me not to drive my own car — that was my business, not his.

Since we had no permit to travel on that road, we turned meekly around, Valodya taking the wheel, and came back home. It seemed that Nell was more annoyed than I, although she had not been very keen to try to go beyond Zagorsk in the first place. She couldn't resist waving to the MVD station that we passed as we came back through Zagorsk. When we got home I tried to console myself by the thought that after all, even though we had only been trying to seek out whatever attractive and interesting side there might be of Russia, it was their country and not ours. Nevertheless, I had no further desire for anything Russian.

Late in the evening we went to the Leningradsky Station to say good-by to Durbrow. It was very hot, and the waiting rooms were crowded. I have almost never been conscious of any of the smells for which Russia is supposed to be famous, but that crowded room was heavy with humanity. It was nearly midnight when the train left, with Derby and small Bruce, who has recently been creating a bit of a disturbance by giving away copies of *Amerika* on the street, waving from the window. As we went out from the station into the fresh air the sky was white with the combination of evening and approaching dawn. In the middle of one of the still-crowded streets was a very very drunk citizen with a belted white embroidered Russian blouse and a walking stick, reeling and weaving in aimless circles while the traffic carefully avoided him.

We were awakened this morning by a sudden blast of excited Russian from the loud-speakers in the plaza outside the Embassy, followed by martial music that was so commanding and authoritative that one felt as if one should get up and do something. Nell was so startled that I asked her why she was disturbed. "Perhaps they are mobilizing!" she said. It proved only to be election day, and the loud-speakers were to urge each citizen to go to the polls and vote.

For weeks the *agitpunkts* have been hung with slogans and draped with crimson flags. Every neighborhood has its *agitpunkt*, manned by professional "agitators" whose business it is to stir up enthusiasm for the Party and to advertise its achievements.

Not long ago a Russian told me a story. "A girl died and went to heaven," he said. "Things went well enough there until one day she caught a glimpse of hell. And there in hell they were having the most wonderful time, playing on accordions, singing and dancing. She watched them often, and at last went to those in charge of heaven and asked if she couldn't be released, to go to hell instead. It was very boring in heaven in comparison with all the accordion playing and dancing that was going on in hell. They let her go, but she soon found out, when she was in hell, that she had been seeing only one of their *agitpunkts*."

In Russia the political anecdote travels in the same way as the off-color story does in America, and perhaps for the same reason. It has the fascination of the forbidden. I never hear one that I do not think of the informer, Varya, whom I have never seen before or since the night she told me of her broken mother in Siberia.

6. THE GLORIOUS FOURTH

FOR SOME REASON, MOSCOW, where dogs are rarely seen, has suddenly been alive with cats. I was startled in the middle of the night to see a huge cat slip noiselessly past the bathroom door and disappear down the hall. I started to search the apartment for him and finally found him, a sort of ghastly pale gray color, sitting in the middle of the living room, glaring at me. Finally he gave way and scurried out through the ventilator fan in the kitchen.

There are no cats at Spiro House, yet McMillan said that he was wakened in the middle of the night, his hair standing on end, because of a sudden and violent cat fight directly under his bed. Nell also said that she thought a cat jumped over her bed during the night recently, but then decided she had been dreaming.

After going to sleep over a nice comfortable tale of witchcraft, such invasions are enough to give one the creeps.

After seeing Laurence Olivier in *Hamlet* at the British Embassy, I was very much ashamed of the American movies that we have here in ours. They are so uniformly bad that one comes to half-believe all that the Russian papers say about their being the mirror of a careless and decadent civilization. If good American pictures are made nowadays, we seldom see them here.

We also went to a cocktail party at the Philbins' on Ostrovsky Street. The entrance to their apartment house was dirty and unpaved, looking like that of the worst sort of tenement, and the long climb up the stairs was past walls crusted and scrawled thick with children's writing. Colonel Philbin, although an assistant military attaché, is a graduate of the Navy language school. He looks like a cherub, but is tough, hard and understanding, and Anne, his wife, is a dark Madonna.

The gentle, courteous little Danish Minister had an excellent dinner in his Legation for the Danish trade delegation which has just finished its dealings here in Moscow. Some of the delegation had been here in former years. They said that although people seemed somewhat better dressed now, they could see no essential change for the better. Perhaps the excellent fragrant French wine had something to do with it — in any case I talked more than usual. Perhaps that is one reason why the evening seemed so enjoyable to me.

General Carter and two or three assistant military attachés were watching some planes practicing for the forthcoming Air Fleet Day from their car which was parked on the public highway. Red Air Force officers came up and told them that they could not do that. When they said that the Americans should go with them to the commanding officer of the airfield, Carter refused. They kept his diplomatic card, however, and he doesn't yet have it back. Nor have he and Macon succeeded as yet in making an appointment with Serayev to discuss the matter.

I asked a Finnish acquaintance if he happened to know the Finn with whom I shared a compartment on the way back from Leningrad, remarking that he seemed a very pleasant person.

"He's a communist," growled my acquaintance.

"He didn't talk like it — quite the contrary," I replied.

"Nevertheless he's a communist. Perhaps he talks one way and thinks another."

It is typical of the complexities of dealing with any aspect of the communist world that many of our own people regard the Finn with whom I was talking as himself a communist.

The Moscow theatrical companies are out in Siberia and the provinces for the summer and some of the provincial troupes are playing in Moscow. Nell and I went to a summer theater in Sokolniki Park to see a troupe from Rostov-on-the-Don play a musical comedy called *The Tobacco Captain*. It was a show about Peter the Great, and it would be generous to call it amateurish. They had a bacchanalian ballet as an *entr'acte* which was downright embarrassing. The costumes looked as though they had been made at home by loving hands, with the result that some of the tights looked more like long winter drawers. None of the ballerinas were remotely good to look at, and they could not even dance well. One wonders why there should be such discrepancies in the efforts of a people which has such real talent.

Still, it was pleasant to walk out through the trees during the intermissions in the long summer evening, even though the park was a little draggled and dirty. That effect may come largely from the wide dirt sidewalks, for even when there is plenty of grass and turf one is always kicking along through the dust and dirt of the walks. The trees of Sokolniki were distinctly northern, with many hemlocks and birches. After the performance, during our long walk of a kilometer or more from the theater to the gates of the park, they gave a theatrical effect to the whole place.

On the way a drunken Russian came staggering down the path. He made some sort of a pass at a woman walking near us, a pass so vigorous that, when it missed, he went down. He lay there, and people just went around him as they walked past, as unconcerned as if he were not there. It does not pay to be curious in Russia.

In addition to the official Embassy Fourth of July party, Ambassador and Mrs. Smith had a special party the day before for all the Americans in Moscow at the Embassy *dacha* at Tarasovka. Unfortunately, it drizzled rain, with sometimes a brief downpour, so none of the outdoor things that had been planned could come off. It is a big *dacha,* set among big trees, and there was plenty of room indoors for people to play bridge and Ping-pong or to dance.

On the way out to Tarasovka it was evident that the summer is already wearing itself out, for many of the trees have lost their greenness and have taken on a distinctly autumnal yellow. The road, which is the beginning of the Yaroslavl Chaussée, seems much more built up than last summer. There certainly are some big new prison camps along the way, with their high fences of new boards and their wooden guard towers at all the jogs and corners.

John Emmerson did one of his piano acts, and it was a great and well-deserved success. I particularly enjoyed Mrs. Morris, the dark-haired busy wife of the new first secretary who has just arrived from Berlin. She and the Emmersons had been in Tokyo at the same time that Ralph Ofstie was naval air attaché there before the war, and she told me how the irrepressible Ralph never failed to sell each newcomer tickets to "see the executions." We decided that we might try that one here in Moscow.

The party was a hospitable one, with gifts for everyone as at Christmas, fountain pens that require no filling, compacts, yo-yos to relieve frustration, and such things, and there were hams and turkeys and plenty to drink. When it finally broke up after midnight, it was in a blaze of glory provided partly by a fight among some of the Russian help.

Fourth of July night the Navy dressed up in whites and did its best to help out at the Ambassador's diplomatic reception. Nell wore a gray evening dress of net and lace, and we stood in the reception line. We were supposed to take the Russian guests to a special room for food, but someone changed the rules while we were in the line. Although several people ended up where they weren't supposed to be, everything went off well, and the reception was a terrific success.

There were turkeys and hams, *ryabchiki,* caviar and champagne. Two or three of the foreign guests remarked to me that they had never seen such hospitality and had never had such a good time in Moscow. Serayev and Pasco were there, and also the heavy-set, baldish General Slavin of the Red Army. There were a few Russians from the Foreign Office, a couple of whom had been on duty in Washington. Even the Russian guests seemed more relaxed and friendly than I have ever seen them. It was broad daylight when the music stopped.

Dr. Vaughn told me that he had just come from the French Embassy, where he had had the unpleasant duty of pronouncing their new Minister-Counselor dead from suicide — hanging. The Russians had, of course, been notified, and there were two or three of their doctors there. Vaughn said that when he went through the routine step of injecting adrenaline directly into the heart in an emergency effort to revive him, the Russians buzzed excitedly as if they had never seen such a thing.

The French Minister had been in Moscow only one week. He was said to have been very low and depressed over the death of his wife some six months before. What a place to send anyone in a depressed mood! The Soviets are not apt to try to make propaganda capital out of it. They are perfectly capable of doing so, but in this case it would backfire.

The Sunday night American movies at Spasso House have been so consistently bad that I have often rebelled mildly at taking Nell to see them. "Why don't you be like Henk Geomans, the Dutch Counsellor?" she once said. "He says that he doesn't go to see the movie, but to see his friends." The next time I offered to go on that basis Nell swept coldly away alone saying that I didn't have any friends to see. You can't win.

For once, the movie itself was a sufficient attraction, for it was Charles Laughton in *The Suspect*. It was a tense sort of thing about a murderer whose conscience does him in in the end. One gets to view things through Soviet eyes almost as second nature. The Soviets would never permit their own people to see this movie because, in spite of its moral lesson, it is not sufficiently black or white in its portrayal of character. It is a good movie for anybody, and Charles Laughton still remains the greatest character actor alive.

7. THE MIDNIGHT SUN

GENERAL NORDENSKJOLD DID NOT FORGET his promise to take me fishing in Lapland; indeed he followed it up with a recent reminder that midsummer was a good time to go. It was necessary for me to go somewhere to get in my routine flying, so I was more than pleased to make arrangements to go to Sweden. General Nordenskjold and Captain Gallagher, our naval attaché in Stockholm, were to meet me on the field there, and we were to leave at once in the amphibian for Lapland.

In the seat beside me on the plane was a tall, faded girl with very blue eyes, from one of the Western missions here in Moscow. She was on her first visit home from Russia in some two or three years. We passed over the Volga near Kalinin, the mighty river shining wide and peaceful in the morning sunshine. Then the clouds began to crowd until we lost sight of the ground, not to see it again until we came down through the clouds over Tsarskoe Selo in the approach to the Leningrad airport.

On the way, the blue-eyed girl had squirmed around and crossed and uncrossed her legs so often that it seemed to me that perhaps she wasn't used to riding on planes. I made a delicate remark about how surprisingly clean the rest room was on this Russian job. But she said that her restlessness was due to her legs going to sleep, so my tact was wasted.

The ruined buildings on the airport at Leningrad still looked like those of most European airports three years ago. There were scores of German prisoners in their dusty gray-green work clothes and their peaked caps, leisurely and ineffectively working about the place, but few signs of reconstruction. For some reason the Russians always use fewer guards for their German prisoners than for their fellow Russians.

A big truck backed up to the plane to take everyone's luggage to the customs except that of the Western girl and myself, since we were the only ones who had diplomatic passports. The Soviets did not touch my luggage, but asked me what money I had with me.

Since I expected to return by train, I had nearly a thousand rubles. They took it away, giving me a receipt with which they said it could easily be redeemed on my re-entry into Russia. This was my fourth trip out of Russia, and the first time that such a thing has happened, but they assured me that they always did that with everyone, regardless of diplomatic status or *laissez-passers*. It was no use telling them that I had been through Leningrad by air with no such troubles, and no good wondering about what could be used for rubles on the train after crossing the border at Vyborg on my way back.

The tall girl, however, provided a bit of philosophy. "If you were in China," she said, "and they took all your money away from you, it wouldn't bother you a bit. You would just regard it as a strange Chinese custom. Every country has its own customs, and to me it is just as interesting to note the Russian customs as it would be to be among the Chinese."

There is much truth in that. It is quite possible that the reason why Soviet vagaries are so annoying is because of the illusion of Western civilization that one has while in Russia. When one realizes that it is only an illusion, and that the busy streets and big buildings of Moscow and Leningrad are only a sort of front to a very primitive country, it helps. A large part of the pattern of inconvenience which continually plagues foreigners can be charged to other things than sheer spite and malice.

After a long wait, the luggage of the other through passengers was carted back to the plane and we took off for Helsinki. By this time the clouds had broken up, but we gave the city of Leningrad a wide berth, seeing only its golden spires shining in the distance. The fortress island of Kronstadt was clear, but too far away to see any details. Soon we were over the innumerable islands and lakes of Finland. Its dark green forests looked wild and desolate, even where they were to be seen only in patches around the rocky outcrops between green glades and clearings.

At lunch in the Helsinki airport my girl friend told me that she had lived for a couple of years in Paris and also in Stockholm. She said that she felt much more at home in Moscow than she had in either of those two places. People thought too much about food in Sweden, and too much about clothes in Paris. There was too much competition in those lines to be healthy. When she added some familiar remarks about the Soviet Union being the only country where the common man really had a chance, I hoped that it would be possible for me to keep my mouth shut for the rest of the journey. Actually it wasn't difficult, for sleeping was good on the Swedish plane from Helsinki to Stockholm.

I walked out of the plane at the Bromma Airport directly into the hands of friends, for those fine Swedish people immediately made me feel that I was one of them. General Nordenskjold and Ferd Grumme, who was to be our host in Lapland, had postponed their trip when they learned of my delay, although doing so had cut deeply into their free time. Grumme was big and blond, with a big, gentle smile and a never-failing gentle manner. In twenty minutes I was ready to take off again in the U.S. Navy amphibian that was waiting. "A regular old fishing hat!" said Nordenskjold, looking at the brown civilian hat that I always wear for best in Moscow.

I soon went up in the second pilot's seat to get in some of my flight time, and found myself again in the blue-and-silver paradise, with a smooth, misty sea that was so indistinguishable from the horizon that I had to fly on instruments. Commander Bengston, the pilot, was a quiet, sandy-haired lad with a deep scar down one cheek. He had put in a couple of years in carriers, and was in one of the Black Cat squadrons in the South Pacific during the war.

We flew directly up the Gulf of Bothnia until finally, above the misty sea and far in the distance to the left, the dim tops of mountains could be seen. The forested land, spotted with lakes and streaked with shining rivers, rose gradually beneath us until it broke into cliffs and mountains. White streaks and spots of snow began to show increasingly. Some fifty or sixty kilometers north of the Arctic Circle we sloshed into a creamy green landing in a mirrorlike mountain lake. All around were snow-capped mountains, with their valleys hardening into glaciers, more and more lofty and rugged as they marched away to the Norwegian border.

Three or four boats with outboard motors circled around, came alongside, and loaded ourselves and our gear. The plane took off while we droned up a placid emerald-green river in the boats.

Another river came tumbling down to join us in a smother of heavy white rapids, and at the juncture lay the little village of Kvikkjokk, a half dozen dark reddish-brown cottages with a high wooden church of the same color, looking strangely pagan and savage in spite of its cross. We kept on up our green river, whose banks were lined with pines, willows and birches, all stunted and small because of the high altitude. The water, although very green, was as clear and light as air, and every stone and pebble on the deep bottom could be seen as clearly as in the lovely rivers of Florida. We passed a Lapp tent, built exactly like an Indian wigwam from a skeleton cone of straight birch boughs. After an hour we began to smell sweet wood smoke. In the distance ahead we could hear the roar of fast water which prevented the boats from going further.

The mosquitoes had been annoying on the way, but I had some of Dr. Vaughan's oil of pennyroyal which seemed to keep them off. There were such swarms of them on shore that the wood fire did little good, so we put on nets. Gallagher, in a green net, sprayed some shaggy little ponies with DDT while Nordenskjold, in a bright blue net, helped some men strap the gear onto skids or sleds to be drawn by the ponies. My own net was brown. It gave a golden autumnal color to everything as we went off at a fast walk along the trail through the woods. We walked for more than an hour in a wilderness of fragrance from wild flowers and stunted pines. The midnight sun was dodging between the mountain peaks when we finally reached the end of our journey, a beautifully designed log lodge, lost in the woods on a high rocky knoll. It seemed a long time since breakfast in Moscow.

Mannborg, Grumme's man of all work, was half Finn and half Swedish. His trousers were tucked into boots, Russian fashion, and he carried his head down, so that his china-blue eyes looked out from under his eyebrows like those of a lowering bull. Since it was too warm to start the central heating plant, we started a birch fire in one of the big stone fireplaces.

The lodge was luxurious, with electric lights from a completely silent generator, thick blankets on the ship-type bunks, a room-size polar bearskin in one of the living rooms, many skins of wolves and bears that had been shot in the vicinity, and gigantic seats around the windows, soft with heavy gray reindeer pelts. Reindeer skin must be the warmest skin there is, but it is much too thick for ordinary wear. There was a Finnish steam bath in the basement, a shower, toilets, and everywhere were cunningly designed cabinets and storage places for tools and gear and equipment, with great stacks of skis and snowshoes and dog harness. Grumme, who was a commander in the Swedish navy during the war, is a chemical engineer by profession. He likes to tinker with things, so he had laid out the whole place himself. Among other things, he is the outboard motor champion of Sweden. For supper, together with cheese, sardines, coffee and wine, we had smoked reindeer meat. Sliced thin, it was deliciously tender and sweet, the color of liver and about the consistency of smoked salmon.

It never did get dark, and it was hard to go to bed. The Swedes said that no one pays any attention to day and night in the summertime so they always lose sleep, but they have the winter darkness in which to make it up. Outside the lodge the sun merely passed behind a mountain and came out on the other side. Everywhere was a wilderness of heavy squat hemlocks, but with no really big trees, for within a mile to the west and north was the abrupt end of the timber and the beginning of the tundra. This marked the true polar regions. The timber line, which is different from the tundra line and depends on altitude in all latitudes, was very sharp and low on all of the mountains around, with the bulk of each mountain rocky and bald. Behind the lodge rose a great mountain, streaked with snow, with a profile like that of a face. Its nose was flattened like an Eskimo's.

"I was telling a Lapp," said Grumme, "about the uneasy state of the world. He said that the Mountain would undoubtedly punish the world for its wickedness. The Lapps still worship their old gods, and you can see many places of sacrifice where they leave reindeer meat and skins for their gods." At last we sprayed the bedrooms with DDT to clear out the last mosquitoes, and I slept untroubled for two or three hours until Nordenskjold pulled me out to go fishing.

The pennyroyal kept away the mosquitoes so well that I never bothered with a net any more. We walked a long way through the fragrant woods in a profusion of wild flowers and bracken, with thick, green, soft bear moss underfoot, or big patches of reindeer moss, which is a big gray lichen. Always we could hear the roar of the river, and at last we came out on its rocky, mossy banks.

And what a river it was! The Skarra was its name, and it was too heavy to fish anywhere except in its little side pools and backswirls. It was much too fast to wade. I found one wide shoal and went out in the middle to the riffle where two fast streams came together around an island. There I got strike after strike on dry flies, hooking an occasional trout but losing him immediately every time. My feet and legs were so numb with the icy glacial water that I had some doubt if I could make it back to the shore again.

I fished upstream through a wizard land of huge rocks and deep pools, leaving the others far behind, and finally came to a beautiful gorge. Within the gorge the water was exactly like emerald, a clear, deep green, but filled with air and bubbles like the flaws which all great emeralds have, thundering along in a series of falls, with heaving, glassy, treacherous pools at the foot of each falls. I fished there for a long time, getting occasional strikes but never landing a fish, until the realization came that I had been away from the others for a long time.

I walked back through the moss and ferns and heavy, squat trees and found that the others had become worried about me, for it is not good to be long alone in that wilderness. Nordenskjold had landed one nice trout, about a three-pounder. In the arctic day, people keep going until they get weary and then sleep for two or three hours without any regard to clocks.

There were several reindeer around the house, and all of the others had seen them several times. During the summer the Lapps let their reindeer range, and in the early fall they round them up in big herds of a couple of thousand or so, using lassos like American cowboys.

After some salmon mayonnaise and cheese — everyone had lost track of what meal it was supposed to be — Grumme and I started fishing alone, heading for the emerald gorge. He was very picturesque in his fringed buckskin jacket. It came from America. He told me many things about the Lapps, saying that even he, who has lived long amongst them, felt that they were a strange and alien nation. They still practice witchcraft, and make dolls to melt or to stick pins into.

"I am always uneasy around the Lapps," he said. "One never feels welcome with them, but always as though one is an intruder. Still, if you will come back in the autumn, I have another lodge on a lake a day's journey from here, and I will try to take you to a reindeer roundup. You will like it in any case, for the lake is full of trout and the lodge is quite comfortable. It is really a Lapp winter house. The Lapps are a cruel and primitive people in many ways. There used to be silver mines in the mountains, and the Lapps hauled the ore out over the ice. Anyone whom they wanted to punish they would tie to the end of a rope, cut a hole in the ice, float the end of the rope down under the ice to another hole, and then haul the offender from one hole to the other, just as sailors used to be keelhauled in the old days."

In the gorge, I at last landed a trout. It was not like our trout, but almost black on the back and sides, with a faint sort of stripe like a rainbow and a very few small colored spots like a brook. Grumme hooked and lost what he said was the biggest fish he had ever hooked, possibly a salmon, although the salmon run was over. On the way back to the lodge we saw a big brown capercailzie, bigger than a turkey. We must have been near her nest, for she ran back and forth through the brush around us for some distance.

Gallagher had managed to get a fishhook completely through his finger, so he and the general hadn't done much fishing. But for supper we had the general's big trout and my smaller one, and they were delicious as trout always are. Then we had to decide what to do. Grumme had an appointment in Stockholm the following day, and, although the rest of us could have stayed on or even gone to the Lapp house on the lake, having the plane come back for us, we did not like to remain without our host. Moreover, there was still much flying to be done.

Although we had to get up early in the morning, if one can call it morning when it is always full daylight, we sat around the birch fire and talked for a long time before turning in. Grumme said that it was best there in the dead of winter. If there is not too much snow, one can drive up on the ice along the lakes and rivers, but if the snow is heavy it is two hundred kilometers by dog sledge and ski to the railroad.

"But can you travel that way in the winter darkness?" I asked.

"Oh, yes. There is always an hour or two of twilight in the middle of the day, and, unless it is stormy, the nights are very light with starshine and the streamers of the Northern Lights. The snow reflects what light there is, and when the moon is shining it is as light as day. One can read a newspaper easily by moonlight. The snow stacks up to the roof, and it is very warm and cozy here — a grand place for the children at Christmas."

I asked about the lemmings, those strange little beasties which, for some mysterious reason, every seven years travel in swarms to the Atlantic coast and commit suicide by throwing themselves over the cliffs into the ocean.

"They are rodents," said Nordenskjold, "little things, no bigger than your fist, but tremendously brave. One of them will attack a man without any hesitation, or even a bear. That is the way the Swedes regard the Big Bear to the east — "

"You can well be that way," I said. "It is noticeable that the Russians have a respect for the Swede and the Finn that is really a fear of them. They talk about how they are always being invaded by the rest of the world, and their three great invasions from the west were by the French under Napoleon, by Hitler's Germany, and by the Swedes. They know well that Charles the Twelfth was only turned back at Poltava, in the Ukraine. I have heard Russians say more than once that the Swedes were terrible people. It has not been proved in recent years, but the Finns, who are also terrible to the Russian mind, have proved it amply."

It was difficult finally to leave that attractive place. When I gave Mannborg a few kroner and told him good-by, he bowed clear down to the ground, just like an occasional Russian. On the way down the placid lower reaches of the river we saw several little flocks of small wild ducklings on the water, and my friends reminded me that there would be ducks as well as fish if it was possible to come back in September. The plane was timed to the dot, reaching the lake at exactly the same moment as we, and soon we were breaking the reflections of the tall white clouds with the spray of our take-off. It was with regret that I saw the snowy peaks fade away behind us.

Our Navy amphibian was made by Grumann, who, more than any other maker of aircraft, should be given credit for the winning of the carrier war in the Pacific. Ferd Grumme said that he had met Roy Grumann in America, and that they had decided they were related.

Once, on the ground beneath, I saw a great stone reindeer slaughtering pen, looking like the vast ground plan of some giant's castle. The shining rivers were filled with logs, floated down from the mountains, looking from the plane like so much straw, clinging together at bends and shallows like tiny bits held by surface tension. At Lulea we had a good breakfast of scrambled eggs, reindeer meat and cheese, and soon everyone but me, who had to fly, was doing a bit of sleeping on the way back to Stockholm.

My room at the Grand Hotel was luxurious, with broad windows that opened out onto the quay, to which was moored a wealth of shipping. The Stockholm docks are not at all like docks, but run right up into the shopping part of the city, and they are as neat and clean and orderly as any city street. Maybe there are warehouses somewhere, but if there are, the ships live in the main streets and not in the warehouse district. And along the sparkling freshness of the quay were big dip nets, and the streets were full of brown, fair-haired girls, with unbelievably lovely clothes fluttering about their bicycles.

I got myself dressed and went out on the streets. There I promptly almost went mad from the beauty and luxury of the shop windows full of wonderful clothes, glittering evening bags, soft, rich leather things, at the shadowy neatness of the gardens and parks that fill the streets, and at the dignity and handsomeness of the people. I did a bit of shopping, including some spoons for pike fishing, for Nordenskjold and I were to do some more fishing in the Archipelago to the east of Stockholm over the week end. Most of the fishing gear was made in America, and it was cheaper than the Swedish gear. Americans are so expert at quantity production that their insistence on free markets really means American supremacy.

Having an hour or so yet before a dinner engagement, I sat down in a gay sidewalk café and, over some good Swedish beer, just wondered at everything around me. The Russian people are all right in their way, but they are a primitive people, and they lack ease and assurance. They are not born to fine and dignified things, and they just don't have them. In comparison, these Swedes seemed like people from the bright future of a hundred years ahead.

It was very sweet in the sunshine. The reddish-brown, brick-colored awnings of the hotels and sidewalk restaurants gave a warm color to the clean air. There were long lines of window boxes banked full of red, white and blue flowers, such as used to line Regent Street in London. There were big banks of blue hydrangeas, and beds of a very blue tiny flower that looked like a midnight mist.

It is not easy to put into words the difference between the feel of Leningrad, where the sun also sparkles on the water of the Neva and the canals, and the charm of this place. The differences are many, and some of them are subtle, but one outstanding and unmistakable fact is that for the most part Russians, or at least the Soviet planners, are just simply and plainly devoid of taste.

One evening Nordenskjold and I went to Tivoli, which is the Stockholm equivalent of Coney Island. There a crowd was gathered around an open-air stage, waiting for the Three Parker Sisters to appear. We joined the edges of the crowd and waited too. The Sisters were big, plump, colored lasses, with fluffy long organdy dresses that made them look even bigger. Their carriage was free and easy. They sang in American in their rich voices and the crowd liked them.

As I went to bed that night, I wished mightily that two or three square miles of Stockholm, chosen at random, Three Parker Sisters and all, could be put down in the middle of Moscow. The Muscovites just wouldn't believe it. They would think it propaganda — or an *agitpunkt*. For that matter, such a bit of transplanted Stockholm wouldn't believe Moscow, but at least they wouldn't think it propaganda.

The train from Turku to Helsinki passed through the Porkalla enclave, which is still held by the Russians in accordance with their treaty with Finland. At the edge of the area the train was stopped and a special engine, with Russian personnel, was attached. Efficient external blinds were pulled up over all the windows and all cars were locked. There was much snorting and grumbling at this among the foreigners on the train, but for an hour and ten minutes we rode in darkness, as if in the middle of the night.

The lights were too dim for reading, so everyone on the train went to sleep willy-nilly. It was like coming out of an enchanted forest when the blinds were raised on all the sleeping passengers and things again became normal. Before entering the Porkalla area there was nothing to be seen but woods, but when the light came again, there were familiar Russian troops standing around with nothing but woods for a background.

On another occasion I have flown over this route with a visibility of over a hundred kilometers, and have seen the entire Porkalla area spread out to one side far below as clear as the palm of one's hand. It was completely empty — not a town, not an airfield, not a factory, not a ship, only forests and empty fields. Although one must never forget the Russian skill with camouflage and illusion, it may well be that the elaborate secrecy about Porkalla is symbolic of the Soviet Union as a whole.

8. LYUBOV

WE WERE FOUR IN A ROOM on the hard sleeper from Helsinki to Leningrad. A close-mouthed, hard-bitten Finn shared my compartment, together with a New York fur buyer and his sixteen-year-old son, who were on their way to the big annual fur auction in Leningrad. The ancient Assyrian cast to these last two faces showed them to be Jews, gentle ones, kindly and generous. The train left Helsinki late in the evening, and the oppressive feeling of going out into some sort of dark cloud lightened when I heard the familiar Russian speech once more among groups saying good-by just as in Leningrad or Moscow.

The next morning, after an uneasy night, we stopped in the last Finnish town before the Russian border. Although the train was already full of fur buyers, American, Mexican, English and German, but all of them Jewish, there we picked up four more. Those four would not believe that there was a train only every other day into a great country like Russia. They had started off on their own on a local train two days earlier, confident that they would have no difficulty in getting on through by freight train or even motorcar. When the local reached the end of its run at the border, they commenced "pulling wires," as they said. They even telephoned the American Legation in Helsinki to try to enlist its aid. Of course they met nothing but a baffling blank wall, and not even the Legation could help. They would have gone hungry and would have had to sleep on the station benches or in the open if some kindly Finnish farmers had not taken them into their homes.

Until one has experienced it, it is difficult to realize the complete blankness of that wall at the Russian borders, the utterly unknown nature of everything just a few kilometers further on. Unlike most international borders of the world, there is no passing back and forth of peasants across the boundary. For ten or fifteen kilometers on the Russian side every human habitation has been removed or destroyed, and the resulting wilderness is patrolled with troops, frontier guards and dogs.

It took several hours for the train to crawl across this uninhabited area into Vyborg, so that the frontier guards and customs officials could check up thoroughly on the train and its passengers. A pink-cheeked, worn-looking, efficient middle-aged Russian woman came into our compartment, followed by a battery of assistants; she sat down, and began courteously to question my two companions. She looked as though she had been cast for the part on the stage.

She was very polite, but lightly and gracefully she wormed everything out of them, every book, paper, magazine, letter, piece of money, even the contents of their wallets, giving them all to her assistants to check over in detail. They looked at every page of every book, at every sheet of blank writing paper, and then she began on their luggage. I couldn't help but admire her firm and pleasant thoroughness. Although she spoke quite good English, I translated from time to time when things got complicated. They found nothing. Doubtless they were after messages to individual Russians and evidences of espionage as well as effectively preventing the introduction of any propaganda or unsympathetic ideology.

It was fortunate that my long-delayed *laissez-passer* had at last reached me in Stockholm, for my things were untouched and I was not questioned. When we at last pulled into Vyborg, this pleasant, efficient woman and I met again. I stopped her on the platform to ask her how long we would be there. Her worn pink face lighted up with a smile when she saw me, and she put out her hand to take mine.

We were in Vyborg for an hour or so, so I strolled around the town, always accompanied close by some of the fur buyers. Vyborg was badly beaten up, and the heaps of brick and stone, the twisted ironwork and the shells of empty walls, made a familiar sight. It had once been an attractive city, but the deadly sameness of the Soviets was already stamped upon it in the inconvenient arrangement of the shops and the unappetizing dummies of food in their windows.

Here and there Finnish characteristics showed contrastingly, such as the stone carvings of old, bearded faces on one half-ruined building that was surrounded by the Russian booths and kiosks. In the streets were booted women, and there were many, many sailors, smarter than any other Russians in their wide leather belts and their blue-and-white jumpers and *klyoshi,* which is Russian for bell-bottomed trousers. An old beggar woman crossed herself when I gave her some coins. It was noticeable that the passing Finns gave to her, but not the Russians. The fur buyer's son wanted to take some snapshots, but his father would not let him.

"And what if they wouldn't like it?" said senior. "Then what would I do for a passport to get to the fur auctions next year?"

There was plenty of tea from the samovar in our wagon, and I appreciated the sandwiches I had brought with me. Although the only restaurant in sight in Vyborg would have been welcome had I been on my way out of Russia, it was too soon after the snowy linen and savory food of Stockholm to plunge into it again without holding one's breath a bit. Besides, my Russian money was all in Leningrad. The fur buyers who had been to Russia before had regular commissaries of supplies in their luggage, and were very generous in sharing their food and drink with those who had not.

The train crawled on across Karelia through dense swampy forests, bright with scarlet berries on the trees and cerise clouds of wild flowers in the infrequent meadows. Vyborg is a strictly military town, so nowhere was there any sign of habitation except for an occasional lonely station, only mile after mile of wilderness. Once, curiously enough, there was a freshly painted brand-new small landing barge abandoned in the midst of some thick trees. There was no water in sight in any direction, and it was difficult to understand how it could have been brought there through all the tangle. It was just left, like some toy of which children have grown tired.

We were almost in Leningrad before the low clusters of unpainted log *izba* huts began to appear. They blend into the landscape, and are as typical of Russia as the black, sluglike Bedouin tents are typical of the upland deserts of the Arab world. We came into Leningrad through extensive unkempt, unpainted suburbs, with every little extra patch of land luxuriantly covered with potatoes, interspersed with little parks and inlets of water where people were sun-bathing or swimming.

At the station, we were met by the same peaches-and-cream blonde girl from Intourist who met me once before in Leningrad, her fair hair twisted around her head in heavy, shining braids. Her name was Raya, which is very like the word for Paradise. She took charge of all the fur buyers and their voluminous luggage with calm efficiency, sending me off by myself in a separate car to the Yevropa Hotel. The Yevropa was an older hotel than the Astoria and, since it did not try quite so hard to be Western, more attractive.

"Why did you arrive today?" asked the middle-aged Intourist woman at the Yevropa.

"Why not?" I asked, puzzled at the question.

"We did not expect you until Thursday."

"But I made no hotel reservation for Thursday or any other day."

"Ah, but you have accommodations on the train for Moscow on Thursday night."

There was a small feeling of satisfaction that I had managed to slip into Leningrad a couple of days before the authorities had organized themselves for the occasion. Moreover, I had a ready excuse.

"I have no money," I said. "When I left Russia the other day they took all my money away from me. This receipt they gave me may be good, but in any case I thought I would need at least a couple of days to redeem it. I may not be able to get away even on Thursday."

"Oh, yes, you will," she answered purposefully. "I'll find out where and how you can get your money back." I noticed two evil-looking men examining a stack of passports. They were whispering together behind their hands, peering around like conspirators.

"How about lending me some money," I asked, "until I can get my own?"

Somewhat to my surprise she handed over a hundred rubles. "You are a real friend!" I said.

"Oh, no, I'm not. That's not my money. The rules say I can advance that much to tide people over. Since we did not expect you, there may be some difficulty about a room."

Nevertheless she dug up a room promptly. It was almost an exact duplicate of my former room at the Astoria, being really a small suite, with chairs and divans upholstered in midnight-blue velvet. They had forgotten to remove a framed placard on the wall which said that since this was an Intourist hotel, built primarily for the use of foreigners, any Russian who might be accommodated was subject to eviction on no notice. At first thought it would seem that a knowledge of that rule for Intourist hotels might come in handy to a foreigner, but on second thought it seems doubtful if he would be denied a room without policy — and police — backing.

The buildings that could be seen across the way from my windows were surrounded with scaffolding. Green-gray German prisoners were leisurely repairing war damage to the façades while barelegged Russian women painters swung on the scaffolding and busily plied their brushes. The dark cloud under which it had seemed I was coming was gone for good, and I was caught again by the fascination of Russia.

The Yevropa had a restaurant on the roof. Although it lacked the neatness and fresh charm of Stockholm, its boxes of petunias and nasturtiums gave it a homemade, unprofessional sort of gaiety. It looked out over a wilderness of tin roofs, and in the middle distance was a black dome with a surmounting arc of ladder silhouetted against the sky. It looked like stage scenery for an astronomical observatory, and the illusion was furthered by a bearded, stooped old man, wearing an overcoat and a fur cap on this warm summer afternoon, pacing back and forth along some walkways against the sky.

Kiev cutlets are among the choicer foods of Russia. They are strips of white chicken rolled around some butter, covered with batter and then fried in deep fat. They were still sizzling and sputtering when they came to the table.

After dinner, while I was walking down the Nevsky Prospekt, a woman called me by name from the crowd. I turned around in surprise to find the Bulgarian Mrs. Colonna and the Persian Mrs. Valadier, both of whom were leaving Russia for good with their French husbands the following morning. I talked with them for a while, enjoying their bright, fast Russian speech, and then continued on my way, turning off the Nevsky under the big yellow curving arch of the gateways to the great plaza in front of the discolored green of the Winter Palace, on past the Bronze Horseman, to the waterfront of the Neva.

For a while it seemed as though I had been honored with a *slezhka* and was being followed, but it was hard to be sure. I stopped in an embrasure on the Lieutenant Shmidt Bridge, and a bareheaded man loitered in the embrasure opposite. Always, wherever I went, there was someone at a distance who might have been detailed for me, but it always seemed like a different person. I walked for hours along the river, past the shipping, and deep into Vassilyevski Island along cobbled walks past tall apartment houses.

By the time it began to grow dark, weariness had overtaken me. An ice-cream barrow gave me an opportunity to get some change. The fat, smiling barrow woman told me that a passing streetcar would take me near home. It is always surprising to see the number of crippled and bandaged people that there are in Russia, many of them apparently crippled too recently to be a result of the war. Others have also noticed this, and some think that it is due to industrial accidents. On the tramcar was the usual high percentage of cripples, and the faces of nearly all the Russians about me had that alert characteristic called *khitrost,* which means a sort of cunning or slyness, but without any connotation of maliciousness. It may well be that it is necessary to be *khitry* in Russia in order to survive. Hunted foxes and fish have their own sort of *khitrost.*

Among the passengers were a couple of representatives of that frequent type of military-looking old man who carries a walking stick and wears a cap like a yachting cap but without any insignia. They are always equipped with little white Vandykes. Perhaps they are retired naval people who like to keep a touch of uniform in their civilian clothes.

I slept late the next morning, and was wakened by Intourist telling me to come at once, for they had made an appointment with the customs for me to recover my own rubles. After a hurried breakfast on the roof I dashed down to the Intourist lounge. I should have known better than to have hurried, for there followed a wait of half an hour while they were getting themselves organized to take me to the customs.

One gets conditioned to waiting, and at such times I enjoy saying over my Russian poetry to myself. Also in the Intourist lounge was a sweepingly imaginative mural of Perseus and Andromeda to admire, with a Pegasus that was spotted and prancing like a circus

pony. There was a concert grand piano there that was completely
and elaborately inlaid, as delicately and beautifully as Nell's old
ormulu chest that she got in England. The piano was made by
Lichtenstein and it carried the double-headed eagle, with its inlay
just as firm and sound as when it was first made, a generation or
more ago.

A plump blonde Intourist girl went with me in a little taxi to
the customs. We found that we had mutual friends among the
American naval officers she had known during the war in Mur-
mansk. We had a long ride, going in back of the shipyards on the
left bank of the Neva, with occasional glimpses of cranes and
waterfront. In the customs house, due to Intourist's previous arrangements, they took me to the head of the waiting line and promptly
gave me my thousand rubles. Then back to the hotel and as
promptly back to sleep.

The flies woke me up late in the afternoon, and, since the
Yevropa Hotel is on the corner by the big flower-bedded park in
front of the Russian Museum, I went into the galleries. Apart from
the blue and tan Volga pictures of Levitan, Shiskin's forests, some
of Repin's characterful portraits and some wildly moving sea pictures by Aivazovski, I had already seen the best of this museum.
One of Aivazovski's pictures called "The Ninth Wave" was filled
with a strange wild light shining through the water, and his
"Deluge" should be much more widely known than it is. It is filled
with the desolation and terror of the great Flood like nothing else
I have ever seen.

I went back to the Repins, and found them easily the best of all
Russian painting. I sat before his "Sadko" again for a long time,
and noticed the way in which all of the nonhumans looked secretly
sidewise with their slanting eyes from lowered heads. The Russian
Museum and the Tretyakovskaya Gallery in Moscow are about
on a par. They should both be seen by anyone who ever comes to
Russia.

When the gallery closed, I sat for a while in the little park
among giant dahlias and watched the children playing while their
wrinkled old nurses gossiped. Two of the old nurses near me found
food for much talk and laughter in a not uncommon type of Russian soldier who walked briskly about the gardens. His legs seemed

much too short for his long body and his long neck, and the resulting effect was exaggerated by the wide, low, flaring cut of his riding breeches and his abnormally low boots. His face was all nose and chin, with a big setback to his forehead. His cap was set square, but forward over his eyes, and he was very pompous and very military. This same type is seen so often that it seems it must belong to one of the many Russian tribes or races. At any rate, it amused the old nurses, for they gesticulated graphically and imitated him for a long time.

The Soviets have found another anniversary to exploit, this time the five-hundredth anniversary of the Autocephaly of the Greek Orthodox Russian Church, and the Yevropa was thronged with black-robed priests, on invitation from all over the world where that church thrives. They seemed to fall into two main types, one of big, florid, handsome men, and the other of very pale, ascetic ones. And all of them wore big silver crosses around their necks, and most of them had enormous beards.

Lyubov and I strolled aimlessly along the Nevsky Prospekt. She looked like any other Russian girl in her twenties, neither particularly pretty nor particularly plain, but pleasant and strong and healthy, tall and high-breasted and strong-legged, with clear gray eyes and tawny hair that was bleached out by the sun into two or three varying shades.

She told me that she had started out to become a ballet dancer. That, to a Russian girl, is the equivalent of Hollywood to an American. She had then gone in for sports, running and physical culture. She had been an instructor and had taken part in the Sports Parade in Moscow last year. Then she had left that, and was now secretary to the manager of one of the great Leningrad shipbuilding yards. "Oh-oh!" I thought to myself. "Look out! It just doesn't stand to reason that out of all the millions of people in Leningrad, I should accidentally fall in with one with a job like that!"

We walked through the streets for a long time. She had had a minor accident and so wasn't working for a few days. She told me about her family and her relatives in various parts of Russia. Her grandfather had recently died in Sverdlovsk, after marrying his housekeeper at the age of eighty-one and having a child by her. After that, it was a little easier to believe that she was really from the shipyard.

On my suggestion that we go somewhere for a drink, she led me up to one of the little booths where they sell sweetened water. That kind of a drink was not what I had in mind, but she didn't seem interested in the Leningrad equivalent of night clubs. Since there was nowhere else to go, we walked around until we were weary, and then I took her home. As always with Russians, I left her on a corner and not at her own place, where she said she lived with her mother. She asked if I were busy the next day. I told her Yes, but that if I were free for a while late in the afternoon, I would look for her in the gardens in front of the Russian Museum.

About four o'clock the following afternoon I went to the dahlia-studded park. There was Lyubov, sitting placidly and patiently on a bench. There being nothing else to do, we again started to walk, finally coming out in a big open space in front of the Kirovsky Bridge. In the middle of the space were some low brown stone bastions, with some grass and flowers inside. We stopped to read the inscriptions, and found that it was a little burial place for the heroes of the February Revolution.

It was windy and dusty, so we turned back and went into the Summer Garden, Pushkin's *Letni Sad*. It is a big, rather formal park, with broad gravel walks and, like all Russian parks, a little unkempt. But everywhere along the walks were endless lines of Greek and Roman marble statues, and there were enormous shady old linden trees and little beds of flowers. I remembered having read somewhere that there was a memorial there to Krylov, the Russian Aesop, so we hunted it up. It was well worth hunting up, for around the base of the heroic bronze figure of the man, running around all four sides, was a marvelous high relief in bronze of countless figures from his fables, acting out their parts. All the beasties of Krylov's sly, ambiguous tales were there, bears playing fiddles, goats, sheep, elephants, lions, foxes being *khitry,* cats and dogs. Best of all were the tiny things, clusters of grapes, mice, frogs, and a great swarm of bees, stirred by a bear out of a honey tree. It is probably because of the political meaning that Krylov managed to put into his versions of Aesop's fables that the Russians have come to call such evasions of the censorship "Aesop talk" or "slave language."

In the Summer Garden was an old dwelling of Peter the Great. Lyubov read every word of every long description that was posted by every object. Peter had prided himself on his simplicity and, although well equipped, the house was almost plain. There were Dutch stoves and tiled walls and also some simple, rough, heavy furniture. The physical size of the man was shown by some of his costumes, which would have been much too big for me. Usually the costumes of a past age look ridiculously small, and I have never seen more than one or two suits of armor that I could have gotten into. Peter liked his food hot, so there was a serving window cut directly into the dining room from the big stoves in the kitchen so he could have it that way. Apart from an occasional ceiling decorated with cupids and nymphs and a couple of Rastrelyi busts, it might have been some old farmhouse.

Lyubov said she would take me to a different sort of restaurant than the roof of the hotel, so we found a taxi and went to the Kirov Park of Culture and Rest. It was a very large park, sprawling across some of the islands beyond Vassilyevsky, full of lagoons and pools. It was in more of a natural state than any Russian park I had seen, and was consequently more attractive, being almost like natural woodland. Once we passed a green pool with a big sign saying "SWIMMING HERE STRICTLY FORBIDDEN!" A little naked boy was making repeated dives from the sign itself.

A small youngster came up and asked me for kopecks. "Aren't you ashamed of yourself!" said Lyubov to him. "Begging from people like that!"

"Don't say that," I said, giving him a handful of coins. "Look at his arm!" And when Lyubov saw that his arm ended in a little stump, she started to weep and opened her purse.

We stopped to sniff at an unusually fragrant plant, which she said was flowering tobacco. Its leaves did look like tobacco, but had none of its taste. At last we came to a big restaurant in the park, which was our goal. There was just as much difference between it and the park restaurants of Stockholm and Copenhagen as there was between Russia and the Western world. This restaurant tried, in a shiftless sort of way, to be cultured, but the tablecloths were spotted and soiled and it gave the general effect of a second-rate restaurant in some tiny third-rate American beach resort.

There are many superficial resemblances in Russia to western Europe or to America, but everything is pitched in a different key, and a bit off key at that. Although some of the Georgian wines are not bad, there was no wine to be had here but port, which the other guests were drinking like Bordeaux.

By the time we had finished dinner it was high time for me to get back to the hotel, pack, pay my bill and get to my train for Moscow. I left Lyubov in the little park where she had waited for me that afternoon, still a bit of an enigma, like everything else in Russia. If she was an *agent provocateur* or an attempt to get me into some sort of trouble, it was a strangely halfhearted and aimless attempt. Probably she was just on her own, and the shipbuilding yards were only a coincidence. Coincidences do happen, as I remember well from one time in the big dining room of a luxurious American hotel, when that hotel was brand-new and sparkling. Nell had just told me some tall tale, to which I said, "Why, I would as soon believe that as I would believe that a big rat would run across this floor!" And straightway a big rat ran across that polished, thick-carpeted floor.

This time my Intourist companion to the station was an inoffensive-looking little man. I talked to him in Russian all the way to the station. When we got out of the car, he took off his hat and said, "Please excuse me for having come. Your Russian is so much better than my English that you have no need for any help from Intourist."

Russian railway platforms are always interesting, more so, it seems to me, than the stations in America. There are always knots and groups of people seeing each other off, and there is much more evidence of emotions and tears. But perhaps the Russian people have more real reasons for tears.

It was nice to be in an international wagon again after the trains across Finland, but nevertheless my berth was extraordinarily uncomfortable. There was one vivid dream in which I was flying, at some six or seven thousand feet, in a motor whaleboat without any wings. The engine labored and stuttered, and then stopped with a great rush of sudden silence. The bow of the whaleboat dropped straight down and headed for the deck of a ship far below. I curled myself up and tried to brace myself against the coming crash, thinking calmly, "Well, this is it!" and watched the deck grow bigger and bigger as it rushed up at me. Then I woke up, and saw through the window that the train was just pulling out of Kalinin, and that I had missed an opportunity to see the Volga at close range.

My companion in the compartment was a pale-faced, long-haired, tense, tieless citizen. Two of the prettiest girls I have seen in Russia brought in some breakfast. They were dainty and pert, brown like gypsies, and dressed as if in a musical show, all ruffles and fluff. My companion said that he traveled back and forth all the time between Leningrad and Moscow. I asked him if the station we had just left wasn't Kalinin, knowing very well that it was. Just to make conversation. He said with assurance, "Oh no, that was Klin!" And when we went through Klin, a long time later, he never batted an eye.

He had a row of ribbons on his threadbare civilian coat, and was pleasant enough, in a tense, ghoullike sort of way. The bright red berries of the *buzina* trees were very vivid as the countryside went by, and occasionally we could see tall, narrow stacks of hay, with little peaked wooden roofs built above them to keep them dry. My friend liked to hunt, so, when his vacation begins on October first, he is going to Lake Ladoga after ducks. Vacations are the only thing about which a Russian is never vague. Every citizen is always very sure and definite about when his vacation is to begin — it is never "about such-and-such a time."

Nell was on the station platform in Moscow to meet me, in a pretty blue dress. Zoya was on her vacation, so Natasha clomped and puttered about the house doing everything. While I had been away, Gospodin Elektrik's Russian girl had been arrested, which accounted adequately for her not showing up for lunch one day with Nell as expected. Henrik Madsen was back from Denmark, and even though he had a *laissez-passer* the Soviets had gone over all his luggage and papers with a fine-toothed comb, to his spluttering indignation. Pasco had called up the office to say that the written request for Nell and me to drive to Yaroslavl and back was disapproved. There was a Polish party in honor of their national holiday that night, but I had had enough of foreigners for the moment and found it much more pleasant to stay home with Nell and listen to Chopin's concertos on the record player.

PART VI. DEATH

1. THE DAY OF THE AIR FLEET

EDDIE AND NINA STEVENS had planned a picnic at their *dacha,* but the roads, as is the case with the roads to all *dachas,* were too bad to risk in the frequent heavy showers, so by a great deal of last-minute telephoning they changed the picnic to a party at their house in town. Although it was chilly, the showers had let up, so we spent most of the afternoon in the little garden back of their house. The garden was filled with petunias, nasturtiums and flowering tobacco, and the back fence was all covered with green vines.

Looking down over the garden were the little balconies and windows of a grim slate-gray apartment house, four or five stories high. All the Russian citizens in those neighboring apartments crowded out onto their balconies to watch the party going on in the Stevenses' garden. They watched so solemnly and so unemotionally that it reminded me of something that was difficult to define. Walter Cronkhite perhaps hit on what it was when he said, "Once I sat like this in a little garden that belonged to the head of an institution, and, from all the windows opposite, the inmates of the asylum stared at us with exactly the same expressions — just the way these Russians are watching us now." It is quite true that the little asymmetries and queernesses that one notices in many of the faces one sees in Moscow seem to have something in common with those one sees in institutions.

On this occasion, their deadpan expressions never changed but twice. Once was when a pet squirrel jumped into the fountain and out again with a big splash, and the other time was when some of the children came out to play in the garden. Both times, those grim strange faces lit up with smiles. And it was quite noticeable that many of the Russian women, when they saw that a party was in progress among foreigners dressed in very informal costumes — for we had planned on a picnic — went back into their apartments and soon came out on their balconies again all decked out in lace dresses. They showed us that they, at least, knew how to dress up.

Yesterday we went to the Stoessels' apartment for lunch. They are nice youngsters, and they had an enjoyable luncheon in their fresh and pretty apartment here in Mokhavaya. Dick Davis, who is Freddy Reinhardt's relief, was there, smooth and suave, with an Irish cast of face and high cheekbones that were almost Slavic. He is here for his second tour of duty, so he is a seasoned old-timer. Also there were the Lyons, going through on their way to duty in Vladivostok, newly married and also nice youngsters, he thin and six feet eight tall and she nearly as tall as I am.

The British Ambassador is home in England on sick leave. Roberts, who was British Chargé here until Sir Maurice's return, has come from London for the next British-French-American approach to Molotov on the Berlin situation. The British Embassy had an evening cocktail party for him last night. Ambassador Smith's fishing in Normandy did him good, for he looked better than I have seen him look for months— well, rested, and full of spirit. He said that Molotov was "out of town" and that no one knew when he would return so that the talks could begin. That sort of thing has come to be expected of the Soviets.

I slid away from the party in order to see the Lyons off for Vladivostok. The doors of the Yaroslavsky Station were guarded by their usual soldiers with bayonets in place. This time when they stopped me there was a reason for my being there other than a general interest in everything Russian, so I brushed past them successfully. The great waiting room of the station was a remarkable sight. Everywhere were stacked bundles and bales of all sorts of belongings, suitcases, packages, pieces of furniture, vegetables, bundles made from knotted kerchiefs and from tablecloths, and everywhere were arms and legs and bodies of people lying and sleeping, or just patiently sitting, mixed with all the gear in inextricable confusion. There were hundreds and hundreds of people there, but the effect was strangely static. They were so utterly passive and motionless that it looked like some sort of waiting place between heaven and earth, a sort of Outward Bound.

I went through the big waiting room and on out through some open double doors onto the train platforms. Just at that moment the loud-speaker announced the Vladivostok train, so there was no trouble in finding it. I walked half its length, past car after car as packed and jammed with bundles and arms and legs and groceries as the waiting room, with people lying on little light shelves that folded down in lieu of berths, to the red international wagon which is always in the middle of every important train. While I was kissing the bride good-by through a train window, the long train, as usual with no warning, gave a sudden jerk and started on its long, long journey.

A crowd of young girls swept past me, running to keep up with the train, waving good-by to a couple of carloads of similar young girls, tears streaming down the faces of everyone both on the train and on the platform, weeping, weeping. As the last car went past, the train jolted to an unexpected stop. Then two harassed-looking young soldiers, with all their gear, were literally thrown off the train. They picked themselves up excitedly. Apparently their tickets weren't in order, and yet they had to get where they were going. Perhaps they had been in Moscow on leave and were returning to their units. The MVD began to converge on them and everyone got excited.

Meanwhile several Russians slipped furtively onto the train between the cars before it started up again. Since the railroads belong to the people, beating one's way is scarcely an offense — it is only when one runs foul of the control of movement of the population that it becomes really serious. The two culprits who had been thrown off were submerged in a ring of blue-capped MVD and they all moved off in such a gesticulating mass that what happened to them I never did know.

When I tried to get back into the station, after no more than ten or fifteen minutes on the platform, the big double doors through which I had come out of the crowded waiting room were closed and padlocked with heavy chains as though they had been shut for a month. I had to make my way back to my car by going around the station, through the crowds who were thronging onto the adjacent suburban trains.

On the way back to the British Embassy, I told Valodya that the platform had been crowded with weeping people. "Ah yes," he said, "partings are always difficult. And Siberia is far away. People do not know much about it, and one always fears what one does not know. Once a sailor was asked by a friend, 'Where is your father?' "

" 'My father is dead,' said the sailor.

" 'Where did he die?'

" 'At sea.'

" 'My God! aren't you afraid of the sea?'

"And the sailor asked, 'Where is *your* father?'

" 'He's dead too.'

" 'Where did he die?'

" 'On top of the big stove.'

" 'My God! aren't you afraid of stoves?' "

This seems to be a universal story, as I had read it in a Hindustani grammar, and Nell said she had seen a French version of it.

The British party was still going full blast. The pink-cheeked, vital Mrs. Aldis was there, all bubbling with life. The envoy of one of the free countries told me that he and his wife had just come back from a vacation in the Crimea.

"How did you manage it?" I asked. "They won't even let me go to Yaroslavl."

"I just don't know," the wife answered. "We just asked if we could go somewhere in the South, without saying where."

I couldn't help thinking, as she said that, that one look at her probably gave the clue to the answer. She looks exactly like a communist, with a grim, uncompromising face that is hard and unpleasant, not from strength, but from furtive, plotting, self-righteous disapproval. Eddy Gilmore told me afterwards that my guess had been right. She was a member of the Party.

Die Fledermaus has been playing in Moscow for a long time at the Operetta Theater. It is one of the best shows in Moscow, and the Russians love it. If it could be transplanted to New York just as it stands, Russian language and all, it would stand a good chance of being a hit because of its gayness and brightness, the beauty of its costumes, the endless lavishness of the masquerade scene, the talents of the troupe and the lovely Strauss music. The Russians have turned the masquerade into a show within a show and included some ballet and variety. They have also added the "Vienna Woods" music and other Strauss pieces.

Vlasova, who takes the part of the maid, is so pert, and at the same time so proud. Her voice and her every gesture are delightful. She has picked up a little weight, but she was still trim and alive, whether in her maid's short skirts with her high red Russian boots or in her cat mask and her long, fluffy, billowing train. When she wore that little cat mask at the ball, every movement of her body, and even of her arms and hands and feet, was catlike. And the costume of the Fledermaus herself was nothing short of wonderful, with great wings all shimmering black and silver.

The scene in the prison between the orderly and the governor of the prison is as amusing a drunk scene as there is anywhere, with the orderly pacing off the distance from which no one will be able to smell his breath, and his taking just one more drink every time he finds he is still sober enough to moo like a cow. But the surge of the Strauss music through it all is what really makes it.

It poured down rain all evening long. Just outside the doors of the theater was a great fountainlike arrangement of that extraordinary flowering tobacco, and it was unbelievably fragrant in the fresh, cool, rainy air.

On Sunday was the big annual Soviet air parade, the Day of the Air Fleet, postponed because of weather from the previous Sunday. The road to the Tushino Airfield on the outskirts of Moscow was lined with red flags and banners and salutations to Stalin and the Red Air Force. Great armfuls of flags fluttered together in solid bunches like huge scarlet flowers. All the diplomatic people except Randall, the Canadian air attaché, were in an uncovered stand at one side of the clubhouse. Randall had received a ticket, but when the show was postponed and new tickets issued for the new date he was left out. It might have been due to slipshod Soviet ways, but he was inclined to think that they had just had the word that the Soviet attaché in Canada had been omitted from a tour of the Far Northern flying fields. He is probably right, for, although the Soviet Air Show and the Canadian occasion are in no way comparable, the Soviet mind, or its policy of irritation, seems to work in that way.

It was much like the usual diplomatic receptions to see all the foreigners going around greeting all the other foreigners. There were plenty of secret police in plain clothes in that enclosure, watching everyone vigilantly. The fat, smiling, polite Chinese Ambassador took his camera out of its leather case and started to take a picture of the crowd in the stand. One of the plain-clothesmen rushed up and told him that it was not permitted, although last year, when I was at this same show, everyone who had a camera took all the pictures they wished without hindrance.

Out on the wide green plain below and in front of us were crowds of people, thick in every direction, like the crowds on Epsom Downs on Derby Day. Scattered through the crowds were tall tents and booths, selling sweetened water, ice cream and other refreshments. As far as one could see in every direction the low hills and bluffs surrounding the airfield were black with people like ants. And there were more parked automobiles than one would have thought to find in all Moscow.

A big army band of some four or five hundred pieces came past the diplomatic stand on their way to the open grassy spot directly in front of the clubhouse, led by the tall standards jingling with little bells and decorated with long scarlet and white horses' tails. A row of blue-capped MVD policemen moved across in front of the band and asked the players for their *dokumenty*. As that entire enormous uniformed band flowed slowly past the MVD, every individual dug out his identification papers and showed them to the sharp-eyed police. They were just beneath me, and it was clear that the examination was not perfunctory. The police looked both at the *dokumenty* and at the living faces, to be sure they corresponded. They did not miss a man.

The stands were gay with bright uniforms and big summer hats, Nell's John Frederick openwork Panama job being easily the best-

looking of them all. The only hat that could compare with it had
rows of fluffy white pleating, definitely from Paris, worn by a
tanned Russian woman with big filigree earrings.

The huge band started to play the Soviet national anthem and
we all stood at attention and saluted. Automobiles had been rolling up in front of the clubhouse for the past few minutes, big,
Packard-like Zees limousines, almost always with dark, drawn
curtains across the back and side windows. This time it was Stalin,
short and gray, but strong-looking and healthy. He went into the
reviewing stand, which jutted out from the clubhouse. Today he did
not seem jovial and smiling, as he usually is, but kept somewhat
morosely to himself. Beria and the rest of the Politburo, in their
slouch hats and civilian clothes, grouped themselves close together
against a background of uniforms of high-ranking military officers.
When one looked through binoculars so that their faces and expressions were plain, they looked more than ever as though they
were whispering about some evil plot. The press said that Stalin's
appearance was greeted with thunderous roars of applause. All I
heard was a little scattered hand-clapping in the clubhouse, which
did not last ten seconds. And that was for Stalin alone, no one else
receiving any.

The show itself was so much like the one of the preceding year
that it was not as impressive to me. It began with a perfect formation of planes sweeping across the sky and spelling out "SLAVA
STALINU" (Glory to Stalin). It continued with various formations,
jet fighters and bombers. One squadron of fifteen heavy bombers
roared overhead, indistinguishable, except in tiny details, from
our B-29s. To build them in quantity is itself an achievement. It
was for us during the war. The jets with extreme sweepback of
wings and tail looked like darting arrows, but the speed they
showed was not startling. One thing, however, was fine, and that
was an acrobatic team of five jet fighters in a tight wing-and-tail
formation doing loops and Immelmans and all sorts of maneuvers
as if they had been tied together, as indeed similar acrobatic teams
in our own Navy have been tied.

There was another thing that was spectacular and beautiful.
Group after group of transport planes came over the field. Out of
each transport streamed eight or ten men, until the whole air was

filled with striped and colored parachutes like confetti or colored bubbles of little balloons, blue and red and silver, striped and spotted, fantastic and lovely. There were over four hundred jumpers, each with two parachutes, in the air at one time, and the billowing, dying spots and splashes of color on the green ground as the parachutes were spilled continued the futuristic, exciting picture.

We drove back to Mokhavaya between long lines of white-coated police. Plenty of police must have been needed to control that mammoth Russian crowd. People were even hanging by their arms from the windows on the outsides of the streetcars.

Nell and I took one final chance on the Rostov-on-the-Don Musical Comedy Company, who were playing *The Merry Widow* at the Yermolova Theater. It was terrible, and, much as we would like to see one or two of the other things they are playing, we know that we couldn't face them. The costumes and settings were amateurish and the people were unattractive without being interesting. There was not one thing to excuse it except the music and the quality of the voices. They ought to keep that company off the stage and let them work over the radio instead. Nevertheless, the house was full, and the Soviet audience seemed to enjoy it. They seem to have a greater power of creating illusion for themselves in the face of difficulties than I.

Senta is back from her holiday on the Volga. She said that it had rained all the time. She had spent her time in the town of Ples, which turned out to be the actual resort of artists and literary people which Chekhov had used for a setting for his story of *The Grasshopper* — that characteristically merciless analysis of a woman who had left her good husband for an indifferent artist. They said in Ples that that story was founded on life, with Chekhov himself as the good husband and Levitan as the artist. Chekhov is regarded by Russians as a great humanitarian, but he seems to me to be like a completely impersonal scientific-minded surgeon. He is solely interested in finding the little grain of morbidity in every individual, and any humanitarianism which results is more or less a by-product.

I was glad to see Senta again — she is so intelligent, so interested, and so sensible. She brought a big birch-bark basket full of black cherries. Natasha made them into a pie, since for once we had enough sugar, flour and shortening all at the same time.

We dined with Eddie and Nina Stevens on the roof of the Moskva Hotel. It was cold, and pouring rain, but we sat under shelter, where climbing vines had been trained to grow upward in a mist of green, thus separating the tables into individual booths. We had some very good steaks, and after two or three bottles of Tsinandel wine — deep-red wine from Georgia — an occasional spray of rain felt good. I admired Nina's dress, which was black wool, covered with close, patterned embroidery of gray.

"No one can tell what sort of a dress this is," she said. "It might have come from anywhere."

"No," I replied, and truthfully. "Anyone who has paid any attention at all to the marvelous Russian patterns of that embroidery would know that it was Russian."

Nina was pleased, but deprecated Russian skills a little. I launched, again truthfully, into praise for the Russian people, their sensitiveness, their feeling for effect, their warm emotional qualities, their writers and painters and their many great composers and musicians. She was really touched, and said, "I wish you would tell our young son that. It seems to me that I spend most of my time in having to apologize to him these days for everything Russian."

2. THE LUBYANKA BAR

EDDY GILMORE'S *dacha* is well out in the country to the north of Moscow. To get there Nell and I drove past the big round flower bed of zinnias and snapdragons in the middle of Dzershinskaya Square in front of MVD headquarters and through city streets along which plodded occasional cattle and goats. We went through Tarasovka past the turnoff to the embassy *dacha* and on to the tall domed churches of Pushkino. There we turned off onto a side road, all great ruts and holes, which ran through fields of potatoes covered with white and pinkish-blue blossoms. We bumped through a factory village, past a stadium and Park of Culture and Rest for Railroad Workers, and into a group of log *dachas* set in a pine woods.

Opposite Eddy's *dacha* was a children's camp. For some reason or other parents are not permitted to visit their children within the camp. Instead, they crowded around the open picket fence that surrounded it, playing with their children and passing them little presents through the pickets. Next door was a two-story log house literally swarming with Russians of all ages. Goats ran in and out of the kitchen. Eddy said that seventy people lived in that one *dacha*.

Tamara was gay in a yellow silk blouse and leopard-skin slacks, and Eddy, for all his size, looked comfortable in a sport shirt and checked trousers. I put on some khaki brought for the occasion and we all went down to a dam at the end of the town. There the little river made a nice pool, fringed with willows and edged with water lilies and reeds. Fishing in the pool were several Russian soldiers and uniformed men who might have been from any one of half a dozen occupations that have recently been put into uniform — railroad men, bank officials, river transport workers or such. I cast for a while from the dam, and then worked around the pool and down the clear gravel-bottomed stream.

On the bank was an artist at work on a very competent oil painting. He was hard-bitten and middle-aged, and he wore one of those caps that give a sort of military air to so many Russians. He thanked me for my remarks about his painting.

"A pleasant place," I said.

"Not now," he replied. "But it was once."

Nevertheless, it seemed pretty enough to me, with an abundance of some water plant lying on the surface, with little leaves so fine that it looked like green lace. No fish seemed interested in my efforts, nor did I expect them to be. It was getting on towards dinner time, so we walked back through the village to the *dacha,* where Eddy made some drinks in tall, slender glasses.

For dinner we had what must have been the best steaks in Russia. I told Eddy that it was difficult to understand what seemed to come over so many Americans when they came to Russia for duty. Even the prospect of it seemed to affect them, for a relief we had been expecting for one of my enlisted men had to be diverted at New York on his way here, ending up in a psychopathic ward.

"That's nothing," said Eddy. "During the war, we had an army officer here who walked into our American doctor's office, and, for no reason at all, shot him four times through the stomach."

When we finally left, the night sky was covered with purple cloud, except for one little narrow crack on the western horizon which was so flat and so long that it looked like a searchlight beam in the night. As we drove back through the silent Moscow streets, we noticed that one of them was named "Godless Lane."

Nellie keeps a little bag all packed, in case we should suddenly be sent off to prison. Although I laugh at her for it, sometimes it seems that she's not so dumb. If things should suddenly go to pot, it would be too bad to have to burn all of these pages, so I took them out of the safe and sent them to an old friend in Washington. Perhaps he will find it interesting, for he taught me all I know about fishing — just fishing, without any troubled waters being involved.

After a year of waiting, our liquor has been released from customs. The Embassy succeeded in getting an additional lump-sum exemption, and by a complicated process of shipping some excess supplies back and paying the costs out of our own pockets, most of us can perhaps break even.

I went down into the rainy court to see how my own shipment was making out. Poor quiet Crawford, blond-haired and almost shy, was doing the best he could. Many cases had been battered and had lost all their markings, so that it was impossible to tell whose they were. Nearly every case had at least one or two bottles broken or pilfered. One lot of mine from London was readily identifiable, but it seems to have been the only shipment that had been kept in the railroad yards through the winter and not in the customs warehouse. All of it except some Scotch and sherry had frozen. The corks were all half popped out of the bottles and the good French wine was turned to vinegar. Still, one cannot get vinegar here, so maybe it's another case of an ill wind. The application of insurance, like everything else, is vague, and if it isn't collectable it would have been less expensive to have tried to be satisfied with high-priced Russian vodka. The storage and handling charges we paid for the privilege of having that one shipment frozen came to about six hundred rubles.

Nell played the piano for a long time tonight, some Chopin waltzes, the "Hungarian Rhapsody," "The Siren Song," "Velia," "Gray Days," many old pieces. It is wonderful how she can keep her gorgeous technique when she plays so seldom, and still more wonderful how she can always look so young and vivid.

While Senta was here today, Nell put her head in the door for a minute to ask some question. Senta remarked afterwards that she was so alive and flamelike, saying that she liked and admired such women. I agreed with her, and told her that she herself belonged to the same class, but that she kept her fire under great restraint. She finally admitted that she was possessed of a *byes*. Now *byes* can be translated as "devil," but the two words have different connotations in the two different languages. Its meaning is very close to the ancient elemental beings or daemons which were halfway between god and man. One needs to know a lot of Russian to know what people are really trying to say.

Last night I dreamed that someone was very much interested in a porcelain stove, which, as is customary in dreams, had somehow become a part of our kitchen furnishings. They examined it carefully, and looked inside. There was nothing in it, but, to make sure, they reached inside and felt around. When they pulled their arm out, arm and hand had become suddenly very diminutive. They tried the other arm, and it too shrank to fairy size. Then they poked their head in, and finally, bit by bit, became small enough so that they crawled completely inside. The door of the stove suddenly banged shut and they were caught there. In the morning Natasha came into the kitchen and heard someone calling in a little piping voice. She hunted all over the place, but could find no one. At last she opened the stove, and out jumped a tiny little old man.

I had a feeling of disappointment when I woke up and knew that I would never find out what Natasha did about that.

I never get tired of going into the dramatic tomb of Lenin, whenever it occurs to me and the time is available. Sunday afternoon the long queue of people with the same idea in mind extended for many blocks, the length of Red Square, around the corner of the Kremlin wall opposite the Embassy and far past the Tsar's riding hall. It was plentifully interspersed with sightseers from out of town, Uzbeki in their little round bright hats, flat-faced Buryat-Mongols and visitors from other parts of the Soviet Union. Since foreigners can go straight in without queuing up, I started for the head of the line. Then it suddenly occurred to me that my *dokumenty* have been turned in for some time for their annual renewal and have not yet been returned. Perhaps I didn't look enough like a foreigner, in which case a public argument did not seem attractive.

Instead, I continued on across Red Square to the Cathedral of Vassily the Blessed. In front of the Cathedral is a bronze statue of Manin and Pozharsky, the two patriots who finally brought an end to the Time of Troubles and made possible the long rule of the Romanovs. St. Basil's, which was built by Ivan the Terrible in gratitude for the successful completion of his campaign against the Kazan Tatars, was at last open after a long period of being closed for repairs. I passed between lilac bushes as big as trees and up the steps of a porch made of those elements that are so reminiscent of old-fashioned children's ornamental building blocks.

The interior of the Cathedral was completely unexpected. One might almost say that there is no interior, for there is no nave or any open space at all. It is all bricked and walled and ceilinged off into a maze of narrow, almost secret passages, interconnecting between many small gilded chapels. The low, vaulted ceilings and the walls were completely covered with decorations. The open floral patterns were orange and green and blue, like those in some Oriental rugs, giving an extraordinary effect. In only one little chapel was it possible to see up into any of the pear-shaped domes, and there the inner roof was unique in its possession of a simple but strange spiral pattern made by single red bricks set into surrounding whitewash. In some places the overhead was flat, but still made of bricks, giving a queer feeling of insecurity as one went beneath them.

The church was crowded with sightseers. It is partly a museum, as it contains armor and trophies from the Kazan victory, and many pictures of the Cathedral in earlier days. Some girls, reading the descriptive signs, asked me what was an iconostas. I pointed out to them the altar screen, and asked them in turn where was the tomb of Ivan the Terrible himself. "We're not Muscovites," they said, "so we don't know." So all of us together hunted up a guide, who told us that Ivan Grozny was buried in the Kremlin.

Even in Russia one seldom sees such dirty and slovenly uniforms as were worn by the crowds of soldiers who were going through the place. In the throng I managed to brush against the hump of a hunchback in an embroidered Russian blouse. That should be unusually lucky.

A few doors from MVD headquarters is one of the few bars in Moscow. It is in a basement and so unrecognizable as a bar from the street that I never would have known it existed if a Russian had not taken me there. The low ceilings are arched like those of medieval cellars. All of the ceilings and walls are painted and decorated, and it has pictures on ground glass with lights behind them that give an aquariumlike effect. Midafternoon in summer is not a good time for such bars, as it is too pleasant out on the streets in the sunshine, so the place was more than half empty.

My shabbily dressed middle-aged Russian acquaintance had occupied the same bench with me in the little park beside the Kremlin wall. It was his suggestion that we walk, so we strolled across Red Square and along the Street of the 25th of October to that bar. His name was Vadim. During his early twenties he had left a Russian ship in New York, spending a year or so in America before returning to Russia. He was very eager to hear what America was like today.

"Yes," he said, "Russia does not know what America is really like. Why, when I was there, I was able to dress just like my employer, and I've eaten with him many a time. But then, America does not know what Russia is like, either. She can have no idea of how impossible a thing like that was in the Tsar's time, nor what really terrible things the Russian people have been through."

"Vadim, you know that it isn't communism that America fears. It's the secret police, and the suppression of all opposition, which makes it utterly impossible for anyone ever to do anything about it."

"But you have no idea how much the Russian people need control. They are not yet ready for the sort of freedom that you have in America. After the Revolution they did terrible things, and the control of the secret police is necessary for them. If any opposition were permitted, they would run away with it and spoil everything."

"I've heard that many times, and have thought much about it," I answered, "and it seems to me that the Russian people deserve much better than they receive. Perhaps they cannot be as free politically as Americans, but a government should at least give protection, even against itself."

During the war Vadim had come to know an American officer in Russia for whom he had unbounded praise.

"They say he has been put back in rank since returning to America. What a wonderful man he was, courteous, patient and understanding. He spoke Russian almost without an accent, and could pass for a Russian any time he wanted to. They say — it may be only gossip — but the Russians say here that the reason he was put back in rank and has never been sent back to Russia is because he liked Russia and was a friend to us."

"I don't think that that is true," I replied. "The Russian people has many friends in America, and there would be many more, if your government, which they do not like, would give them half a chance to be friendly."

We sat over our mugs of sweetish Russian beer and listened to the people talking at the nearby tables. There were two lads who were grumbling openly about how little they got out of life in return for their hard work. At another table, two pompous fat men talked oilily about Comrade Stalin and what he had done for the people. "Both those lads and the fat ones are Russia," said Vadim.

There was also a young couple, better dressed than those one usually sees, who had brought some sausage of their own to eat with their beer. Everyone had hard-boiled eggs. Later, at home, I asked Natasha how much eggs were in the markets. For some reason, the hard-boiled eggs in that bar were about half the price of fresh eggs in the market.

"Doubtless they weren't very good eggs," said Natasha, with her nose in the air. But that is not so. Natasha, moreover, is not holding out on the price of eggs, for Nell has been doing much of her own marketing lately. Perhaps the convenient nearness of that place to MVD headquarters had something to do with the price of eggs. That circumstance would also explain why people did not flock there to get a bargain. But why did Vadim take me there?

3. I CANNOT HELP HEARING

I HAPPENED TO GO DOWN to the doctor's office, and there, waiting in the little hall outside the dispensary, were Nell and Zoya, all pale and shaky and with traces of recent tears. "Good God!" I said, "What's the matter now?"

Nell said that she had heard Zoya cry out, and had gone to the living room to find out what was wrong. There lay Zoya, literally bathed in blood. One of the huge studio windows had suddenly blown loose, swinging violently in and gashing poor Zoya deeply in the head. Part of Zoya's head was shaved and the wound stitched up. Dr. Vaughn said that Nell looked as if she needed attention more than Zoya. She had had her hands full in getting Zoya cleaned up and over to the dispensary.

Nell was indeed fairly well done in with all the tension around here, so she asked me to go without her to a buffet dinner at the Canadian Legation. Although the party was a nice one, I did not stay long. On my return home, every light in the house was blazing. "Anything wrong?" I asked Nell.

"No," she answered. "Only the telephone keeps tinkling slightly, as if someone is dialing out from the extension. When I'm downstairs, I think it may be going on upstairs, and when I'm up there, it seems to be from the downstairs telephone. I just felt a little more comfortable with all the lights on, upstairs and down!"

In the middle of the night Nell woke me quietly. "What is that ticking?" she asked. I listened, and sure enough, there was a deep, steady, slow beating sound. "I've heard of embassies getting bombed," Nell said. "You don't think that that could be a time bomb, do you?"

I got up and followed the sound around. It came from outside, from a level below our balcony. "It must come from the street," I said, "at any rate, it's not in our place." And I went back to bed.

But Nell threw on a wrap and went out on the balcony to see for herself. Down on the pavement below was a squad of women. They were working with picks which were muffled in some way so as not to disturb sleeping people with their noise. That was considerate of them.

In the late afternoon Nell and I walked all the way around the Kremlin. We started with the idea of trying to see for sure if the Tsar Bell, which sits somewhere there on the ground and which is always associated in my mind with pictures of Napoleon, can be seen from anywhere outside the Kremlin. It was dusk by the time we got to any place where that might have been possible, so, as usually happens in Russia, we did not find out.

However, it was a pleasant walk, and the clusters of gilded domes and golden crosses over the Kremlin churches were very lovely against the sky. As we followed close behind a couple of Red Army officers, it was easy to do a bit of eavesdropping. They were talking about the hard conditions somewhere in northern Siberia. I do not know whether their conversation had reference to something that had happened recently or long ago, but a chill ran down my back as they discussed expertly the details of cannibalism.

Eddy Gilmore is sick in bed, and Dr. Vaughn, who had gone out to his *dacha* to see him, seemed quite disturbed because he was obviously followed on the way. Something that is also disturbing is a request he has had for a cyanide capsule, or its equivalent, supposedly needed for a Russian who is about to try to escape from the country. Maybe so, but some Russian is always trying to frame the doctor with requests for morphine or other drugs, and it should be obvious that no cyanide is being given out except under orders.

All week long it has been breathlessly hot, with occasional thunderstorms which did little to cool the air. It has been hot like Washington, and not dry, as is usually the case here. In the evening Nell and I went to the Stanislavsky Theater to see a local amateur production of *Rose Marie*. It was vastly better than the efforts of the Rostov-on-the-Don troupe. The cast wasn't so hard to look at and their voices were better than average, but the show itself still wasn't very good. I must be thoroughly used to Russians by now, for the incongruity of their playing the parts of Indians and cowboys was hardly noticeable — except for some of the costumes, which were more Asiatic than American. One of the cowboys wore a sky-blue set of coveralls, like Winston Churchill's siren suit or a child's slumber suit. It was trimmed with whole skins of red foxes.

The Kasenkina and Samarin case in New York, where some Soviet schoolteachers apparently do not want to go back to Russia, has broken, with all its charges of abduction and force. All my men without diplomatic passports have been warned of possible retaliations. Senta has been all big black eyes to see the American press bulletins.

"What does 'habeas corpus' mean?" she asked. That was something completely unknown to Russian citizens. She got the idea of how we protect the individual citizen against the power of the government itself, but it is doubtful if, even as intelligent as she is, she thinks it is such a good idea for Russia. It may be all right in America, for every Russian believes that the government there is wicked and corrupt, so doubtless the Americans must need protection against it.

Like going to church, listening to the Voice of America is not prohibited in Russia. A Russian once told me that he had taken a radio with him on his vacation. When alone in his room he turned on the Voice of America. Soon there was a knock on the door. A Soviet colonel of infantry stood there.

"Comrade," said the colonel, "please change to some other program."

"But why?" asked my friend. "That is the Voice of America."

"I know. That is why I am asking you to listen to something else."

"But it is not forbidden to listen to that."

"I know that also. But you see, I am in the room next to yours, and the partitions are so thin I cannot help hearing. If anyone knew that I had listened to American broadcasts, these stars you see on my shoulders would not be there for long."

Nevertheless, another Russian has also told me that ninety per cent of the population of Moscow knows what the Voice of America says about the Kasenkina affair within a few hours of each broadcast. The first question that is asked by almost every Russian of everyone he meets is "What does the American radio say?"

There is an inherent situation in Russia which gives America a remarkable potential advantage. Most Russians neither believe nor disbelieve their own radio. They know that it can only exist as an effort of government, and that therefore what it has to say can only be in the interests of their government. They also know from their own experience and education that their government regards objective truth as entirely subordinate to the class struggle throughout the world and to its own power interests. It follows that what it puts out may or may not be true. The Russian ends up a complete agnostic as far as his normal sources of information are concerned. He does not close his ears to Soviet broadcasts, but says to himself: "This may or may not be so. In any case it is not put out to inform me accurately, and so in the very nature of things I cannot know the truth."

When he first hears American broadcasts he has much the same attitude toward them, thinking that objective truth has little to do with their content, since they must be put out with some ulterior motive. But as the Voice of America, which has bent over backward to be objective, has acquired experience, it has become more skillful in introducing material which the Russian has countless ways of checking from his own experience, and he soon ends up by coming to believe the word of a foreign government in preference to that of his own. Of course he always discounts the bourgeois point of view, and if we can learn to be objective about that and really understand his communist conditioning, the situation has tremendous possibilities.

4. UNWELCOME VISITORS

SENTA ASKED ME if I had ever been to Zvenigorod. When I told her that I had fished near there many times, she said that somewhere near the town was supposed to be a very good sandy beach. That put it in my head to go out there, in search of a breath of fresh air from the blanket of heat that hung over Moscow. Perhaps it might be possible to raise a fish. Even when well out of the city there was a hot white haze that hung over the yellowing fields and woods.

Thirty or forty kilometers from Moscow on the Mozhaisk Chaussée we had a flat tire. While Valodya was changing the tire, Nell and I walked through a big settlement that lay alongside the road. It seemed to be all made up of *dachas* and summer camps and children's rest homes, built back into the trees and bushes and surrounded with a variety of fences. Due to the fences and the heavy growth, it was quite difficult to see that it was really a good-sized town. In all countries, of course, especially in England, hedges are used for privacy, but there one does not get the impression of secrecy that is given by them in this country. There was an occasional glimpse of children playing, of people sleeping on the grass, or of women going about their work, sometimes obviously in nothing but a shirt. I had not realized before the literalness of the Russian expression *v odnoy rubashke* — in shirt alone. For some reason, probably because of all the fenced-in trees and bushes, it reminded me of a big zoo or the sort of native settlement one sees at world's fairs. And sometimes there were groups of tiny children, all exactly the same age, looking, with their big heads and their fat little bodies, for all the world like a group of Rose O'Neill's Kewpies.

We pulled the car up by the bridge near Zvenigorod and I started to cast in the clear gravelly river. Except for the heat, it was much like the last time I was there, for everywhere up and down the river were bathers, dressing and undressing modestly on the banks. Most of them wore bathing suits or their underclothes.

One flaxen-haired young girl nearby, wearing only her bloomers, was completely unconscious of her well-budded breasts. And there was no reason why she shouldn't be unconscious of them, for her buxom mother took off her own ample brassière to do some thorough scrubbing, and then followed with the only other item of her costume. There were too many people in the water for any possibility of fish, so, since big drops of rain started to patter down from the edge of a towering thundercloud that sailed by, my desultory efforts were soon over.

We got in the car and drove across the bridge and through the little town of Zvenigorod. Beyond the village, where the road came out again on the river, was Senta's sandy beach. It was coarse gravel, but it was long and clean against the green grass of the meadows. Although nearly everyone had been driven away by the shower, except some dignified portly gentlemen in bright pajamas who had a big umbrella, it must have been far nicer than any crowded place near Moscow.

We kept on for a mile or so, heading for the fantastic domes of the big monastery, following arrows pointing "TO THE CAR PARK." The car park was just outside the monastery gates, obviously a public place. I asked a Red Army officer who was sitting there if we could go into the monastery. "I don't know," he answered. "I'm just waiting for a bus. But there is a reception room just inside the gates. They will tell you."

There was no one in the reception room but an attractive young lady who was reading a novel. "We are foreigners," I said. "Are there any sights of interest here which we could be permitted to see, such as old churches or museums?"

"The church in the monastery here is a museum," she answered, "and I'm sorry, but it is locked up. If I had the key, I would open it for you, but the key is kept down in the village. But if you want to go inside the walls of the monastery, go on ahead. You can walk around all you please, and look at whatever there is to be seen."

Nell and I went on in. The thick, fortified walls were whitewashed, and the whitewash had been covered with a blue wash, of an intensity varying from white to the deep color of the sky above. There was a green lawn, shining with raindrops, and a badly ruined bell tower. Many buildings grew out of the walls in a complex and confusing fashion, housing the complex and confusing life of the place. Here and there the heavy outer walls had been breached to make convenient paths of access, and everywhere women were scrubbing and hanging out clothes and going about the usual village life.

One building had a sign on it saying that it was a storehouse, apparently for food or clothing. The main church in the center, whose golden domes could be seen from far off, was covered with external murals. The road narrowed as it went past the church, and, catching sight of a couple of sentries pacing up and down on the sidewalk opposite, we hesitated. The sentries saw us hesitate, and waved to us. At first we were not sure whether they were waving us back or motioning to us to come on, but after some further gestures, it became apparent that they were telling us that we were free to keep on. They grinned pleasantly as we passed them.

The church was well worth seeing, even if only from the outside. Not only was it ornate with the reds and browns and blues and gold of its paintings of the saints and its scenes from the Scriptures, but it had heavy arabesques running around it in wide bands. The arched doors were also deeply arabesqued, washed with faded red and green and purple, so that the effect was as Arabic as it was Byzantine. We walked around the church, then strolled across the grassy plaza and out through the gates to the car, waving at the receptionist as we passed her windows.

As we got into the car, a brown-faced militiaman stepped up. "What is your name, and what is your business here?" he asked. I told him.

"This place is forbidden," he said.

"The receptionist at the gates gave us permission to go in."

"No matter," he said. "It belongs to the Red Army, and is a forbidden area. How do you spell your name?"

So on our way back to Moscow we thought that one over. I remembered that there was a sign on the road between the town and the monastery announcing an agricultural division of a Red Army rest home, but it was impossible to tell whether it referred to the place we had violated or to some other place in the vicinity. Although such an incident, with its always unknown consequences, didn't add anything to our enjoyment of the day, it didn't seem to amount to anything. Still, one never knows what the Soviet government will do — except that they are very apt to take every little advantage that they can.

On the way back we turned off onto the Ouspensky Road and took another long look at the thick enchanted birch wood which we had found once before. It was just as wonderful as before, without a leaf or a bit of underbrush except for the tossing green at the very tops of the trees, dim and magical in its rich brown and white solid background of thickly crowding trunks. Such things help to compensate for annoyances.

This morning being Sunday, I was just sitting down to a late breakfast when the telephone rang. It was Whitney, Eddy Gilmore's assistant, wanting to know if I had any comment to make on that morning's *Pravda*. He came on over, bringing me the paper. After a silence of several months, the Soviets had broken the Dreher incident in a big spread under the headline "AMERICAN SPY CAUGHT RED-HANDED!"

Pravda left the impression that Dreher was an unknown civilian who, when apprehended by Soviet vigilance, turned out to be an assistant naval attaché. In spite of Dreher's previous long wait for an exit visa, and as though the Ambassador's conversation with Vishinsky and mine with Serayev had never occurred, it said that when the American Embassy was notified that Dreher had been caught in the act of espionage the proofs were so convincing that the Americans did not even attempt to dispute it, and, without any reply whatsoever, had complied with the Soviet demand that he leave the Soviet Union at once.

So I thought that one over, meanwhile having no comment for Whitney that the Soviets would permit him to send back to his press. It seems highly probable that *Pravda's* release was intended to help counter the unfavorable Kasenkina publicity. Also it occured to me that they had an excellent case of espionage against me because of yesterday's incident at the Zvenigorod monastery, for I was certainly caught red-handed or red-footed in coming out of what they said was a forbidden area.

I told the Ambassador of the incident, and he told Kohler to beat the Soviets to it by making a formal report of the actual circumstances to the Foreign Office. So, what with the necessary dispatches and reports to the Navy Department on the Dreher publicity and my own little and perhaps sinister affair, this Sunday was rather well taken up.

We had watermelon for lunch, red, thin-skinned and sweet. They surely have things under control here, for this Soviet watermelon even had red seeds.

This Sunday is Soviet Navy Day. I did not feel that anything was missed when it became apparent that no foreigners were to be invited to any of their Navy Day events. Last year the foreign attachés were invited to some navy boat races and athletic events at the river port of Khimki. Those who had gone said that they had been bored stiff. I might not have been so bored, but I certainly was not in the mood to be polite. In fact, I couldn't help thinking that it would be a bit of a relief if I were declared *persona non grata.*

By Monday, the hot weather had broken and it was rainy and cold. It seemed as though most of the day was spent in explaining the Dreher affair to various people. Henrik Madsen made a special visit for that purpose. He said that on his return from Denmark the customs officials had gone through his luggage so thoroughly that the regular airplane by which he was traveling was delayed and, together with all its passengers, had to stay overnight in Leningrad. The Soviets have apologized to the Danes and said that it would not happen again. Nevertheless, they mentioned that last spring a Soviet assistant naval attaché had been searched by the Danes, in spite of his having been given a *laissez-passer* by the Danish government. Henrik and his legation are now trying to find out if that really happened. They are inclined to believe that, if it did, the Russian's *laissez-passer* had expired.

General Carter and his tall handsome daughter are going back to America to join Mrs. Carter, who went home long ago. They planned to leave by the Red Arrow for Leningrad, but the day of their departure the general found out that the Red Arrow carried no baggage car, so his personal luggage could not accompany him. It is some sort of commentary on the Soviet system that Carter had so little faith in ever seeing his things again, or at least of getting them without endless difficulties, that he changed his plans and caught an earlier train instead, so as to be with his luggage, thereby complicating the farewell parties that had been arranged for him.

On the platform at the Leningradsky Station to see him off were General Macon and a group of Americans who could not speak Russian looking puzzledly at a little old Russian woman. She was talking to them long and earnestly, so wrapped up in her own talk that she did not take time out to wonder why she got no answers. The little old lady was asking why the Americans would not let those two Russian citizens in New York come back to Russia.

"You should let them go," she said, over and over again. "They have already been inconvenienced a lot by missing one boat. And with their fare all paid, too!"

I told her that there seemed to be a great deal of doubt as to whether or not they really did want to come back to Russia, and that perhaps it was only the Russian government who wanted them back. This seemed a completely new idea to her, and she was all for continuing the discussion and learning more, but enough things have happened recently without my laying myself open to charges of undermining the public in the Leningradsky Station.

One of our couriers has arrived without his mail, except for what he could carry in his hands. The rest of it had been in a baggage car, and the baggage car had been detached from the rest of the train during the night. Now the Soviets won't release that mail on the grounds that it did not accompany the courier. They are probably just making a spot check, for they must know that no courier would let any classified material out of his sight.

They say that one of the embassies here in Moscow ordered a safe from home. It didn't show up for so long that they had almost forgotten about it when it finally appeared. Since the need for it had long since been met in some other way, the embassy shipped the safe back home. There someone had enough curiosity to take it to pieces. They found that the mechanism had been cleverly rebuilt in such a way that anyone who was familiar with the job that had been done could open the safe at will without knowing the combination.

Here it is considered a misappropriation of resources and effort to publish any stories or novels that do not have a mission. The Soviets have made me much more sensitive to the lessons that are embodied in such things than would otherwise be the case. Strangely enough, what is called science fiction seems to lend itself unusually well to making a point. Many look down their noses at science fiction, but much of that literature from the days of H. G. Wells's *Time Machine* has much more to it than sheer mood or adventure.

I have just finished an anthology of such stories which has several outstanding examples that are thoroughly adult and go far to disprove the Soviet charge of American sensationalism and decadence in that medium. The Soviets have their own science fiction, notably some of Aleksei Tolstoy's earlier novels, but they all are full of propaganda that is almost as heavy-handed as that in the daily press. I suspect that Tolstoy's were rewritten.

Conversation with a Russian citizen.

"I notice that a great many churches are now being repaired here in Moscow."

"Yes. For a long time they let them stand all ruined and deserted, but now there are many being worked on. They need them, too, for the ones that are being used by the people are crowded."

"And yet the Party and the newspapers always say that there is no need for religion."

"Oh, that is communism! It is not true. There is no need for communism to say that. People are not free here — they are always being interfered with. They are not as free as they used to be."

"How old are you?"

"In my fifties. I can remember the Tsar's times, and the Russian people were more free then than they are today."

"It's dangerous to say such things."

He looked all around and said, "Yes, very dangerous."

I started to quote Lermontov's poem, "Farewell, unwashed Russia — "

He picked it up and added, "The all-hearing ears are still here. All one needs to do is to breathe one word, and — pht! You are completely finished."

"Then you be careful. Don't say one word. Don't even think!"

There was an Embassy picnic at the Tarasovka *dacha*. Nell was in charge of all the arrangements, and she did a good job. When we left Mokhavaya, there was a Belgian car and a Swiss car, both with flags, following ours. If the Soviets follow every ambassador and chargé, we must have made quite a procession through the heavy Saturday traffic.

Although the heads of missions are probably followed to see that they are protected, that reason certainly does not apply to the following of all other foreigners. In addition to Dreher's experience in Odessa, one of our Navy cars here in Moscow broke down on the way to the Vnukovo Airport. There was barely time for one of the passengers to make an outgoing plane to Berlin, so my lads appealed to the following police car for a lift for him. They were met with nothing but stony silence. Luckily some civilians were more helpful.

At the picnic everyone played tennis or badminton, pitched horseshoes, played Ping-pong or cards, swam, or did whatever they wanted to. There was plenty of cold bottled Russian beer. Goffin, the new Belgian Ambassador, was there with his slim, fair-haired young bride, who looks like the pictures of Queen Astrid of Belgium. As Nell said, they are obviously crazy about each other, and it was a delight to watch them. Late in the afternoon it started to grow cool and the sun sent long, level red rays through the pines. We spread our picnic supper, including cold pheasant — Tsar's bird, according to Natasha — and the accompanying cold bottle.

Then, as it grew dark, I lay on the grass and looked at the brocaded pattern of the birch leaves against the sky and listened to people singing. They sang in Russian and in English and in French. Geomans and Goffin are both Flemish, and they knew many Flemish songs. A big moon came up through the woods, looking like a distant conflagration.

5. INTERFERENCE

NELL AND I WENT OUT for a ride, along the Kashirskaya Chaussée. They say that, since about the time I first started to be followed, no one from any foreign mission has succeeded in getting more than about sixty or seventy kilometers from Moscow without being turned back. I wanted to check that for myself, but Valodya, in spite of his orders to keep the car always filled with petrol, showed up with only half a tank, so it wasn't possible to go as far as I wanted.

We were followed by a black Pobeda with two men in it. They could be seen even before we had left the Kremlin, while we were looking back to see if we could locate the huge Tsar Bell. This time we saw the bell definitely, looming as big as a house through some thinned-out trees. Before we got out of Moscow we were held up by a suddenly changing traffic light. Our *slezhka,* a couple of blocks behind, turned into a side street, waited until the light had changed, and then backed out to resume its pursuit. I don't know why it is so annoying to be followed like that, but it is. There is a sort of depression that settles over one. Perhaps if they didn't try to be so secret and sly about it, it would not be so bad.

We did not turn off on the road where we had been before for wild strawberries, but kept on toward Kashira, over rolling hills covered with wheat and hay and potatoes and bits of woodland, past occasional big factories in process of being built, with queer structures whose use could only be guessed. We went through villages with an occasional lovely little naked baby trotting along after his or her mother, over a stream edged as far as one could see with bathers in every stage of undress, and on until we had to turn around lest we run out of fuel.

It was a little over fifty kilometers from Moscow. No sooner had we made our turnaround in a hayfield by the road than we met our black *slezhka.* They were all innocence, keeping straight on and not turning in the good place where we had turned, until a hill put them out of sight. A little later I had Valodya stop to tighten up the spare tire, which was rattling. When we started up again, our followers could be seen pulling out from a clump of trees on the nearest hill horizon where they had been hiding themselves while we stopped.

I had expected not only to be followed, but, if we had only had enough gasoline, to be turned back, so I was a little surprised at our resentment. I think that our sense of justice was offended, for we had as clear a conscience as one would have had on a Sunday afternoon drive in Maryland or Virginia. I couldn't help but remember how wrong I had been in telling the Spiro lads just to ignore their followers. Not only is that psychologically impossible, but it is now clear that the pattern of Soviet action is something that they spin up for themselves. Like their propaganda, it serves an end of its own which has no relationship to the objective facts with which they pretend to deal.

It has grown cold and rainy, so we shivered in the Summer Theater of the Hermitage Park, even though the house could have been opened up much more widely to the air than it was. Part of the roof is of heavy carved beams and the rest of it is movable. All of the decorations except the curtain, which was of crushed flame-yellow velvet, are quite Russian, giving a heavy Oriental effect. There was a silver-haired fine-looking Russian general in the audience near us whom I recognized from published photographs as the airplane designer Tupolev.

The Moscow Dramatic Theater has moved out to this park. They at last put on *Don't Use Your Own Sleigh,* which we had missed when seeing them before. They played with a studied perfection, getting everything that there was to be had from every line and word, and they were attractive people besides. Yet when the play was over, the cast was only called back two or three times. I remarked on this to a Russian on leaving, and he said that occasionally the plays in Moscow are better than the audiences.

We went to Madame Pandit's for dinner. On the way we drove straight into a dramatic clear golden sunset. Moscow was completely overcast with a layer of slate-blue clouds, but between the overcast and the horizon was nothing but limpid clear gold. Madame Pandit's two daughters are dark, delicate, and liquid-eyed. They were very pretty in their plum-colored Indian dress wrapped around them like Roman togas, with sandals on their bare feet.

Nehru is Madame Pandit's brother, so she was much interested in a copy of *Time* which Nell brought her which contained a very creditable account of him. The entire family is so highly intelligent, speaks such excellent English, and is above all so gentle. I remarked that most English and Americans derive their ideas of India from Kipling and E. M. Forster. Madame Pandit said that *Kim* was an essentially true picture of India under British rule.

For breakfast there was some toast made from Natasha's fresh-baked bread. It has always been hard for me to understand why American bakeries do not go in for the chewy, satisfying sort of bread which one gets both in Russia and in England, rather than for the lighter, fluffier American variety. It is almost worth the discomforts of Russia to have such bread, and when one eats it one understands why just bread can be the most important food item of an entire people.

Although I have liked the dark bread of other countries, the famous black bread of Russia often does not seem very good to me. For one thing, it is too sour, and for another, it frequently seems to be adulterated with something besides flour. Even many Russians agree on this last point.

Although it was cold and threatening, Nell and I went for a long drive. It was Valodya's day off, so the dark, bristly-haired Kiril Kovalyov was driving for me. It was annoying to find that, contrary to orders, the car's fuel tank was less than three-quarters full, so we stopped at Spiro, where the gasoline is stored, to remedy that. Day and night the militia stands at the gates of such places as Spiro, American House and Khlebny. I didn't want to attract their attention to the fact that we were taking on fuel as if we were headed for some distant place, but Kiril couldn't find any hose with which to drain some gas from the storage barrel.

Within two minutes every servant in Spiro was rushing around trying to help. It is just a physical impossibility to do anything quietly in Russia. Although we were starting during the usual lunch time when most of the trailing cars are busy following people around to wherever they may go for lunch, the lads at Spiro later said that there were two cars on our heels as we pulled away from there. I spotted one of them following us long before we got out of Moscow.

We drove through Komsomolskaya Square past the three great railroad stations that are there and on past Sokolniki Park. We intended to take the chaussée that goes towards Vladimir and Gorky, the old Nizhni Novgorod, but none of the highways are marked and we must have missed the way. About twenty kilometers or so from Moscow we went through Shelkovo, a big town with many big factories. It was apparently a textile-weaving city. Around it were two or three good-sized airfields. A twin-engined helicopter was flying over one of the fields, and over another was a Russian transport plane towing a big twin-boomed glider.

Beyond Shelkovo the road became rough and narrow, paved alternately with cobblestones and with asphalt. Whatever the paving, it was bumpy and filled with great holes. Our follower, as usual, lingered far behind, but never quite lost sight of us. We stopped two or three trucks and country busses to ask where we were heading. They all told us that the road didn't go anywhere in particular, and that there wasn't any way to get off it onto any other road. It started to sift rain from the dark skies, and we finally got into the wildest and most desolate part of Russia that I have yet seen. There were long stretches of forest which were so thick with underbrush that it was impossible to see more than a few feet into it in any direction. The sad rain added to the dreary, oppressive atmosphere.

Our follower apparently had better sense than we, for at last he passed us and jolted out of sight on ahead. We kept on, expecting to be turned back every minute, but there was nothing to be seen but the dense woods, broken by an occasional dark pool or a glade where women were busily cutting and piling black peat in the rain. The road got steadily worse until we were hardly ever able to get out of low gear. Kiril was getting more and more worried for fear our low road clearance would wreck something underneath the car, so at the sixty-nine kilometer mark we turned around and came back to Moscow through the cold, dark, misty rain.

It seemed that the very people of that countryside were different than those one finds in other directions. They were darker, smaller, grimmer looking. As a matter of fact, they probably were different, for Russia is essentially a very primitive country, and the people, always provincial, have never had much means of incentive for moving about, although they sometimes like it when they can.

Nell had let the servants go, so when we got home she produced some scrambled eggs and chicken livers as if by magic. She is always mysterious about how she is able to produce such unusual things, but she finally admitted that Milly Feldman had sent the chicken livers, tinned, from America. Milly is a lovely person, and those chicken livers put her a little deeper in my heart.

Most of the day has been taken up with another crisis. The Soviets, having recently doubled our rent for space in their customs to four hundred dollars a month, have just informed us that the increase in rent is retroactive for the last eight months. The commissary is already in serious difficulties, and perhaps the worst of it is that we are never able to find out just where we do stand financially. I have tried hard to understand the Soviets and to see things from what might be their viewpoint, but this last imposition seems to be nothing but sheer dishonesty and extortion.

Tarkhanov, a beloved Russian actor, has died. We have seen him play in *The Cherry Orchard* many times, and he always got a big hand from the audience. He was very old, and he always took the part of the ancient family servant who was left to die in the house through the sheer Russian footlessness of the landowning family. His body lay in state at MXAT one night and the queues of people waiting in line to walk past extended for blocks. A government decree now sets up several scholarships in his name, gives his widow a considerable cash sum and a pension for life, and the funeral is at state expense. This sort of thing chalks up a big mark on the credit side of the Soviet ledger. They need it.

I worked all afternoon on a pen-and-ink of the long line of people which can be seen from the windows of our apartment waiting to see Lenin's body. It was interesting to work on it, and it is turning out fairly well, with a sort of *skazka* effect of soaring towers. It must be grand to wander through the world doing nothing but making pictures. Yet it becomes steadily harder to go to interesting places in this modern world. Here in Russia one can sketch only from Embassy premises where the all-seeing eye can't do anything about it. If I ever get caught up with all my work I shall make a real effort to find out if that is really true.

Today's papers carried an announcement of the death of Rybalko, the famous general of tanks. I wonder sometimes if the Soviets don't deliberately foster the air of secrecy and suspicion that exists within Russia itself. Of course everyone must die some time, but without the universal curiosity of a free press and the facts which it can dig up, everyone wonders about the real causes of death and the whole place becomes a hotbed of rumors. Fear and uncertainty can build up legends of power and omniscience which might be effective in helping to control this vast land. Perhaps there is very little substance to the true direct power of the secret police. Still, there is a scientific thumb rule which says that, of two adequate explanations for anything, one must always take the simpler in preference to the more complex. Being Russian, the regime cannot very well do away with secrecy and suspicion. One becomes more and more impressed with the resemblances between tsarist and Soviet Russia, particularly in the darker aspects. In any case, it would be less than prudent to assume that power here is based more on psychology than on material force.

Goloway and Philbin set out by car for Maloyaroslavyets, where there had once been a famous battle with the French second only to that of Borodino. They told me that their *slezhka* eventually pulled ahead of them, just as ours had done in the grim, rainy forest country. As the Russian car went past, Goloway recognized one of the plain-clothesmen in it as one who had frequently been assigned to follow him.

Within a few minutes they were stopped by a white-jacketed militiaman. He was the same individual whom Goloway had recognized in plain clothes. He was young, and apparently had not realized that Goloway was in the American car, for he seemed surprised and nervous. He asked for their papers, and started looking through them with shaking hands.

"You will have to go back," he said. "Your car isn't properly registered."

Having been stopped on the roads a few days before for the same reason, Goloway had sent over to get the car's papers in proper order, and had been told by the authorities that there was nothing the matter with them. But it was no use. Goloway and Philbin were sent back to Moscow, feeling a bit sorry for the agitated young policeman who must have been only carrying out his orders. The devious pattern of those orders is slowly becoming more clear.

6. INSIDE THE KREMLIN

ALTHOUGH ANNA AKHMATOVA IS ONE of the few really great lyric poets of modern Russia, her poems cannot be bought in any bookshop in her own country. I have tried ever since I have been here, without any success. There is no published list of books that are suppressed, nor is any announcement ever made that they are forbidden. Occasionally, when returning to the same used-book shop time after time and asking for the same books, a clerk who has come to know me has said, "No, we do not have that book, and we do not expect to have it." That is proof positive that its sale is forbidden, and that, in the clerk's opinion at least, the ban will last for a long time. My copy of Akhmatova was given me by a Russian friend who told me that, although Russians could no longer read her poems, Akhmatova had been given a pension by the government which has never been withdrawn. Born in 1888, she is still alive in Leningrad.

The poem of *Lot's Wife* is in itself sufficient to put Akhmatova under the ban:

> *After the envoy of God went the righteous man,*
> *Great in the eyes of the world, by the black mountain.*
> *But alarm spoke loudly to his wife —*
> *It is not late, you may yet look*
>
> *On the beautiful towers of your native Sodom,*
> *On the square where you sang, on the court where you spun,*
> *On the empty windows of the high house*
> *Where you bore children to your dear husband.*
>
> *She looked, and, rooted by a deadly pain,*
> *Her eyes could look no more;*
> *And her body became transparent salt,*
> *And her swift feet grew to the ground.*

Who will weep for this woman?
Does she seem the less for her losses?
Only my heart will never forget
A life given for a single backward look.

This is far more poignant in Russian than in my literal translation, and its beauty is enhanced by its poetic form. Everyone in this land expects to find parables and Aesop talk in much that they read, and no Russian can possibly miss the analogy that this exquisite poem holds.

At last Nell and I got into the Kremlin. Every few months a small party of foreigners is permitted to go through, and we had long been waiting our turn. We were to meet at the far corner gate at eleven in the morning, so in order to be sure that we didn't miss our one opportunity we were there in the car in plenty of time. When the rest of the party showed up, we sent the cars away and went on through the great medieval walls on foot.

A tall, round-faced, bookish-looking man in the gray uniform of the Foreign Office went with us, together with a stubby, polite little officer of the Kremlin Guards, a dumpy black-skirted woman guide, and a red-haired Russian girl from our Embassy to interpret. Dick Davis had asked if I wouldn't act as interpreter, but I had told him that the other Americans and I would be better off if he sent a professional.

Once through the mysterious gates, the road climbed a steep hill and opened up into a wide drive on the crest, edged with northern-looking pines. It was a strange feeling to look down rather than up at the towers and walls, for one does not realize that the Kremlin is actually set on a high hill. It was as peaceful and quiet there as in some country estate. The only signs of activity were occasional little groups of guards who marched briskly past, swinging their arms wide and stamping heavily in something that was reminiscent of the old Prussian goose step, yet Russian rather than German. Here and there were little guard booths, striped like barbers' poles, as they have been in Russia since far back in the days of the Tsars.

The big palaces along the drive were heavily covered with

arabesques in high relief on their columns and façades. We went first to the Cathedral Square which was surrounded with churches. There were soft, colorful wall paintings around the doors and high above. The square is dominated by the huge gold bulbous dome of the Ouspensky Cathedral, where all the Tsars of all the Russias were crowned and which dates from 1457. It is flanked on one side by another cathedral in which are the tombs of the Tsars down to the time of Peter the Great, and on the other side by still another church whose doorways were covered with paintings and Byzantine carving. Nearby was another building whose walls consisted of separate embossed stones, giving it an unfamiliar effect. As we moved on out of the square a sudden burst of golden domes and great heavy chained crosses came into view.

At last it was possible to have a good look at the Tsar Bell, the Emperor of all Bells. It was the biggest bell that has ever been cast, slate-gray in color and enormously thick, as could be seen from the big broken place in its skirt. Into the molten metal at its casting the people of Moscow threw their personal jewelry. It has never rung, having been dropped and cracked in the effort to raise it to the tall bell tower of Ivan the Great. Part of the inscription on one side was illegible, but the guide did not know if the inscription had ever been finished, or if it had flowed and distorted from a great fire to which it had been subjected. They said that the big bell which hangs in the Kremlin bell tower, and which is rung on holidays, is itself the largest bell that has ever sounded. But the Tsar Bell must be added to the long list of unfinished projects which Russian enthusiasm and imagination are still enscribing.

I asked where Stalin's quarters were in the Kremlin and immediately knew, from the look on the Russian faces, that that was dangerous ground. No one knew where he lived and worked in the Kremlin, or even if he actually slept there.

The Tsar Gun, another project that did not pan out, is as big as the biggest modern mortar. It is a fantastic casting of faces and foliage, all worked in bronze. Beyond it was a building that had hundreds and hundreds of Napoleon's cannon with muzzles bristling forth from its foundation.

Then we went into the Kremlin Museum. It is as difficult to describe as is the Hermitage in Leningrad. One should go to the pages of Théophile Gautier to get an adequate description of that treasure. My principal impression was one of fabulous wealth, wealth in jewels and precious stones and gold and silver on the scale of the national debt of a great nation. There were literally dozens of crowns of the Tsars, all encrusted with diamonds and enormous rubies and emeralds, including the famous fur-trimmed bowl-shaped crown of Vladimir Monomachus which was traditionally used in subsequent coronations. Throne after throne after throne, likewise heavily crusted with jewels, diamonds as big as quarters and emeralds and rubies as big as half-dollars, with an occasional chunk of emerald as big as one's fist, among them the double throne of Peter the Great and his sickly half-brother, Ivan V, with its secret compartment behind, from which their sister Sophia used to tell them what to say. Scores of jeweled saddles, bridles and stirrups, studded with turquoise, sapphires, and the endless rubies, emeralds and diamonds. Horse blankets sewn thick with jewels and great pearls. Some of them were on real horses that had been beautifully stuffed and preserved. Of all the riches that were there, perhaps the most impressive were those of the Church, all the trappings of religion. There were ikon frames, jeweled crosses and miters. Some of the robes of gold bullion thread were solid with pearls and jewels, weighing up to forty kilograms.

The coronation dresses of many Tsaritsas, including that of Catherine the Great, most of them of silver bullion thread, and the coronation clothes of the Tsars, were echoes of the pageantry of the Romanov court. One of the later Tsars was unwilling to unbutton his jacket in order to be anointed on his breast, so he had a little pocket made in his jacket, with succeeding pockets through his shirt and underlinen, for that purpose. Costumes of guards and soldiers were worn by dummies. But the dummies had no faces. Where a head should be was only a wrapping of white cloth. This gave an eerie masked effect to the whole place.

Case after case of jeweled swords, inlaid guns, and trophies chronicled the many wars of Russia, particularly those with the Turks. Among the decorations was the famous white-enameled George Cross for which so many Russians have struggled, schemed, and died. Peter the Great's enormous jackboots which he himself had made with his own hands were there. There were scepters blazing with jewels, and there was armor. Some of the chain mail that hung over the face added to the strange effect given by the faceless dummies, as though there were masked conspirators there behind one's back. A helmet and some rusted chain armor had been worn by the father of Alexander Nevsky in the year 1230.

An elaborate clock of Catherine's still ran and performed its many wonders, and a golden bird on its top dropped a diamond from its beak regularly to mark the passage of the seconds. The biggest topaz that has ever been found, as big as a sea coconut, was like a huge smeared and melted piece of crystal.

Jeweled Easter eggs of the Tsars were solid with precious stones. One, a gift from one of the Tsars to his Tsaritsa, was made up of emeralds and diamonds that were brilliant-cut in the modern fashion. Most of the Easter eggs had various things inside. A tiny model of the Tsar's yacht was inside a crystal eggshell. One egg contained a little train with several coaches, all of solid gold, and, with typical Russian lavishness, the engine was of pure platinum. It wound up with a tiny spring and an almost microscopic key, and it ran.

One of the most Russian things in all the Kremlin was a big bronze bell without a clapper. It had once rung out the signal for a revolt of the people in Catherine's time. In punishment, she had had its tongue torn out so that it could never speak again.

7. ZHDANOV'S FUNERAL

ALL OF THE NEWSPAPERS THIS MORNING were edged in black, announcing the death of Zhdanov, the first member of the Politburo to die for a long time. He has been the intellectual interpreter of Marxism-Leninism and the purger of the musical, artistic, and literary worlds. There have been rumors that there was some sort of internal struggle in the Politburo, with Zhdanov representing the leadership of the more or less anti-American part. It is probably not that simple, for they must all be anti-American by their own definitions of themselves and that for which their philosophy stands.

There may well have been dissension, for Zhdanov seems to have begun to build up a personal following, supported, after the manner of politicos everywhere, with his own appointments in many important places. And contrary to the usual practice, the death has been announced as due to natural causes — announced by no less than five doctors. Like the Player Queen, the lady doth protest too much.* At any rate, Zhdanov is dead, and outside the window as I write, long lines of blue-capped MVD soldiers are being stationed to control the movements of traffic when his body is brought to lie in state in the Hall of Columns of the Home of the Soviets.

A military band began to play Chopin's Funeral March, very slowly, with a sort of sad triumph bannering out from the soft brass. From our balcony we could see along Okhotny Row, into which a line of troops and automobiles was slowly turning from

* In January, 1953, the Soviet regime itself announced that Zhdanov's death was not a natural one. The statement that the doctors themselves were responsible, together with the Kremlin's dark, tangled web of anti-Semitism and charges of foreign interference and espionage, constitute a typically Russian enigma. It is probable that it was a major incident in the unfolding of a great purge which was diverted from its course by Stalin's death a few weeks later. The subsequent reversal by Stalin's successors of the charges against the doctors adds further complications to the strange case of Zhdanov's death, which is perhaps the most important mystery in history.

the direction of the railroad station where Zhdanov's body had arrived. The head of the column, led by two men carrying a gigantic portrait of Zhdanov, stopped at the entrance of the Home of the Soviets, and the coffin was carried through the doors.

The coffin was a vivid scarlet, and it was shaped in at the top and bottom so that its section was diamond-shaped, not boxlike. Soon the automobiles began to leave singly, each car with closely drawn blinds so that it was impossible to tell who might be in them. Thus people with rank and position usually travel through the streets of Moscow.

That night Nell and I went to dinner with the bright-eyed Prices in their room at the Metropole. We had no trouble getting through the long lines of militiamen that still marked off the central part of Moscow while Zhdanov's body lies in state. Outside the French windows of the Prices' room was an inner court of the hotel. Its irregularity and its age gave the place much more of a Russian atmosphere than Mokhavaya House has. Rocky Winters and several other Americans came in after dinner and we talked economics until long after midnight.

That young company doubtless put me down as a reactionary because of the viewpoints that have grown up in me only since being in Russia. They seem so simple that they must be wrong, but it is difficult to see how the welfare state can avoid eventually becoming the police state if it is to enforce its will in any way other than by education.

When we walked home, a line of troops had started to form along Sverdlovsk Square in front of the Metropole. Since they were not yet very effective, we went through them regardless of their telling us we could not. There was another close line of troops across the entrance to Okhotny Row. The others were all for going through those troops also, but, since they looked well organized, the older generation took charge and made them all walk around the block instead.

Our balcony was crowded with those who had come to watch the state funeral of Zhdanov. OVS had called up to find out if the service attachés were in town, but nothing further came of the call. No invitations were issued to foreigners, but heads of missions were told over the telephone that they might be present in Red Square if they wished. A few of them went, in their shiny silk hats.

Long lines of troops marked off the route from the Home of the Soviets to Red Square. They blocked all roads, so that there was no traffic at all in the center of Moscow. It was a showery afternoon, with little intervals of pale, cold sunshine between heavy, tumbled dark-blue clouds. Big blocks of troops were lined up in Manezhny Place in front of the Embassy, frequently soaked with heavy showers. Many of the blocks wore the blue caps of the MVD, and an occasional senior officer was conspicuous in his decorations and his blue-green parade uniform.

The center of Okhotny Row was such a great mass of flowers and wreaths that the people carrying them could scarcely be seen. Long lines of individuals and organizations streamed into Red Square, carrying red banners and red and gold slogans. There were vivid splashes of white, green and orange wherever several of them protected themselves from a shower by spreading over themselves a transparent, colored raincoat. A peculiar reflection from the stormy sky turned the distant roofs of the city to a color as blue as the MVD caps, but which slowly faded back to its usual rusty gray.

At last, well beyond the scheduled time, the bands began the slow, sad, majestic Chopin music and the huge portrait of Zhdanov started down Okhotny Row. It was followed by a train of Marshals of the Soviet Union carrying Zhdanov's orders and decorations in their hands. Then the crowded heaps of flowers and wreaths started to move behind them like a forest.

After them came four men carrying the scarlet, ominous shape of the coffin's lid, and then, half propped up in the red coffin, riding on a gun caisson, the body. Its face was deathly pale, yellowish-waxy, and so startlingly different from all the thousands of other faces that it was easy to pick it out as far as the cortege could be seen. It was Death itself — the Great Doom's Image. The Birnam Wood of green wreaths and flowers went down the defile between the Historical Museum and the Kremlin into Red Square, which was massed solid with red-bannered crowds.

And behind, trudging on foot, came the Politburo, with Stalin, swart and stocky, wearing uniform, in their ranks. Zoya was on the balcony with all the Americans. It was the first time in her life

she had ever seen Stalin, and she was vivid and excited. A long line
of civilians, probably the top people of the government and the
Party, followed the Politburo.

Then came some of the most beautiful matched horses I have
ever seen, hauling some light artillery. Their hoofs sounded like the
steady beating of surf, or like the hollow rolling of rocks by the sea.
The rhythmic hollow tramping of five thousand troops followed
them as the blocks of soldiers swung into the procession. The windows of Mokhavaya House rattled to the salute of the guns as
Zhdanov was buried by the Kremlin Wall.

As I came in from the balcony I could not help but think that
there are now too many Russians who have seen Zhdanov as dead
as Lenin for anyone to arise in true Russian fashion and announce
that a trick had been played on the people and that he himself was
the real Zhdanov.

8. THE HUMPBACKED PONY

IN THE LATE AFTERNOON WE DROVE OUT to Seryebranny Bor, the Silver Wood, on the outskirts of Moscow, past neat, small, new apartment houses covered with a pink wash that was already fading and running. I had heard much of the Silver Wood, but was disappointed to find it just some more pine trees plentifully interspersed with *dachas*. Although the hard road gave out early, we kept along a trail until we came to the river. The Moskva ran full and peaceful through meadows, reflecting the rosebud-shaped domes of a little church which stood on the far bank.

We had been followed all the way from the center of Moscow, and as we circled around through first one and then another of the bad roads in that vicinity in an attempt to find some real charm in the Silver Wood itself, we twice ran into our own *slezkha*. Each time they looked very startled to see us coming back before they had caught up with us, but each time they continued to try to conceal themselves around corners and in the by-lanes.

We lost them finally on the way back home, for there was no sign of them when we stopped to get out and look at a marvelous triple rainbow spanning the poor brown hills and rising clear and brilliant among tumbled black clouds.

To use a Russian idiom, opera has never been for me. It seems to me that it is all out of balance. There is so much realism in the settings, the costumes and the acting, that the singing becomes incongruous. People just don't conduct themselves that way. Nell and I went to see *Eugene Onegin* at the Bolshoy. In addition to the natural hazards of opera, this production set up one of its own, for Shpillyer, the buxom lady who sang the part of Tatyana, was much too big and heavy to be able to do anything but destroy illusions. She is said to have once been Stalin's pet.

The settings were lavish, and the fine voices made the most of Tchaikovsky's melodious score. A famous basso named Mikhailov, who played the part of Tatyana's husband in the last act, sang in such a way that every tone was music. His cheeks blew out like bellows, and the sounds were really thrilling. Like many other Russian singers, he received his training in the Church.

Nell had a luncheon, with a ham and some hoarded American baked beans as the *pièce de résistance*. Foreigners, and Americans as well, go for them in a big way because of the magic that Nell can work with a touch of garlic. General Juhlin-Dannfelt, the new Swedish military attaché, was among the guests, rather stiff and formal as are many Swedish people of rank, and with tight, curly, graying hair.

There was a discussion on overrating Russian military strength and ability. Those characteristics were overrated for a generation or more after they threw out Napoleon, and something of the same sort may be going on now after Hitler's defeat. The Russians are not to be underrated in their numbers nor in their land, both of which they have in vast quantities, nor in the simple soldierly virtues and their willingness to fight for their land, but it is very hard to believe that the Soviet Union is the great and powerful technical and industrial country she would have the world believe.

The play at MXAT was changed without warning at the last minute, and once more we saw Ostrovsky's *The Last Sacrifice*. It is a good play and really enjoyable, but after a dozen different Ostrovsky plays one has had about enough Ostrovsky. Chekhov and the wonderful *Dead Souls* seem to stand up better than anything else as a steady diet.

If one is genuinely interested in the Russian language, the theater here will never pall. I at last went to see Shaw's *Pygmalion* and found that it was better to keep my eyes shut. The Russian version is really remarkable. Once on hearing part of it on the radio I had praised it to some Britisher. He asked me how they managed "Not bloody likely!" — so I was on the lookout for it tonight. They did it very neatly with the expression *chorta c dva*, which is just as untranslatable in its way as the English phrase. Literally, it's "from two devils," but it really means "That's what *you* think!" But the art of the translation is apparent only when you realize that *chort* is a bad word in Russian — what they call a "black word" — carrying just about the same shade of impropriety as "bloody" does in England.

For some reason I used to think that Russian must have some soul-shaking oaths which one doesn't usually encounter in print. Actually their swearing, although picturesque, is very mild, *chort* being a very strong word. The thing at which they really excel is obscenity, and the heights of obscenity are reached in connection with the Russian word for "mother." There is a special verb from the root for "mother" which means to curse in that fashion, and a similar special adjective which describes the result.

Winters and I were discussing the way the Politburo can control the Five Year Plan and alter it to suit internal or external situations at will. Without the dictatorial power of the Politburo, the Five Year Plan would be completely unwieldy and extremely difficult to alter with changing conditions. This being so, perhaps state socialism and state planning are incompatible with American democracy and our form of government. Perhaps that is the reason why Congress is endlessly confronted with an impossible task, why its work is never done, and why there are so many boards and commissions that are never properly assimilated into the rest of government. Far from offering socialist attractions, all the evidence of Russia seems to me to point in the other direction. It seems increasingly clear to me that we will never have any more peace until our state gets back to its proper business of defining and policing wrongdoing.

The Soviets have said that our Spirodonovka House is to be torn down and that the naval officers there must move within six weeks. I went to look at the house they offered us on Granatny Street and found that it would be an improvement. Spiro is a bit on the shabby side, whereas the Granatny place, although smaller, is handsome and dignified within, with several picturesque porcelain stoves. Unfortunately, it will require an unusually large number of servants to keep it going because of those stoves, for there is no other means of heating or cooking. The Spiro officers will have trouble in swinging this new place, for it is only the Navy which must pay for servants abroad out of their own pockets. One has to live abroad to realize how impossible it is to do the work oneself.

The Italian Ambassador had a small dinner dance at the Grand Hotel. On the way out of the Grand, Nell dropped a sparkly earring. We went back to look for it, and told the doorman and the inevitable militiamen who guard the place to keep an eye out for it. As we finally went away toward Gorky Street one of the militiamen came running after us, having found it. Considering its apparent value and the fact that in the eyes of Soviet propaganda we must be parasitical, exploiting capitalists (how little they know!), that was a very honest thing to do. It is impossible to give people like the militiamen anything, but Nell did a good job with her evident gratitude and appreciation, coupled with an impulsive holding out of her hand. For a brief second she thought that he was not going to respond, but he was pulling off his glove to bow low and graciously over her outstretched hand. I shouldn't think a militiaman would get in trouble for that.

The Russian imagination is at its best in its *skazki,* and it is a very fine best. They are peopled with animals with peculiarly Russian mentalities. The ballet of *The Humpbacked Pony* that we saw at the Bolshoy was a wonderful thing. I had never heard of the Humpbacked Pony until Lewinkov, the gentle, efficient Russian baggagemaster of the *America,* gave me a copy of it on the ship on my way to Europe and Russia. He told me that one who knew it thoroughly could speak Russian as the people speak it. It was written in 1834 at about the same time that Pushkin produced his remarkable writings which crystallized the Russian language, and, like Puskin, Ershov used the old *skazki* in his long poem, which begins like the *skazki* themselves:

> *Over the mountains and over the sea,*
> *Over the forests, broad and free,*
> *Not in the sky, but lower down,*
> *Lived an old man in a little town.*
> *He had three sons, so the story is told;*
> *The oldest one was wise and bold,*
> *The middle son was half and half*
> *And the youngest only good for a laugh.*

The settings at the Bolshoy were filled with great bursts of color and splendor, with a fantasy that had nothing vague and misty about it but which was as real as the flames from a diamond, and with an archaic touch that was as good as anything the Middle Ages of Western Europe can offer. There was one scene in the submarine empire of the Sea Tsar that made it difficult to believe that it was not actually under water. Long trailing seaweed hung from above and the scenery swayed and shifted as though carried by the currents of green water. Fish that seemed to be very real swam past, and now and then there would be a sudden bright streak of phosphorescence.

The dancing was varied and extraordinary, with Tatars and Circassians, Ukrainians and Great Russians. The unbridled savagery of the Tatars was more convincing than any portrayal I have ever seen of our own Red Indians. And the whole thing was genuinely and uproariously amusing with its dainty little humpbacked pony who worked the magic with the help of the Fire Bird's feather, and with Ivanushka, the classical younger son who is more than a bit of a fool but yet the hero. Ivanushka stole the show by his antics with the Khan while the lovely Tsar-Maiden and the enchanted beauties did their remarkable ballet dancing.

The Moscow Zoo is in a small park near the center of the city. Its entrance is surmounted by a blue-and-white Wedgwood-like fresco of beasts which, like the park itself, somehow contrives to look tinselly and tawdry. Indian Summer, which the Russians call Old Wive's Summer, has come, so this Sunday afternoon there were great crowds of people in the *Zoopark*. Half of them were children, with never a smarty or a show-off to be seen. Out of all the thousands of people we saw only one crying brat. Pulling their ears seems to be a substitute for spanking, for the embarrassed father eventually achieved discipline by doing just that.

Large crowds were gathered around the only elephant in the Zoo. The huge beast seemed very conscious of the fact that he was putting on an entertaining show by digging up dirt with his long tusks and then throwing it over his back with his trunk. Other crowds were around the concrete tanks of the hippopotami, the enormous yellowish-white polar bears, the monkey houses, and the lions and tigers and beautiful spotted leopards, who were being fed. But everywhere were crowds, particularly in a little jam-packed smelly aquarium which was half underground. The only unusual sight among the animals were several hybrids of wolves and German police dogs. Perhaps even this was not in fact unusual, but the placards said that only Soviet scientists had succeeded in interbreeding them. They were almost indistinguishable from true wolves, or, for that matter, from the usual Alsatians.

In the middle of the park was a good-sized lake, dotted white with swans, with an occasional scarlet-beaked black swan or a shaggy-crested white heron. The water of the lake was scummy and littered with trash all along its shores. Like so many other things in Russia, it seemed as though it could have been so much better with a little more care and thought and effort.

The people were fully as interesting as the animals, with many big-bearded peasants who wore belted Russian blouses and baggy trousers stuffed into their Russian boots. There was an occasional neat young soldier or officer who looked exactly the same as the most attractive sort of nice young soldier or officer one might see in the United States.

Last night the house began suddenly to shake with periodic gunfire. I went out on the balcony to find out what was up. For no apparent reason Moscow was all ablaze with periodic synchronized bursts of colored rockets. There were no crowds on the streets, no excitement, and no special decorations, only the gun salutes that accompanied the green and red of the rockets and a blue weaving of searchlights in the sky overhead. It stopped as suddenly as it began, and it was only in the papers this morning that I found out that yesterday was Tank Day.

Several Russians have told me that there is a Soviet writer named Grin who is now dead, but who had written some things full of mood and atmosphere that were remarkable in that they did not try to teach a lesson. Russians are often impulsive and generous, and one of them gave me one of Grin's books. In it was a story named *Crimson Sails* which has been made into a ballet.

Consequently Nell and I went to the Bolshoy Filial to see

Crimson Sails. The Filial is built on the same horseshoe plan as the Bolshoy itself, but falls far short of it in magnificence. The ballet was attractive and interesting. The story is a rather charming one, of how a little Cinderella comes to believe that some day a fairy prince will come in a great ship with crimson sails to take her away from her poverty and misery, and of how a greathearted man brings it really to pass. Such themes are dear to the Russian heart — a fairy-tale ending for all their misery and oppression.

At a party in the evening an Eastern European sought me out. He showed an extraordinary familiarity with the Soviet navy and a still more extraordinary willingness to tell me what he knew. I played dumb, for one doesn't know whom one can trust in these damnable countries of communist intrigue. Moreover, his wife, who carries the characteristic Party look, was right at his side.

PART VII. THE BORDERS OF ASIA

1. NIGHT FLIGHT

MY NEXT JOURNEY TO SCANDINAVIA in search of flying time was complicated by an intermittent low-grade fever and by the fact that the Finns objected to my flying over Finland off the regular airlines for fear that the Soviets would interpret it as aiding and abetting some sort of espionage or preparations for war. My flying at last accomplished under these restrictions, I stood at the Helsinki airport, waiting for the Russian plane to come in for its turnaround. Out of the plane came Medvedeff, plunged in gloom and dejection, looking much as I must have looked when leaving Russia a few days earlier. That hunted, downcast air lasts only for the first few moments, however. He told me that the Navy had been dispossessed of its office space and crowded into cramped quarters elsewhere, which has been long scheduled to happen. But he also told me that all embassies and legations had received a note from the Soviet Foreign Office limiting their movements to fifty kilometers from Moscow. The note of the Foreign Office was a bit complicated in its wording, but that was what it seemed to mean.

The only other passenger on the Soviet plane was a French courier who couldn't speak anything but French. On the front bulkhead of the plane was a big picture of a Red Army fighter with fifty-seven red stars on it, indicating enemy planes shot down in combat. The pilot of the transport was a red-faced, long-haired, heavy, gray-eyed, competent booted and belted Russian. On his jacket was the star and red ribbon of a Hero of the Soviet Union, so when he came through the passenger compartment I asked him if the picture on the bulkhead was of his machine. He said No, that he had never flown anything but heavy aircraft. The weather was . good, with a few scattered clouds and a strong tail wind, so in an hour and a half we were on the ground in Leningrad.

There was a strong cold wind blowing, with an occasional little drift of hail from an occasional isolated cloud. It was bitter cold on the ground, where we had no heat. There was an interminable passing in and out of frontier guards, customs inspectors and officials. When I greeted some of them, they surprised me by re-plying with the respectful old-Russian hissing sound at the end of their words. There seems to be no connection between that Russian sound and the polite hissing of the Japanese, for it is merely short for *sudar,* or "sir."

Some sort of extremely concentrated cargo was loaded in in small unmarked boxes, so heavy that each small box could be barely lifted by four men. Then the tank truck that was to replenish us with fuel went wrong and couldn't pump any fuel. It must have been the only tank truck on what was one of the most important fields of Russia, for we sat and waited for an hour or more while the Russians tinkered with it.

The pilot sat down, accepted a cigarette, and talked freely with me. He had flown a Soviet plane all the way to San Francisco at the time of the first United Nations conference. He had been around Europe quite a bit. "London — it doesn't please me. Too gloomy. And Paris. I don't like the French women. They are too thin. They don't feed them enough in France. Amsterdam is the finest foreign city I have ever seen. San Francisco has too many hills. Los Angeles is a fine city, though. But no matter where one goes, home is always the best."

At last the plane was fueled and we took off into a burning red sunset which still managed to look bleak and cold. The low hills to the south of Leningrad looked mountainous for a moment until we rose above them, and the white walls and windows of Leningrad in the distance stood out against a cold blue background like lights and fires in the reflection of the dying sun. Very soon we were flying over the vast darkness of Russia. Only here and there, at rare intervals, would there be a tiny group of faint lights marking a village, showing that the forested, wild country was really as desolate as it looked in the daytime.

At last we reached Moscow, a vast bed of glowing ashes in the darkness. It seemed several times bigger than it seems in daylight, stretching as far as one could see in the night. Vnukovo Field was as dimly marked as any wartime field, and we landed almost as in wartime. There was only the glow of our own landing lights and the announcement of our arrival by a single white star from a Very's pistol. Nell and Mac were waiting for me on the field, and it was good to be back home in Moscow once again.

My new office is cozy and warm but badly crowded for the other naval officers and, since it is on the street level, noisy. Just outside the doors is a swarm of Russians — chauffeurs and help of all sorts — through which every visitor must come.

The Foreign Office note on travel restrictions was partly in line with what Serayev had hinted several times. He had asked me if a statement of where we could go and where we could not would fill the bill, but this was a statement of only where one could not go in the Soviet Union. That covers all the border regions and a great many other places, but, by implication, there remain vast areas where perhaps one can go. The limitations on Moscow itself, however, meant that there were only certain roads by which one could leave the city to the fifty-kilometer limit. It seems clear that Burobin's fishing and shooting preserve is now a thing of the past. That is no loss, however, to anyone but the American Navy, for we remain the only ones who were ever able to enter it, the few Poles and Englishmen who tried being confined to the lodge at its very edge for lack of rugged transportation. Also my hope of getting lodgings of some sort next summer far out from Moscow is definitely gone, although it has long since faded to only a dim glimmer.

There are many things about the new travel order which are still not clear, such as whether one may go by automobile, train, or plane, and whether or not one can cross a prohibited area in order to reach a destination that is not prohibited. If one cannot do that, not only is all of the Soviet Union closed, but one cannot even leave the country by any route. A note has been sent to the Foreign Office asking for such clarifications.

There was no doubt but that my temperature was up, which Dr. Vaughn checked as soon as he saw me, sending me promptly home to bed. So I'm taking it easy, with all of the back office work brought up to me by the delightful, effective Kidder.

Natasha brought me a recent book, Polevoy's *Story of a Real Man.* It is not clear whether she gave it to me or lent it to me, but it is considerably better than most contemporary Russian literature. It opens with a splendid description of the winter forest, in early spring, through which a wrecked aviator with both feet broken crawls alone for eighteen days before he reaches some partisans who are living underground. After that it tends to be a glorification of the Soviet Man, telling how the hero was fitted with artificial legs and eventually became a pilot again. It is founded on fact, but no one, let alone a Russian, can be such an uncomplicated paragon of all the virtues as the central character. There is even the usual dig at America and England for not starting a second front earlier, which always seems particularly graceless when it was the Russo-German pact that unleashed the need for it.

Not only is the content of literature under the Soviets adulterated, but the language itself is being impoverished. Russians have told me that few of their countrymen today thoroughly understand all the richness and variety of the vocabularies of Leskov or even Goncharov, and it is entirely possible that very soon they will become as obsolete and obscure as the most difficult passage of Shakespeare, for no modern writer seems to be able to command such language. The very few Soviet authors who could do so, such as Aleksei Tolstoy and Vyacheslav Shishkov, were already writing at the time of the Red Revolution and no others have risen to take their place. What a marvelous tongue Russian could have been, if it had really been free to flower! But its literature today is in the Horatio Alger stage, and it is kept there by the utilitarian needs of the regime.

One of our couriers has just come in from Helsinki, and again a car full of surface mail pouches has been detached from the train and failed to show up when he arrived. He said that the Intourist girl here in Moscow seemed very much disturbed when she heard of it.

"How awful!" she said, "to have this happen a second time to you! And just when we were supposed to be particularly nice to Americans!"

Maybe — just maybe — things will be all right.

General O'Daniel, the new military attaché who has recently arrived as Macon's relief, was the first to try the reality of the new regulations on travel. Much to everyone's surprise, he actually got away a couple of days ago by train with his wife, an enlisted man and Colonel Urban as interpreter — for Stalingrad!

Also Alan Little has definite train reservations and is leaving tonight for Mahachkala in Daghestan and Astrakhan at the mouth of the Volga. I would have headed for there if my fever — and my disposition — had been fully recovered. Those two characteristics seem to be interrelated.

This little temperature has been running now for about a month. Dr. Vaughn and I have decided that if it doesn't come down in another two or three days we'll start in with some tests in the Russian Polyclinic. It's probably Malta fever, for I had a touch of what they thought was that in Germany at the end of the war. It would be interesting really to see the inside of a Russian hospital as a patient, although it wouldn't be a terrible stroke of bad luck to be sent back to the wonderful Navy hospital at Bethesda in Washington for a bit.

Chekhov's *Sea Gull*, which provides MXAT with its insignia, has not been produced on the Moscow stage recently, so I read it. It is a grim, almost terrifying psychological drama, ending with a suicide. Yet its title page says "The Sea Gull — A Comedy"!

Conversation with a Russian:
"What a terrible thing was that earthquake in Ashkabad the other day! In the dead of night, with no lights or anything. How terrified people must have been!"

"Yes," I reply. "Earthquakes are always bad in cities, where there are many people. In the country, they are soon over, and things do not become so disorganized."

"The old people say that some day Moscow will disappear."

"What! From an earthquake?"

"I don't know. But that's what the old people say."

2. FRUSTRATION IN A MONASTERY

MY DAMNABLE TEMPERATURE has gradually become completely normal, and I feel better than for a long time. Consequently on Saturday afternoon, although it was damp and raw and overcast, I went to the Novodevichy Monastery to see if formal permission could not be had to make some sketches there. The monastery is classed as a museum because of its historical interest, and since it seemed probable that the administrative organization was separate from the spiritual organization, I went to the Director of the Museum.

He had his office in his living quarters within the thick walls. The potted plants, the warm air and the smell of fresh baking within his apartment made me think of houses of my childhood. The Director was a little gray goat-bearded fellow, not fine-grained enough to be one of the real intelligentsia and too gentle to be a politician.

"*Pazhaluista,*" he said, "of course you can sketch. All you want to. Why not? But only inside the walls. That is all over which I have authority. If you want to sketch from outside the walls, you will have to get permission from someone else."

It was too late to do much then, so I thanked him and said I would be back the next day. Sunday was also raw and overcast, and although I didn't feel much like going it seemed desirable to do so because of what had been said.

On entering the grounds I wished that I had been able to work rapidly enough to sketch some of the ragged poor who were sitting beside the walks to the churches. The combination of shrewdness, patience and resignation in their faces was remarkable. One old man with very blue eyes had a great square-cut white beard curled across his faded blue jacket. Both his jacket and trousers were heavily wadded for warmth, with the wadding stitched in place. His trousers were stuffed into *valyenki,* and on his patriarchal silver head was a towering hat of dirty white wool, curling like his beard and almost as tall as the bearskin shako of one of the Coldstream

Guards. He looked as though he had stepped out of the pages of Tolstoy or Dostoevsky, except for his heavy *valyenki*. He should have been wearing shoes made of bast, with their fastenings wrapped round his trouser legs like the pictures of prerevolutionary Russians and of northern peoples from the Middle Ages and before. One seldom sees those bast shoes nowadays, for they were made by hand, and the felt *valyenki* and everything else the Russian wears are now made by machinery, and not very well made at that. The poor devils haven't even been able to get quantity in return for the quality of their homespun.

Being quite sure that any attempt to draw those faces that were so full of personality and character would only attract a lot of undesirable attention, I picked out a spot in an angle of a hedge that could not be seen from the paths and walks and started to lay out a sketch of one of the squat, half-ruined medieval towers at a corner of the great wall. A house crouched against the tower, with a line of washing fluttering in front of a set of massive barred gates. I had no sooner made a beginning than a dirty, hard-faced man in a wadded jacket came up. He looked like a laborer in his grimy clothes.

"Have you got permission to draw here?" he asked.

"Yes."

"From whom?"

"From the Director of the Museum."

"Let me see it."

"I don't have written permission. He told me to go ahead and draw all I wanted to."

"You must have written permission. That is the law, and you can't draw here without it."

So I folded up my things and went to the Director again, telling him what had happened. He had been so cordial that I expected his support. Nor was I disappointed.

"Oh, that's all right," said the Director. "You don't need written permission."

"But others say I do. It seems to me that I'll have to have it to keep from being stopped again."

"Can you write Russian?"

"Of course."

"Well, you write out a request for permission, addressed to me. I can only give you oral permission, so I'll have to get you your written permission from the head of the bureau under which I come. There will be no trouble about that. I'll do that immediately, so it will be ready very soon. In the meantime, you go on ahead and draw, and if anyone stops you, you send them to me. Don't be disturbed. Everything is in order."

So I went back, got out my gear, and started in again. Very soon the same dirty laborer came up.

"Didn't I tell you once," he said vindictively, "that you couldn't draw here without written permission? Why are you at it again?"

I had no idea what his status was, but judged him to be a Party member on a low level. It was no use to make a scene.

"All right," I answered. "You come with me, and we'll both talk with the Director."

I folded up my gear again and we went across the yard and through the dark passages into the Director's apartment. Without a word my Russian stepped into the Director's Office and shut the door in my face. In a few minutes the Director came out alone.

"Excuse me!" he said, spreading out his hands. "I have tried to reach the head of my department, and to my great regret, I find that it is his day off. There's nothing that can be done."

I couldn't resist saying that this was no surprise.

"But why?" he asked, wonderingly.

"Things aren't made easy in Russia for a foreigner," I replied.

"Then why doesn't America conduct herself better towards Russia?" he asked, becoming suddenly belligerent.

"How do you mean?"

"Well, how about our schoolteachers whom the Americans kidnapped in New York? And why won't America keep her trade agreements and sell us things that we need?"

I tried to tell him that the Russian teachers were completely free to go back to Russia if they wished, but that they didn't want to. As for selling things to Russia, why should we sell anything that might be of help in a war against us?

"That proves that you want war."

"It doesn't prove anything of the sort," I said, feeling myself become heated.

"But is it all right to sell arms to Greece and Turkey, and not to Russia?"

"Yes."

He smiled knowingly and waved his arms. It was no use trying to talk with him, and besides, I had come there to try to draw and not to get into a political argument.

I still don't know why I felt so bitterly about that little experience. It seems to me that it was because of an injured sense of fairness more than anything else. It might have been expected if I had not taken considerable trouble to hunt up the Director in advance and do things properly. There is absolutely no doubt in my mind but that he was not truthful about the "day off," for that is too familiar an excuse for the runaround. And yet, on the other hand, what would have happened to him if he had gone out of his way to help me? Why should he take the risk of being denounced in the next Party meeting? I understand more and more how a foreigner in Russia can lose his objectivity after he has been here for a while. It takes an increasing effort to see the glint of sunlight on the golden domes of Russia instead of the tarnish, the gaping holes and the broken, tilted crosses that crown them.

We put in a request for Ensign Goloway to visit Odessa. The Foreign Office had told the Embassy that Odessa was forbidden because it was on the borders, but OVS has said that it was open. It is undoubtedly the MVD and neither the Foreign Office nor OVS that makes the decision, and it is probable that even the MVD does not set the policy that governs the decision. Our request not only came back approved, but Goloway was singled out by having a young woman share his apartment on the Odessa train. She must have been very tired, for she started removing her clothes for bed as soon as the journey began. The Soviets seem to have overconditioned us to their solicitude, for Goloway said that all he could think of was the probability that she had been put in his compartment to compromise him. Goloway kept his distance. Besides, she was not very pretty.

A heavy fog obliterated the city during the entire three or four days of his stay, so that he was almost ready to believe that the Soviets had even the weather under control. Only potatoes were to be had in Odessa, no other vegetables, not even the universal cabbage, and there was no hot water in the hotel except on Saturday nights. Nevertheless Goloway liked Odessa, saying it was more like a French or an English city than like a Russian one. Although he was followed closely and continuously, many Russian friends of Bob Dreher, hearing that there was an American in town, called up on the telephone or came to see him.

I walked over to the iron-colored Lenin Library and dithered as to whether or not it was worth the effort of trying to get into it. With a great deal of time and patience an occasional foreigner who has a good command of the language has managed to do so. Even then no one has been given real access to its contents. One is not permitted to see any listings of what they have but must ask for a definite book or publication by name, being meticulously careful to make no mistake in title or author. Sometimes the item requested will be produced for reading on the premises, but often it is being "repaired" or is simply not available.

Perhaps it was due to the gloomy autumn day, but I was not in the mood for another long bout with Russian deviousness and so continued on along the Arbat. I wandered for some time, stopping in an occasional old bookshop, but seeing only dingy, badly worn books on technology and sociology. At last a park bench in the ragged gardens that run along the middle of Gogolevsky Boulevard was welcome.

A big seated statue of Gogol broods over the beginnings of the parkway, with a procession of all the characters from his books, delicately and finely done in bronze, going around its base. But all I could see was the appalling faces of most of the people in the gardens, hard-bitten with suffering, ignorance and suspicion, and their poor makeshift clothes and footgear.

Then I walked along the ring of boulevards through Nikitsky and Tverskoy to Pushkin Square, stopping on the way three or four times to give something to the old women who were frankly begging in the streets. Each time they crossed themselves and blessed me.

I dropped in to the bar that is in the vicinity and had a couple of mugs of sour-sweet beer. But that place was just as bad as the streets. There was never an open, cheerful face to be seen, but always a sort of distortion or caricature. And that after thirty years of communism, for surely the Germans haven't left their marks on everyone. It seemed that it was not the world we know, and that it was more and more hopeless to try to rationalize it into the same sort of world. Russia could still be so possible if only the Russians were not endlessly the victims of Russian institutions. A young man came up to my table and started talking to me, urgently and excitedly.

It was some time before what he wanted was clear. Part of it had already been satisfied by my buying him two hundred grams of vodka, and then he wanted either a bottle to take home or a loan of a hundred rubles so he could buy his own bottle. He showed enough of the symptoms of an alcoholic for me to refuse. He tried to press his identification papers on me to keep as security until he would repay the loan. *Dokumenty* are essential to every Russian, and his willingness to pawn them was offered as proof that he would repay. I paid my bill and left, but he followed me all the way down Gorky Street, plucking at my sleeve and weeping. The crowds went past us with unseeing eyes, and when I finally went in to the Embassy the militiamen at the gates did not seem to notice as he spat on the ground in disgust.

The Czech Ambassador sent us tickets for a concert at the Great Hall in honor of the thirtieth anniversary of the founding of the Czech Republic, which has recently ceased to be a republic in our sense of the word. The USSR Government Symphony Orchestra was led in a program of Czech music by Karel Ancher, a graceful Czech conductor.

A brown-haired clear-eyed Russian girl played Dvorak's violin concerto as magnificently as Oistrakh, the greatest Soviet violinist, could have played it. The orchestra was all in white ties. Some of them had turned down collars with their white ties and almost all of the shirts were dubiously clean. Of course that isn't important, but such artists deserve far better.

For two or three days there has been a white fog, so thick that for many hours nothing could be seen from our windows but a blind whiteness. Only wisps, however, trailed down the street level. The clouds hang low here in Moscow.

The Soviet Union has just used her veto in the Security Council of the United Nations to prevent a peaceful settlement of the Berlin crisis. Bourgeois institutions should be used, according to Lenin, not to solve problems, but to demonstrate continually that those problems are insoluble within anything but a communist framework.

Yesterday being Sunday, I went down to my office on the ground floor and made a sketch of one of the militiamen on duty at the Embassy entrance. The only place from which he could be seen without arousing his attention was from between the window hangings, and then only when he stood in one place. Even so he did not stand still long enough for me to get a very good likeness. The uniform turned out better than the face, which, although there is a definite resemblance, turned out to be a little more soulless than I hope he really is.

Today, by one of those coincidences which seem so well timed here, some Russian workmen appeared in order to frost over the windows of my office. They were told that I did not want my windows frosted, but they insisted that it was the Ambassador's orders. I sent them away, saying that I would wait.

Wherever it has appeared throughout the world the Soviets have protested the showing of *The Iron Curtain,* the movie of the Canadian spy trials which involved their Embassy at Ottawa. A special showing was held at Spasso House. It was a tense, exciting picture, particularly to one who has lived in Russia.

The Soviets say that it is all propaganda and lies, that their code attaché had made it all up to cover the fact that he had stolen money from their Embassy, and that nobody but a Fascist-dominated government would have even pretended to believe his story. I have never yet succeeded in identifying Fascism or lying propaganda in the words or acts of the Canadian or American governments, but I have seldom been aware of anything but distortion, dishonesty and deliberate misrepresentation in the continuing picture of America which the Soviet government gives to its citizens.

Outside, preparations are going on tonight for the November 7th Parade. The rays of two powerful searchlights lie long and level and very blue along the plaza in front of the Embassy. Swarming through the blueness is a swirling myriad of white snowflakes.

Revolution Day, November 7th, was cold. Ragged clouds lowered over Moscow and frequent little flurries of icy rain swept the streets. The parade was almost indistinguishable from the May Day parade, except that it wasn't quite so lavish nor nearly so long. The same floats, the same paper flowers, and the same rivers of marchers converged to stream through Red Square. The same clichés, such as "All Roads Lead to Communism" and "Proletarians of All Countries, Unite!" stared from placards carried by the crowds, but there were no anti-Western slogans or posters to be seen. Yet Timoshenko, the principal speaker, for the first time identified the Warmongers and Inciters of a New War as the English and the Americans. Having at last come to realize that nothing one does, short of becoming one of them, can affect the basic Soviet attitude toward foreigners, I left after a couple of hours, just before the parade ended.

Molotov's reception that night also seemed much less lavish than is customary at an official Russian reception. At the reception a rabbit-faced man displayed across his civilian jacket the unusual sight of five Medals of Lenin. Everyone said he was Kapitza, the atomic scientist. Even Sophronia, the Russian correspondent, swore by her head that he was Kapitza. He did not look like my idea of Kapitza, so Nell, who has few inhibitions, asked him. He wasn't.

Then a Russian general refused to autograph Nell's postage-stamp-sized little gold book for her, saying that he was illiterate. Someone said that he was Konev. Nell asked him, and he wasn't. What a place for misinformation. No wonder there are so many conflicting ideas of Russia.

Nell and I went again to the Lenin Museum. The space given to Stalin seems to have definitely increased since the last time we were there, for we noticed two or three exhibits featuring him that we could hardly have missed earlier. If this goes on, he will crowd Lenin out of his own museum. It is very noticeable that most Russians regard Lenin with veneration, believing that things would be different if he had lived. It is very doubtful if this belief would have been realized, for the Stalinist regime seems to be only the logical development of what was implicit in Leninism.

As we entered one of the rooms, there was no one in it but two teen-aged girls with shining pigtails wrapped around their heads. I heard one of them say, "What's in that case, Marthushka?"

"Oh," answered the other girl in a bored voice, "probably something to commemorate another earth-shaking remark!"

Then they were suddenly aware that someone else was in the room with them, and they went all wide-eyed and frightened. I could not help but laugh. Their relief was obvious, and they began to giggle, but the giggles were subdued and embarrassed.

3. THE FROSTY CAUCASUS

THE FOREIGN OFFICE HAS TOLD US that travel by automobile would be permitted to Zagorsk and to the home of Tchaikovsky and Tolstoy. Tula is out of bounds, so, although we may pass through it on the way to Yasnaya Polyana, we cannot pause there. To offset this sharp restriction on motor travel, it seems possible to go by train or Soviet airline to many places where we could not go before. But Kiev, Kazan, Samarkand and the Khorazm — all the places listed in my ignored request of many months ago — are still within the area where no foreigners are permitted. Even if it continues to be possible to go to all the places that are presumed to be open just because they have not been declared closed, which is doubtful, the fact remains that not since Perry opened up Japan has any supposedly civilized country put such restrictions on the movements of foreigners as Soviet Russia has now. And the capital cities of two members of the United Nations, Minsk and Kiev, are as forbidden as Lhasa.

It has been almost a year and a half since Nell has been away from Moscow, so Intourist was asked for reservations for the two of us to Tblisi, as Tiflis is now called in Sovietland. The train leaves at seven in the evening and Intourist was unable to inform us if they had space until three in the afternoon of the day of departure, so for a week Nell and I kept packed up and ready to go, making no other engagements. Two or three other foreign attachés, including Hulton, the new pink-cheeked acting British military attaché, were also trying to get to Tiflis.

At least four different theories for the delay were put forth in various embassies: one, that the brief honeymoon of liberalized travel by train was already over; two, that the Soviets were accumulating requests so as to herd as many foreigners as possible into a single group; three, that they need time either to conceal something of special interest to foreigners or to prepare it for their eyes; four, that there were too many big shots in the Soviet government who had first to be given reservations.

The first two theories proved wrong when Intourist telephoned one day to say that we should be at the Kursk Station for departure within an hour. Even though our things were packed, we barely made it. We hurried through the steaming crowds in the station, through the muddy tunnel under the tracks where we passed a group of Russians carrying a legless soldier in their arms, and breathlessly onto the train. Soon after we were snug in our compartment in the international wagon, the captain of the train came to ask if everything was satisfactory.

Although the engineer was much more careful than usual in stopping and starting the long train, I spent a restless night. Once I wakened and looked through the window. We were stopped in some town, but there were no lights in the windows of the houses, no street lights, no one to be seen. Only the weak light from a watery moon that was half-hidden by clouds glittered sadly on the snowy roofs.

We were wakened in the morning by music from the loud-speaker, a popular song of Shostakovich's about the mountains. That song was repeated again and again during the journey of over three days until its refrain of *"Gorý, gorý, gorý"* was indelibly impressed on our minds. The restaurant car appealed to me more than to Nell, who contented herself with coffee and sweetened cream from a tube like toothpaste which the Swiss Mrs. Schnyder had given us for the journey, while I ate eggs that were still sizzling in the skillet in which they were cooked.

The snow was gone, except for patches. The train rumbled on through a gray-white fog, through which could be seen glimpses of rolling treeless hills, sometimes covered with grass, sometimes plowed, and often thatched white cottages, banked with drab shocks of corn to keep out the winter cold. At Belgorod, on the edge of the Ukraine, an armored train was on a siding, its gay camouflage and the concentrated effect of its armor making it look like a child's toy. There have been many rumors about disorders in the Ukraine, and the Ukrainian newspapers have been full of brief, ambiguous notices of various officials who have died while carrying out their routine responsibilities. One could not help but wonder if the armored train had anything to do with those items.

The platforms at Kharkov were crowded with people, more

poorly dressed than even in Moscow, often literally in rags and patches. Yet it was a colorful crowd, with the rose, crimson, and paisley-colored kerchiefs of the women. Here and there was a deer-skin coat, or one made of some other spotted fur, or a pair of red or purple *valyenki*. Garments like ski pants kept the children warm, but the little girls never failed to wear in addition a short little skirt, their heavy braids of sunburned hair also indicating their sex. The many faces in the crowd were full of character, strong, bearded faces, cunning faces, faces lined with a thousand wrinkles. The women seemed bigger and stronger than those in Moscow, and they pushed and shoved as energetically as the men to get a place on the steps or between the cars of the packed suburban trains.

The fog grew thicker beyond Kharkov, with only an occasional hedge of brush to be seen flitting past in the gathering gloom. At one stop I was fascinated by a lone Ukrainian who was for some reason pacing back and forth in deep dejection, with his hands clasped behind his back. His cap was pulled down over his eyes, and his baggy trousers were stuffed into big boots. He looked exactly like my old friend Bruce Johnson — the same brown eyes, small brown mustache, flattish nose. But there is no one in this world more dapper and lighthearted than Bruce, and to see him here in such a masquerade, trying to seem downcast, opened up avenues for the imagination.

When the music from the loud-speaker wakened us the next morning, we were crossing the ice-fringed Don on a long tempo-rary bridge. Rostov, a forbidden city, was already behind us, its blue and green cathedral rising above its many hills. There is no word for plain "toast" in the vocabulary of the Russians, so my efforts to describe it and tell how it was made again resulted in only more scorched black bread. The sunburned waitress, with. skirts almost as short as those on the little girls in the Kharkov station, made up for it with an omelet and cocoa.

The fog had begun to thin, but it was still too misty to see the sweep of the Kuban steppe. Much grassland rose high and flat, with haystacks built square, the more distant ones looming through the mist like big barns. An occasional windmill stood like a Doré illustration. Pink brick houses, sometimes with an edging of white, and all of them thatched, had well-worn paths leading to nearby big open-air stoves. The scrubby trees were thick with the huge nests of some sort of bird. One patriotic station had "GLORY TO STALIN" marked out on the ground with pebbles in letters ten feet wide.

Between the restaurant car and our own wagon, two grubby men and a rather handsome but soiled young woman stood on the wind-blown platform. A woman train official reached the door at

the same time as we, and we heard the girl plead softly with her —"*Matushka!*" (Mother dear!). They had no tickets and apparently her plea was successful, for they were still standing there at lunch time.

Wherever the train stopped, the station platforms were full of people selling eggs, dill pickles, or roast chickens. A stately be-medaled Soviet general carried the chicken he had bought by one leg, held at arms length so it would not spot his red-striped blue trousers. We tried one, and found it juicier and sweeter than it looked.

By evening the mist was gone. Tumbleweeds rolled across the

empty steppe, and a long low line of ruby mountains glowed against the horizon in the rose and blue of the sunset.

We supplemented our chicken with beef strogonov in the restaurant car. Such cars in Russia have no partitions for kitchen or pantry, so that they give the effect of three or four tables set more or less at random in the midst of the supplies and cooking activities. The brown, short-skirted girl was expertly slicing a flat loaf of bread with a long, murderously thin knife when the train slowed down for a stop. Immediately everything was confusion. Cooks and waitresses rushed about putting away food and covering it up. They were just in time, for as the last box banged shut, a savage-looking crowd was storming the doors of the car. Although pushed and pulled, the girls managed to keep them near the doors. There was a brisk trade in cigarettes, but, in spite of many urgent requests, no bread or other food was sold. The bold eyes of the crowd darted here and there, but the girls stood their own. When the train pulled out and the last of the local customers was pushed off the platform, out came the food again and things went on as usual.

The following morning we were somewhere in the Caucasus Mountains. The rocky slopes went up at a steep angle into the clouds, with here and there traces of snow. Huge ferns grew close to the roadbed, covered white with thick frost. In a few minutes we were running along the edge of the Black Sea, rosy in the morning light, the coast of Colchis, that land at the world's end where Jason and the Argonauts went to find the Golden Fleece, the home of Medea and her dark sorceries. The water lay so flat and calm that it looked like an enchanted sea. As the day went on, the effect of enchantment was heightened, for never once was a boat or sail or moving thing to be seen on its shining waters. Anywhere else there would have been fishing boats, but these towns might just as well have been far inland, for there was no sign of a craft of any sort or any indication that the towns were on the water's edge, and the Black Sea remained as empty as though swept of all life by some spell. Once we saw an MVD guard with two police dogs on leash.

The air was fresh and springlike. In Sukhumi, tremendous cypress trees shadowed a little park through which wandered the ubiquitous sailors. The waiting room, where we bought some runty pears and tangerines, was decorated with geometric Asiatic patterns and smelled of saffron. When the train swung away from the sea towards the great humped plain that runs all the way to the Caspian Sea and separates the North and South Caucasus, we went for a long way through thickets of bracken and brush. One of the passengers said that this area was only now being cleared and settled, with the aid of prisoners in such numbers that he used the word which means both "darkness" and " countless thousands."

The houses were now tiled instead of thatched, often on stilts to keep them from floods. Festoons of drying tobacco hung on the houses, and the corn was put high in the trees, above the reach of the cattle. The Chinese-red balls of passion fruit hung thick on the bare branches of the trees. The fences were of woven wattle, and sometimes there would be buffalo skulls on the entrance posts. The slow-moving buffaloes themselves were huge, lowering, brutish-looking animals, with rubbery muzzles and flat horns that swept back from their low brows. One would have expected to see color-ful Eastern rugs in those houses, but the open doors showed nothing but rags and bareness, and the people along the roads were ragged and dirty.

At Mikha Tskhaka, near which began the only stretch of elec-trified railroad that I have seen in the Soviet Union, a yoked pair of big buffaloes crouched kneeling with their heads stretched out flat in the dust in front of them, where sat a woman veiled to the eyes in black, holding a long-legged lamb on her lap. At Samtredia a tall tribesman in a long *cherkeska* with cartridge pockets across his broad chest flirted through the open window with our short-skirted waitress. He was so effective that she cut a great gash in her thumb while slicing bread with her long sharp knife, and was very grateful when Nell bandaged it for her.

The faraway ridge of the Caucasus is very rich in minerals. Strabo, the Greek geographer of about the time of Christ, says that the legend of the Golden Fleece came from the pierced sheepskins with which the people of the Caucasus wash gold from the moun-tain streams. As we climbed up on the plateau, the countryside began to look more like that of southern California, tawny and dry. Above the acacia trees the blue sky was dappled with clouds, glowing with color from the sunset. The mountains ranged up and up, and through the bright clouds were occasional glimpses of higher and higher peaks, until to the south could be seen the far Turkish mountains beyond which lay Ararat and perhaps Noah's Ark. In the north, Elbrus, far higher than any peak in Europe, the highest peak this side of the Himalayas, caught the rosy light.

The train was late. The samovar for tea had been long since shut down, the other passengers were all busy getting their belongings together, and the lights of the train were too dim for reading. It was nearly midnight when the lights of Tblisi began to jewel the darkness. We were met by a brown-eyed Intourist girl with a clear oval face. Her name was Aksinya, and she seemed more fluttery and shy than those self-assured young ladies usually are. She led us to a special red plush entrance, where a rattly little car was waiting.

It was a wild drive to the hotel, the chauffeur feeling that he had the town to himself at that late hour. Although the streets were almost empty, once he had to put on the brakes and honk his horn loudly to keep from running over a little group of people in baggy Eastern trousers and turbans of saffron and maroon. "Who were they?" I asked.

"Poor people," Aksinya answered, "very poor people, who do the commonest sort of work."

"But what nationality?"

"They are Asiatic tribal people, Kurds. Others in Tblisi pay no attention to them because they are so poor." Aksinya was much too gentle to be snobbish. She was just stating a fact.

4. TIFLIS

NEVER HAVE I SEEN SERVANTS as grim as those in the Intourist hotel at Tiflis. Tight-lipped and stony-faced, they took us to our big high-ceilinged rooms, whose walls were covered with something that looked like dark red brocade. There was no hot water in the stark, high-ceilinged bathroom. A red satin chair and sofa were spattered with ominous dark stains. "I hope it isn't blood," said Nell, eying them with mistrust.

In the morning there was still no hot water, but about the bathroom hung a mephitic odor which Nell said hopefully might be due to sulphur water. This time the toast turned out to be fried. Nell, who will never eat eggs unless they are cooked hard, decided on some fried eggs. My Russian words must have overemphasized that point about frying them until they were solid, for she was presented with two hard-boiled ones. The Russian language, usually rich in verbs, is poor in those that have to do with cooking. I strongly suspect that the reputation for good cooking which the Russians once enjoyed was due largely to their French chefs.

On the street the air was exhilaratingly bracing, although the sun was warm. Rustavely Boulevard, named for the half-legendary poet who wrote the weretiger epic nearly eight hundred years ago in the golden days of the great Queen Tamara, is lined with evergreens, sycamores and palmettos. Stalin's homeland of Georgia is said to be especially favored by the Soviet regime, and the many new public buildings bore this out. Except for a greater proportion of men in khaki uniform, the people on the streets bore a strong resemblance to these in Moscow, with the same poor clothes and the same rundown shoes.

Aksinya had showed up with a sallow, sharp-featured guide. As we walked along the boulevard I told her that we had not wanted a guide, but this only brought her to a state of mildly agitated worry. "But you are supposed to have a guide!" she said. We left the boulevard and went into the old part of the town, through narrow stone streets past houses with carved enclosed balconies, complicated external staircases, and drab wash hanging from every window and in every court. Their walls were so old that the bricks were often eaten out and honeycombed, and, since the plaster or cement had also long since disappeared, it was difficult to see what kept them together.

It would have been charming if there had been any color in the wash, or in the hangings and bedding that were put out on the balconies to air, but everything was of the utilitarian dark blue of our overalls, and their bloomers, or gray and dingy. There was a soiled griminess that seemed out of place in the winelike air, and this, together with the seedy monotony of the passers-by, drained away any picturesqueness and made it seem as though the dead hand of Soviet mediocrity had been placed on everything.

We went to a seventh-century church whose roof was starry sky with clouds and cherubs overhead. It was part church and part museum, filled with looms and rugs and claptrap. A few things, such as some silver work and embroideries, were good, but, although the old hand looms were there as curiosities, the rugs were machinemade. "We much prefer the rugs made by machine," said the guide. "They are so much more uniform and regular, and they are economical of labor, too."

In the old town were streets with a few jewelers and a few hand-workers who made hats. We were given to understand that those artisans did not exactly work for themselves, but had some sort of co-operative arrangement with the state. Just now artels are being squeezed and discouraged in Moscow, but perhaps the Caucausus is different. My fancy was taken by a black caracul *kubanka,* a tall fur hat such as one sees worn often by Soviet army officers, but when the price came to the equivalent of a hundred and fifty dollars, my interest waned.

Finally we came to the swift river, the chalky green Kura, running deep and treacherous through Tiflis, with a drop of some sixty feet within the city limits alone. Its banks were sheer rock topped by old fortifications and a gloomy stone prison on the far cliff. A vivid realization of the great age of the city was given by the alternate layers of brick and stone that extended far down into the face of the cliff, foundations of old structures that had been swept away by time.

We went into a mosque near the river. It was empty and un-adorned, except for its symbolic hands and its honeycombed clusters of Arabic decoration. The guide was not interested in it, saying that it was doubtless kept as a sort of museum, but Aksinya said that the Kurds, the "poor people," were often to be seen in it.

The mountains of the Caucasus are remarkable for their many tribes and nations, the debris of history. Romans, Avars, Huns, Mongols, Khazars, and the Crusaders have swept across the Caucasus, and fragments and splinters of them have remained where the remoteness of the land and the inaccessibility of the snow-covered mountains made it easy for them to keep their individuality and their strange, anachronistic customs.

The Russian claim to the Caucasus dates from 1561, when Ivan the Terrible took a Kabardin princess as one of his many wives, presumably inheriting her lands. In the time of Catherine the Great the conquest of that rugged land was undertaken seriously, but it turned out to be a hundred years' war that lasted until the latter part of the nineteenth century. During that long era the Caucasus was the frontier of romance to the Russian. It was there that the young officer sought active service and glory. Since military service was expected from almost all, the Caucasus became embedded in the lives and writings of many of the Russian writers from Pushkin to Leo Tolstoy. Lermontov's *Hero of Our Time,* which is laid in the Caucasus, is still one of the great romantic novels of the world.

Some of the more remote mountain tribes were never conquered, even by the Soviets, and all of them continued to retain their individuality and their peculiarities. Several of the larger nations were made into autonomous republics after the Revolution. In Tiflis we had hoped to see some of the tribal people which have always given the Caucasus so much of its color.

"They seldom come to Tblisi," said Aksinya, "and never at this time of year. They are always *chuzhoy* (alien). The Chechen language, for instance, has more than fifty different consonants. Many of the Chechens helped the Germans during the war, and hundreds of thousands of them have been sent somewhere in Siberia."

I remembered the Janissaries, and the Circassian beauties who were famous for centuries in the harems of the East, and Shamil, the Hereward the Wake of the Chechens. Like Russia itself in

ancient times, the Caucasus has done more than its share in con-
tributing slaves to the world. But now it is not a matter of raids
and private deals, for government itself has entered the business
on a vast scale, moving entire populations for "re-education." How
much sad and tragic drama there must be in the deportation of such
numbers of a proud and fiery people!

"All these people look like Muscovites," I said. "Aren't there any
to be seen who are really different?"

"Only the very poor," replied Aksinya. "You can see them beating out the wash on the stones up this little stream."

The stream along which we walked was fed by hot springs, with
big, ramshackle public bath buildings along its banks. Except for
an occasional shepherd in a huge bushy hat of dyed sheepskin, the
outcast Kurdish women, ragged as they were in their sweeping
trousers and their faded yellow, blue and cerise turbans, were the
only bit of Eastern color that we saw in that ancient Asiatic city.

The sound of bells came from somewhere below the hotel, so
Nell and I went out and made our way through the narrow cobbled
streets of the old town, past vine-covered crumbling walls to the
seventh-century church. There the Archbishop of Georgia was cele-
brating mass. His fine, white-bearded face beneath his golden miter
was patriarchal and serene. As we stood in the heavy, incense-laden
air of the church and looked at the strong, rapt faces around us, it
seemed that the Soviet stamp of mediocrity was confined to the
things they wore and possessed rather than being printed on the
people themselves.

The plateau that connects the Black Sea with the Caspian is
broken by many groups of rugged hills. Tiflis is in the midst of
one such group, and in the middle of the city is a steep hill nearly
a thousand feet high, flattened into a small plateau on top which
runs back into the higher surrounding hills. Nell and I took the
funicular railway that runs up to the top. Halfway up, in a wooded
cleft in the hill, was a little conical church where are buried
Griboyedov, the great playwright of Pushkin's day, and Stalin's
mother.

A white pavilion whose purpose seemed vague perched on the

plateau. It would have been a dramatic place for dining or listening
to music in the evening, but it was just an empty pavilion. There
was a forest of evergreens covering the hills behind, and many
evergreens about the plateau. Also many MVD guards and sentries.
To the north there was a spectacular view. The city was spread
out below, its broad, tree-planted boulevards contrasting with the
narrow, tortuous lanes of the old town and the swift Kura swinging in a green arc through the far borders. Here and there little
columns of smoke rose straight up in the clean bright air. Beyond
the river were low tawny bare hills and beyond them the desert,
rising up and up until it was lost in a confusion of clouds in the
lower reaches of the mountains. And above the clouds, far, far
away, soared the mighty snow-covered ridge of the Caucasus, with
Kazbek standing out as a separate sharp-pointed peak. There Prome-
theus climbed to steal the first fire from heaven, and it is somewhere
in the snows of Kazbek that he still stands, chained to a rock, while
every day an eagle devours his liver, which renews itself every night.

5. A RARE BIRD

WE DID A BIT OF SHOPPING, and we went to the theater. Aksinya accompanied us to the opera, but she was as helpless as we in understanding it, for it was in Georgian, an heroic drama of the past, with settings and costumes that looked like leaves from an illuminated Persian manuscript. Nell came back wide-eyed from the rest room, saying that there was no mirror, no wash basin, no anything, only a hole in the floor.

We tried restaurant after restaurant where we ate shashlik and good tough Georgian bread from flat loaves, and where we enjoyed the red Tsinandel although we asked in vain for Kakhetinoye, which is said to be the best wine in Georgia. The Georgians, easily heated by their wine, lived up to their reputation of being a spirited race. Two or three times hotheaded quarrels sprang up at the tables in the restaurants, and once the mustachioed, popeyed manager hustled two of his proletarian customers out of the place by their coat collars. He was horrified that such scenes should take place in front of foreigners and apologized to us profusely.

Our British friends the Hultons showed up, and we went to their room for a spot of gin before dinner. "At least they have good coffee here," said Hulton. Since he was English, we did not go into the fact that, just as there are differences between Russians and Americans in the conception of freedom, there are differences between the English and Americans in the conception of coffee. The English should really have some other name for the "coffee" which they drink and like.

On the train from Moscow, the Hultons had found an Armenian girl in another wagon who spoke English. She had come with her family to Soviet Armenia from America, lured by tales of the promised land. They had brought with them an electric washing machine, refrigerator, vacuum cleaner, radio — all the gadgets of their nine-room American house. Even a piano. The combined wages of the family proved insufficient for a living in Soviet Russia, so, when they had used up their savings, they sold their household things one by one. They decided they could not make a go of it and must return to America, but they could not get an exit visa. A Soviet official promised to get them a visa in exchange for the last bit of money that they could scrape up, but he was either a scoundrel or was himself caught in the attempt. In any case, they still had no visa, so the girl had gone to Moscow to see what could be done, and was returning to tell her family that the effort had been a failure. She said that she had been prevented by the Soviets from going to the American Embassy in Moscow, although there was little that that Embassy could have done but protest. The tears rolled down her cheeks as she said that she did not know what would become of them, and she ended by hoping that some way would be found of getting a warning word to others in America who might be similarly lured.

The Hultons had, like us, taken the funicular up to the plateau. From there, they struck out in a brisk walk into the flanking hills. Soon they were aware that they were being followed, for out of the corner of their eyes they could see a man behind them, slipping stealthily from tree to tree. Thinking that there was a chance that their follower was a brigand, they turned and retraced their steps. The supposed brigand, suddenly caught without cover in a grassy spot near the road, unbuckled his trousers and squatted down in the grass in an awkward attempt to appear to be occupied with his daily routine. A few yards farther along the road, a squad of soldiers were so obviously startled to meet them that they decided that the soldiers also had been following them. And then, behind the soldiers, they came on a little group of the MVD, following the soldiers. Hulton stopped and told the MVD that they should keep their eye out for a suspicious-looking character who had been following the two of them, and described his actions, saying that he might possibly be a brigand. An MVD officer gave the whole ridiculous show away by replying, "Oh no, he is not a brigand. He is an honest man!" He used the word *chestny,* which has overtones of respectability in addition to common honesty.

"Then why was he acting so queerly?" asked Hulton.

"He was looking for a rare bird!"

Mtskhet, pronounced exactly as it is spelled, is twenty or thirty kilometers from Tiflis. There, where the famous Aragvi drops from the high mountains to join the Kura, the Georgian Military Highway takes off to cross the high Daryal Pass. Kazbek has looked down on the Daryal Pass to see many a marauding army directing its invasion sometimes to the south and sometimes to the north. Mtskhet was long the capital of Georgia, until, at the end of the fifth century, the government was moved to Tiflis.

With the Hultons and Aksinya we went to Mtskhet in two Intourist automobiles. On the way we passed oxcarts that were painted with blue and yellow flowers on a bright red ground. Over the necks of the oxen arched huge, brightly painted oxbows. Mtskhet is only a village now, but there is an imposing cathedral there that stands in a broad, low-walled yard of willow-green grass, the Church of the Twelve Apostles and the Living Tree. The present tall church was built of brick in the early part of the fifteenth century, replacing one that was razed by Tamerlane when he built his piles of skulls from end to end of Georgia. The original church was built where stood a cedar tree, beneath which was buried the robe of Christ, brought from Golgotha by a Mtskhet Jew of that time. On the outside of the medieval church that is still standing is the sculptured hand of the architect, with an inscription asking God's forgiveness for his sins, if any. Neither Aksinya nor the Hultons' guide seemed to have a clear idea of why the hand appeared to be severed.

The interior was lighter than most old churches, for the walls had been whitewashed. In places beneath the whitewash could be seen old frescoes, whose faces had the same large dark eyes and gave the same soft effect of weakness as those one sees at Pompeii. The Bagration family, to which Queen Tamara belonged and which has many famous names in Russia even outside the Caucasus, ruled Georgia for a thousand years, so there were many tombs of Bagrations in the cathedral. Most of the inscriptions were in the beautiful, flowing Georgian script, so that the marble slabs looked as though they were covered with graceful flowers.

Rags are a commonplace in Soviet Russia. But it was a shock to see a priest with his robe as patched and tattered as that of the priest who stood sadly against a colored column for some reason clutching a daggerlike knife. There is another church in Mtskhet, much smaller, darker, and colder than the cathedral. It had good rugs on its stone floors, and its black marble tombs dated from the fourth century.

Not far from the churches is a still more ancient burial place, discovered when the Georgian Highway was put through in 1871. The lower levels of this graveyard show evidences that it was used in the beginning of the iron age, a thousand years before Christ, and in the upper levels have been found coins of the Roman Emperor Augustus. The oldest burials were in huge pottery jars, some of them still lying about.

In the Tiflis Museum is one of the huge jars from Mtskhet with a human skeleton neatly curled up inside. Although it was very cold in the museum, being out of the warming sun, the museum was an interesting place, less so because of the guns and swords and trophies of the many Russian wars than because of the amount of archeological and anthropological material. Many ancient phallic bronzes were there, and there was a chariot that dated from 2000 B.C. Aksinya had said that some of the remote tribal nations still come out occasionally from their stone castles among the cliffs and peaks wearing chain mail and carrying battleaxes.

The Svaneti live in such inaccessible places that the Soviet regime is said not to have bothered about trying to communize them. Although they are Christians, they believe also in other gods — gods of the hunt and of game, and in angels of the woods. When one of them goes to hunt, he goes as on a sacred errand alone, separately from the others, in the early morning, after sacrificing to the Protector of Wild Beasts, and he returns only in the darkness. They eat from round wooden plates and drink from the horns of cattle. Marriage contracts are made in early childhood, and if, on reaching maturity, one or the other does not wish to complete the marriage, the refusal is avenged in blood.

The tsarist priest Gulbian, who was an authority on the Svaneti, says that they are much given to unchastity, incest, oath-breaking, extortion and hypocrisy. They were known to the ancient Greeks, when they must have stood on a higher level of culture, for among their crags and glaciers are numerous ruins of shrines, castles and towers that contain fragments of wonderful frescoes. The Tiflis

Museum has many of their dishes, horns and weapons, animal masks that they use in their sacrifices, and models of their dwelling places.

The day before we left Tiflis, Nell and I started in search of the Botanical Gardens. When we came to the hot springs where the outcast Kurdish women beat their wash, I stopped a strong, high-cheekboned middle-aged woman who was walking past, and asked her the way. While she was telling me, two or three MVD officers came past. One of them called to her from across the narrow street, "It's forbidden to talk with a foreigner!"

The woman turned on him and shouted back savagely, "You fool! Don't try to tell me what to do!" Then she said to me, "I'll show you the way. It's easier than telling you."

"But what about the police?" I asked. They had not stopped, but were looking back over their shoulders.

She shrugged her shoulders and turned down the corners of her mouth. "*Svoloch!*" was all she said, which is a most impolite word for a no-goodnik. In a few short blocks we learned that she was a doctor who served in one of the hospitals. Her Russian father, who was doubtless the source of this characteristic willingness to tell all, had married a Georgian mother. There was the usual conversation about how long we had been in the city and how long we were going to stay. When she asked how we liked Tiflis, we told her that it would probably have been much more interesting if we were not always singled out as foreigners.

"It is a fine city," she said. "I am sorry that you are going so early in the morning. Promise me that when you come back to Tiflis, you will come to stay with me. Then you can forget that you are not Russian. I would like so much to have you do that, and I will show you many things that you would never see otherwise."

When our warmhearted woman doctor left us, we climbed up a long, steep hill to the gardens we were seeking. Georgia is said to be the land of the Amazons of the old Greek tales, in proof whereof certain vestiges of matriarchy are cited, together with the curious fact that the word *mama* means father in Georgian, and *deda* means mother. Our stouthearted friend with the Georgian mother was further evidence to bolster up that belief.

Like most Russian parks, the Botanical Gardens were a little unkempt and bedraggled, but they were bright with small chrysanthemums and green with hardy palms and many varieties of strange trees. Over them, on a ridge that rose still higher, loomed an enormous, castlelike fortification. The warm stream from which Tiflis gets its name, which means "hot," smoked and steamed far below at the bottom of the gulch. On the other side of the black, precipitous rocks was a Mohammedan graveyard with the neglected, abandoned look that so many Eastern cemeteries have.

6. THANKSGIVING DAY

IT WAS THANKSGIVING MORNING, still dark and very cold when Aksinya came to take us to the airport, thoughtfully bringing with her from her home a kettleful of hot water for us. We rattled and bumped in the darkness over an unbelievably bad road, and the sun was just turning a tumbled mass of storm clouds to liquid gold when we took off for home. There was little to be seen from the air, for there were storm clouds all around, with worse ahead. The Black Sea was completely hidden in clouds and rain, so it was a relief when we landed on the bare, muddy field at Sukhumi.

It was a long time before we were permitted to leave the plane, and when we were, I followed two or three of the Russian passengers through the mud to the little boothlike buffet on the edge of the field. One was a tall blond artillery captain who would have been handsome if it had not been for a squinched-up quality to his face. We all had a round of vodka. The artillery captain, who said he was going home to Tambov on leave, insisted on paying for it. The bill for the next round was footed by a little man who bore a startling resemblance to Lenin — the same domed, half-bald head, the same Tatar eyes with the Mephistophelean eyebrows, the same neat little mustache and beard. He must have been aware of the resemblance and tried to cultivate it. He came from Odessa and was on his way to Moscow before returning to the Ukraine. I tried to pay for the next round, but was forestalled by a genuinely handsome dark young Georgian officer in a high astrakhan cap. It was at last my rightful turn, but when I handed the attendant some rubles on ordering, he refused to take them, for the Lenin-like Ukrainian had managed in some way to get there ahead of me. A laugh went up from them all, and before we had finished that round someone put his head in the door to say that it was time to get aboard the plane again. We agreed to have another drink in Kharkov, and my companions promised me faithfully that they would then be my guests.

On the plane, half of the passengers were gathered around Nell, laughing and talking animatedly. The first solid step in friendship with a Russian is when he shows you snapshots of his family. Nell had several such family pictures in her hands, and was listening to the details of how old the children were.

We all took our seats for the take-off, but nothing happened. Then someone in the front of the plane told a long story, followed by someone else. Everyone strained their ears to listen, but the speakers were too far away for me to get their points. The stories seemed to be either personal experiences or parables. The little Ukrainian told a complicated one which ended in a question: "Who is the greater sinner, you or the thief?" Nearly everyone nodded their heads approvingly when someone said "The thief," but one old man said, "No!" That started an earnest argument which went on until at last the plane's engines were started and we took off.

Three or four of the passengers came back to present Nell and me with passion fruit, or with tangerines or mandarin oranges. Having seen the prices of fruit in the markets in Tiflis, we were touched by their generosity as well as their genuine simplicity and friendliness. Most of the time the ground was out of sight. The weather grew steadily darker and more threatening, until we were flying in occasional flurries of snow. The Ukrainian hauled out a suitcase, fished around in it for a while, and then came beaming back to show us a copy of *Amerika*. Although it was the latest number, only a week or ten days old, it was soiled and dog-eared as though it had been through fifty hands. Perhaps it had.

The copilot came through to tell us that the weather was so bad towards Kharkov that we were landing at Rostov-on-the-Don, where we would spend the night. So there we landed, in bitter cold and deep snow.

We stood around in the wide hall of the barracks to which we were all taken. Through the doors at the end of the hall could be seen the iron beds of a dormitory. Nell looked around, then asked in Russian, "Where do we sleep?"

The question was addressed to no one in particular, but our Lenin raised a general laugh with his reply, "All together!" The laugh was tinged with embarrassed surprise at his boldness.

Just then an orderly came up and took Nell and me to what must have been a room for visiting general officers Two sagging iron beds, a large round oak table and three or four chairs stood starkly about. We were still getting unpacked when there was a knock at the door. It was Lenin, his little pointed beard quivering with excitement at the luxury of our quarters, for the rest of them were indeed sleeping "all together" in the big dormitory. While Nell freshened up, he and I went out through the blowing snow to the buffet to let me get the drink that had been promised at Sukhumi.

But the buffet was stuffy and crowded, with no chairs, and so tiny that if our two friends showed up there would not be room for them.

"I have a better idea," I said. "Today is Thanksgiving Day, which is a great *prazdnik* in America, when everyone eats all they can hold. You saw our room, where there is a big table and chairs for all four of us. Let me get vodka and some food to take with us, and you can round up the others so we can all sit in peace and eat and drink to our Thanksgiving *prazdnik*."

He agreed enthusiastically, and we went out into the snowy darkness and on to the barracks with our arms full of vodka bottles, sausages, cheese, caviar, bread — everything we could see that looked good. As we carried our bundles into Nell's and my room, the tall Tambov artillery officer was coming down the hall.

"There comes one we want, right now," I said. "The two of you round up the Georgian with the *kubanka* while we are opening the vodka."

We opened the packages and pulled a couple of corks. Nell sliced some bread and laid out heaps of caviar and sausage. There were even glasses in the packages. When everything was ready, we sat down and waited. It was a long wait. Everything was strangely quiet outside, except for the regular pacing of footsteps in the hall. Already we knew what had happened. I went to the door and looked out. There was no one in sight but a big, hard-looking MVD major, pacing up and down outside our door. I shut the door, and Nell and I had a large vodka to the Thanksgiving *prazdnik*.

Later in the evening I went out into the hall adjoining the dormitory. The MVD major was sitting with his feet on a chair, reading a newspaper. The artillery officer and the handsome Georgian were seated at a table playing dominoes. I stood and watched their game for a few moments. Neither of them looked up. There was not a word, no sign of recognition, only the sound of the dominoes as they slapped them hard on the table.

It was so cold that night that we slept in all our clothes, on the most uncomfortable beds we had experienced for many a day. In the morning, while waiting to go on board the plane with our party food under our arms, not one of all the passengers who had been so kind spoke to Nell or me, or seemed even aware of us. But as soon as we were in the air they were twittering around us, being friendly, pressing more little oranges on us and telling us more about their families.

At Kharkov it was even colder, and a piercing wind blew the dry snow across the field in clouds. There two thinly clad passengers were put off, although they were Moscow-bound. It seemed rather heartless to leave them in a strange city, particularly when they were dropped in order to permit two big bags of rice to be brought on board. One wondered what Party banquet that high-priority rice was for.

I asked the Tambov artillery captain point blank what had happened the night before in Rostov and got nothing but evasions.

"Then where is the little Ukrainian who looks so much like Lenin?" I insisted.

"Oh, he caught an earlier freight plane that was going through to Moscow."

I had heard the pilot talking about the weather, and I knew that ours was the first plane out of Rostov for Moscow that day.

7. THE INDISPENSABLE BOOK

THE ARMY-NAVY FOOTBALL GAME has come and gone. At Spasso House arrangements were made to listen in on a special rebroadcast of the game from Berlin. We got enough of it to know that it ended in a 21–21 tie. Since the Navy was enough of an underdog for me to get odds for once, I came away from Spasso with a handful of General O'Daniel's rubles. Mike O'Daniel is a fine, straight-thinking, straight-talking officer, with a world of common sense. Even the Polish general told me that he was very fond of him, because Mike is a soldier's soldier. More than once our telephone has rung with a call from the O'Daniels: "Will you please tell our maid to go home? There is nothing for her to do, but we can't make her understand!"

Last night Nell and I went to the small, low-ceilinged, uncomfortable Gypsy Theater to see *Grushenka.* It is based on Leskov's *The Enchanted Stranger,* a remarkable book, full of tales within tales which show an adventurous, wandering side of Russian life which is seldom encountered in literature. The play was well acted, but it would take more than the resources of the Gypsy Theater to put across the charm of the book.

Although gypsies have many similarities throughout the world, there is a special tradition that attaches to them in Russia. Russians have a love for lavishness and display, for living in the grand, extravagant manner; for them, perhaps because of the contrast with the severity of their climate, it is very forgivable to bring one's family to beggary through prodigal entertaining and a gay life. In tsarist times the peak of revelry was to bring in the gypsies, who though remaining strangely inscrutable and apart became a symbol of spendthrift Bohemianism.

Although Russia is far from being a land of plenty, lavishness is still a Russian trait. The *pir,* or feast that lasted for two or three days, has not yet entirely disappeared, and the Russian table, on special traditional occasions, is extraordinarily generous, even though there may be little to eat between times. Once Serayev said, when complimented on the food at a Soviet party, "Yes, we Russians have rich banquets" — and the choice of the word "rich" is noteworthy. This can also be seen in their embassies abroad. Such embassy lavishness may be incompatible with the dictatorship of the proleteriat, but it seems to be part of the semi-Asiatic Russian nature.

Yesterday the telephone rang in my office. It was the scholarly, aristocratic little old man whom I had come to know at Peterhof. He was in Moscow for a day or so on business, and he would like very much to renew our acquaintance. He agreed that perhaps it would not be well for him to come to the Embassy, but he was staying at the Grand Hotel and would welcome my coming to his room for the afternoon.

After hanging up, I started to worry. The last thing in the world that I wanted to do was to get this gentle old man, one of the very few Russians who I felt was really a friend, into trouble, yet it seemed that this was what would happen, just as night follows the day. It is only since being in Russia that it has become clear to me that what passes for Soviet justice is not based on what people have done, but what they might do. Since from this point of view most of the damage had probably already been done by his telephone call, which was undoubtedly monitored by his hotel, I went to see him, taking a couple of bottles of wine and some tobacco.

He was the same warm, charming gentleman that I remembered, a little older and a little frailer, perhaps, but eager to talk about Russian intellectual life and the outside world. Time after time, when his voice would rise emphatically to make a point, it was necessary for me to make gestures which said that the walls had ears. Some of the hotel rooms even have concealed cameras. Nevertheless, it was an interesting afternoon, and when he accompanied me to the door of his room, he beamed and said, "This shows that it is entirely possible for us to see each other."

"You are not yet out of Moscow," I answered rather grimly. "Tomorrow, just before your train leaves, call me from a pay telephone in the station, and perhaps I will believe you. Don't call my office, for I may not be in, and it would not be wise to leave messages. Nell will be in my apartment, and when she answers the telephone, just say *'Vcyaw v poryadkye!'* (everything's all right). She will be expecting such a call."

Today, when I came home from the office for lunch, all the Russian servants from the nearby apartments were gathered around our door, chatting excitedly. "Gospodin Admiral," said one of them, "some Russian has just called on the telephone. He said that he was a friend of yours, and to tell you that everything was all right. What do you suppose he meant by that?"

Naïveté and a clear conscience must have brought to destruction vastly more Russians than anything they themselves ever did. Or maybe — just maybe — my friend was forced to seem free.

The Soviet press is continually telling its readers to go to the *Short Course in the Party History* in order to find the answers to problems which may be puzzling them, and several times Russians have given me the same advice in answer to my questions. At last I have gotten around to reading it. Few foreigners seem familiar with it, but that is not surprising, for it was published in 1939, just before the Germans went into Poland, and the war overshadowed everything else for years. It has supplied something which for me was lacking in all that was said about the Soviet regime, and gives a key for understanding that seems even more important than Hitler's *Mein Kampf* was in its way.

The *Short Course* is not the party line, but an orientation course in communism, an authentic education in how to figure out the party line for one's self. The party line changes continually, but this book, which is required reading for all Russians whether or not they are party members, has not been changed an iota since its publication. It is not the dogma that I had expected, growing out of the text of Lenin and Stalin, but a guide to practical action in accordance with a basic philosophy of crude materialism. It reaffirms what is widely known, that Bolshevism differs from all forms of socialism in that it holds that the common man throughout the world can never permanently improve his lot through any processes of compromise or evolution, but can do so only by seizing and holding power by force. Pseudoscientific arguments are set forth to prove this thesis, and, although they leave me cold, they are so full of ambiguities and semantic thorns that they must seem convincing to many.

What impresses me more than anything else about the *Short Course* is the light that it sheds on the international and domestic actions of the Soviet regime, which is, of course, the Bolshevik Party. Under its philosophy, power becomes a built-in prerequisite to everything else, and the regime can never be expected to lessen its power for any consideration, unless it is literally forced to do so. The moral questions that seem to us to be involved in the terrible persecutions of the peasants, and all interests which are not completely and actively identified with the regime and its power, simply do not arise within that philosophy.

The same pseudoscientific arguments are used to prove, not only that everything but what the regime embraces is an opponent, but that no genuine compromises are possible and that all differences should be made sharper, all wounds rubbed with salt. It has always been difficult for foreigners to understand just why, in Russia's own self-interest, foreigners were not handled in a way that would at least permit sympathy rather than insure irritation. The *Short Course* gives a satisfying answer. In effect it says that there is no such thing as friendship — there is only the party, which is the Soviet government, and its enemies, and that enmity should always be stimulated and increased except when important tactical reasons make advisable a temporary course to the contrary. It also becomes clear that the whole chronic situation of propaganda and strain is not simply due to the fact that the Soviets view things from an angle that happens to differ from ours, but that it necessarily involves deliberate deception and troublemaking — salt-rubbing.

It is obvious that not everyone would be conscious of the fact that such things are either explicitly or implicitly in the *Short Course,* but it is difficult to see how they can be escaped by anyone who has seen their day-to-day manifestations and who has independent standards of comparison. Unless and until the Bolshevik Party changes its basic philosophy, it is a grim outlook for international relations. The touchstone by which it will be possible to tell whether or not the Party ever does change will be the rewriting of the *Short Course* and the publication, both within and without Russia, of new editions which, like the present book, run into tens of millions of copies.

Tolstoy's *Anna Karenina,* which we saw tonight at MXAT, is impressive theater, with Elanskaya as a completely satisfying Anna. Scene after scene was staged with that incomparable skill which belongs only to MXAT. There were brilliant satires of tsarist social life as seen at the races, and at the opera, where the stage was empty except for a couple of overhanging boxes like those at the Bolshoy. Yet through it all was a deep sympathy which seems to me more and more to be ingrained in the Russian people. It was not a sympathy for outmoded social classes — MXAT could never get away with that, and there is no reason to believe that it would want to — but a feeling for life and its problems. After reading the *Short Course,* it seems entirely possible that some day even this much feeling can no longer be evidenced in Russia. The big scene in this production was when Anna throws herself under the train in the bleak railway station. The huge oncoming engine grew larger and larger until the audience cowered in their seats before its onrush.

One notes how much of the great Russian literature is so Victorian in its attitude toward marriage and the family. Society is shown as having even more power than in Victorian England, with resultant torments of conscience suitable to the Russian temperament. Now all children here in Russia today must read those things at some time in their lives — Tolstoy, Chekhov, Turgenev (Dostoevsky is rapidly going under the ban) — and it would be interesting to know if they regard them merely as survivals of another age, or as something valid in themselves. I mentioned this to a fairly young Russian the other day, and he said that unquestionably the coming generation would be far different from his own, which, strangely enough, he called a generation of freedom. Perhaps he foresaw worse in the future.

A dispatch has come calling me to a conference in Washington in early January. It is strange now to think of how eager I was to get back to Russia on my first trip to Stockholm, for another breather will now be very welcome. It seems to me that those foreigners who become the best adjusted to Moscow are those who continue in a state of passive puzzlement about the place, without ever arriving at any positive ideas of their own.

8. EMBARRASSMENTS

THIS YEAR WASHINGTON HAS ANNOUNCED that every naval officer over a certain age must have an electrocardiogram incident to his regular annual physical examination. Dr. Vaughn has no electrocardiographic equipment, so, although there would be no difficulty in getting the requirement waived or postponed under the circumstances, he suggested that it would be interesting to have the Russian Polyclinic make a cardiogram for me.

We went to the Polyclinic, and found it clean and neat. An elderly woman doctor strapped some unusually heavy and cumbersome equipment on me, and said that we could have the results of the test if we cared to wait a few minutes. When she returned, she said that she wanted to talk with Dr. Vaughn alone. I had been doing what interpreting was necessary and there was no one else available who could speak both English and Russian, but she now steadfastly refused to talk with Vaughn through me. Although suspecting what was up, I felt fine and was more amused than anything else at the impasse, but Dr. Vaughn seemed quite disturbed. He made arrangements to get the completed cardiographic record.

Today he brought me the record, together with a translation of its interpretation. It is no longer amusing. The report on my annual physical examination now recommends hospitalization in Washington to make a survey of my heart. Vaughn says that if the results bear out the Russian findings they will retire me immediately from active duty, on the spot. Apparently the Russians were surprised that I was still alive. He told me the usual things that are told to sufferers from heart trouble — that if I take things slow and easy I might live for a long time, but under no circumstances to exert myself. That prescription appeals to my natural inclinations, but the elevator is broken down at the moment, so it won't always be easy. Vaughn has also broken the news to Nell not to expect me to return to Russia.

Everyone probably wonders what his own reactions would be to news of this sort. It is surprising to find that mine consist largely of relief that if something is really seriously wrong with me I should feel no worse than I do. For one thing, no change in my immediate plans is involved, for I am about to leave for Washington in any case.

It is Christmas, and very cold. It is impossible to see through the windows without first melting holes in the Jack Frost patterns, which are richer and more fernlike than ever before. There has been a heavy schedule of parties, but everyone has been wonderfully thoughtful and considerate of me, insisting that I sit down, and waiting on me hand and foot. My trouble, if any, has its compensations.

Nell's punch bowl, which is one of the few in Moscow, has been working overtime. Whenever she needs it, it takes plenty of advance notice for it to appear, for the servants pass it from place to place. The other day she recognized it at a Finnish party.

The Christmas party for the Russian children at Granatny did not seem to me up to last year's party at Spiro, in spite of the beautiful tree, the gifts, and the dancing and singing, but perhaps that was only due to my mood. A Russian named Prokofiev, some sort of kinsman of the composer, played the piano. It was never quite clear to me how he fitted in with the rest of our Russian help, but he added greatly to the party. The thought kept coming up in my mind that perhaps this was the last Christmas that I would ever see.

Eddy Gilmore has returned from a trip to Berlin. He said that when he first brought his typewriter and his automobile to Russia they were entered in his passport. This time the customs officials held him up for a long time trying to decide what to do because he did not have those two items with him as listed on his passport. He was traveling by air.

For days the loud-speakers have been blaring in Manezhny Place and the colored lights have been playing on the open-air Christmas trees. Pushkin Square is not decorated at all this year, possibly due to one of the spasmodic economy drives. There are only a few people in the streets, and Moscow seems rather dull for the Russians. It has been bitter cold, with a sift of dry snow. Last night we drove to Sokolniki, and found that, except for the fountain of lights on a tree in the square, it was the same dull New Year there. When I got out of the car to take a closer look at the tree, the crackling cold burned and seemed to grab me by the throat.

The Sokolniki area has an evil reputation, as do two or three other areas in Moscow and its suburbs. No woman will go there alone after dark. Zoya, who lives in Sokolniki, is always met at the subway. If it is too late for the Metro to be running, she stays with us.

New Year's Day is just another working day in England. Envious of American plans for that day, and desiring to attend many of the parties, several Britishers talked Ogilivie-Forbes, their blond, soft-spoken air attaché, into working on their Ambassador. Ogilivie-Forbes thought that it might be appealing to remind Sir Maurice that New Year's is also Hogmanay and a holiday in Scotland. "Sirrrr," said the Ambassador, "as far as I am aware, the Scots have no embassies and no foreign office, so ye'll just have to abide by the rules."

Krasny Krest was burglarized and robbed yesterday. That was the Red Cross house during the war, which is still used by the Embassy, and where Ireland, Risk and Stefan live. We were there for cocktails the other day and enjoyed sitting in front of one of the few fireplaces in Moscow. Of course, no crime of any sort is ever reported in the Soviet press. The formidable reputation of the Russian police seems to be founded on their ability to terrify an innocent population rather than malefactors.

Two or three of our newspapermen came to ask if I could make any sense out of the crackdown on the quantum theory that has suddenly hit the front pages of the Soviet press. The featured item of news in today's newspapers was a long article on the subject by Vavilov, the President of the Academy of Sciences. The *Short Course in the History of the Communist Party* gives the clue to understanding. According to the communist philosophy, the physical world is all that exists, consciousness being at best nothing but the passive reflection of that external world. Since the quantum theory accepts the existence of a random factor in the physical world which can be dealt with only statistically, acceptance of the quantum theory as anything other than a convenient temporary tool tends to destroy the communist thesis that everything is knowable and to wash away the logical and scientific foundations on which their whole ideological doctrine, the necessary justification of their power to even their own peoples, is built.

The Soviet regime does not persecute academic freedom of thought capriciously, just for the sake of persecution, but only in cases where viewpoints can undermine the power of the regime or interfere with its operations. If the Western world would study the scientific and other intellectual controversies that rock the Soviet Union, with a view to identifying the threats to the regime that are involved, and would then throw its own intellectual weight into those controversies, it might go far in loosening the hold which communism has on millions of minds.

For some time the Navy pool of chauffeurs has included a good-looking ex-soldier named Osip. Osip, having been in the Soviet army that liberated Austria, had a broad chest covered with medals — and a wife who worked in a Moscow factory. After having seen how well the poor Austrians lived under the heel of capitalism, he made no bones about wondering why the Soviet regime could not do more for the Russian people. The naval officers at Granatny told him often that he should keep such speculations to himself.

"Oh, no," Osip would say, "you do not understand that Russia is really a free country. We all have the right to ask questions and criticize. Not only that, but I am a soldier who has been wounded in defense of the fatherland, so I am even freer than others to speak."

Then Osip's wife lost her job. "There are stories going round," Osip said, "that that was because I work for the Americans, but that is not true, for I have permission to work for you. There has just been a stupid mistake. If I can get to the right people, it will be remedied." Meanwhile, in spite of repeated warnings, he continued to point out ways in which the lot of the Russians could easily be raised more nearly to the bourgeois level he had seen in Austria.

Now Burobin has told us that Osip's certificate permitting him to work for us has been withdrawn. This patriotic well-meaning young Russian and his wife have been absorbed back into the countless masses of Russians and no one knows what will happen to them. The problem of the soldier who has seen the outside world is a serious one to the Bolshevik regime, for it knows that similar circumstances during the Napoleonic Wars had much to do with the Dekabrist revolt. Yet the problem seems to be well in hand.

For five days we got up before dawn every morning to wait at the Vnukovo Airport in weather far below zero. On the fifth day I left for America in the brown and rose sunrise of midmorning. I remember that my low-grade temperature had returned, and I also remember that one morning, although the plane was canceled, a note of reprimand had been put on my ticket because we were a few minutes late in arriving at the field.

The sun was setting when we landed at Kaliningrad, which was once Königsberg in East Prussia. We had a load of high-ranking Soviet officers and their families, bound for Berlin. One of them was a very beautiful girl child with big violet eyes and pigtails. The visibility was unlimited, so we were told to stay on the plane, as we would go on to Berlin after refueling. Soon we were told that the flight had been called off. No sooner were we off the plane than we were herded back on again, the pilot saying there had been a mistake. It was dark when he came back from the operations room, slapping his fleece-lined gloves in frustrated disgust, to tell us that "some blockhead" would not let us continue that night.

The barracks were empty and dark, for whoever ran them had gone into town. As we stamped our feet and thrashed our arms to keep warm, the Russian officers were outspoken in their remarks about the confusion, not because of their own inconvenience, but because of the women and children. The little violet-eyed beauty had begun to cry with the cold when one by one the help began to show up, the lights came on, and we were at last taken care of.

In my room was a Russian charcoal-fired stove against which my broken-springed bed was moved for warmth. The Russian language has a remarkably varied group of words to describe what happens when stoves are zealously fired by unskilled hands, and I learned the reason for this rich vocabulary, for I woke in the morning with a splitting headache.

During breakfast in my room, a diminutive Russian soldier with an enormous sweeping red mustache knocked at the door and clicked his heels to announce that a taxi was waiting to take me to the plane. The taxi turned out to be an open truck, and although the plane was only a few yards away my soldier insisted that I ride in it. His mustaches waggled violently as he apologized for the fact that the taxi had no seats — some *sukin syn* (son of a bitch) had stolen the chairs that were ordinarily provided. So I stood up in the truck and rode in state to the plane.

The skyscraper tower of the spotless white naval hospital at Bethesda looks far out over the sweet, familiar fields of Maryland. I was petted and spoiled by all my friends, who seemed to think I had been through some real hardships. Freddie Lang, who had himself done a tour of duty in Moscow during the war, took wonderful care of my case. Test after test not only showed nothing wrong with my heart and failed to duplicate the tracings of the Russian cardiogram, but the Russian equipment itself seemed to be unfamiliar to the American experts. They held the prints from Moscow sidewise and upside down trying to decipher them, as one who is unfamiliar with the Cyrillic letters might hold a sample of Russian handwriting. The traces of fever made my pleasant stay at Bethesda unusually long, but, after exhaustive study and experiment, Freddie decided that the temperature could only be due to the fact that, like Mrs. Gummage, I was more sensitive than others. Whereupon the fever went away, and I started on the long journey back to Moscow.

The train from Berlin carried much the same passengers as usual, the same strong-faced Russian officers, the same plump high-breasted wives, the same well-behaved children bundled up like little rabbits. One mother, with enormous braids of corn-colored hair coiled above her pretty face, half terrified and half delighted her big-eyed children by threatening to throw their dolls off the train because the dolls didn't have tickets. But it seemed to me that, even in the short time I had been away, there had been a noticeable tightening up in the handling of foreigners. For one thing, the loud-speaker which used to put forth only music and cultural entertainment now spewed venom against America. Although the trains were crowded, there was no one to share my compartment.

In the station at Warsaw a bristling little officer with a peaked, ratlike nose and a medal which showed him to be a Hero of the Soviet Union came up to me and insisted that America wanted war. Several other passengers intervened to stop the resulting argument, telling him that it was *niprilichno* (undecorous) and "not good." Later the Hero came into my compartment to continue his verbal attacks, only to be again stopped by others. He decided that I was "a very backward person," too far gone to be worth saving.

During the long wait at the Russian border a green-capped officer of the frontier guards came in and sat down. He asked me how old I was, and then said that his father was exactly the same age and looked very like me. I told him of my own Stevie, and he was very much struck with the fact that he and Stevie were of the same age. He recommended that I read Aleksei Tolstoy's *Journey Through Torment,* saying that there were two sides to the civil wars that followed the October Revolution.

At Brest-Litovsk the station was, as usual, packed with troops. In the restaurant there, a clean-looking wholesome young soldier asked me diffidently if he might sit down at my table. He was followed by two others, very worn-looking and tired, still boys. They asked me what I was, and when I told them, their eyes lighted up with interest in America. In a moment a man in civilian clothes came up and whispered to the two weary ones. Without a word, they got up and went away.

"We are only little people," the remaining boy said to me. "I'm surprised that they bother with us, for we are of no importance. They are letting me stay because I have always taken my political education seriously. And perhaps because I have a new uniform."

But very soon a whisper came in his ear too. The child looked startled, rose, and bowed stiffly to me. "I am very much embarrassed," he said, and walked proudly away.

Something went wrong with the electricity, and the lights in the restaurant went out. The waitresses bustled around with candles. I sat in the flickering, shadowy darkness and listened to the sad, nostalgic Russian music of an accordion, played softly by a soldier at a table nearby.

At Moscow Nell met me, looking like a Russian in her gray Persian lamb hat, coat and muff, fur-edged boots and bright red scarf and mittens. As we drove from Vnukovo to the warm apartment in Mokhavaya that is now home, it was a comfortable thought that only a Russian wind could whistle around the car so like a flock of birds that the driver peered eagerly to see them through the flurries of drifting snow.

PART VIII.
"FAREWELL, UNWASHED RUSSIA"

1. GRIM RIVER

IT IS A PITY THAT NO ONE has yet undertaken the difficult job of translating Vyacheslav Shishkov. I had heard of his *Grim River* in Russia, but only succeeded in getting a copy in New York. It is a thick book of eight or nine hundred pages, but I read it while in the hospital and finished it soon after reaching Moscow again. My copy is one from a memorial edition of Shishkov published in 1947 after his death, although the book was begun in 1918 and finished in 1932. It would be interesting to compare it with an earlier edition, for there are evidences of rewriting in a few places where class consciousness and party interests seem to be dragged in by the heels. It is a book vast and vital enough to take that in its stride without detriment.

Grim River is a great slice of the earthiness, the hot passion, the drunkenness, the eeriness and the beauty that is Russia. The grim river is the Lena in Siberia and the story is one of the many loves, the bawdy vicissitudes and diversions and the final disintegration of a fascinating character who makes a fortune from the wilderness in the days just before the Revolution. Tramps, Cossacks, escaped convicts, aboriginal natives, shamans, swindlers, murderers, prostitutes — all the lawless underworld of Siberia swagger through its pages almost in flesh and blood. Shishkov's eye is only for atmosphere, beauty and drama, never on social significance or a moral.

His women are magnificent and unashamed. An American mining expert who always gets his Russian proverbs mixed, the *chertoznais* who can see through the ground and, with the aid of unclean spirits, sense the presence of gold, and a betrayed Asiatic friend who devotes his life to a creepy and fantastic revenge, have all the complex reality of living people. Some of his drunken scenes are so vivid that one feels drunk while reading. One also feels that *Grim River* was written not to edify or entertain, but to express moods and feelings that no one has expressed before, and to do so in vivid language.

The night was all in lunar silver. Dew lay thick. The church cross shone with a phosphorescent gleam. The white hut of Father Aleksander had become blue, and through the blue glass windows a little red flame winked in an ikon-lamp. For the human ear, there was only a thick silence. But everywhere was an imperceptible humming; the flood of moonrays, cutting through the broad spaces above the earth, fell on the sleeping world of the taiga, quivering and ringing. The taiga, laden with sleep, answered them with a rustle, a murmur, a delirium of evanescent dreams, sharp, like frankincense; the taiga became perfumed and fragrant.

Prokhor dreamily breathed that stupefying aroma of the woods and felt how his will, shackled by the conventions of life, had become free. The moonlight floods pierced his nerves like arrows, whipped his blood. Already something had triumphed in him, drawn him into something like a drunken revel. This silvery night sucked at a man's heart like a serpent. It was sad for a man, lonely . . .

The cook complained that the house-goblin had been choking her for three nights—on the fourth, she slept with the coachman. . . .

Like a squirrel with its tail, he covered his face, puffed-up from hard drinking, with his beard. . . .

He tried to channel his consciousness, which had disintegrated like mercury on glass. . . .

He thrust his calloused hands into his hair and shook all over with sobs that were as dry and cold as a crackling shroud. . . .

So the song, gray with age, poured forth and spread its peacock's tail. The modulated tone of the horns was throaty and strong. Softly and singingly, with some sort of tormenting pressure, flew the sounds, now like round balls, now like a smooth, taut string. Particularly expressively spoke the horn of the littlest shepherd, Eroshka. Popping out his greenish eyes and puffing out his belly-ing cheeks to their limit, Eroshka carried the main melody with all passion. And it seemed as though a strong woman's voice from all her broad breast and her very heart is sounding without words. And if you shut your eyes — you will see the Russian peasant woman, exuberant, magnificent and rosy-cheeked. All in red bunt-ing, crossing her sunburned hands on her breast, she swims over the fields in the sunlit air and sings, sings, not knowing why, not knowing for whom. . . .

The hair stirred on the back of Prokhor's neck. Wrapping his dressing gown close about him, he ran to the fireplace. Empty. Only fear was thickening in the corners. . . . The room is empty. In its corners cowers fear, silent, cold, terrifying. Fear is waiting for night, so that, growing strong, it may rise to the ceiling, freeze the burning brain of Prokhor, and, having frozen it, cast it into the flames of delirium. . . . Fear fills the whole house, the kitchen, the servant's quarters. Fear, like *ugar,* sweeps far on all sides . . .

and here my translation goes to pieces on the word *ugar.* It means carbon monoxide, the invisible vapor of burning charcoal, it means the poisoning that can come from it, and it also means drunken-ness, revelry and madness.

One of the characters that are scattered through the pages with Russian prodigality is this:

Ilya Sokhatykh is red-headed and curly-haired; his face is so thick with freckles that from a distance he seems to be rosy-cheeked; in actual fact, he is meager and sickly, but he has a weak-ness for the female sex. In the village he is the foremost dandy, always in collar and cuffs and bright ties; the head of his cane is also not of the retiring sort; his cigarette case is entirely proper externally, but you open the top — and there is the devil knows what: even Father Ipat, when he saw it, spat. Ilya Sokhatykh also had a couple of dozen disgraceful postcards; the lads in the eve-nings hugged their bellies at them and the girls raised a decorous squeal — "Akh, you should be ashamed of yourself! Phooey on you!" — but their eyes burned naughtily and they clung secretly to the forbidden fruit.

Ilya Sokhatykh loved to perfume himself with cheap scents, they wafted from him for three kilometers like dill and garlic. Rings, cufflinks, tiepins played with a false glassy color, gold-plated watch and chain shone. All this "civilization" — he loved to bruise the heads of the lads and girls with a complicated word — was picked up by him in the chief town of the district. . . .

One day Nell asked Valodya how many rooms there were in his apartment. "Three rooms," he replied.

"I understood that only great ballerinas and important people in the government had apartments that big," said Nell, thinking for a moment that Valodya must have the concealed rank of at least a colonel in the MVD to live in such luxury.

"There are three families in our apartment," Valodya explained. "Each family has one room, and then there is the kitchen besides, which we all share. We have drawn a line on the kitchen table with chalk, so that we each have our own space."

"How do you manage about the stove?"

"If people really want to get along, they have no difficulty. Of course, if someone wants to cook something that takes a long time, they must get up very early in the morning to get it over with so that it won't interfere too much."

Sadko is at last on at the Bolshoy. Though it is rich with *skazka* magic, *Sadko* is one of the *bylini,* those long half-historic epics which are still in the memories of specially gifted peasants in the remote parts of Russia. I have two thick volumes of them that have been written down and published by learned societies of tsarist times, and *Sadko,* from which Rimsky-Korsakov took his opera, is included. It is difficult to understand why some of these magnificent Russian shows are not put on in New York. Probably the cost of the big casts and the costumes and settings, which are what really make them so spectacular, would be too much of a speculative investment.

At the Bolshoy we hear the "Song of India" rising clear and sweet above the colorful polyglot crowds on the docks of Novgorod in the days when it was a great commercial city and Moscow, if it existed at all, was only a trading post in the forests. Looming high overhead were the bright, fantastic prows of the Novgorod shipping, carved like those of the Vikings, but with a proud archaic crudeness that is the stamp of the Russian. There was an underwater scene that used the same techniques as *The Humpbacked Pony,* with phosphorescent things that flashed and darted to give something of the effect of the Repin picture.

On the way home from the Bolshoy we saw a crowd gathered around a little Pobeda automobile. Three militiamen were trying to get it to move on, but the two Russians who were in it were a bit under the weather. They had told some friends they would meet them there, and how could they meet those friends if they moved on? The crowd laughed approvingly, and the argument was still going on when we left.

At one of the many national holidays which make Moscow embassy life a continual round of receptions, I was talking with a Soviet official. Since he had never heard of *Grim River,* I told him something of it and remarked on the freedom with which the American Mister Cook and many foreign travelers and explorers in other books that were not fiction had once moved around in Siberia.

He laughed and said, "That was in the Tsar's time. Just try to do it now!" Then he clapped his hand over his mouth and rolled his eyes around to see if he had been overheard.

The price of beer has come down from nine rubles to five rubles and sixty kopecks, which means only seventy cents for a big glass mug. Pleased with such a reduction in the cost of living, I sat quietly this evening in the bar at Pushkin Square and watched a grimy-looking couple at the next table beat their whole dried fish against the table to loosen the succulent morsels from the tough skin. The walls were of imitation marble, with Grecian columns at one end of the room framing a blue and white cameo effect of goddesses in flowing robes. On the side walls were hung pictures of still life — glasses of beer beside a dead duck or a dish of straw-berries, exactly like old-fashioned beer advertisements without the advertising.

A little black-browed man with no collar and a very dirty shirt asked me if the other seat at my table was taken. When I told him *"Pazhaluista!"* he sat down and immediately plunged into con-versation, but when I told him who I was he went through the same period of preoccupation which I have seen on several occa-sions. He was a typesetter for *Pravda,* and he asked me what I thought of the paper. I gave him my frank opinion, which is not very high. Forrestal's suicide is being handled by the Soviet press in a particularly brutal and shocking manner. I told him of For-restal's services to his country, his sincerity and open-mindedness, and ended by saying that it was difficult to understand how honest people could continue to publish the innuendoes and deliberate lies about America and Americans that one sees daily in every paper in Soviet Russia.

The standard time for a Russian to make up his mind that he is in safe hands is about seven or eight minutes. After a comparable period, the little typesetter's face cleared up. He looked around, then said: "Don't worry about propaganda against your country. We Russians do not believe it. Whenever you read such things, it is a sure sign that the Russian people, the *narod,* thinks otherwise, and the sharper the propaganda, the stronger their beliefs to the contrary."

He must have thought better of his decision to talk freely, for the usual flow of grievances against the government did not follow and he left soon afterwards. One thing that he said might be taken ambiguously: "We Russians are all nihilists. No matter where the power may lie, we do not trust it and we do not like it."

Although this typesetter was an exception in his sophistication, it is noticeable that Russians, particularly on the middle and lower levels, are generally more politically and economically minded than Americans from corresponding walks of life. Their education is a warped and one-sided one, they are walled off from alien systems, but they are familiar with and interested in concepts that are apt to be boring to the usual American, and they should not be under-rated in those respects.

In the Tretyakovskaya Galleries an old, pink-cheeked *babushka,* all bundled up in a wadded jacket and *valyenki,* followed me around with interest and curiosity popping out of her eyes. Our conversation was more rewarding to me than it was to her, for I have grown chary of trying to explain America to simple people. When we stopped in front of Savitsky's "Meeting of the Ikon," she said that in the "old days" the whole city would go out to fall on their knees before a specially holy ikon.

"Everyone would go, sick and well alike. But it was particularly the sick and the cripples who went, for sometimes the ikon would heal them. Nobody knows where all the cripples came from. There were many *klikushi* also in the crowd."

My interest was well caught, for the *klikushi,* or shouters, were certain ones who were seized with hysteria or a religious ecstasy. They have always been numerous in Russia, and what is really involved is very complex. Sometimes it may be connected with epilepsy, sometimes with whatever it was that caused the manifestations of medieval witchcraft, sometimes even with the gift of tongues of the Bible.

"Yes," the old woman went on, "there were many *klikushi* then. Perhaps they were possessed by devils, or perhaps it was due to a deep belief, for there were also *klikushi* among the priests in the churches, and devils could hardly get hold of them."

"Are there still *klikushi* in Russia, *matushka?*" I asked.

"Of course. Only the other day a *klikusha* cried out in one of the churches that, when Easter Sunday comes, snow will be knee-deep in the streets, and that forty days thereafter blood will flow knee-deep in the streets of Moscow. Haven't you heard that? All Moscow is talking about it."

I tried to get her on the subject of witchcraft, but she was of a pious turn of mind and not inclined to discuss the workings of the "unclean spirits." She did tell me that once she had seen a priest cure a woman who had gone out of her mind from seeing all her family shot during the partisan wars. The priest burned her leg with a white-hot iron. Perhaps shock treatment for the insane has a longer ancestry than is commonly believed.

Tom Ireland and I went to see a Soviet court of justice in action.

Apparently any citizen who wishes can attend, for we had no trouble in getting in without even showing our *dokumenty*. The case was one against some of the administrative staff of Moscow University who were charged with diverting to their own use part of the produce from one of the collective farms run by the University.

One of the difficulties in trying to appraise the true output of Soviet industrial establishments is the number of extraneous activities in which they become engaged. Soviet industry is not only young, but it cannot develop naturally — its growth must be planned. Only the major industries — steel, coal, petroleum and the like — have been brought into existence, for there have not yet been time and ready resources to plan the minor supporting industries. There is no hardware industry, for example, and, except for big planned production jobs, each Soviet factory has to divert part of its effort to making the sort of bits and pieces that are ordered from a stock catalogue in America. There is an electrical industry, but factories have to design and build their own elevators and countless things for which an older industrial civilization has long since developed sources of supply. Many organizations do their own construction work and provide their own housing, and still more of them raise their own food. Moscow University seems to be no exception.

The regime seems to be particularly plagued with diversion of state resources to private use, for it is a chronic source of complaint in the press. When a political aspect is involved, the press is silent, as it is on crimes of violence. I do not know what sort of courts handle the latter, nor if the public is admitted, but political offenses — and they are legion — are dealt with under special laws and special procedures, usually within the dread framework of the MVD.

In this courtroom the woman judge sat behind a table draped in scarlet. She was broad-shouldered and squat, with the toughest, hardest face I have seen in many a day. When she waddled in, the chills ran down my back at the thought of being brought to justice before her. Nevertheless, appearances may have been deceiving, for she seemed surprisingly mild-mannered and equitable as she ran the proceedings, which were informal to the point of being free and easy.

Three or four of the accused sat in the front row, better dressed than anyone else in the room, and seemingly not greatly concerned. They and the lawyers, as well as what appeared to be mere visitors in the audience, interrupted testimony at will to ask questions. There was no evidence of animus or dramatics on the part of any-one. However, during the time we were there the testimony was identification and verification of the trucks which were supposed to have made away with the vegetables, the status of the drivers, the amount of potatoes involved and such routine matters. The trial had been going on for two or three days, and there may have been other times with bigger moments.

Nell and I went to see Moussorgsky's *Boris Godunov,* which is probably the greatest of Russian operas. It lived up to its reputation in every way. The expert use of perspective, in which the Russian stage designers excel, gave the huge log walls of the old Kremlin a medieval atmosphere of tremendous strength, and over their gate was a gigantic ikon, shedded under its own roof, which produced a corresponding atmosphere of mystic piety. The scene within the Kremlin itself was rich beyond words with the furs and robes of the huge cast, and it blazed with cloth of gold and ikons.

There is a long, meandering solo in *Boris,* sung by a *yurodivye* — one of "God's fools" — wherein voice, make-up, setting, acting, even the music itself and the way it was sung, combined to give an extraordinarily strange and moving effect. The *yurodivye* shade off at one extreme into the *klikushi* — and beyond that into the imposter — but at the other extreme they are genuine saints and prophets.

Boris Godunov was a Tatar, or at least had a large admixture of Tatar blood, and the same is true of Karamzin, the great his-torian. Pushkin was part Negro, and Lermontov of Scottish an-cestry. A list of the great Russian names whose ancestors were not Great Russians would be interesting, and probably impressive. It would include Zhukovsky and Fonvizin, de Tolly, Gogol, Gribo-yedov, Dostoevsky, Nekrasov, Glinka, Dahl, Turgenev, Hertzen, Catherine the Great and all her successors, Trotsky, Lenin and Stalin, and undoubtedly many, many others that do not occur to me or of which I have never been aware. The common English expression "I wonder if . . ." cannot be translated into Russian, so, to express it as a Russian would, "it would be interesting to know if" a case could be made for the Great Russians as reapers of profits, exploiters of those with other blood. Many an Irishman and Scotsman say that this is the way England became great.

2. UNFINISHED PROJECTS

THE PAPERS ARE FULL of a grandiose plan to connect the great northward-flowing Siberian rivers with the Aral and the Caspian Seas, which are gradually drying up and changing the climate of the cotton-producing areas for worse. Some of the foreigners here take this seriously, but no one should hold his breath until it is done. Although the Russians have done much under the Five Year Plans, those accomplishments are difficult to appraise because no firm basis for checking ever emerges from the percentages in which they are expressed. It is not as much as most Westerners have been led to believe — and the West has provided most of even that. The Russian imagination has a noble sweep, for an Atlantic-Pacific Canal has been proposed more than once. Yet even the Don-Volga Canal, only a few kilometers long and child's play compared to the Panama Canal, has been on the books ever since Peter the Great, and is still unfinished.*

Perhaps the remarkable organization of the Party which is the Soviet Union, the terrible will of its hard core, will bring more of the bright dreams to reality than in the past, but some of the dreams are still very Russian. Certainly the regime did drive through the White Sea Canal and the Moscow-Volga Canal — by the slave labor of hundreds of thousands of unfortunates and a blood-curdling cost in human life.

Someone should make a study of the Unfinished Projects of Russia, from Peter the Great's project to make the Russian Navy the greatest navy in the world, through Tsar Paul's campaign to seize India in the early days of the Napoleonic Wars, to the road-building plans of the Soviet Union, not forgetting the construction of a new strategic trans-Siberian railroad far to the north of the present one. What became of the Holy Alliance, and the Third Rome, and Pan-Slavism? What happened to all the liberal projects of the revolutionaries of tsarist days? Human rights and freedom of speech were always a prominent part of their platforms, and

* This canal is believed to have been finally completed in 1953.

there even seemed to be a better understanding of those things then than now.

The great bell and the Tsar Gun of the Kremlin were to be the greatest in the world, and the new Home of the Soviets in Moscow was to surpass the skyscrapers of New York. The bell is cracked and broken, the gun a museum piece, and the Home of the Soviets a gaping hole in swampy ground, surrounded by a high board fence to keep away the curious. One of the most beautiful churches in Russia was broken up and torn down in order to make that hole, and a Russian once told me that the ambitious skyscraper would never be finished because the very ground was cursed because of that. Incidentally, there was an unintentionally amusing article in the Moscow papers on the shocking way in which the tall buildings of America swayed in the wind. Soviet engineers would build the Home of the Soviets so that it would be absolutely rigid against the wind. The Russians really produce some good engineers, so it is to be presumed that they know their stresses and strains better than the author of that article.

Literature has its share of unfinished projects. Among the most beautiful books of Russia is a series of monographs on Russian artists and their work, under the editorship of Igor Grabar. The first volume, on Vrubel, which was published in 1911, lists forty volumes in preparation. Over the next twenty-five or thirty years no more than five or six have been published, although they are of the highest standard, and the series now seems to have died away.

I have a copy of the *Tale of the Host of Igor* published in 1891 as the first of a series of fifty books of the "Russian Classroom Library." Although I have hunted far and wide, there are no copies of the other forty-nine to be found, and it is probable that that is another project that died. It is a pity, for this was an ambitious and scholarly plan and, unlike the Grabar books which were published at around fifty rubles (secondhand copies now cost up to two hundred rubles), put out in an inexpensive format. *Igor* is the earliest literary production of the Russian language, corresponding roughly to the English *Beowulf*. This edition has the original text with a translation into contemporary Russian in parallel columns. It also has literary translations by three or four different Russian poets, seven easy articles on various aspects of the work, and a glossary of unusual words. All at the publisher's price of thirty kopecks. Passed by the Censor to boot, as shown on the flyleaf.

Many of the tsarist books, of course, perished in the Revolution. Natasha, knowing my interest in Russian books, once said, "Oh, Gospodin Admiral, how many books were burned during the Revolution!"

"Why?" I asked, thinking that the Bolsheviks had never been known to resort to such crude Nazi tactics of censorship.

"Just to keep from freezing to death!" was the answer.

Although Natasha herself did not tell me, books were also used for fuel during the last war. They say the works of Lenin were superior to those of Stalin even in this respect — they gave more heat. Doubtless this is literally true, for earlier publications were on paper of better quality

The *History of the Civil War* is an unfinished Soviet project. Only two volumes of this official history have appeared, taking the story only through November, 1917, the month following the Red Revolution itself. The first edition of the first volume has Radek's name as one of the authors. My copy, which was published in 1936, omits Radek, but the names of two of the editors and one of the writers are obliterated with the familiar indelible ink. Further volumes of this project have long been awaited with interest, but it is quite possible that the rewriting of history is so full of booby traps that even so basic a work as this will take its place among the Unfinished Projects of Russia.

Interplanetary travel is just the thing to catch the Russian imagination. Among my Russian books is one which is a serious technical discussion of just that, written simply and clearly in 1903, although my copy is one of fifty thousand of the tenth edition, published in Leningrad in 1935. There is an excellent chance that the Russian engineers, who do not lack for brains, will pioneer in this field.

The Soviets are beginning to jam the Russian broadcasts of the Voice of America on a massive scale. Those broadcasts come on many different wave lengths, but whenever you turn to any of them, a horrible grinding sound drowns out everything. This can only mean that the broadcasts are effective and that the regime is afraid of them.

George Morgan, the scholarly, distinguished-looking first secretary who relieved Dick Davis, is trying to round up enough Russian-speaking Americans to make a round-the-clock check to find out if this goes on continuously. Already we have found that, like most Russian efforts, the interference is spotty, sometimes breaking down enough to let the words come through. But the rapidity with which they open up on so many different frequencies indicates that they are not just experimenting, but have put important resources to work.

More than one Russian has told us the same thing that the *Pravda* typesetter said — as long as the Soviets attack America, it is a sign that the Russian people believe in America.

Sometimes Natasha and Zoya seem like Russian cats, with a fierce, defiant look in their eyes that are at once opaque and mysterious. That is usually at the rare times when they are quarreling, but now for several days their eyes have had that uncanny expression while the two of them seem to get along with each other better than usual. Certainly Nell and I have not aroused their disapproval, for Natasha has just looked in where Nell is reading and I am writing, and I heard her say: "What a quiet, noble family!"

The Indians in Moscow are beautifully educated, nearly all of them speaking excellent English — English English rather than American English. They are an attractive lot, particularly the women, with their bright saris, their small-boned little figures, and the red caste marks on their foreheads. I sat next to one of them at dinner tonight. She was completely at home in discussing both England and America, familiar with Western literature and culture, broadly liberal and enlightened in her views. Yet the deep psychological differences which make foreign peoples so fascinating showed up when she told me in all sincerity that going barefoot was good for the eyes, and that a sapphire was the cause of Mrs. Schnyder's present illness.

"Tell me," I said, "is it really true that Tibetan lamas and certain holy Hindus can leave their bodies and travel freely in time and space?"

"Of course it is," she said earnestly. "If you go to India and are sympathetic and understanding, you will see such things with your own eyes, as I have done."

We went to the Bolshoy to see *Bakhchisaraisky Fountain,* a ballet based on one of Pushkin's long poems. Spring has come with a rush to Sverdlovsk Square, for in its center is a big plot of garden, bright with tulips and fragrant with lilacs and apple trees in blossom. For some reason there is an ugly, unpainted wooden fence all around this freshness, but perhaps it is there only while the planting is being done.

Pushkin's poem has a familiar theme, the love of a Russian for a woman of one of the invading Asiatic tribes. For many centuries in historic times what is now European Russia was occupied jointly by the Russians and first the Pechenegs and then the Polovtsi, who were followed by the Tatars. The history of those times is complex with alternating wars and alliances, the Dukes of Muscovy in particular not hesitating to use the Mongols for their own conquests even while paying tribute to the Golden Horde at the mouth of the Volga. Romantic intermarriages were common, for the Asiatic women were a skilled and attractive lot. If the American Indians had been as sophisticated and as effective, resolute and strong as the settlers of North America, perhaps our own history of border warfare would have more nearly resembled the situation in Russia under the Mongol yoke. In any case, the wild savageness of the barbaric Asiatic tribes inspired similar feelings in the Russians.

The ballet was full of this atmosphere, and it was also full of the color of the East, with scores of whirling booted Tatar dancers, naked slender waists and bare ribs showing between short fur jackets and wide striped and spangled Eastern trousers. In one scene the trousers were of narrow, multicolored strips of ribbon that belled out like circular rainbows as the dancers spun in complete abandon. In another scene lassos, like those used by our own western horsemen, were used with the utmost skill.

.   .   .

We went out one of the roads that is still permitted to us, through the crowded streets of Moscow, through what was the foreign suburb when the Russia of the Tsars was less of a closed land than the Russia of the Soviets, past a tangle of railroad yards, past an enormous collection of rusty steel scrap that seemed to extend forever, past grim factories and the last scattered log houses of the city with colored Easter eggs wrapped in cotton displayed in their windows of wavy glass, into the oceanlike swells of the open country. Apple trees and cherry trees looked like little white clouds on the low, misty hills that smoked with dust, and the lilacs were blossoming in the villages. Here and there was a dark pine forest, a wood of shining birches, or a broad black scar where women were digging peat, guarded by other women with rifles. At the forty-eight-kilometer mark was a guard post where we were told we could go no further.

We left the car by the road and crossed a little field beyond which was a graveyard. It was old and populous, so old that its walks were worn down into the ground like English country lanes. Although there were many cut and withered flowers about and various signs of affection, the whole place had an air of disorder and neglect. The tombstones leaned at odd angles, most of the crosses were drooping and askew, and bits of broken glass lay in the unkempt grass that half-obscured ambiguous little hollows.

The grassy mounds which had no relation to the size of human beings were often surrounded with unsubstantial enclosures. Sometimes the little enclosures were made of sheets of metal from which spoons and kitchenware had once been stamped. Most of the graves had crosses, many of them painted an off-color blue, others welded together from rusty tubing. One grave of an aviation major had only the red star of the Soviet Union on top of its shaft, but a small, broken marble cross was laid unobtrusively on the mound. Thick hedges of bridal wreath were in and about this place. The air was so heavy with their fragrance and so loud with the hum of bees that Keats's nightingale kept coming to my mind.

There were many brightly kerchiefed women in the fields along the road back to Moscow, their skirts flying in the wind about their bare white legs as they planted potatoes. One seldom sees a woman without her kerchief, for it is not proper for a woman to be seen with her head bare. Yet in one place by the road where some old peat diggings had been flooded with clear, dark water, a slim young woman stood naked and white and lovely against the black background of the peat as she coiled the heavy braids on her head after her bath.

Before the May Day Parade there was rain, and the pools of water in the streets looked like pools of blood as they reflected the scarlet flags and banners with which the city is decorated. One of the foreign attachés forgot his card of admission to Red Square. He appealed to OVS's Pasco, who was standing nearby and knew him well. Pasco told him gravely that there was nothing that could be done for him, so that attaché missed the parade.

When in the attachés' stand, I noticed that the dim ancient figures that had spread their great wings near the Kremlin gate behind Lenin's tomb were gone. Where they had stood for centuries, the Kremlin wall is now faced with new utilitarian brick. Not only does the tower outside our apartment have a shiny new top, but a new brick facing has been put around its base. Perhaps the uses to which it was put by men and boys who could not wait to find greater privacy had something to do with that. In any event, it seems that the charm of Moscow is continually being chipped away by the sort of minds that prefer machinemade rugs.

The parade itself was indistinguishable from those that I have seen before — the same jowls quivering in unison as the infantrymen stamped past, the same paratroopers sitting stiffly erect in the carryalls with the chin straps of their hard helmets framing their faces into grim Asiatic masks, the same tanks crawling swift as armored saurians out of geologic time, the same torrents of civilian marchers carrying the same slogans and the same paper flowers. Russians have told me that one cannot just decide to join in with the parade, the "popular demonstration," but must be part of some organization that participates. This is nevertheless rather a loose arrangement, for a member of a participating factory or other organization can sometimes bring a friend. More than once foreigners, including an officer from my own office, have in this manner appeared in one of the big parades.

Knowing how impressionable the Russians are to medals,

General O'Daniel wore every one he had, and they were many. His uniform jacket was literally covered with medals from top to bottom, and the Russian officers in the attachés' stand looked at him from all angles and walked round and round him as they counted them. When the civilian demonstration was well under way he whispered to me, "Steve, I can't take much more of this. The ground is beginning to crawl."

I knew exactly how he felt, for our eyes had become so accustomed to the moving line that everything else at which we looked crawled dizzily, setting up a disturbing effect of nausea. Although more than one Russian officer had commented approvingly on how last year I had stayed through until the end, it seemed to me that it would be altogether too much of a sensation if Mike and I should both start staggering and perhaps pass out, so I followed General O'Daniel through the crowds out of Red Square.

For some time the little windows in the attic of the medical department of Moscow University across from our apartment have been boarded up. We wondered what was going on there to be concealed from the eyes of the Americans, and when Mike and I returned to the Embassy we found out. On the occasion of every parade, some of our people have gone on the roof of the Embassy to get a better view of the fly-past of airplanes. Since the Embassy is the equivalent of American soil, our people were also free to use cameras. This May Day, as they were following their usual routine, someone noticed a recurrent whirring sound. They looked around to locate its source, and finally, through a chink in the blinded windows of Moscow University's attic, they caught a glimpse of a movie camera taking pictures of them as they took pictures of the planes overhead. American Spies Caught Red-Handed!

The Soviet press has shouted loudly about the improvements that have been made in airplane service this season, announcing with much boasting that the daily flights to Yakutsk, among other places, had been doubled. Throughout the winter, traveling in the Soviet Union has been too rugged for us. The last trip that was made before winter really set in was by Colonel McMillan to Ufa, in the Bashkir Republic this side of the Urals. He found a temperature

of forty-nine degrees below zero in Ufa, and a wind whose leakage through the joints and cracks of his closed windows made the curtains stand out straight. Mac's Marine pride was touched to the quick when they searched him for fleas before letting him occupy those quarters. Now that the weather has opened up, the process of feeling out where we are permitted to go has begun again.

Yakutsk is on Shishkov's grim river, in the heart of the Siberian gold fields and the concentration camps. It didn't stand to reason that a foreigner would be permitted to go there, but it is in the middle of a vast area that is not on the long list of forbidden regions and so is presumably open.

I tried to go to Yakutsk. Aeroflot, which runs the airlines, said that only Intourist handled plane tickets for foreigners. Intourist said that they had nothing to do with travel to Yakutsk, which was handled solely by Aeroflot. Then Aeroflot said that there were no services to Yakutsk. When they were shown the glowing statements in the newspapers, they agreed that there must be such flights, but insisted that they knew nothing of them. Intourist said the same thing. The Embassy then wrote a polite letter to the Foreign Office reviewing all those circumstances and asking only for advice as to where to go to take advantage of the improved services that had been publicized. No reply is expected.

On hearing of this, a Russian told me that Aeroflot, Intourist and the press had all been right. The catch was that the line to Yakutsk, which branches off from the main trans-Siberian route at Krasnoyarsk, is operated by the MVD, to serve the prison camp enterprises on the Lena. No Russian can get passage on that branch without special reasons and a clearance from the MVD itself. "There are many places," he said, "where Russians are not permitted to go. All of the Crimea has been closed to us for some time, for my uncle, who has relatives in Sevastopol, has tried to go there and been refused."

It seems rather remarkable that the women, who do so much of the work of Russia that they are the ones who really make it go, are seldom found high in the hierarchy. They maintain their place among doctors, engineers, and judges, and there has been an occasional woman minister or ambassador, but they disappear almost entirely at the higher levels. It has often been said that the Soviet constitution merely gives women the right to do the heaviest sort of work, but that does not explain much, particularly in view of the influence they have always wielded in Russian political life, and when one realizes the active part they took during the long history of the revolutionary movement.

Russian women are quite capable of doing men's work in other ways than laying rails and chopping wood, or even engaging in the professions. There were two women in Kamo's band that staged the robbery in 1907 in the Caucasus which gathered in well over a quarter of a million rubles to finance the revolution, and women play important parts in every revolutionary activity. One is struck by the large number of women among the conspirators and assassins, from Sophia Perovskaya and Vera Zasulich to Dora Kaplan, and the women in Lenin's and Trotsky's lives helped the Revolution in many ways other than domestic.

It is quite possible that the women of Russia could have a greater proportion of high position — if they wanted it. This passage from Tolstoy's *Cossacks* expresses a relationship that is essentially true of Russians other than Cossacks:

> The Cossack looks on woman as an instrument of his well-being; he permits young girls just to gad about, but he compels his peasant woman to work for him from youth even to advanced old age, and he regards a woman with an Eastern demand for submission and labor. As the result of such a view, the woman, who develops intensively both physically and morally even though she is externally submissive, obtains, as generally in the East, an influence and weight in domestic life that is beyond comparison greater than in the West. Her removal from social life and her habituation to heavy masculine work give her still greater weight and force in domestic existence. The Cossack, who in the presence of strangers considers it improper to speak affectionately or idly with his woman, involuntarily feels her superiority, and sees eye to eye with her. The whole house, all the property, all the domestic economy have been acquired by her and are held together only by her labors and solicitude. Even though he is firmly convinced that work is shameful for a Cossack and proper only for the workers from the Nogaisk steppe and for women, he still feels confusedly that everything he uses and calls his own is the product

of this work, and that it is in the power of the woman, mother or wife, whom he counts his serf, to deprive him of everything that is of any use to him. Moreover, the continual masculine, heavy work and the worries that are entrusted to her hands have given a particularly independent, masculine character to the hill woman and to a surprising degree have developed in her physical strength, decisiveness and firmness of character. Their women are, for the most part, both stronger, wiser, better developed, and more beautiful than the Cossack men.

Bismarck once called the Russians a "female people." Although in most countries it is probably true that women pursue men more than is commonly admitted, there seems to be something in the Russian man that demands this reversal of the usual relationship. The spirit of Tatyana's letter confessing her love to Eugene Onegin is repeated over and over again throughout Russian literature, sometimes subtly, as in Turgenev's women, sometimes baldly and directly, as over and over again in *Grim River*. This aspect of Russian psychology has depths that have attracted little attention.

The overhead of universal planning is appalling. Bureaucracies have a strong tendency to spawn and spread, for every force that is organized to deal with a problem finds several other problems for which further organizations should be set up. It seems as though one out of every three or four Russians one meets by chance are planners. The struggle to reduce overhead personnel and costs is a perennial one in the Soviet Union.

The latest urge for economy has taken the form of a requirement that theaters become self-supporting. That will be a great blow to the Russian theater, particularly since there is no indication that there will be any further relaxation in ideological requirements of what is produced. State support will be continued only in certain cases.

The Bolshoy seems to be one of the exceptions to the new order, for we found Borodin's *Prince Igor* as lavish and exciting as anything we have ever seen. The opera, based on *The Tale of the Host of Igor*, opposes the Slavic world of Kiev with its chivalric lances and battleaxes to the bows and arrows, curved swords and lassos of the savage Polovtsi from the Asiatic steppes. The Russians do this sort of thing with enthusiasm and abandon, not only in the wild dances of the Asiatics with feathered and fringed rainbow-hued billowing trousers and jeweled harness crossed over bare brown chests, but in the awe-inspiring drunkenness of some of the mob scenes. In *Prince Igor* the huge felt mushroom-shaped *yurts* — the movable homes of the nomads — made an unforgettable scene that was more vivid because of the exotic music and the rich voices. And there was a slim brown girl who will always make the music of the dance of the Polovtsi maidens seem something special to me.

While walking home from Sverdlovsk Square we were close on the heels of Paul Robeson, who is greatly admired in Russia for his fine singing. He was talking in English with a blonde girl who accompanied him, he in his deep musical voice and she with a marked Russian accent. She seemed to be an Intourist girl or her equivalent, who was making arrangements for what he might see the following day. After the services he has rendered communism, I would have expected him to be lodged in the Kremlin, or at least the Moscow Hotel rather than the National, and to be dined and lionized and surrounded with admirers. His apparent mess of pottage seemed to be rather thin, for his leisure time appeared to be managed like that of any other foreign visitor in the hands of Intourist.

A new edition of Pushkin has just been published in one big, fat volume. Such things are put out in enormous editions, but this one was completely sold out the day it appeared in the bookshops and it was only because of the thoughtfulness of a friend that I got a copy. The book is really complete, except possibly for some of Pushkin's correspondence — a wonderful thing to have. Even the missing stanzas of *Eugene Onegin,* as far as they have been recovered, are in the notes. I had heard that those stanzas were omitted under both Tsar and Soviet because of their highly erotic nature, but such does not seem to be the case, for the *Gavriliad,* which gives ample grounds for exclusion on that score, is included in its entirety.

Whenever one goes in an old bookshop one becomes the center of a little crowd of ever-curious Russians. The other day in a remote part of town I went down my usual list of books that are difficult or impossible to get, and the clerk said No to every name. As I walked down the street towards my car, a hand plucked at my sleeve. It was a thin, poorly dressed man in a greasy cap.

"I heard you ask for some books by Ilf and Petrov," he said. "You know, those books cannot be sold in our shops any more."

"Yes, I know," I replied, "but sometimes the shops get careless."

"I have a complete set of all that Ilf and Petrov have written. I will let you have them if you would like. They are good books, and there is nothing wrong about them. Ilf and Petrov only laughed at things in the Soviet Union, and it is a good thing to be able to laugh when things are no laughing matter."

The set of Ilf and Petrov is now safe in our apartment.

The Turks have been informed that one of their diplomatic couriers committed suicide on the train in the Caucasus while traveling alone on his way out to Turkey. He was in excellent spirits when he left Moscow, where he had bought several little gifts to take home to his family and friends. Moreover, when the Turks examined his body, they found that he had killed himself in an extraordinarily difficult way, for the shot entered the base of his skull from behind, in the same way that people are executed in Russia. Although only an obscure courier, he was given a state funeral in Istanbul, with much of Turkey's high rank attending.

Ilf and Petrov's *Twelve Chairs* and *The Golden Calf* are picaresque tales of the ingenious and sometimes spectacular ways in which one Ostap Bender made a living in Soviet Russia. The two books are genuinely funny, and they have something of the quality that Mark Twain managed to put into *Huckleberry Finn*. At least one of them has been translated into English, but one should have lived in Russia to get its full flavor.

The Golden Calf begins with Ostap successfully raising eight rubles and some ration tickets in the office of the city Executive Committee by palming himself off as the son of Lieutenant Shmidt. While he is still in the office, a stranger enters with the same idea, claiming the same hero of the 1905 Revolution as his father. The ever-resourceful Ostap embraces the startled stranger and greets him as his long-lost brother.

When the two are safely out on the street, they see another citizen going into the office they have just left. "See that man in the straw hat?" the second son asks Ostap.

"I see him," Ostap replies superciliously. "So what? Perhaps he is the governor of the island of Borneo!"

"That," comes the answer, "is Panikovsky, son of Lieutenant Shmidt."

"'The Lieutenant had three sons," says Ostap, "two wise ones and the third a fool. He must be warned."

"It's not necessary," is the reply. "Let him find out what it means to break the agreement."

Throughout the whole country from Minsk to the Bering Sea, swindling and begging were "false sons of Karl Marx, nonexistent nephews of Friedrich Engels, brothers of Lunacharsky, cousins of Klara Tsetkin, and, at a pinch, descendants of the well-known anarchist Prince Kropotkin." So many sons of Lieutenant Shmidt were competing with one another that they finally called a convention where there appeared "thirty sons, from eighteen to fifty-two years old, and four daughters, stupid, not young, and very plain." They had agreed to divide the Soviet Union into thirty-four parts and each member of the convention was given one part for his exclusive exploitation.

It is far easier to suppress Ilf's and Petrov's books, which were tremendously popular in the thirties, than it is to suppress the *samozvantsy* of Russia.

3. WITCHCRAFT

NELL'S FACE WORE A QUEER FAR-AWAY EXPRESSION when I came home from the office today. She had just returned from the market and seemed to be pondering. Natasha, with Valodya carrying her bundles, had gone to another part of the market, leaving Nell alone. At that moment a deaf and dumb woman for some reason chose Nell, who still has enough difficulty in understanding spoken Russian, out of all the hundreds that crowded the market and began to talk on her hands to her. Nell, fascinated with this doubly complicated problem in communication, could find no way of telling the woman that her message wasn't getting across, but the woman only became more excited and stamped her hands and twinkled her fingers more rapidly.

Finally Natasha showed up. Aided by pantomime on the woman's part, Nell and Natasha decided that she wanted change for a ruble so she could put the kopecks in a pay station. They couldn't make exact change, but they did have enough kopecks for the call, so Natasha went with her, perhaps to be sure that the kopecks really ended up in the telephone, perhaps to help her.

Nell is still wondering how a deaf and dumb woman could make a telephone call even if she had a pocket full of kopecks, or how Natasha could find out what the woman wanted to say so that Natasha could make the call for her.

An attractive lad from one of the countries which, although still free, is close enough to the Russian Bear to feel its hot breath, was sent to the Soviet Union by his family for an education in aeronautical engineering. This lad can speak no English, but a genuine friendship has grown up between him and some of our younger officers who speak Russia. They often went swimming together at the big beach in Khimki, and he liked to come to the American parties.

The other day this young foreigner was denounced at his engineering school as a spy for the Americans. I know that the charge

is preposterous, for not only is a student not likely to be taught
state secrets, but he was very careful not to talk about his school,
shying away from any questions so obviously that his friends never
brought the subject up. This well-bred, prepossessing boy, a stranger
in a strange land whose only offense was that he found Americans
congenial, was read out of his school and told that he was to be
escorted under guard from the Soviet Union. Having no embassy
status, he was first arrested, stripped and subjected to fifty terrible
continuous hours of questioning in an attempt to make him admit
his guilt.

After what happened to the Turkish courier, all couriers now
travel in pairs, and everyone was very much concerned at the statement that this lad was to be escorted out of the country by the
Soviets. His embassy finally succeeded in making arrangements for
him to leave in company with their own couriers, and he has now
managed to reach his own land in safety. The whole affair has been
very depressing. What a shame to Russia such things are!
Chaadayev wrote of the Russians over a hundred years ago: "We are
not of the West or of the East, and we have the traditions of
neither."

I must have missed much of *Ruslan and Ludmilla* when I saw it
in Leningrad, for on seeing it again at the Bolshoy it seemed like a
completely new show. In any event Russian productions are not
standardized and there is much room for individuality. The field of
bones was there, but without the gigantic arrows, and in Moscow
the great head was even better than in Leningrad, bearded and
terrible, eyes, lips and eyelids moving as it spoke, and even the
whole head twisting and bowing with its moods. And I do not
remember seeing earlier the starry sky with stars ranged on nets so
that you could see that they were in space and not on a backdrop,
nor dancers swinging through the sky among shooting stars, nor an
army of silken tents that rose up out of the ground as if by enchantment.

Some of the magic scenes were remarkable. Chernomor the
sorcerer, who has a beard thirty feet long, steals Ludmilla on her
wedding night and takes her to his city. That city is fantastic with
thin spires, mushroom-shaped stupas and tall twisted columns on

top of which stand little dwarfs with long spears. There Ludmilla's couch hangs in mid-air in such a way, as Chernomor weaves his spells, that it seems impossible that there could be wires or anything but magic that supports it. One of our American sergeants told me that he had been to *Ruslan and Ludmilla* eight times and intended to keep on going until he could figure out how that was done.

We walked outside the theater during one intermission. It was still broad daylight, and on the pavement in front of the Bolshoy were half a dozen booted men with enormous black beards, wearing tall black astrakhan hats, wide baggy trousers and short jackets like boleros. Two of them were sitting cross-legged in the middle of the street, and one was rocking a little baby in his arms.

A converted Lancaster bomber that brought a new British ambassador to the Soviet Union took me out on its return trip, swiftly and luxuriously. The outside world had changed much more than Moscow. There was a new neatness to Berlin, a prosperity and a great air of confidence and assurance. Pinky Schuirmann had long since gone, and John Wilkes, who took his place as Commander of our Naval Forces in Germany, had given up the dreaming green gardens of Wannsee for a place in town. Because of the airlift, his Navy plane was based in Bremen, which now became my base.

From Bremen I ranged from Vienna, whose streets seemed to echo at night with intrigue, to the familiar rumble of London. Between flights there was sweet brown Löwenbräu to be had at the hotel in Bremen, and a piano player who could wring your heart with Brahms's *Wiegenlied*.

It was in Bremen that I was taken to a dinner party where I met the daughter of the Grand Duke Cyril whose father was the brother of Alexander III and uncle of the last Nicholas. An exquisite, contained woman, now married to the son of the German Crown Prince, she had played as a child in the endless rooms of the Winter Palace, and she had a thousand questions to ask about Russia and its people. Through her I had a glimpse of a side of Russia that is gone forever, seen through the eyes of a child, yet it seemed that the perennial land and its enduring people had laid the same nostalgic hand on her heart that it has laid on that of so many Russians.

I returned to Berlin by the airlift, a bit soiled by the cargo of coal we carried, and the next morning found myself in a palatial new airport in the Russian Zone waiting for the plane to Minsk and Moscow. One Russian mystery that will never be solved is how they can manage to obtain the off-key effect that is so oppressive in what would otherwise be a good effort. The private lounge in which I waited was new, spacious and airy, quite unlike the usual gloomy Russian waiting rooms that are overcrowded with heavy leather chairs and couches. Blue is normally a restful color, but these walls were decorated with some strange shade of blue that vibrated and jangled until it actually hurt the eyes. It was only by looking through the broad window and concentrating on the huge beds of pansies outside that I managed to hang on to my eyesight and keep from flying to pieces. That was such an unusual experience that I could not help but wonder if the effect was not consciously and deliberately fostered.

Although my luggage was well overweight with presents and food supplies, it was taken onto the plane without question. The passenger traffic was light, only a bright-eyed Russian girl and her Georgian husband and two or three dignified colonels in the Red Army. At the customs in Minsk no attention was paid to me, but an hour was spent in opening every box and bag of the Soviet passengers and going through all their belongings in the most minute detail. One of the Russian colonels trembled with suppressed indignation as they searched his pockets.

It is easy to start an argument in the *narodny* bars of Moscow. Two middle-aged Russians, who were probably more expediters or draftsmen than the planning engineers they said they were, were upholding to me the desirability and necessity of the single-party system in Russia. "Your American idea of freedom seems to us to be nothing but confusion," they said. "People just become muddled with all sorts of misleading arguments, when there is always one course that is correct, and those who do not agree with it must be forced to agree. There would be no order or control in Russia if we followed your ideas, only chaos, for everything would rapidly get completely out of hand."

A group of four at the next table began to take an interest in our discussion. One by one they hitched their chairs over and joined in. Soon I was being attacked on all sides with so many arguments that they could not be answered separately. Again the workings of the Russian mind were very different from ours. I remembered that even Plekhanov, one of the great thinkers of the revolutionary movement, who was much milder than the Bolsheviks and eventually broke with them, said early in the century that if elections should turn out ill in a new democratic Russia it would be necessary to dissolve the results of the elections within two weeks. So I fell back on the one sure-fire thing that has never failed to make an impression on a Russian.

"In my country," I said, "when anyone is sitting in prison, his friends and neighbors, or even someone who is merely curious, can always find out exactly where he is, how long he will be there, and the exact reason why he is in prison. Is that true in Russia today?"

A little man who had been particularly violent in his attacks stared into space, as though other scenes than that bar were before his eyes, and said quietly, "He speaks the truth!"

Several started to talk excitedly at once. One of them got up and took the little man's arm: "Come on, Tikhon Pavlich, it's time to go."

But Tikhon Pavlich was in no mood to go. "He speaks the truth, and you all know it," he said, banging his fist on the table.

As the argument grew hot among themselves, and the little man's friend still tried futilely to drag him away, I left unnoticed, sorry that I had not had enough sense to keep away from such matters.

At last I have found a Russian who knows something about witchcraft and is willing to talk about it. It began when I quoted a passage from *Eugene Onegin* and asked if Russians still told fortunes with wax.

"Of course they do," she said.

"Just how is it done?"

"They light a candle and let the wax drip into a pan of cold water, then take the casts that have been formed and hold them in various positions so that the candle will throw them in shadows on the wall. Some people are very good at telling the future in this way. And at christenings, they cut off a little of the baby's hair, roll it in a ball with wax, and drop it in the christening font. If the ball sinks, the baby will die. If the parents walk around the font three times, spit, and say 'Renounce Satan!' it will sometimes help to keep the baby alive."

"Have you ever heard of the devil appearing in the form of a pig?"

She thought a moment. "No," she said, "but in my village there was a woman who had a bad scar. She hated her husband. One day a huge pig appeared in the village and followed her husband everywhere. He could not drive the pig away, but at last he wounded it in the back. Perhaps that pig was a devil, but when the husband returned home he found his wife bathed in blood from a wound in her back. She still carries the scar from that wound."

My friend told me that there was a witch in every village. "In Kolumna there is a very famous witch. She is a terrifying woman, taller and heavier than a man, with her legs all wrapped up strangely. She can heal, and she can tell the future exactly. People come from far away to seek her advice. And the witches are not only in the villages, for I know of one in Moscow. A soldier whom I knew married a girl and moved into the same big apartment where that witch lives. The witch made the girl waste away and die."

She told me that wax dolls were made from the hair combings and nail cuttings of the intended victim, who wasted as the wax melted in a flame. In addition to this classical method, which is as old as the earliest records of ancient Egypt, the Russian witches of today make little bags of rags and other personal belongings of those whom they wish to harm and put them under their mattresses. She said that there was a time when all the churches would have been destroyed if it had not been for the fact that so many of those who were tearing them down fell from the high belfries to their deaths that the people were afraid to continue with the destruction. She told of several typical poltergeist manifestations, although she did not recognize them as such.

"In my village," she went on, "there was a *strashnaya doroga* (a terrible road). It ran out of a wood across a swamp. In the wood it was just an ordinary road, but something happened to it when it reached the swamp. Nobody in the village would go on it after dark, for in some way people were lured off the road into the marsh and were never seen again."

And the woman who told me all this is not an old unreconstructed *babushka,* but a young and personable product of Soviet times and Soviet education. She agreed with my own conclusion that the reason one seldom finds witchcraft mentioned in Russian literature and why devils are usually grotesque and laughable is not because of any lack of deep and wide belief in them, but because it is best not to discuss them, or, if faced, to face them courageously.

"Gospodin Admiral," said Natasha, "is it true that the Americans have a bomb which is so powerful that, when it goes off, all the people up to sixty-five kilometers away turn black and die?"

"I was at Bikini," I told her, "and I was very much closer to the bomb than sixty-five kilometers. Have I turned black and died?"

Recently pamphlets have been sold in large numbers in the street kiosks telling the Russians the facts about the atomic bomb. Having been through the big blitz in London in 1940 as well as at Bikini, those pamphlets seem to me to be realistic rather than being the desperate attempt to mislead the population which some see in them. In any event, they are obviously intended to provide a stabilizing influence if things should go wrong, but one wonders how much belief the statements of their government inspire in the people here.

Someone should make a thorough and profound study of the psychology of the informer. Whoever undertakes such a job will find a wealth of material in Russia. Allied fields for research are the psychology of the defector and the double agent. All these subjects require the insight of an artist as well as an academician, a Shakespeare as well as a scientist. Tyutchev says in a much-quoted passage that Russia can be understood only through the heart and not through the mind, and Sir Bernard Pares points out that much Russian thought and action demand of the student "not only often a very wrestle of thought but also a very special gift of sympathy."

In speaking of the double agent, Pares also has this to say: "There was something in the Russian temperament and scene that engendered these men of ambivalent spirit and double role, these Gapons, Azevs, Kaplinskys, Bagrovs and Malinovskys — figures without parallel in the police and revolutionary movements of other lands."

Nevertheless, there is much in the Russian character that resists these dark tendencies. Some say that since the war it is increasingly difficult to recruit effective informers. Perhaps this might be due to feelings of comradeship that were developed during the war, or perhaps the continued disappointments of the people have brought about a final cynicism. Whatever the reasons may be, this fact, if it is a fact, could be one of extraordinary importance. Bolshevism may well carry the seeds of its own decay within its inherent need for forced control of the people, and an effective universal informer system is essential to that control. The apparent invulnerability of the Bolshevik regime rests on such a system to so great an extent that any illness here may well prove fatal.*

Foy Kohler, who has been acting ambassador since the departure of General Smith, after many longing looks on my part, has given me a copy of a Russian translation of the memoirs of the Marquis de Custine, the French traveler who visited Russia in 1839 hoping to find there grounds for the defense of autocracy to which he had reason to be inclined, since both his father and his grandfather had died on the guillotine in the French Revolution. He came away from Russia so appalled by what he had seen, and what he had seen so parallels what goes on in Russia today, that his remarkable book is still of extraordinary interest. Hertzen said of it in 1843, "Without doubt, this is the most diverting and the wisest book that has been written by a foreigner about Russia."

It was not until after the Revolution that any translation, other than a brief censored condensation of 1910, appeared in Russia. In 1930, a fairly full and completely uncensored translation was published in Moscow by the All-Union Society of Political Ex-Convicts and Exiles. That Society has since been liquidated, and it would not be surprising if the long introduction which prefaced the Rus-

---

* The XIX Congress of the Communist Party of Soviet Russia in late 1952 laid unusual emphasis on the necessity of Party members informing on each other. If all were well with the informer system, the regime would be unlikely to stress this point.

sian translation of Custine was one of the reasons, for it is a good example of the "slave talk" of recent years. Just as the Russia of Nicholas I in Custine's book provides an excellent parallel to the Soviet Union, the history of the treatment of that book by the tsarist government, which is set forth in detail in the Society's introduction parallels the treatment today of books that criticize the Soviet regime. Since Custine could not be attacked on the grounds of the justice of his observations, his character and capabilities were attacked.

Alan Kirk has arrived and taken over his duties. He is an excellent ambassador, dignified and suave, and both he and the engaging Mrs. Kirk know their jobs thoroughly. The senior Embassy personnel went with the new Ambassador into the Kremlin, where he presented his credentials to Shvernik, the President of the Presidium of the Supreme Soviet. He is often regarded by foreigners as analogous to the President of the United States, though of course the real power lies in Stalin. The fact that Shvernik is not even a full member of the Politburo, being only a candidate or alternate, shows how false this analogy is. It was a stiff little ceremony in a room with a polished parquet floor, bare except for busts of Lenin and Stalin. Shvernik, short and stocky, with black hair and eyebrows and a gray mustache, looked in his dark suit as respectable as a banker, but he had a vague air of not being completely at ease.

4. SIBERIA

NOVOSIBIRSK IN CENTRAL SIBERIA has no Intourist connections, so it is necessary to make one's own way in all respects if one wishes to go there. It is in an area that has not been declared closed to foreigners, and, unlike Yakutsk, is not chiefly dependent on concentration camps for its economy. Because of the risk of sudden fits of despondency ending up a "suicide" like the Turkish courier, I took with me Lieutenant Commander Whited, the graduate of the Navy language school who had eventually been assigned to our office. Airplane tickets were obtained from Aeroflot with no difficulty, and we sent a telegram to the local hotel and another to the mayor, or head of the Executive Committee of the city, asking if he would be kind enough to assist us with accommodations in case the hotel could not take care of us. That seemed desirable, because Commander Cosby had had to spend the night on the streets on a recent trip to southeastern Russia.

The white light of day had already come when we took off from the Vnukovo Airport at two o'clock in the morning. All my previous flights had been in Russian-built Dakotas or C-47s, but this plane was a new Ilyushin of Russian design. But the engines, equipment and general type of construction were copied more or less directly from American models. Whited and I agreed to talk with each other only in Russian, and we adhered to this rigidly throughout the whole trip. He said that he had been puny while a boy, and so had taken up weight lifting. Weight lifting is to be highly recommended, for he is certainly now a *silach,* or strong-man athlete.

The forbidden city of Kazan was black in the far distance as we crossed the Volga, with a long smear of smoke from its many tall chimneys trailing across the river. Asia begins at the Volga rather than at the Urals as the geographies say. The houses beneath were not set in straggling yards along a single village street, as in Great Russia, but each was built around its own courtyard, pushed up against a broad space that should have been a road, with its kitchen garden trailing out into the countryside. There was never a road to be seen, only trails. For a long time we followed the Kama, a tributary of the Volga almost as broad and burnished as the great river itself, with many rafts and river barges. At Chistopol a peculiar cloud of thick yellowish-green clung close to the ground, obscuring the town. We passed other towns with such intriguing names as Yelabuga and Arsk.

This part of Russia is made up of several autonomous republics, inhabited largely by the Finno-Ugric aborigines who were there when the Great Russians took over, or by the remnants of the Mongol invaders. It was in this country that human sacrifice took place even into my own lifetime, and where it may even still occur. About the time I was a small child, on a footpath in the forest which now lay beneath us, appeared a corpse without a head and without a heart and lungs. Bodies whose heads or right hands had been cut off had been found before in that locality, but the inhabitants, by means known only to themselves, had led the authorities to list them as the bodies of animals. The local priests had been ordered to bury them. But rumors of rites, and even of cannibalism, were whispered, so in this case there was a thorough investigation.

Seven Votyaks were brought to trial and charged with murder and with drinking human blood. They were found guilty. The local senate annulled the verdict and directed a new trial in Yelabuga. They were again found guilty, but the senate found irregularities in the court procedure, and the case was taken to the highest court in Kazan. There the seven Votyaks were finally released, the court saying that since "now, on the threshold of the twentieth century, human sacrifices take place among a people who have been living for more than three centuries within the limits and under the civilizing influence of a Christian government, the basis for a sentence of guilt must be subjected to much stricter examination than those motives and data which lead to a finding of guilt in commonplace murder." If these seven were guilty, so was the whole Votyak nation, or at least an entire section of it.

I have a pamphlet, written and published locally at the time by a priest, Blinov, that gives the details. Blinov, being a member of the Imperial Russian Geographical Society, was disturbed by the lack of information about an entire nation, made evident at the trials and in the comment they aroused in Russia, so for a hundred pages he gives a wealth of fascinating ethnographic data and speculation on the religion of the Votyaks, tracing it to Buddhism from the Altais fifteen hundred years ago that had become debased by merging with the beliefs and customs of north-central Asia.

We crossed a corner of the Bashkir Republic and imperceptibly were in the Urals, landing at Sverdlovsk, the Ekaterinburg where the last of the Romanovs were slain. Sverdlovsk lies in a broad gap, or rather a gentle swelling saddle between the North and South Urals. That saddle is nowhere as rough as eastern Ohio, and it is more open meadowland than forest. But far to the north and south spread the taiga, an unbroken expanse of dark pine forest that covered the low mountains. In that saddle was the only road that we had seen since leaving the Volga, indeed the only road that we saw all the way across Siberia to Novosibirsk. It was unpaved, but graveled where it climbed through hills and woods. An occasional swift, clear stream could be seen which looked like trout water. Whited and I had time for some beer while the plane was being refueled, but there was no food to be had. In the little buffet they said that they had not had any bread for many days.

We slid down the long saddle into Asia proper. Not far from Sverdlovsk the trans-Siberian railroad splits into two branches that run parallel as much as a hundred miles apart until they come together again almost five hundred miles to the east at Omsk. Both lines are single-tracked, so that it seemed more like following a branch railroad in the western part of the United States than flying along the great trunk line that is the only link between European Russia and the Pacific. Grassy steppes and a few big farms lay along the railroad and as far as we could see to the north and south.

As we neared Omsk the whole sky became filled with dark clouds. We came down low to keep under them, and flew across a corner of Omsk. The names of Omsk and Tomsk have always seemed to me to have a barbaric majesty like the beating of drums and a mysterious echo like the names of unknown Gog and Magog. What impressed me most about Omsk at the moment was the small size of the city. It lies in a vast, empty country, and its population under the Tsars was only about fifty thousand. It still looks from the air no bigger than an American city of about that class, and does not seem nearly as large as, say, Lincoln, Nebraska. Part of that is due to its greater compactness, and also to the manner in which Russians are crowded into their living spaces. It seems to me that most Russians do not resent their crowded quarters as much as we would under similar circumstances; it is not only that few of them have been used to anything else, but that they seem to like to crowd together. There are limits, of course, beyond which all privacy is broken down, and those limits probably would not be exceeded by most if they had their way.

We flew low through streaming tendrils of cloud over black-and-white barracklike houses, and on along the double-tracked railroad into the Barabinskaya Steppe. By this time the clouds, spitting a little rain now and then, had forced us down to within fifty or a hundred feet from the ground, so that it was almost like looking from the windows of a train to watch the monotonous landscape slide past. It was very bumpy, so rough that we had to strap ourselves in our seats to keep from being thrown out. Omsk itself, in the center of the vastest of continents, is only some two hundred and fifty feet above sea level, and the Barabinskaya Steppe is part of one of the greatest marshlands of the world, reaching for thousands of miles from the foothills of the Altais to the arctic tundra. It stretched flat and level, as far as the eye could reach, with never the slightest rise or change. Everywhere was lush green grass, standing high and reedlike to what appeared to be more than the height of a man. This endless green expanse was regularly broken by small clumps of silver birches growing thickly together, bending almost to the ground under the strong wind.

Very rarely one would see a little hayfield wrested out of the swamp, or a miserable little village of four or five houses, decrepit and half-drowned in mud, huddled against the railroad. Never a road was there in all that wilderness, only now and then a wagon track which opened and spread like an unraveled rope wherever the going got too soft. It is difficult to see how anything but a horse or the railroad could cross that terrible dreamlike monotony. Little round peat ponds were dotted through the green, growing larger and larger as we swept on to enormous lakes, and always there was the grass and the little tossing clumps of birches. It was beautiful in the rain under the dark sky, but, by the time we had seen two or three hundred miles of it, it seemed like the end of the world, and the dream became oppressive — like a nightmare of an enchanted land of grass and water and wind that would never end.

A thin flaxen-haired girl who was part of the plane's crew came up to us. She had a cast in her eye so that she looked at us obliquely as she said that there would be a car from the Gorkom, the city committee, waiting for us on our arrival in Novosibirsk. We felt quite pleased with our foresightedness, and regarded the Soviets with a new warmth for taking such good care of us. Unlike Omsk, from the air Novosibirsk gave the impression of a very large city. We were still flying low, but in flat country one can see a long distance from an airplane, and the opposite ends of the city were never in sight as we circled over its edge to land well beyond its outskirts.

When we climbed out of the plane into the drizzling wind-blown rain, there was not a car in sight and the girl with a cast in her eye was not to be found. The lone woman who seemed to be in charge of the airport said that the plane was late, although our watches, set four hours ahead for the time difference, checked with the schedule. There had been a car there, but it had waited for us for two hours and then gone away. That did not seem to us like even Soviet efficiency, particularly where foreigners were involved. We asked the woman if she would call the Gorkom, but she said they were now closed. She said that there was no way of calling a taxi, but that if we would wait for a while perhaps one would show up. There seemed to be nothing to do but wait or walk, and since the road was long and muddy we waited.

At last a taxi drove up, driven by a squat, flat-nosed young man with a hoarse loud voice and a breezy manner. Almost every other word in his conversation was "Yei bogu!" (by God!). He had been a paratrooper during the war, and he liked driving a taxi, except that his hours were too long. Yes, this was a wonderful country for duck-shooting — it was nothing to come in with two or three hundred ducks from a morning's shooting. And fish! More than you could carry home. Cold in the winter, though. Last winter it was fifty below zero, with snow filling the road to the level of those high banks on each side, so that cars could not get through to the airport for days. Of course Russians love Moscow and do not like to go to the "periphery" to work, but this is not the periphery, it is a metropolis as good as Moscow.

We bumped and rattled over the irregular cobblestones as he punctuated his garrulity with *yei bogus*. A woman with a load of wood on her shoulder did not move aside fast enough when he blasted his horn, so he had to swerve sharply to avoid hitting her. "*Yei bogu, korova!* (cow!)" he shouted at her as she gave him a black look. "*Yei bogu,* these women are long on hair and short on brains!"

I have often thought that from almost any place in every Soviet city and town of any size you could look around and sooner or later spot a prison camp. I tried it as we came into Novosibirsk, and three times the familiar guardhouses were to be seen at every strategic angle of the fences surrounding three different building jobs. Some have tried to explain them by saying that they are merely to protect the materials from theft, but that does not seem true, for there are many places where similar work is in progress that have the fences, but not the booths and the guards with rifles and machine guns.

Although almost all of the intersecting streets of the city were unpaved, we had pavement of a sort all the way. The streets were broad and the houses low and far apart. The tsarist town from which Novosibirsk has grown was a tiny place, but in spite of its newness the city already looked gray and old. "Yeibogu" let us out at the Sovetskaya Hotel in the center of the downtown area, whose buildings were of about the same size and number as those of a Middle Western American town of ten or twenty thousand inhabitants. The Sovetskaya was three or four stories high, neater outside than within.

A composed, fine-looking girl presided over the desk. Yes, we were expected, but the plane was so late that she had had to give the room that was being saved for us to someone else. We would have to wait and see what showed up. It was clear to us that we were going to get a room, for the first thing that we were required to do after showing our documents was to pay for it. We had some much-needed stroganov and some good Georgian wine and then did our waiting.

The calm girl at the desk of the hotel was good to look at, for she had a lovely creamy skin and heavy braids of pale hair coiled above her oval face. There was no doubt about accommodations being in short supply, for a dozen times we watched her turn people away by telephone or in person. Her neck ached, for she twisted it continually as she peacefully told the inquirers that there was no room for them. One strong, square-faced Russian continued to sit by his luggage in the lobby regardless of her repeated assurances that there was no chance of anyone leaving at that time of night. "Why don't you go to the community house?" she said to him. "There you will at least have a place to sleep." That pointer seemed to me worth remembering for use in further travels in the Soviet Union, but the man continued to sit patiently by his luggage. He was there when we first came to the hotel, and he was still there three hours later when we were finally shown to a room.

It was a very narrow room whose single window did not seem to have been washed from time immemorial. All the space was taken up by three cots. Our consciences hurt us a little for not offering the extra cot to the man who was waiting so patiently below, but, after all, the girl at the desk, not we, was in charge, and we did not know but that we would still have a roommate. Also there was always the community house, whatever that might be, for him. We had to make our own beds, for blankets and sheets were neatly folded on each cot, and this was a standard procedure: each day we found them folded instead of spread.

A futile effort had been made to sluice down the common wash-room, but it was nevertheless so pungent that it stung the eyes. Never yet in the Soviet Union have I seen any toilet paper — even in luxury accommodations, which means sit-down toilets. But then, as they themselves say, what would they do with *Pravda?* Here one sees a minor example of the difference in values between Russia and America, for it is difficult to imagine an American Five Year Plan, no matter how austere, that would not include that item. Although the Russians try to be Western, they show a remarkable insensitivity to many of the details which go to make up the complex of Western customs and habits. Yet there were no bugs in the beds, nor have I ever seen any in Russia.

We had a gorgeous sleep, broken in the morning by the crowing of roosters as numerous and as triumphant as if we were on a farm instead of in the center of the biggest city in Siberia. By the time we were up and about, breakfast was over and all the restaurants were closed. Every time we stopped a passer-by to ask where we could get some coffee and a bite to eat, we became the center of a crowd of Russians, all trying to be helpful, and at last we were led to a little dining room where we had some bread and butter, cheese and tea.

There was intermittent rain from the gray clouds that were so low it seemed as though one could almost reach up and touch them, but the air was soft and springlike. We went to the Gorkom to pay our respects, but were told by the suspicious young lady in the ante-room that all of the members of the Gorkom were out of town or ill, so we left our cards. Then we thought we would get a taxi and see the town. Several taxis were in evidence, but every one of the drivers told us he had an engagement and could not take us any-where. We ran across Yeibogu's car parked near the railroad sta-tion.

"*Yei bogu*," he said, "I would like to take you around, but *yei bogu*, I'm waiting for a couple who have already engaged me. Just one little minute — I'll telephone to tell them that since they are so late I'm going to take you instead."

He disappeared into the station while we climbed into his car to get out of the rain. In a few moments a young man and woman came up to the car. "What are you doing in our taxi?" they asked angrily. Just then Yeibogu returned and greeted them heartily by name. "What are these people doing in your car?" they asked ac-rimoniously. Yeibogu shrugged his shoulders and looked at us in surprise as though he had never seen us before. Having lost our support, there was nothing to do but yield.

So we made our way on foot to the famous theater, one of the largest in the Soviet Union. When the girl at the ticket office told us that all seats were sold out, we asked to see the director. We were taken into a comfortable office, where the gentle little old man who was in charge beamed when we told him that his theater was known even in America as one of the finest in the world and that it would be a sin and a shame for us to have to return to Moscow and tell our friends that we had been unable to see it. He took us courteously around. The huge amphitheater was so free from the usual ornate decorations that it seemed bare, but the seats were very comfortable. When we thanked him on leaving, he invited us to come to the production that night as his guests, saying that there would be seats at the box office for us.

Since there were still no taxis to be had, we saw the town on foot through the occasional showers. The Siberian architecture is plainer than that of Russia and the woodcarving of the windows and gables less ornate, but the people on the streets looked exactly like those to be seen in Moscow. Perhaps they were a little more countrified and a little freer in their manners — in fact, one had the feeling that this was almost a frontier town — but their clothing and their faces were the same as one sees everywhere, without any traces of Asia or any more signs of the tribal peoples than there are signs of Indians in Topeka. One tiny square green cottage had on it a brass plate which said that it had been Kirov's home in 1908.

Once we fell in with some very young girls. They were schoolteachers from Leningrad, but they looked like children. One of them came up to me and said, "What's your name?" When I told her, she asked if she could introduce us to her friends. Her name was Shura, and there were three others with her. "Youth in America cannot possibly be as free as in Russia," they said, and urged us to go to the movies with them. They were disappointed when we declined, and far down the street we could see them looking back and waving good-by to us.

Although the river Ob flows through Novosibirsk, we could not find it. What seemed like valleys cutting across the streets ahead turned out to be nothing, or we were blocked by the railroad. When we became thoroughly confused and lost, we asked a broad-shouldered man in boots and carrying a whip which direction we should take. "Follow me," he said, and set off at a brisk pace. He led us through a tunnel under the trans-Siberian and through a maze of dirt roads crowded with cattle and goats looking much more like the streets of a market town than of a big city. There were many beggars in this part of town, unbelievably ragged, some of them legless and armless ex-soldiers still wearing uniforms that were barely recognizable as such. When we came out on the river our guide had vanished before we could thank him.

The turbid waters of the Ob were very wide, with mud flats showing here and there. On the far bank, dim in the gray distance, were what seemed like gigantic factories, although there is something about the Russian atmosphere that makes buildings loom so portentously that it is difficult to get any idea of their true size. A straggle of discolored and unlovely river boats and fishing craft lay alongside the near bank seemingly deserted, but not a boat moved on the broad yellow surface of the river.

At the end of the sloping road ahead sprawled a flat low bridge with no overhead structure and little or nothing in the way of guardrails, the only bridge to be seen except for the railroad bridge far in the distance that leads almost immediately to the great Siberian taiga. Close to this shore was a section which could be used as a draw to let the river traffic pass, marked by huge wooden lanterns set on posts. Where the bridge began was a guardhouse opposite which stood two sharp-eyed MVD, checking the documents of the country traffic that streamed across in a long line of cattle, horse-drawn carts and small trucks. It took no effort of the imagination to picture the melancholy lines of convicts and exiles driven on foot into the endless Siberian wilderness.

Although we stood some distance from the guardhouse, an MVD trooper suddenly appeared at our elbow. "Your *dokumenty!*" he said, regarding us suspiciously. He looked at them for a long time. "What are you doing here?"

We told him truthfully that we were seeing the sights of Novosibirsk on foot, and added with equal truth that we would be very grateful for a taxi to take us back to our hotel. Even if we had not been very weary, to attempt to cross that bridge seemed like a hopeless show of impertinence. An empty taxi came chugging up the slope while the trooper was thinking hard. We shouted to the driver, and fortunately he stopped. Whited and I piled in, leaving the MVD undecided as to whether or not they had missed a chance for glory in letting two public enemies escape.

We congratulated ourselves on at last having a car at our disposal, but when we asked the driver to drive us around a bit, he said surlily that he had to meet a train at the station and dumped us off at our hotel. Anyhow, we had had no lunch and it would soon be time for us to eat if we were going to get to the theater without having to rush.

Dinner in a big restaurant on the main street was very welcome, savory with fried onions and lamb cutlets. As we were dining, a sturdy Russian stopped at our table for a brief moment as he was leaving. "You are Americans," he said in a low voice. "It is dangerous for me to stop to talk, but I want to tell you that we Russians will never forget all that America has done for us, from the days of the great famine to those of the war." And he was gone before we could get a good look at him.

Mazeppa was on at the Novosibirsk opera house. We had seats in the very middle of the front row, and for the first time since being in Russia I was presented with a free program. Mazeppa, who is a patriot and a hero to the Ukrainians, is regarded by the Russians as a scoundrel and a traitor. Some of the music of the opera was haunting, but the passion and sincerity of the artists was memorable. At the close, the leader of the orchestra applauded the cast, and then they all applauded each other.

Although it was very late when we got back home and the streets were generally empty, there was some excitement going on across the street from the hotel. A three-story building with living quarters above a food shop on the ground floor was blazing merrily. The fire was in the food shop, but smoke and flames wrapped the whole building. A small crowd had gathered in the street to watch the firemen, who wore huge bronze helmets, crested like those of Achilles and Ajax, at work leading out the fire hose. A diminutive fire engine, shining with brass, wheezily supplied pressure to the hose.

It occurred to me that in all the time I have lived in Moscow I have never seen a fire. That is remarkable, for fire was once one of the terrors of Russia. Electrification may account for part of this anomaly, but it also seems probable that the Russians have had their fingers burnt so often that they have become abnormally careful in dealing with fire. One still sees burned-out ruins in the villages, where there are many thatched roofs. In England a thatched roof makes fire insurance almost prohibitive in cost.

Even this midnight fire in Novosibirsk had its touch of the strangeness that seems so inseparable from Russia. On such an occasion in America the dwellers in the apartments above would have been rushing around saving their books and clothes and other possessions, but here there was no such excitement. A man in his shirt sleeves and a woman in a wrapper sat in front of an open window immediately above the hottest part of the fire, leaning their elbows unconcernedly on the windowsill and calmly enjoying the scene while they exchanged wisecracks with friends in the audience below.

It is difficult to tell whether or not the taxi drivers of Novosibirsk had been told by the secret police to be non-cooperative, but we never did succeed in getting to look around in any other way than on foot. When we finally left, we were up early so as to be sure not to miss the Aeroflot bus which ran out to the airport. The bus turned out to be an open truck with benches in which we rode through the rain, jammed in between a neat Mongol lieutenant colonel and a drowsy unkempt soldier. Before we had left the Barabinskaya Steppe the weather had cleared up, continuing fine all the way to Sverdlovsk. There it was again bad to the west, so we waited for an hour and a half for a clearance.

We left the buffet and followed the slant-eyed colonel to stretch our legs on the grass at the edge of the flying field. A soldier stepped in front of us to bar our way, his rifle held suggestively ready in his hands. No passengers were permitted on the field unescorted. Another puzzling example of inconsistency, for when we had been there before, we were permitted to come and go alone without question and now the stoppage seemed directed towards a Soviet officer rather than towards us as foreigners. Perhaps an MVD transport that had just landed had something to do with it, but there were no signs of activity about that plane as we sat in the grass in front of the buffet and waited.

The ceiling was low and we were well off our course by the time we had passed through the storm front, for we had a good look at the forbidden city of Gorky, the old Nizhni Novgorod. It is now a very large city, extending for miles along the sandy banks of the Volga. In the Ivanovo area the harvest was being gathered, and although almost none of the boasted mechanized equipment was in evidence, we saw many horse-drawn reapers. Twice we saw long tables set out in the fields for the harvest dinner, which, from the activity about, seemed to be more of a festival than an ordinary workers' meal.

As we neared Moscow there was a tremendous black thunderstorm ahead. We flew round and round, over country that was completely unrecognizable to me, wild and desolate and black with vast peat fields. Whited and I hoped mightily that the Russian pilots were watching their supply of gasoline, for we had been in the air a long time. They doubtless were, for since the storm did not blow over, we went in to a dirt field some distance from Moscow which I did not know even existed. But it was a long, long wait before our car, which had been waiting at Vnukovo, finally showed up to get us.

5. THE PIG MARKET

IT IS RATHER REMARKABLE that one never hears anything of Rasputin. The enigmatic priest whose very name is suggestive — *rasputnik* means "libertine" — and who exercised so much influence over the last Tsaritsa is never mentioned in the propaganda, nor do any of the people, even the old ones, talk of him. In answer to my questions, one Russian said: "Rasputin said in his lifetime that if he were killed Russia would be destroyed with him. Did not this prove to be true? He had tremendous strength, and to speak his name now might release him."

Another said that he was the voice of the people and the voice of God to the Tsar: the regime does not make propaganda capital of him because it knows that this is true, and their consciences are guilty.

Still another told me that he thought that Rasputin's case led to certain ideological difficulties. After all, Rasputin was a man of the people, a product of the Russian masses, and, since many of the masses still cling to their religious beliefs, the regime would have trouble in explaining to them how the instinctive proletariat could produce such an evil man.

This is the third year that I have seen the Soviet air show on Air Fleet Day. Except for a few more jets and some experimental planes, it was almost indistinguishable from the preceding shows. One has the feeling that one has seen it all before, the same sensation of "this is where I came in" that one gets at a continuous motion picture show.

Henrik Madsen gave me a copy of the Danish Communist paper, published immediately after the air show. It showed two pictures from Moscow side by side, one of a group of laughing, cheering Soviet boys and girls looking and pointing at the sky, and the other of Mike O'Daniel and me, also looking up and with what seemed to me to be rather quizzical expressions on our faces. Beneath our picture was the following legend: *"This shows the Amer-*

*ican Military Attache and Naval Attache, whose interest by no
means appears less, but whose expressions indicate that their pleasure in the results of the Soviet pilots by no means equals that of the
young Soviet citizens."*

In the southern part of Moscow is the big Kalitnikosky Market
which does a retail business in animals. We set forth for it on a
warm Sunday under a blue sky dotted with little half-formed clouds
whose bases faded out into nothing. Valodya had great difficulty in
finding it, for few seemed to know it by its right name and those
who called it the "bird market" did not recognize it as the "horse
market" and vice versa. It was a big enclosure in the fields opposite
a treeless cemetery.

We knew we were getting near from the number of people we
met leading cows and pigs. The pigs had ropes around their mid-
dles. When they were carried, they were mostly in bags, but sometimes they were kicking and squealing in the arms of the delighted
purchaser. Scrubbed very clean, they looked like fat little dogs. Men,
women and children alike carried them with affection, like pets —
and perhaps that is what they were, for a time, at least — rubbing
their cheeks against them and talking to their squeals.

As we neared the market the squealing grew louder, and, once
inside, the ground was covered with moving, jumping bags. Big
wicker baskets were piled high, and from them too came squeals.
Clean white pigs, brown pigs, black pigs, spotted ones. It was more
of a bazaar than a market, for it had streets and districts in which
different beasts were sold. The dog district had many police dogs
and Siberians, with a few Samoyeds and bird dogs. Cages and baskets
and pens were alive with fluffy puppies. One street was lined with
cages in which Angora rabbits wrinkled their pink noses, and another was populated by kittens and cats. The cows and horses were
bony and gaunt, not sleek like the smaller animals. Peasant women
in wide skirts and bright kerchiefs milked cows and goats on the
spot. Goats, chickens, ducks and brilliant yellow-beaked geese added
to the din and confusion amidst the barnyard smells. The geese and
rabbits were placid, and only the pigs seemed to rebel.

All of the collective farms for a radius of scores of kilometers
from Moscow must have brought their animals to the Kalitnikosky

to sell. Peasants and city folk were in their Sunday best, and lace underskirts would be swept up so that some tired woman could sit on her blue denim bloomers rather than her finery. Many came up to us — "Want to buy a cow?" — "Fine chicken cheap, feel how fat she is!" There were thick bushy beards and long straggling ones. Some of the men wore homemade bast or reed shoes over rags which were wrapped up their legs. And everywhere were the wonderful faces of the people, shrewd, sunburned, curious and patient. They liked the animals, for they were forever petting them, but a bony cow with a bloody rag wrapped around one of her horns and a poor famished police dog with enormously swollen testicles attracted no attention.

The pigeons were with the stock, possibly because they were used for food, but a corner of the market was piled high with wooden cages and wire cages filled with canaries, small parrots and love birds — red birds, blue ones, birds of pastel tints. The fish section was entered through a lane lined with fishing poles, crude reels, coarse lines, sinkers, homemade hooks, some of them very tiny, and nets, including even the big dip nets for the *lyulki*. Everyone who wanted fish brought their own containers, for bottles and even cans are so hard to get that they are prized. Goldfish, guppies, and Siamese fighting fish flashed like jewels in glass jars of every conceivable shape and size on counters that were also covered with seeds, cress, and heaps of tiny red worms. One glass tank was filled with diminutive fish that were sold for a ruble each, tiny fish less than an inch long, so transparent that their little skeletons could be plainly seen, but gleaming and glittering with a shifting, opalescent glow. The bearded old man who sold them, seeing my interest, said: "Buy some of these and you will soon be rich. They are very lecherous and hot, and will quickly throw a whole aquarium full."

There is a river-boat service that runs down the Ob from Novosibirsk to Kolpashevo, well north of Tomsk. I still cling to the belief that many of the annoyances and delays to which foreigners are put are also suffered by Soviet citizens themselves, and that if one had the time, patience and endurance to sit it out long enough in some provincial town, one might still succeed in seeing something of Russia that is off the beaten path — either that, or perhaps end up in the pokey. But something which never seemed possible has happened to me — patience and endurance are at a very low ebb, and, now that my days here are few, time has also run out.

So our Marine colonel went to Novosibirsk to try to beat out a trip on the river boat. At first he could find out little or nothing about the river line, and then day after day he was put off. There would be no boat that day, but perhaps the next. Then the boat was broken down, and no one could say when it would be running again. This went on so long that his patience and endurance were also almost exhausted and he had reached the conclusion that no foreigner would be permitted to go on that river journey, when he became acquainted with the Russian who occupied the adjoining room. Mac had often been kept awake by endless nervous pacing back and forth next door, but any annoyance disappeared when he learned that it was because the man had a very sick child at Kolpashevo. The only means of transportation was by river boat, and this Soviet citizen could find out no more than Mac when, if ever, he might get to what was for him home.

But time ran out even for Mac, who returned to Moscow without ever learning whether or not a foreigner could reach Kolpashevo, leaving his friend still pacing back and forth and worrying about his sick child.

This year, for the first time, Dostoevsky is omitted from the college entrance requirements. It seems as though the day is not far distant when this greatest of all Russian writers will be only an obscure name to the people whom he understood so well. The regime has in the past gone to some pains to point out wherein Dostoevsky was "mistaken" and to explain him away in terms of class background and the state of development of society of his day, but it is easy to see why he has now been completely done away with.

Any thoughtful Russian must be impressed by the analogies with the present regime that can be found in Dostoevsky's books. The theme that freedom is too hot for the individual to handle, so that world-wide salvation can be had only through world-wide oppression, is found not only in the Grand Inquisitor passage of *The Brothers Karamazov,* but is developed by Shigalyov in *The Pos-*

sessed. This latter book, which is founded in part on the actual character of Nechayev who was brought to justice in 1871 for organizing a widespread conspiracy, sets forth the technique of the cell, or group of five. The surest way to guarantee security and control is to arouse in the cell suspicion of an informer, for when the informer is finally murdered, no member will dare to betray the cell lest he himself be betrayed as a murderer.

Prince Mishkin's insights at moments of approaching epileptic seizure in *The Idiot* give some remarkable glimpses into the Russian soul. Dostoevsky is deep stuff, often morbid and sometimes

obscure, but he is of such stature in Russian literature that no honest government could do with him what is now being done by the Soviet regime.

There is a unique fascination about trying to trace anything down from published Russian sources. The volumes of all Russian encyclopedias under both Tsar and Soviet have always appeared serially over a considerable number of years. I tried in the *Great Encyclopedia* to find out something about the All-Union Society of Political Ex-Convicts and Exiles which published Custine's absorbing book. Sure enough, the society was listed under "All-Union," but only with the statement *"See Society of."* There were scores of societies in the "S" volume, but not one word about the one that interested me. A look in the front of the volumes showed that publication of the "S" volume had not been reached until after the Great Purge, many years after the early volume that contained the Russian equivalent of "All-Union."

Then I tried the *Little Encyclopedia,* which, being a less ambitious effort, was completed in less time, and whose "S" volume might have gotten in under the wire. In it there was nothing under "S," but it was no procrastinator, for it had plunged boldly into the subject under All-Union.

The society helped its own members and their families, maintaining sanatoriums, homes of rest and children's homes. It had fifty divisions and groups, with a total membership of about three thousand, forty-three per cent of them Bolsheviks and the rest non-Party. This was no fly-by-night minor organization, and it is difficult to imagine one with a better claim to revolutionary legitimacy or better intrenched. Yet, like the Society of Old Bolsheviks, it disappears from Soviet history and reference books without a trace, sometime during the Great Purge.

One who attempts to do research among Russian sources must pay attention to the date those sources were published. He must also know the history of the censorship in both tsarist and Soviet times, and the policies of the censorship at the time of publication. Successive editions should also be compared with those points in mind.

There has been much cold rain and the days are rapidly getting shorter. Nell and I have been to see *The Cherry Orchard* and *Dead Souls* for the last time, for my orders home have arrived. Last night we saw *Romeo and Juliet* danced to Prokofiev's music. One scene in it was unforgettable. Tybalt's body is borne in, carried high on its bier, and Lady Capulet gives a wild demonstration of emotional grief that would be hard to match. She literally tears her hair and rends her garments, and then throws herself on Tybalt's body, to be finally raised with him on the bier and carried away sobbing and screaming, her long hair flying against a somber, lurid background. It was hair-raising. Even the final scene of wholesale death was given such an emotional content that it was very affecting.

As we left the Bolshoy, we saw in the crowd one of the MXAT actors who often plays the boorish Yasha in *The Cherry Orchard.*

There was no mistaking him, for we have seen him in many other things. Theatrical make-up is remarkable here in its use of wax, cotton and other material to change the contours of a face, and there was little in common between the intelligent alert face of this young man and that of Yasha.

Both the British Aldises and the Dutch Geomans have gone. When they left, I heard a Russian say that they were "real democrats." And now Eddie Stevens and Nina are leaving for a new assignment with his paper in Rome. So many whom we have known and liked have gone that Moscow does not seem like the same place. Eddie has been envious of my tsarist five-volume edition of Afanasyev's *Skazki,* but he has a translation of the *Thousand and One Nights* into Russian that I would like to have. For some reason those tales are much more effective in Russian than they are in English, probably because of the naturalness of the translation.

Eddie has a tsarist edition of Tolstoy. Once I went through a whole volume to compare it with a Soviet edition. The Tsar's censors were more honest than the modern ones, for omissions were always indicated in the text. In this case nothing in the old edition was omitted from the Soviet version, and all the old omissions were filled in. All of the cuts had to do with what might be construed as casting reflections on either the Orthodox Church or the Tsar and his family.

I share Eddie's aversion to Klyuchevsky, the great historian whom the Soviets regard so highly. Klyuchevsky's history is wholly in terms of social and economic conditions, which is all very well, but when you want to find out what happened it is far better to go to Karamzin or Solovyov. As far as I know, neither of them has been translated into English, but they are mines of curious information. I have a complete set of Karamzin, with his thousands and thousands of footnotes containing the things of most interest, but have tried to get Solovyov volume by volume. Complete sets are very rare and very expensive. It has been fun to hunt for them that way, but even though they still cost more than I should have put into books, it looks as though I shall leave Russia with six of his twenty-nine volumes still missing.

Braham, the commercial counselor of the British Embassy and

a gentle, sensible person, lives in a *dacha* among tall pine trees on the northern edge of Moscow. The school year has opened and his lovely little English daughter had just returned from her first day in the very first grade of a Russian school in the vicinity. We asked her what she had learned in school.

"I learned to march," she said, "and to play a game and to sing a little song." And this is the little song:

> *Lenina i Stalina*
> *Lyubit detvora,*
> *Leninu i Stalinu*
> *Ura! Ura! Ura!*

Which means "Children love Lenin and Stalin, to Lenin and Stalin — Hurrah! Hurrah! Hurrah!"

The *dacha* where the Brahams lived had formerly belonged to Allan Monkhouse, the British engineer who was one of the defendants at the famous trial of the Metro-Vickers engineers in 1933. There is an incident in Monkhouse's book which seems to me to be very significant. He had lived in Russia since tsarist times, and he gives a conversation he had with two intelligent, educated military Russians on the eve of the First World War. When he explained to them the way golf was played, one of the Russians expressed his astonishment that one player could trust another not to improve the lie of his ball when he was caught in the rough. The other Russian agreed that the game required too much mutual trust between players to be satisfactory.

To this day there is not a single golf links in all the Russias. Of course this is a little thing, but few of us realize the contributions that are made in the West by our comparative freedom from mutual suspicion and the way our civilization would break down if it were otherwise. Most Americans at home find it difficult to believe that no Russian trusts another except within the intimacy of a family, and by no means always even then. And when wider interests are involved, even to the welfare of some important branch of the national economy, the differences between our conditions and those in Russia begin to be more clear.

6. SHORT-TIMERS

AMBASSADOR KIRK HAD VISHINSKY to Spasso House for an informal luncheon as a gesture of courtesy to him on the day before Vishinsky's departure for a session of the United Nations in New York. Two or three secretaries in our foreign service and I were included. Admiral Kirk is a fine host, so the luncheon was pleasant and amiable. It was hard to believe that the agreeable, smiling Vishinsky was the grim prosecutor of the spectacular trials of the Great Purge. Perhaps there is something in one of the theories that attempts to explain the Cheka and the NKVD — that if they ever lose the belief that they are right in what they are doing, they will go mad and start tearing each other limb from limb.

Vishinsky said that Spasso House was once the residence of Chicherin, who was Foreign Minister in the early days of the Soviets, and that before that it had belonged to a textile manufacturer. Vishinsky showed that he knew all the answers, for when it was suggested to him that it would be a wonderful thing if perhaps one or two of the great ballerinas whose dancing was so admirable might be permitted to come to Spasso House some time, he replied, "But you see, they dance only for the people!"

I asked him why such aboriginal nations as the Mordvi and the Chuvashi had never been assimilated into Russia. Instead of denying that this was so, as might have been expected, he said that it was doubtless because the Tsar was more interested in providing them with vodka than with education.

Outside the Embassy in Manezhny Place, women are laying new asphalt paving. They work like ants, stopping only for their lunch of water and bread whacked off in black chunks from big loaves. Strapping girls dig up the old pavement with pickaxes, spread the new asphalt, tramp it down by hand with heavy weights, then roll it with new steam rollers, made in Belgium. Crowds of people examine the equipment with curiosity. The Belgians must live somehow, but it is a pity that Western trade strengthens a regime which continually seeks the overthrow of the West. Trade goes on in spite of the vilification of the West and the announced intention of helping to bring about the historical processes which will lead to One World — a communist world under the control of the Bolshevik Party of Russia. Even before the war this intention was clear, but it was more understandable then, for the anti-Western propaganda, although always present, was more muted. Perhaps it seems worse to me now because I have just finished reading George Orwell's *1984*. One should read that terrible book in Soviet Russia to experience its full impact, for it seems to be the Russia of today, lacking only the technical gadgets and a few refinements which time can bring.

A broad new road is being driven across the southern part of Moscow, but this construction is being done by troops. Hundreds and hundreds of soldiers are at work running bulldozers, jacking up and moving houses, digging ditches, moving telephone and light lines and laying conduit. It is difficult to compare either the Soviet economy or the Soviet armies with Western ones when one sees evidences of so many troops engaged in commercial or industrial operations. They have not run out of German prisoners, for prisoners are at work on roads in the northern part of the city. A big group of them is busy on the road that runs to the Embassy. Not only do they wear the familiar caps and greenish uniforms, but signs in both German and Russian have been put up in that vicinity for their guidance.

We had difficulty in getting through the new construction and the swarms of soldiers, but finally made our way to Kolonenskoye on the southern edge of Moscow. Few seem to have heard of Kolonenskoye, but there were three or four things there worth going to see. One of them is a tall church, built by one of the early Ivans. Its galleries look out over peaceful meadows where Bolotnikov's attack on Moscow was defeated some three hundred and fifty years ago. Among the fascinating things about Russian history are the parallels with modern times that can so often be found. Class warfare is old in Russia, for the serf Bolotnikov raised the people under the slogan of the land to the peasants, urging the serfs to kill their masters and take their wives and daughters and all their possessions for themselves.

In a yellow autumn wood nearby is a log *izba* that Peter the Great built with his own hands on the Dvina River in the far north. It was moved bodily from the Arkhangelsk area to its present location and kept intact with all its contents. Dishes and crude household implements, old prints, big iron-strapped psalters and pieces of embroidery showed the decorative richness which is characteristic of Russian handwork. The strange *alkonost*, that bird with a human face, was often to be seen in the prints and carvings. Such work is interesting, but it is characteristic that it is never fine, as in the corresponding work of European peoples.

We went into the Church of the Kazan Virgin, where a few calm-faced peasant women were leaving from some sort of services. In it the ikons were black with the smoke of the red ikon lamps, and their rich jeweled and beaded canopies were thick with dust. I looked into a little separate alcove and saw a diminutive figure, dark and barefoot, sitting peacefully on a chair. The image was so lifelike in the gloom that for a startled moment I thought it was a real child.

At one of the farewell parties for us everyone was congregated around the punch bowl when Nell came up to me. "Don't look now," she said, "but when you get a chance, take a good look at that man's necktie and tell me if you see the same thing I see."

I stole around and looked. It was a hand-painted tie, worn by a kindly-looking stranger who seemed as homelike and competent as a Rotarian. On the tie was emblazoned the ornate Soldiers' and Sailors' Monument which stands in the middle of Indianapolis. "It looks like your monument," I said to Nell, who was born and raised not far from Indianapolis.

From then on, we had a firm friend. Ed Dowling had accomplished the unheard-of feat of getting himself into the Soviet Union. He has a great curiosity about the world, and, having been nearly everywhere else, he talked the Soviets into giving him a visa to Moscow in order to investigate the possibilities of marketing Russian champagne in the United States. He was serious about it, but already he had found that the champagne was not up to customary standards and had seen enough to know that the regime was up to no good, either abroad or at home. Most short-time visitors never get into the back streets, and leave Russia after having been impressed by the vodka and caviar treatment, but Ed was no social scientist but a hardheaded businessman with a special gift of curiosity and a clear vision. He is a living refutation of the Soviet propaganda that Americans are only interested in making money, and after coming to know him my faith in American businessmen was well shored up.

Ambassador and Mrs. Kirk are going out to Paris soon, so we have accepted their invitation to go in his plane. Always on leaving a city where one has lived for a long time there are many things one would like to do that can only be done there. Moscow goes in heavily for museums. There is even a Police Museum listed, but Russians always looked at me sidewise and shrugged their shoulders when I tried to find out where it was and how to get into it. We went to the Tolstoy Museum, which was the great novelist's city dwelling, and to the Polytechnic Museum, filled with examples of labor-saving equipment and safety devices to show how the interests of the people were fostered. The Revolutionary Museum was one we were glad we did not miss.

It is in what was once the old English Club of Tolstoy's *War and Peace*. Outside stand some of the strange stone lions which are also near the Gogol monument. I have never been able to find out where they were from or what they signified, but their archaic, grotesque shapes never came from the West.

The rewriting of history is very apparent in the Revolutionary Museum. The figure of Trotsky never once appears in the many paintings, although they say that some of those pictures once showed him. But the most interesting part of the museum is the big room in which are displayed the presents to Stalin. Almost every conceivable kind of present is there — pipes, chess sets, jeweled swords, working models of machines and equipment, rugs with Stalin's portrait woven in their designs, malachite pen and ink sets, musical instruments, even a combination pistol and dagger sent for unknown reasons by some American admirer.

I also covered all the old bookshops for the last time, and succumbed to a complete and unbroken set of the last tsarist encyclopedia that was published before the Revolution — which I had long been eying. Its ninety-six volumes of comparatively uncensored information will be difficult to carry back, but it is worth it.

In addition to a last roundup of the museums, we went once more to Klin and also to Zagorsk, where pious peasant women literally beat their foreheads on the floor before kissing the ring on the withered finger of Saint Sergei, who lay covered with a red cloth on top of his silver coffin. Driving back through the autumn rain from Zagorsk we noticed that there was not a village which did not have radio antennae on some of its houses. Collective farms, MVD stations and administrative offices can be expected to be equipped with radios, but these were on the tiny *izbas,* sometimes elaborate and well-made above the shaggy thatch. There are many parts of Russia where the Voice of America still comes.

Peter the Great, whose huge bronze equestrian statue still stands near the Neva, built St. Petersburg almost on the bones of thousands of Russians on low-lying land that is exposed to winds from the Finnish Gulf. Pushkin's poem of *The Bronze Horseman* tells of how Eugene's sweetheart, with whom he used to sit beneath the statue, was torn away and drowned by one of the many floods driven into the city by continued storms. Eugene goes mad and wanders about the city, an object of pity. One night he finds himself beneath the statue. Something stirs in his bewildered mind, his memory returns and he curses the bronze rider.

> It seemed to him that the face of the terrible Tsar, suddenly blazing with wrath, turned silently. And he flees through the silent square and hears behind him a heavy, ringing gallop like the rumble of thunder on the shaking pavement. And, lit by the pale moon, hand raised on high, behind him rides the Bronze Horseman on his galloping horse; and all through the night, wherever the poor witless one turned his running steps, behind him galloped the Bronze Horseman with heavy, ringing hooves.

The Bronze Horseman has just been made into a ballet and everyone is eager to see it. Twice we have gone to the Bolshoy for that purpose, only to find that it was postponed and replaced with something else. Possibly the delays were because of ideological difficulties, for there are obvious problems in presenting Peter the

Great as a great national hero and there are always comparisons to be drawn with the present regime. At last whatever troubles there were were cleared up, and it has become a part of the Bolshoy's repertoire.

It was the last show we saw in Russia. Just as Americans long went to *Ben Hur* for the chariot race, Russians will go to *The Bronze Horseman* to see the flood scene. The Petersburg streets are gay with people, lighthearted as in another Paris. The skies darken as a black, threatening storm begins to appear. Big drops of rain patter on the pavement, singly at first and then more steadily. The gutters overflow and water runs in the streets. Ladies lift their long skirts and pick their way carefully through the water. Then the wind strikes. Lurid flashes of lightning show the people fleeing in terror through the rising water. The flood rises higher and higher in the streets until it is waist deep, carrying wreckage and debris swiftly along in its current. Higher it rises — chest deep — over one's head — boiling and swirling, foaming and tossing.

How that illusion was obtained is still not altogether clear to me. At first, from the splash of the drops, I thought that it was real water and that the stage was some sort of tank. Perhaps it was, at first, but that water rose above the edges of any tank, higher and higher, and what kept it on the stage was a mystery. The audience, including ourselves, hung onto the arms of their chairs and were ready for a running start in case the thing got out of hand. I could see that the rushing, swirling flood consisted of scores of little separate parts of semitransparent scenery in echelons of depth, moving rhythmically according to a complex scheme, and that they were given unity by motion pictures thrown upon them by unseen projectors. At least that is what I think I saw, and the trick of perspective by which one knew that the water was many feet deep without seeing it in cross-section remains unsolved.

The flood scene of *The Bronze Horseman* was for us a grand climax to many delightful evenings of illusion and entertainment in a land that would have been less bright without them.

On the day we left Moscow, we rode to the airport for the last time, through little flurries of occasional snow from the broken clouds. We were sorry to leave old Natasha and Zoya, Senta and a dozen others, for there was a good chance that we would see the foreigners again somewhere, some time, but not these Russians. I had sometimes had visions of myself declaiming Lermontov's "Farewell, unwashed Russia" from the platform of a departing train, but that did not seem appropriate when the Navy contingent piped me aboard the Ambassador's plane with a bo's'n's whistle they had conjured up.

EPILOGUE

The Bosporus runs like a swift deep river to Istanbul, the "Tsargrad" of the Russians, with its Byzantine churches, its colored minarets and its red and white encircling wall, from the Black Sea. As I sat on a vine-covered terrace where the sea pours into the Bosporus, my thoughts were always of Russia. The Russian proverb came to mind which says that in every tale there is a grain of truth. Russia is like an optical illusion wherein a flight of stairs at which one has looked steadily for some time suddenly turns inside out and reverses its direction.

The sun had set. The western sky was still bathed in shining gold, but already darkness had come over the Black Sea, white and angry beneath broken storm clouds. There was a brooding sense of mystery in the far distance. There night had fallen on the cities and towns of the Caucasian coast, the Crimea, the Ukraine and on the vast, endless lands that lay beyond. Russian faces came before my eyes, clear blue-eyed faces of boys and girls, bearded faces, sly cunning faces, and the wrinkled faces of the old women with the fine, peaceful, extraordinarily appealing and attractive expression which they so often carry.

The optical illusion righted itself when those faces appeared. It is difficult for reason and logic alone always to say in which direction the flight of stairs really runs, and it is then that the heritage of common decency must be applied. Underlying all the dualities which the Russian nature has beneath the external conformities which are forced on it if it is to survive, and in spite of an inherent partisanship which makes genuine compromise to them a betrayal of one's cause, in spite of their extremes of violence and of passive submission, the Russians to which decency must be applied are themselves basically a decent people. Decency is difficult to define, but it comes in large part from the heart.

As I looked out across the Black Sea towards the darkness that was Russia, I realized that the chances of my ever seeing that land again were very slight, and, because of that, a sort of sadness and depression, that which the Russians call *toska,* settled over me. Yet I know that as surely as light follows darkness, the problems created in a decent people by the forced maintenance of power will somehow in the end destroy that power.

INDEX

INDEX

555